CONTENTS

✱

D0017834

PENGUIN  CLASSICS

THE NIBELUNGENLIED

The *Nibelungenlied* was written in about A.D. 1200 by an anonymous poet, probably a professional entertainer, for performance at court in Austria somewhere between Vienna and Passau.

•

Arthur Thomas Hatto was Head of the Department of German, Queen Mary College, University of London, from 1938 until his retirement in 1977, and was Professor of German Language and Literature at the same university from 1953 to 1977. He is now Professor Emeritus in German in the University of London. He was assistant for English at the University of Berne (1932–5), and during the Second World War worked in the Foreign Office (1939–45). Since 1960 he has been a Governor of the School of Oriental and African Studies, University of London, where in 1970 he gave the Foundation Lecture, with the title 'Shamanism and Epic Poetry in Northern Asia'.

His other publications include *The Memorial Feast for Kökötöykhan* – a Kirghiz epic, edited, translated and with a commentary. His translations for the Penguin Classics are Gottfried's *Tristan* and the fragments of Thomas's *Tristran* (together in one volume) and the *Nibelungenlied*, and with Wolfram von Eschenbach's *Parzival*, his third volume for the series, he has made available to the English-reading public a substantial portion of the finest narrative poetry of the medieval German Golden Age.

Professor Hatto is now living in retirement in the enjoyment of a Leverhulme Emeritus Fellowship in support of his studies of epic poetry in Central Asia and Siberia. He is married and has one daughter.

THE NIBELUNGENLIED

A NEW TRANSLATION BY
A. T. HATTO

PENGUIN BOOKS

PENGUIN BOOKS

Published by the Penguin Group
Penguin Books Ltd, 27 Wrights Lane, London W8 5TZ, England
Penguin Books USA Inc., 375 Hudson Street, New York, New York 10014, USA
Penguin Books Australia Ltd, Ringwood, Victoria, Australia
Penguin Books Canada Ltd, 10 Alcorn Avenue, Toronto, Ontario, Canada M4V 3B2
Penguin Books (NZ) Ltd, 182–190 Wairau Road, Auckland 10, New Zealand

Penguin Books Ltd, Registered Offices: Harmondsworth, Middlesex, England

This translation first published 1965
Reprinted with revisions 1969
17 19 20 18

Copyright © A. T. Hatto, 1965, 1969
All rights reserved

Printed in England by Clays Ltd, St Ives plc
Set in Monotype Baskerville

FOREWORD

*

THE *Nibelungenlied* is a heroic epic surpassed only by the *Iliad* of
Homer. It was written at about A.D. 1200 by an unnamed poet,
for performance at court in Austria somewhere between Vienna
and Passau. In it there culminated a tradition of heroic poetry
reaching back to the sixth or fifth century A.D. in the lands of the
Germanic peoples, and so well did it succeed in its own age that,
for want of copying, all earlier poems on the theme in German were
lost for ever. Modern poets and poetasters have often returned to
its subject, prominent among them Richard Wagner with his
gigantic music drama *Der Ring des Nibelungen* with which (as with
his *Parsifal* and his *Tristan* – whatever their merits as modern works
of art) he has unfortunately harmed the cause of medieval
German poetry by intruding reckless distortions between us and an
ancient masterpiece. Thus those who come to the *Nibelungenlied*
from Wagner will be much surprised by what they read in it.

The story which our poem tells is one of murder and of revenge
long-nourished, and it ends in the destruction of two armies. The
avenger is a woman; the avenged her beloved husband; her vic-
tims are her brothers and kinsmen. This, in its crudest terms, is the
plot: having won the amazonian Queen Brunhild for King
Gunther in exchange for Gunther's sister Kriemhild, the mighty
King Siegfried is murdered by Gunther's vassal Hagen after a
quarrel between the Queens; for which Kriemhild, at long last,
avenges him.

The action thus has two crises, of which the first is subordinated
to the second, but less emphatically than one would expect in a
story of revenge. (In the Japanese *Tale of the Forty-Seven Ronin*,
for example, the Provocation is dealt with briefly, though firmly.)
Yet despite its two crises,[1] the plot of our poem is single-
stranded to a remarkable degree. Apart from incidental tourna-
ments it knows no women or greybeards on the city-walls as
onlookers, nor is there an upper storey from which Heaven may
watch and intervene. (The miraculous escape of the chaplain in

1. The reader might be misled into thinking that Siegfried is the hero
of the epic, and that the poet is at fault in causing him to die at its mid-
point: but its true heroes are Kriemhild and Hagen, as the sequel shows.

7

Chapter 25 is an isolated incident.) Its actors of the moment are held in the limelight and left godforsaken and alone to work out their own destinies, while all others, even those who were talking and doing but a moment before, are blacked out till required again. But on the margins of light and darkness there is, either present or evoked from the future, a chorus of widows and young women whose inarticulate weeping points to woe, or woe to come. Comparison with the *Iliad* confirms the markedly linear nature of the plot. For whereas Homer selects but a few days from the whole action of the Rape of Helen and the Siege and Sack of Troy, thereby anticipating the three unities of Greek drama, our poet narrates all significant events from Kriemhild's girlhood till her death as a woman of advanced years. In order to do this, the poet passes over vast lapses of time during which nothing happens and concentrates on brief periods full of incident with peaks of tense dialogue, which in their turn foreshadow modern drama. The poet is able to do this thanks to the strength and directness of his plot, as, step by step, he confronts the implacable wills of his great protagonists, Kriemhild and Hagen. He thus achieves a work the finest moments of which would come through even in pidgin-English and positively thrive on the prose of Damon Runyon. Indeed, I once read a gripping essay on the plot of the *Nibelungenlied* by an undergraduate who knew (or pretended to know) no better than to treat it as a thriller.

The *Nibelungenlied*, then, should appeal on the one hand to those who have read the *Iliad* and the *Song of Roland* with pleasure, and on the other to readers (though scarcely to addicts) of the tougher novels of our day, but also to many in between; and they could enjoy it in English better or worse than mine. Yet a word of warning is due to them. Owing to the weight which the poet gives to the events that lead up to the quarrel of the Queens and the death of Siegfried, the story unfolds slowly at first. Indeed, it begins almost like a fairy-tale, with a Princess averse to love and a Prince Charming destined to win her. But at length this crystal casement is shattered, to reveal a stage on which imperious wills, guile, treachery, loyalty of many hues, some chivalry, sublime tact, and desperate courage, all play their fateful parts.[1]

Queen Mary College, London. July 1962   A.T.H.

1. The *Nibelungenlied* is an enigmatic poem. For those who become engrossed in its problems I have provided an Introduction to a Second Reading, pp. 293ff.

ACKNOWLEDGEMENTS

*

To acknowledge my debt in full for all the help that I have received whilst preparing this book would involve the compilation of a bibliography of the subject; for so vast is the literature on the *Nibelungenlied*, the epic poem of one of the more learned tongues of the world, that I have inevitably profited from works I shall never read, by authors whose names I have never seen. I am therefore all the more happy to confine my acknowledgements to recent and living authors.

I wish to thank the following for the gift of offprints of their illuminating articles: Professor Werner Betz, Professor Jean Fourquet, Professor Hugo Kuhn, Dr Emil Ploss, Professor Friedrich Neumann (whom I have quoted as near as English would let me), and Professor Peter Wapnewski. I was grateful to receive an offprint from the late Dr J. Knight Bostock, whom on one occasion I quote verbatim. If through inadvertence I have failed to acknowledge any debt under this head, I am truly sorry.

To name only some of those whose writings have been an especial stimulus to me, I have further profited from books or articles by Professor Joachim Bumke, Professor G. Fenwick Jones, Professor Dietrich Kralik, Professor Wolfgang Mohr, Dr Bert Nagel, Professor Hans Naumann, Professor Otto Höfler, Professor Hermann Schneider, Professor Julius Schwietering, Professor K. F. Stroheker, Professor E. Tonnelat, Professor K. Weller, Dr R. Wisniewski, and Professor O. Zallinger.

I am greatly indebted to an article by Professor Heinrich Hempel, whose argument that the strophes which concern Passau must be interpolations, I have adopted and, I hope, reinforced.

I am particularly grateful to Dr Helmut Brackert, who placed a summary of his challenging book on the manuscript relations of the *Nibelungenlied* at my disposal in advance of publication, and for answering some stiff questions arising therefrom; to Dr Emil Ploss for very generously allowing me to read in typescript a chapter of a treatise he was preparing; and to my colleague Dr Paul Salmon for showing me an article which he had hastened to put on to paper so that I might read it before going to press.

9

Acknowledgements

Following up Professor Hempel's ideas already referred to, I got out of my depth in the Danube somewhere between the River Enns and the River Inn, and was promptly hauled out, on receipt of my S.O.S., by Professor Erich Zöllner of the Institut für österreichische Geschichtsforschung of Vienna, far downstream, and given the full benefit of his deep learning in medieval Austrian history. It is thanks to him, and to the staff of the Oberöster-reichisches Landesarchiv in Linz, that I have been able to set forth certain facts of local Austrian history *c.*1200 with confidence, despite their problematic background, in my Appendix 2. But it goes without saying that I must take the entire responsibility for the literary use to which I have put this information. Here I must warmly thank the Director, Secretary, and Librarian of the Austrian Cultural Institute of London for their kind mediation and generous loan of books procured from Vienna and Linz.

My debt to Professor Helmut de Boor, editor, commentator, and verse-translator of the *Nibelungenlied*, and to Professor Maurice Colleville and the late Professor Ernest Tonnelat, joint translators of the epic into French, is recorded at a more appropriate place below.

No writer on any major aspect of the *Nibelungenlied* can pass by the name of Andreas Heusler, the great Swiss scholar of Basle, to whose monumental work reference is also made below.

I wish to record my gratitude to my tutor, Professor Frederick Norman, O.B.E., and our colleague Dr Herbert Thoma for their having answered, independently, four pages of searching questions on points for which I needed other opinions; and I must thank the former, the leading authority in this country on the whole subject of German-cum-Germanic heroic poetry, for giving me of his knowledge and advice whenever I felt the need for it, and also for lending me rare works. The blemishes of this book, however, are all mine, and it would be lamentable if because of a close association with it the faults of the pupil were attributed to the tutor. Professor Norman has read my proofs on this occasion, too, a kindness for which I also have to thank my colleague Dr Rosemary Combridge once more, as also for advice on legal problems in the text. I am deeply grateful to them both for removing so many blemishes from my work.

As before, my College Librarian, Mr Adrian Whitworth, M.A., and his whilom Deputy, Mr C. P. Corney, M.A., have given tireless assistance in the provision of books and articles.

I owe a deep debt of gratitude to my wife Margot for once

Acknowledgements

again listening to my readings, and to Professors John Brough, Bernard Lewis, and Ralph Tymms, who read the translation in typescript and gave it the benefit of their sharp-sighted and balanced criticism.

I am very grateful to de heer Lambertus Okken of the University of Utrecht for having compared my translation, as reprinted in 1966, with the original in its entirety and lending me his notes, as a result of which I have been able to render numerous passages more accurately.

These acknowledgements would not be complete without a word of thanks to Dr E. V. Rieu, the veteran Editor of this series, who has given his contributors the guidance and encouragement they needed with so light and sure a touch. I am proud to have joined him here with a translation of a great heroic epic. And, as in my comments on the *Nibelungenlied* below, my poem is made to salute the *Iliad* from time to time, as it must, so I myself salute Dr Rieu, not only for his *Iliad* and *Odyssey*, but also for the wealth of fine literature from all over the world which he has caused to be laid before us in good English.

THE NIBELUNGENLIED

CONTENTS

*

Contents

CHAPTER ONE

Kriemhild[1]

*

WE have been told in ancient tales many marvels of famous heroes, of mighty toil, joys, and high festivities, of weeping and wailing, and the fighting of bold warriors – of such things you can now hear wonders unending!

In the land of the Burgundians there grew up a maiden of high lineage, so fair that none in any land could be fairer. Her name was Kriemhild. She came to be a beautiful woman, causing many knights to lose their lives. This charming girl was as if made for love's caresses: she was desired by brave fighting men and none was her enemy, for her noble person was beyond all measure lovely. Such graces did the young lady possess that she was the adornment of her sex. She was in the care of three great and noble kings, the renowned warriors Gunther and Gernot, and young Giselher, a splendid knight, and she was sister to these princes who had the charge of her. These lords were of high race, magnanimous, strong, and brave beyond measure, altogether rare warriors. Their country was called Burgundy, and in days to come they wrought mighty wonders in Etzel's land. They held sway at Worms beside the Rhine, and were served in high honour by many proud knights from their territories till their dying day, when the enmity of two noble ladies was to bring them to a sad end. The great queen their mother was named Uote, and their father, who had bequeathed them their heritage, was called Dancrat. A man of abounding valour, Dancrat too had won great fame in younger days. These three kings, as I have

---

1. At the head of Chapters 2–39 I have translated the traditional subtitles. There is none for Chapter 1, and I have supplied one of my own. The chapter-divisions go back to the archetype of our text: but whether the sub-titles do so or not is disputed.

said, were of high courage and they also had as their vassals the best warriors whose deeds were ever told, strong, brave, and resolute in sharp encounters, Hagen of Troneck and his valiant brother Dancwart, Ortwin of Metz, the two margraves Gere and Eckewart, and Volker of Alzei, a man of flawless courage. Rumold, who was Lord of the Kitchen and an excellent knight, and lords Sindold and Hunold, all vassals of the three kings, were charged with maintaining their court and their renown, and they had many other men besides whom I cannot name. Dancwart was Marshal, his nephew Ortwin was the King's Seneschal, Sindold was Cup-bearer – he was a splendid knight – and Hunold was Chamberlain. These were well able to maintain the court's high honour, and indeed none could recount to the full its power and far-flung dominion, or the glory and chivalry those lords rejoiced in all their lives.

Living in such magnificence, Kriemhild dreamt she reared a falcon, strong, handsome and wild, but that two eagles rent it while she perforce looked on, the most grievous thing that could ever befall her. She told her dream to her mother Uote, who could give the good maiden no better reading than this: 'The falcon you are rearing is a noble man who, unless God preserve him, will soon be taken from you.'

'Why do you talk to me of a man, dear Mother? I intend to stay free of a warrior's love all my life. I mean to keep my beauty till I die, and never be made wretched by the love of any man.'

'Do not forswear it too firmly,' rejoined her mother. 'If you are ever to know heartfelt happiness it can come only from a man's love. If God should assign to you a truly worthy knight you will grow to be a beautiful woman.'

'Let us speak of other things, my lady. There are many examples of women who have paid for happiness with sorrow in the end. I shall avoid both, and so I shall come to no harm.'

Kriemhild set all thought of love aside, and after this conversation the good girl passed many a pleasant day unaware of any man whom she would love. Yet the time came when she was wed with honour to a very brave warrior, to that same falcon whom she had seen in the dream which her mother had interpreted for her. What terrible vengeance she took on her nearest kinsmen for slaying him in days to come! For his one life there died many a mother's child.

CHAPTER TWO

Siegfried

*

DOWN the Rhine, in the splendid, far-famed city of Xanten in the Netherlands, there grew up a royal prince, a gallant knight named Siegfried, son of Siegmund and Sieglind. Fired by his courage, he tried the mettle of many kingdoms and rode through many lands to put his strength to the test. Later, in Burgundy, he was to meet a host of valiant knights. Of his best days, when he was young, marvels could be told of the honours that accrued to him and of his handsome looks, so that women of great beauty came to love him. He was reared with all the care that befitted his high station, and acquired many fine qualities of his own. It gave lustre to his father's kingdom that he was found altogether so distinguished. He had now grown up sufficiently to ride to court, where many were glad to see him. Indeed many ladies, both married and maidens, hoped he would always wish to come there; for (as lord Siegfried was aware) no few were well-disposed towards him.

The young man was never allowed to go riding without escort. By Siegmund's and Sieglind's command he was dressed in elegant clothes, and experienced men well-versed in matters of honour had him in their charge, as a result of which he was able to win all hearts. He had grown to be strong enough to bear arms expertly, and he possessed in abundance all the needful qualities. As to the lovely women he wooed, he showed discernment, and they for their part would have done themselves high honour in loving fearless Siegfried.

When the time was ripe, his father Siegmund had it made known to his vassals that he wished to hold a festivity in company with his dear friends, and the news was borne to other kingdoms. The King bestowed horses and fine clothes on native and stranger alike. And wherever there were noble squires of his line of an age to be knighted, they were invited to his country to take part in the festivity; and when the time came they received their swords in company with the prince.

It was a magnificent feast, and well did Siegmund and Sieglind know how to win esteem with the lavish gifts they made, so that many people from other parts came riding to their country. Four hundred knights-aspirant were to be attired with Siegfried: thus many comely young ladies, wishing him well, toiled busily, setting in gold brocade jewel upon jewel, which, as custom required, they planned to work with silk-and-gold trimmings into the proud young warriors' clothes.

Then, at midsummer, when his son was knighted, the King commanded seats to be set for the valiant company, whereupon a host of noble squires and knights of high rank repaired to the minster. The older men did well to wait upon the novices as they had been waited upon at their own knighting; it passed the time agreeably for them, and they had hope of pleasures to come. Mass was sung to the glory of God, and at once there was a great press where, in accordance with chivalric custom, the squires were to be knighted amid such splendour as can scarcely be seen again.

They ran to where many chargers stood saddled, and the bohort[1] in Siegmund's courtyard grew so tremendous that the palace thundered with the din which those spirited warriors made, while you could hear thrust on thrust by young and old, so that the shivering of shafts rang loud on the air and you could see all these knights send the splinters flying far and wide before the hall – so zestfully did they set to.

Their host asked them to make an end, and their mounts were led away. You could see many strong bosses all broken, and precious stones that had been torn from gleaming shield-plates and strewn upon the grass, the work of mighty lance-thrusts.

1. An equestrian exercise, half pageant, half sport, with shields and lances, the latter generally blunted.

Then the King's guests went and sat where they were bidden. The profusion of rare dishes and the excellent wine that were set before them in great abundance banished their fatigue – all honour was paid to both friends and strangers. And although they well amused themselves the livelong day, there were many strolling entertainers who, in their eagerness to earn the rich gifts to be had there, put all thought of rest aside, so that Siegmund's whole kingdom was gilded by their praises. And now the King commanded young Siegfried to bestow lands and castles in fee, as he himself had done when he was knighted, and Siegfried enfeoffed his companions richly, so that they were well pleased with their journey there.

The celebrations had lasted for a week when, in honour of her son, Sieglind dispensed gifts of red gold, in accordance with ancient custom, for she well knew how to win the people's favour for him. No wandering minstrel remained poor there – it rained horses and clothes as though their donors had not a day to live! I cannot imagine that any royal household ever practised such munificence.

Those who had come to the festivity dispersed in grand style. Powerful nobles were afterwards heard to say that they would gladly have the young man for their lord: but handsome Siegfried did not want it, Siegmund's and Sieglind's beloved son did not wish to wear the crown[1] so long as both were alive; yet as a valiant knight he aspired to dominion that he might ward off all the violence which he feared for his country.

1. That *the* crown of the Netherlands is meant, and not merely *a* crown, is evident from Siegmund's abdication in favour of Siegfried in Chapter 11, p. 98.

CHAPTER THREE

How Siegfried came to Worms

*

THIS prince was never troubled by heartfelt sorrow. But one day he heard a report that there was a maiden living in Burgundy who was of perfect beauty; and from her, as it fell out, he was to receive much joy, yet also great distress.

The young lady's most rare beauty was known far and wide, and many warriors had also learned of her spirited disposition, so that her perfections attracted many visitors to Gunther's country. But however many suitors came to woo her, Kriemhild never admitted to herself in her inmost thoughts that she wanted any as her lover, since as yet her future lord was a stranger to her.

Siegfried's thoughts were now bent on a noble attachment, and beside his claims to favour all others were as nothing. Brave Siegfried was well endowed to win the hearts of lovely women, and in the event noble Kriemhild became his wife.

Seeing that he aspired to a constant love, his kinsmen and many of his vassals counselled him to woo a lady of suitable standing. 'I shall take Kriemhild the fair maiden of Burgundy,' he answered boldly, 'on account of her very great beauty, since even if the mightiest of emperors wished to marry, I know he would not demean himself in loving the noble princess.'

The affair came to Siegmund's ears through the gossip of his courtiers, who said that Siegfried meant to woo the noble maiden, a design which grieved his father deeply. Queen Sieglind learned of this too, and, having no illusions about Gunther and his men, she feared greatly for the life of her son. Thus they tried to turn the young knight's thoughts against this enterprise.

'But, dear father,' answered Siegfried, 'rather than not

23

woo where my heart finds great delight, I would quite forgo the love of noble ladies. All would be in vain, whatever anyone should say.'

'If you are set on it, then I am heartily glad of your intentions,' replied the King, 'and I shall help you to accomplish them to the best of my powers. Yet, remember, Gunther has many proud vassals. Were there no other than Hagen, he has such haughty ways that I fear we might regret it if we asked for the Princess's hand.'

'How should that trouble us?' asked Siegfried. 'Whatever I fail to get from them by friendly requests, I shall take by my own valour. I fancy I shall wrest their lands and people from them.'

'What you say distresses me,' replied King Siegmund, 'since if this were repeated at Worms they would never let you ride into Burgundy. I have known Gunther's and Gernot's ways for a long time now. I have been told on good authority that none will ever win the girl by force. But if you mean to ride there in the company of warriors I shall put our friends to the test and summon them at once.'

'It is not my wish and indeed I should regret it if warriors were to accompany me to Burgundy on a warlike expedition to win the handsome girl, for I am well able to gain her by my own unaided powers. I shall go to Gunther's country as one of a band of twelve, and you must help me to get there, father.' Following this his stalwarts were furnished with clothes lined with vari-coloured squirrel.

This came to the ears of his mother Sieglind, too. Fearing to lose him at the hands of Gunther's vassals, the noble Queen shed many tears in sad concern for her darling son. But lord Siegfried went to see her and, addressing her kindly, said: 'You must not weep for me, my lady. I shall not go in fear of any fighting-man, I promise you. And if you will help me on my march to Burgundy by providing me and my followers with clothes such as proud warriors may wear with honour, I shall thank you most sincerely.'

'Since you will not be dissuaded,' answered the lady Sieglind, 'I will help you on your journey, though you are my only son, and I shall give you and your companions to take with you ample stocks of the finest clothes that knights ever wore.'

Young Siegfried thanked the Queen with a bow. 'I intend to have on my journey twelve warriors all told,' he said, 'and it is for them that the clothes must be made. I should much like to see how matters stand with Kriemhild.'

Thus lovely women sat day and night with scarcely any rest till Siegfried's clothes were ready, since he was firmly resolved on his journey. His father commanded the knightly equipment in which Siegfried was going abroad to be richly adorned, while gleaming corselets, sturdy helmets, and fine broad shields were made ready for his companions.

When the time drew near for them to set out for Burgundy, people began anxiously to wonder whether they would ever return; but the warriors themselves ordered their clothes and armour to be loaded on to pack-horses. Their chargers were handsome and their harness shone red with gold; and if there were any men alive who were prouder than Siegfried and his companions, they had no cause to be so. Siegfried now asked leave to depart for Burgundy, and the King and Queen sadly granted it, at which he consoled them affectionately. 'Do not weep on my account,' he said. 'Never fear that I shall ever be in danger.'

The knights were sorry at his going, and many young ladies wept. I imagine their hearts had truly foretold them that it would end in death for so many of their friends.[1] They were lamenting not without reason, they had good cause to do so.

A week later, in the morning, Siegfried's valiant company rode on to the sandy river-bank at Worms. All their equipment shone red with gold, their chargers went with even pace, their harness was good to see; they bore bright new shields of ample width, their helmets were very handsome, and never were such magnificent robes seen upon warriors as when Siegfried rode to court in Gunther's land. The points of their swords dangled beside their spurs, and these

1. As the story is told, Siegfried alone of all the party dies.

excellent knights carried sharp spears – Siegfried's had a head two spans across, with fearful cutting edges. Their hands held golden bridles, and the poitrels were of silk.

In such style did they arrive. Crowds began to stare at them on all sides as many of Gunther's vassals ran out to meet them. Proud warriors, knights and squires alike, they went out to those lords as they were bound to do and they welcomed the strangers to their master's country and relieved them of mounts and shields.

The squires were about to lead the chargers to stable, when brave Siegfried quickly said: 'Leave our horses where they are. We shall soon be riding away, for such is my intention. If anyone knows where I can find the great King Gunther of Burgundy, let him tell me frankly.'

'You can easily find him if you wish,' answered one of their number who knew. 'I saw him with his warriors in that spacious hall. Go there, and you will find him in the company of fine men in plenty.'

Now it was announced to the King that some gay knights had arrived, clad in dazzling corselets and magnificent robes, though none in Burgundy knew them. The King was curious to know where these lordly warriors were from, in their bright clothes and with their fine, broad, new shields, and he was sorry that none could tell him. But Ortwin of Metz, who was accounted both mighty and brave, made answer: 'Since we do not know a man of them, send for my uncle Hagen and let him take a look at them – he knows all the kingdoms and foreign countries – so that if these lords are known to him he will tell us.' The King accordingly summoned Hagen and his men, and as they came to court they made a splendid sight.

Hagen asked the King's pleasure.

'There are strange knights within my walls whom nobody knows. If you have ever seen them, Hagen, tell me who they are.'

'I will do so,' answered Hagen. Going to a window, he directed his gaze to the strangers. Their whole turnout pleased him greatly, but they were total strangers to him here in Burgundy. He declared that wherever these knights had come from to Worms, they must be either princes or princes' envoys, judging by their handsome chargers and splendid clothes, and that whichever land they had left, they were men of spirit.

'Although I have never seen him,' said Hagen, 'I dare assert my belief that the knight who makes such a magnificent figure there is Siegfried, whatever his purpose. He is bringing unheard-of news to this country, for this warrior slew the bold Nibelungs[1], the two mighty princes Schilbung and Nibelung,[2] and marvellous are the deeds he has done since in his great strength. Riding unaccompanied past the foot of a mountain (as I was truly told), he chanced upon a host of valiant men whom he had never seen before, gathered round Nibelung's[3] treasure, all of which they had borne out from a cavern. Now hear the strange tale how the Nibelungs were intent on dividing it! – Siegfried marvelled as he watched them, for he came so near that he could see those warriors and they him. "Here comes mighty Siegfried of the Netherlands," said one of them; and mysterious were the things which he experienced among them. Siegfried was well received by Schilbung and Nibelung, and these noble young princes begged and implored the handsome man by common consent to make division of the treasure, and this he promised to do. He saw so many precious stones, we are told, that a hundred baggage-waggons could not have carried them, and an even greater quantity of red gold of Nibelung's country; all of which bold Siegfried was asked to divide for them. They gave him Nibelung's sword in payment, but they had scant profit from the service which the good warrior was to render them. He was unable to finish his task, so enraged were they. But although they had twelve brave men among their friends there – mighty giants they were – how could it avail them? Siegfried slew them in a

1. A dynastic name, see pp. 386, 403.
2. A personal name.
3. Nibelung was apparently the eponymous founder of the Nibelung dynasty, and father of Schilbung and Nibelung II.

fury and he also subdued seven hundred men of Nibelung-
land with the good sword Balmung, so that, in dread of this
sword and also of brave Siegfried, a host of young warriors
yielded the land and its castles to him as their lord. Further-
more he slew the mighty princes Schilbung and Nibelung,
and he came in great peril from Alberich who hoped to
avenge his masters there and then, till Siegfried's huge
strength was brought home to him; for the powerful
dwarf was no match for him. They then ran towards the
cavern like raging lions, and here he won from Alberich the
cloak of invisibility. Thus Siegfried, terrible man, was now
lord of all the treasure.

'All who had dared fight lay slain there. Siegfried com-
manded the hoard to be taken back to the cave whence
Nibelung's men had fetched it, and, after swearing oaths to
Siegfried that he would be his humble servitor, Alberich was
made lord treasurer. Indeed, he was in all ways ready to do
his bidding.

'These are the deeds that he has done,' continued Hagen
of Troneck. 'No warrior was ever so strong. But I know more
concerning him. This hero slew a dragon and bathed in its
blood, from which his skin grew horny so that no weapon
will bite it, as has been shown time and time again. We
must receive this young lord with more than usual honour,
lest we incur his enmity. He is so valiant and has performed
so many marvels thanks to his bodily strength that it is best
to have his friendship.'

'I am sure you are right,' replied the great King. 'Just
see how he stands there all eager for battle, together with his
men, the image of a fearless warrior! Let us go down to
meet him.'

'You may do so without loss of honour,' said Hagen, 'since
he is of noble race, the son of a mighty King. I'll swear from
his manner that it is no trifle which brings him riding here.'

'Then he is welcome,' answered the King. 'You have told
me that he is both well-born and brave, and he shall profit
from it here in Burgundy.' Thus Gunther went out to

Siegfried and, accompanied by his warriors, received their visitor with flawless courtesy, so that the handsome man inclined his head in thanks for their fair welcome.

'I should very much like to know where you have come from, noble Siegfried, and what business it is that brings you here to Worms on the Rhine?'

'This I shall not hide from you,' the stranger answered him. 'I was told repeatedly in my father's country that the bravest warriors that King ever had were to be found with you, and I have come to see for myself. I have also heard such warlike qualities ascribed to you that (according to many people in all the lands about) a more valiant prince was never seen; nor shall I desist till I know the truth of it. I, too, am a warrior and am entitled to wear a crown, but I wish to achieve the reputation of possessing a land and people in my own sole right, for which my head and honour shall be pledge! Now since (as they tell me) you are so brave – and I do not care who minds – I will wrest from you by force all that you possess! Your lands and your castles shall all be subject to me!'

The King and his vassals were amazed to hear this news that Siegfried meant to deprive him of his lands, and as Gunther's warriors listened they felt their anger rise.

'But how have I deserved that through the strength of any man we should lose what my father so long maintained in honour?' asked Gunther. 'Were we to let this happen it would be poor proof that we, too, practise the art of war.'

'I shall not yield my claim,' answered the fearless man. 'Unless you can protect your country by your own valour I shall rule the whole of it: but if you can wrest my inheritance from me this shall be subject to you. Now let us stake our patrimonies one against the other, and whichever of us two proves victorious let him be master of both lands and peoples.'

Hagen and Gernot were quick to advise against it. 'We do not aspire to gain any land by force at the price of the slaying of one warrior by another,' answered Gernot. 'We possess rich territories that render service to us as to their rightful lords, nor could they be in better keeping.'

The King's friends stood round him with fierce anger in their hearts, among them Ortwin of Metz. 'These terms displease me greatly,' said he. 'Mighty Siegfried has challenged you without provocation. Even if you and your brothers lacked forces to defend you, and he came at the head of a royal army, I fancy I should compel him with very good reason to have done with such swaggering!'

This stung the warrior from the Netherlands to anger. 'Do not presume to raise your hand against me: I am a mighty King, while you are but a king's vassal. I tell you, a dozen such as you could never face up to me in battle!'

True nephew of Hagen that he was, Ortwin shouted for swords. The King was sorry that Hagen kept silent so long. But Gernot, as brave as he was unabashed, intervened.

'Put your anger by,' he told Ortwin. 'My advice is this. Lord Siegfried has done nothing to us that we cannot settle courteously, so that we may have him for our friend. This would be more to our credit.'

'We, your knights, have every cause to resent his riding here to Worms to battle,' declared mighty Hagen. 'He ought to have refrained. My lords would never have wronged him so.'

'If what I have said irks you, lord Hagen,' retorted Siegfried, the powerful man, 'I will show you that I mean to have the upper hand here in Burgundy.'

'It falls to me to prevent it,' rejoined Gernot. And he forbade all his followers to say anything in arrogance that might arouse Siegfried's displeasure, while Siegfried, too, was mollified by thoughts of lovely Kriemhild.

'Why should we fight you?' asked Gernot. 'For all the warriors that must die we should gain little honour and you small profit from it.'

But Siegfried, son of King Siegmund, answered: 'What are Hagen and Ortwin waiting for, that they and the many friends whom Hagen has here do not rush into the fray?' –

But these had to keep their peace as Gernot had commanded them.

'We bid you welcome,' said Uote's son,[1] 'together with your comrades-in-arms who have accompanied you! I and my kinsmen shall be glad to attend you.' Word was given to pour out Gunther's wine in greeting, after which the King declared: 'Everything we have is at your disposal, provided you accept it honourably. Our lives and our wealth shall be shared with you in common.'

Lord Siegfried was somewhat appeased. Orders were given to store their gear away, while the best possible quarters were sought for Siegfried's squires, and they were made very comfortable. In the days that followed, Siegfried was a most welcome guest among the Burgundians, and, believe me, he was honoured by them for his manly courage a thousand times more than I can tell you, so that none could see him and harbour any grudge against him. When the kings and their vassals sought recreation, Siegfried was always the best, whatever they did: he was so strong that none was a match for him, whether at putting the weight or throwing the javelin. And whenever gay knights were passing the time with the ladies and displaying their good breeding, people were glad to see him, for he aspired to a noble love.[2] Whatever the company undertook, Siegfried was ready to join in. Meanwhile he cherished a lovely girl in his heart and was cherished in return by this same young lady whom he had never seen but who in her own intimate circle nevertheless often spoke kindly of him. When the young knights and squires had a mind for some sport in the courtyard, the noble princess Kriemhild would often look on from the window, and as long as it lasted she needed no other entertainment. Had Siegfried but

1. The context favours the identification with Gernot, yet the formula belongs to 'Young Giselher' (see p. 326), an identification which MS C makes explicit at this point.

2. In accordance with the theory of the Minnesinger that love uplifts and purifies a man, Siegfried is elevated by his love for Kriemhild, so that he becomes acceptable to courtly society.

known that his beloved was observing him, it would have been a source of unending delight to him, and if he could have seen her I dare assert no greater pleasure could ever have befallen him. And when he stood in the courtyard among the warriors to pass the time, as people still do today, Sieglind's son made such a handsome figure that many fell deeply in love with him.

As to Siegfried, he often thought: 'How shall it ever come about that I may set eyes on this noble young lady? It saddens me that she whom I love with all my heart and have long so loved, remains an utter stranger to me.'

And whenever the great kings rode on circuit through their lands, their retainers perforce accompanied them and Siegfried among them, much to Kriemhild's regret, while he, too, was often in great distress from the love he bore her.

Thus Siegfried, you must know, lived with those lords in Gunther's land for a year on end without ever having seen the lovely maiden who was to bring him much joy and yet much sorrow, too.

CHAPTER FOUR

How Siegfried fought with the Saxons

*

STRANGE tidings were on their way to Gunther's country, borne by envoys that had been sent to the Burgundians from afar by unknown warriors who nevertheless were their enemies; hearing which, Gunther and his men were greatly vexed. I shall name those warriors for you. They were Liudeger, the proud and mighty sovereign of Saxony, and Liudegast, King of Denmark, and they were bringing a host of lordly intruders with them on their campaign.

The messengers whom these enemies of Gunther had sent into his country had arrived, and the strangers were asked their business and at once summoned into the presence of the King, who gave them a friendly greeting. 'You are welcome!' said the good King. 'Now tell us who it was that sent you here, for I have yet to learn it.' But they were much afraid of Gunther's wrath.

'If you will permit us to tell you the message we bring, Sire, we shall not stay silent but shall name you the lords who have sent us. They are Liudegast and Liudeger; and they intend to invade your country. You have provoked their anger and, truly, we were told that these lords bear you great hostility. They mean to launch an expedition against Worms on the Rhine, and you can take my word for it that they have many knights to support them. In twelve weeks from now their campaign will be launched, so that you must soon let it be seen whether you have any staunch friends to help you to guard your lands and castles; for the men of Liudegast and Liudeger will hack many helmets and shields to pieces here. But if you wish to treat with them, send a message to that effect, and then the numerous forces of your mighty enemies will not draw

33

near to do you such harm as must lead to the destruction of countless gallant knights.'

'Now wait a little until I have considered this affair,' answered the good King, 'and then I will tell you my mind. I shall not keep this momentous news from whatever trusty followers I may have; rather shall I complain of it to my friends.'

Mighty Gunther was deeply downcast. He kept the matter privy to his own thoughts, sent for Hagen and others of his men, and summoned Gernot urgently to court. When the noblest that could be found were assembled, he addressed them.

'Our country is threatened with invasion by strong attacking forces. I call on you to support me!'

'Let us ward it off, sword in hand,' answered gallant Gernot. 'They alone die that are doomed. Leave them for the dead men they are. Such things shall not make me forget my honour! Our enemies are welcome!'

'I would not advise that,' said Hagen of Troneck. 'Liudegast and Liudeger are of arrogant temper, and we cannot muster our forces so soon. But,' added the valiant warrior, 'why do you not tell Siegfried?'

Word was given to lodge the envoys in the town,[1] and whatever the hatred that was felt for them, it was right of mighty Gunther to have them well cared for till he should learn from his friends who was going to stand by him. Yet the King was in great anxiety and distress, and Siegfried, gay young knight, seeing Gunther so downcast, asked him to tell him all about it, since he could not know what had happened to him.

'I am much surprised,' he said, 'that the cheerful demeanour which you have shown us all along is so altered.'

'I cannot tell everyone of the vexations I have to bear, locked away in my heart,' answered handsome Gunther. 'One should complain of one's wrongs to proven friends.'

Siegfried turned pale, and then red. 'I have never denied you anything,' he answered the King. 'I shall help you to

1. Presumably outside the castle walls.

avert all your troubles. If you are looking for friends I shall assuredly be one among them, and I trust I shall acquit myself honourably till the end of my days.'

'May God reward you, lord Siegfried, for I like your words. And if your manly courage never comes to my aid I shall nevertheless rejoice that you wish me so well, and if I live for any time you shall be well rewarded. I will tell you why I am downcast. I have been informed by my enemies' envoys that they intend to attack me here, a thing that warriors have never done to us in Burgundy before.'

'Do not let that weigh on you,' said Siegfried, 'but calm your fears. Do as I ask – let me win honour and advantage for you, while you on your part summon your knights to your aid. Even though your powerful enemies had thirty thousand knights to help them and I only a thousand, I should face them in battle. You can rely on me!'

'I shall always seek to repay you,' replied King Gunther.

'Then muster a thousand of your men for me (since apart from a dozen warriors I have none of my own with me) and I shall defend your lands – for Siegfried will always serve you loyally. Hagen and Ortwin, Dancwart and Sindold, your beloved stalwarts, must help us, and brave Volker must ride with them – indeed Volker must bear your standard, since there is none I would give it to more willingly. As to the envoys, let them ride home to their lords' countries and inform their masters that they shall see us very soon and to such purpose that peace shall be assured for our cities.'

The King summoned his kinsmen and vassals accordingly.

Liudeger's envoys went into the presence of good King Gunther, and were glad to learn that they were soon to go home; and when he offered them rich presents and gave them a safe conduct they were happy indeed.

'Now tell my mighty enemies that they would do well to stay at home with their expedition,' said Gunther, 'but that if they insist on invading me here they shall learn what trouble is, unless my friends should fail me.' Thereupon magnificent gifts (of which Gunther had plenty to bestow) were placed before Liudeger's envoys; nor did they dare decline them, but, taking their leave, departed in good spirits.

When they arrived in Denmark, and King Liudegast heard the news which they were bringing from the Rhine, he was incensed at his enemies' disdain. The envoys told him that the Burgundians had brave men in great number and that they themselves had seen standing among them a warrior called Siegfried of the Netherlands – news that Liudegast did not like at all when he learned its import. But having heard it, the men of Denmark made haste to round up even more of their friends, until Lord Liudegast had enlisted for his campaign twenty thousand knights from among his warlike subjects. King Liudeger of Saxony like-wise summoned his vassals, till they had upwards of forty thousand with whom they planned to march on Burgundy. For his part, here at home, King Gunther had mustered his kinsmen and his brothers' and Hagen's men, of whom they had great need (though good warriors had later to die for it). They prepared themselves for their march, and when they were ready to cross the Rhine from Worms, valiant Volker was told to bear the standard, and Hagen to be captain of troops. With them rode Sindold and Hunold, who were well able to earn Gunther's gold; while Hagen's brother Dancwart, with Ortwin, had good claim to a place of honour on this expedition.

'Stay at home, my lord King, since your knights are ready to follow me,' said Siegfried. 'Remain here with the ladies and be of good cheer, for I dare assert I shall guard your lands and honour well. I shall take good care that those who would attack you in Worms stay at home, for we mean to ride so close to them in their own country as will turn their arrogance to fear.'

They rode with their warriors from the Rhine through Hesse towards Saxony, where there was fighting later. They laid waste the countryside with fire and pillage, to the great distress of the two kings, when they came to hear of it. Never had the Saxons suffered greater loss from invasion.

And now the Burgundians had reached the frontier, and the squires drew away.

'Who will take charge of our train here?' asked mighty Siegfried.

'Let brave Dancwart have charge of the youngsters,' they said. 'Put him and Ortwin in command of the rearguard, and we shall lose all the fewer to Liudeger's men.'

'And I myself will ride out and reconnoitre the enemy,' said valiant Siegfried, 'until I have made out their positions exactly.'

Fair Sieglind's son was soon armed. Before leaving, he entrusted the army to Hagen and valiant Gernot, and then rode off alone into Saxony – and many were the helmet-straps he cut through on that day! Soon Siegfried saw lying on the plain the great army which to the forces he could rally opposed a seething horde – forty thousand or more! His spirits rose at the sight of them.

On the other side, too, armed to perfection, a warrior had set out towards his enemy to reconnoitre, and him lord Siegfried saw, as the valient man saw him, so that each began to watch the other fiercely. I shall tell you who it was on outpost duty with his bright shield of gold held in readiness – it was King Liudegast guarding his army! Towards him the noble intruder galloped in fine style, and now lord Liudegast had marked him down, so that the two of them set their spurs to their chargers' flanks and vehemently levelled their spears at each other's shields, with the result that the King was soon in jeopardy. In the train of these thrusts, these princes' mounts bore them past each other at such a pace that they might have been wafted by the wind; whereupon, wheeling with splendid horsemanship, this fierce pair tried their fortunes with their swords. Then lord Siegfried struck blows that filled the plain with their sound and sent fiery sparks flying from his enemy's helmet as though from huge torches. Each met his match in the other, since lord Liudegast struck many cruel blows in answer, and the strength of each was brought mightily to bear on the other's shield. Thirty of Liudegast's men were patrolling in that quarter, but before they could come to his aid, Siegfried had won the victory with three great wounds which he dealt through Liudegast's bright corselet, stout though it was, drawing the blood with his two-edged sword, and damping all his ardour. King Liudegast asked Siegfried to spare him; he offered him his lands, and told him his name was Liudegast.

At this moment Luidegast's warriors arrived on the field. They had clearly seen what had passed between the two outposts, and, just as Siegfried was about to lead Liudegast away, they charged him, thirty strong, whereupon the hero defended his mighty captive with tremendous blows. Nor was this the last damage the handsome young knight inflicted, for he slew these thirty in a most warlike manner, leaving but one alive to ride off at speed and report what had happened there, with his bloody helmet for proof. When the Danes heard that their lord was a prisoner they were fearfully afflicted, and when his brother was told of it he began to rave with boundless anger, for it was a cruel blow to him.

Siegfried led valiant Liudegast away by sheer force to Gunther's men and handed him over to Hagen, who, learning that it was the King, was not unduly sorry.

The Burgundians were ordered to lace on their pennons. 'Forward!' cried Siegfried, 'If I remain alive, much shall be achieved here before the day is done that will sadden many a fine lady in Saxony! Keep me well in sight, you warriors from the Rhine, for I can lead you straight into Liudeger's army, and then you will see such a hacking of helmets by stout fighting-men! Before we turn back they will know what trouble means.'

Gernot and his men raced to their chargers. Lord Volker, the burly Minstrel,[1] seized the standard and rode at the head of the column who, for their part, were all splendidly equipped for battle, though, apart from Siegfried's Twelve, they brought a mere thousand to the field. Clouds of dust

1. Although he is a nobleman, and the minstrels were plebeians of the nondescript class of entertainers, Volker bears the sobriquet of 'the Minstrel' or 'the Fiddler' because he in fact sings and plays the fiddle and entertains his comrades from time to time (see p. 337).

rose up over the ways, and many fine shields gleamed among them as they rode across country. The Saxons, too, had come with their divisions, bearing keen swords which (as I learned since) bit deep when wielded by those warriors – they meant to defend both their castles and their lands from these intruders.

The captains of the two kings led their forces on, and Siegfried, too, had arrived with those whom he had brought from the Netherlands. Many a hand was reddened in the blood of battle that day. Sindold, Hunold, and Gernot slew many warriors in combat before these had really grasped how daring their slayers were, so that afterwards many ladies had to weep for them. Volker, Hagen, and Ortwin, who knew no fear in the fight, dimmed the brightness of numberless helmets with streams of blood in the fray, and Dancwart performed marvels.

And now the men of Denmark tried their hands. You could hear the clang of countless shields under the impact of their charge, and of the sharp swords, too, that were swung there in plenty, while the valiant Saxons also wrought much havoc.

When the Burgundians thrust into the battle they hacked wound on gaping wound, and blood was seen flowing over saddles – so boldly did those knights woo honour. And when the stalwarts from the Netherlands pressed after their lord into the closed ranks of the enemy, their keen swords rang loud and clear as they wielded them – they went in with Siegfried like the splendid young fighting-men they were. Not one of the Rhinelanders was seen to keep up with Siegfried; but as his blows fell you could pick out the rivers of blood running down from his enemy's helmets, till at last he came upon Liudeger at the head of his companions.

Siegfried had cut his way through the enemy there and back for the third time, and now Hagen had come to help him to have his fill of fighting, so that many excellent knights had to die that day from the pair of them. Finding Siegfried before him and seeing him swing his good sword Balmung so high and slay so many of his men, mighty lord Liudeger was seized with fierce anger. There was a grand mêlée and a loud ringing of swords as their retinues closed with each other. Then the two warriors made harsher trial of their prowess, till the Saxons began to give ground. Bitter was the strife between them! The lord of the Saxons had been informed, to his great wrath, that his brother had been taken prisoner, but he was unaware[1] that Siegfried was his captor, since the deed was ascribed to Gernot, though later he learned the truth of it. Liudeger dealt such powerful blows that Siegfried's horse stumbled under him; but when the beast had recovered itself Siegfried raged terribly in the fight, in which he was aided by Hagen, Gernot, Dancwart, and Volker, so that many men lay slain there. Sindold, Hunold, and Sir Ortwin, too, laid low many foemen. These princes were locked in battle. You could see javelins beyond number hurled by warriors' hands flying over helmets and piercing bright shields, with buckler after buckler all stained with blood. Many knights dismounted in the thick of it – Siegfried and Liudeger assailed each other on foot amid flying spears and keen-edged javelins.

Siegfried of the Netherlands was bent on wresting victory from the brave Saxons, of whom many were now wounded, and the weight of his blows sent the bolts and braces flying from their shields. And oh, the bright mail-corselets that Dancwart burst asunder!

Then, suddenly, lord Liudeger descried a crown painted on Siegfried's shield over the grip, and he knew at once that the mighty man was there.

'Stop fighting, all my men!' the warrior shouted to his friends. 'I have just recognized mighty Siegfried, son of Siegmund. The Devil accurst has sent him here to Saxony!' He ordered them to lower their standards, and sued for peace. Peace was later granted him, though, overwhelmed as he had been by fearless Siegfried, he had to be a prisoner in Gunther's land.

1. With the editor of the text I read *niht* for *wol*, which, though vouched for by all the MSS, is clearly an error.

By common accord they ceased their fighting, and the Saxons laid aside their helmets and broad shields which, one like the other, were pierced through and through and blood-stained from blows dealt by the Burgundians, who now made captive whomever they pleased, since theirs was the power to do so. Warlike Gernot and Hagen had the wounded placed on litters and they took back to the Rhine as prisoners five hundred fighting-men.

The Danes rode back defeated to Denmark, nor to their shame had the Saxons fought so marvellously as to earn themselves any glory. The fallen were deeply mourned by their kinsmen. Then the Burgundians ordered their armour to be transported to the Rhine. In company with his stalwarts, gallant Siegfried had done what he had set out to do, and he had so distinguished himself that all Gunther's men could not but admit it.

Lord Gernot sent messengers to Worms to inform his friends at home of his and his men's success, and how honourably those bold men had acquitted themselves.

The pages spurred hard and made report, and those who had been downcast were overjoyed at the glad news that had reached them, while noble ladies were heard eagerly inquiring how the King's vassals had fared. One of the messengers was summoned into Kriemhild's presence, and this was done in great secrecy – she dared not do it openly, since among those who had fought was the darling of her heart.

When she saw the messenger entering her chamber, lovely Kriemhild said very kindly: 'Tell me the good news, and I will reward you with gold; and if you tell me truly I shall always be your friend. How did my brother Gernot and other of my relations come off in the fighting? Have we perhaps lost many dead? Or, tell me, who acquitted himself best there?'

'There were no cowards on our side anywhere,' the page was quick to answer. 'But, my noble princess, since you have asked me, no man rode so well in battle as our noble guest, brave Siegfried of the Netherlands, who worked miracles there! Whatever all those warriors – Dancwart, Hagen, and the other royal vassals – did during the fighting, and however they strove to win honour, they achieved nothing compared with Siegfried, King Siegmund's son. They killed a host of warriors while the battle raged, but none could tell you all the marvels which Siegfried performed whenever he entered the fray, such sorrow did he bring to ladies by slaying their kinsmen! The lovers of many ladies fell there too, never to rise again – his blows rang on their helmets so mightily that the blood came streaming from their wounds! He has all the qualities that go to make a brave, good knight. But whatever the exploits of Ortwin of Metz – all he could reach with his sword fell wounded or for the most part dead – your brother inflicted the greatest anguish possible in battle. One must concede the truth to these rare warriors: the Burgundians bore themselves so manfully that their honour is free of all tarnish! They emptied saddle after saddle with blows from their shining swords that echoed loudly over the plain. Indeed, the Rhenish warriors rode to such purpose that it would have been better had their enemies refrained. When the armies met with all their forces, the brave knights of Troneck inflicted fearful losses and valiant Hagen himself dispatched a great number, of which there would be much to tell on arriving back here in Burgundy; while Gernot's men, Sindold and Hunold, and fearless Rumold, too, performed such feats that Liudeger will always rue having sent messengers to the Rhine to declare war on your kinsmen. Yet from beginning to end of the battle, Siegfried did the greatest deeds that were ever witnessed anywhere – and with what relish! The splendid man is bringing back to Gunther's land captives of great rank, subdued by his strength and courage, for whom King Liudegast and his brother Liudeger of Saxony must bear the loss. And now listen to the news I bring, most noble Princess! Siegfried captured them both! Thanks to his prowess, never were so many prisoners brought back to this country as are coming Rhinewards now!'

No news could have been more welcome to Kriemhild.

'Believe me, my lady,' the page continued, 'more than five hundred able-bodied men are being brought to Burgundy and eighty bloodstained litters of men who are sorely wounded, most of them hewn by brave Siegfried. Those who in their pride sent their challenge to the Rhineland are now perforce Gunther's prisoners, and are being led here with rejoicing.'

A blush suffused Kriemhild's fair cheek when she learned the news, her lovely face blushed red as a rose on hearing that handsome young Siegfried had happily emerged from great peril. She was also glad for her relatives, as indeed she should have been.

'You have brought me good news, and for your pains you shall have some fine clothes and ten marks of gold I shall have fetched for you.' (Such gifts encourage one to tell such news to great ladies.)

The messenger received his reward of gold and clothes, whereupon the windows were thronged with pretty girls who kept lookout over the road along which a host of proud warriors was riding back to Burgundy.

And there came the hale and hearty, together with the wounded. They could hear their friends' welcome without shame. The King rode out cheerfully to meet his guests, for his great sorrows had yielded to joy. He received his own men honourably, and the strangers[1] too, since to have done otherwise than to thank those kindly who had come to his aid and won a glorious victory would have ill beseemed a mighty king.

Gunther asked for news of his friends and inquired who had been killed on this campaign, and he was told that he had lost no more than sixty. They had to be resigned to their loss, as still happens when heroes are slain.

Those who were unwounded brought back to Burgundy many a shield and helmet battered and cut to pieces. The army dismounted before the royal palace, where glad scunds of welcome met the ear. The King had the warriors quartered in the town, his guests well cared for, and the wounded

1. Siegfried and his men.

tended and given every comfort, while his treatment of his enemies bore witness to his quality.

'You are welcome,' he said to Liudegast. 'Owing to you I have suffered great harm, but, if I am lucky, this will soon be made good to me. God reward my friends, they have done well by me.'

'You may indeed thank them,' replied Liudeger. 'No King ever won more prisoners of such rank. If you will treat us well while we are in your custody, and act mercifully towards your enemies, we shall pay you handsomely.'

'I shall leave you your personal freedom, the two of you, provided that my enemies remain here with me,' answered Gunther. 'And I require sureties that they will not quit my territories without leave.'

Liudeger gave his hand on it. They were then led to their rest and made comfortable. The wounded were kindly put to bed, and for those who remained whole, mead and good wine were poured out. These warriors were as happy as could be. Their battered shields were taken away to store, and orders were given for the bloodstained saddles (of which there were so many) to be hidden away lest the ladies be moved to tears. And still many good knights were arriving, weary from campaigning.

The land was full of both friend and foe. The King entertained his guests with unheard-of magnanimity, commanding that the sorely wounded be tended with great solicitude. Thus the pride and swagger of the invaders had been brought very low.

Physicians were offered rich rewards of unweighed silver, and of bright gold too, if they would heal the combatants now that the stress of war was past; in addition to which, the King gave lavishly to his allies there. Those of them who wished to set out on their journey home again were asked to stay, as is the custom with friends. And now he took counsel how he might reward his vassals who had fulfilled his wishes so triumphantly.

'Let them ride away now,' advised lord Gernot, 'but invite them to return in six weeks' time for a festivity, when many who are now badly wounded will have recovered.'

Thereupon Siegfried of the Netherlands asked the King's leave to depart. But on being acquainted with his wish, King Gunther most amiably begged him to stay, a thing Siegfried would not have done but for Gunther's sister. And although he had well deserved the King's friendship, like that of Gunther's kinsmen who had witnessed his feats in battle, he was too exalted to accept a reward. Thus Siegfried decided to remain there for the sake of the lovely young woman whom he hoped to be able to meet. And indeed he did so, later, for he came to know her as well as he had wished, and rode back happily to Siegmund's land.

By royal command, knightly sports were held continuously, and many young knights followed them with zest. Meanwhile on the river bank below Worms the King had seats set up for those who had been invited to Burgundy.

Towards the time when the guests were expected, it came to the ears of lovely Kriemhild that her brother wished to give a feast in honour of his esteemed allies, and, accordingly, fair ladies gave assiduous attention to the dresses and wimples they would wear. When queenly Uote heard of the proud knights who had been invited, she had some magnificent fabrics taken from the chest and clothes got ready for love of her dear children; and with these many ladies, maidens, and young warriors of Burgundy were adorned; but she had many fine robes made up for the strangers, too.

CHAPTER FIVE

How Siegfried first set eyes on Kriemhild

*

THOSE who wished to attend the festivity could be seen riding towards the Rhine daily, and many who came to Burgundy for love of the King were given chargers and splendid robes. Their high seats were ready for them all at that festival, the noblest and most exalted, to the number, so we are told, of two-and-thirty princes, in expectation of whom fair ladies vied in adorning themselves. Nor was young Giselher idle. He, Gernot, and their suite extended a kindly welcome to friend and stranger alike, saluting the knights with all due ceremony.

Their guests brought with them to this festivity by the Rhine numerous saddles red with gold, and sumptuous shields and robes. Many who had been wounded now appeared cheerful again; while those who were bedridden and harassed by their wounds had to forget death's harshness. But to the loss of those who were languishing the others perforce resigned themselves: one and all, they looked forward with pleasure to the festive days ahead, and to the gay life they meant to lead with the entertainment offered them. Their delight knew no bounds, their hearts overflowed with happiness; and throughout the length and breadth of Gunther's realm there was great rejoicing.

At Whitsuntide one morning, five thousand knights or more emerged from their quarters for the festival to greet the eye with their delightful clothes; and at once in many places the entertainment began, each man striving to outdo his fellow.

The King was observant enough to have noticed how deeply Siegfried loved his sister, though Siegfried had never set eyes on her, whose great beauty was admitted to surpass that of all other young ladies.

46

Then Ortwin addressed the King. 'If you wish to win full credit at your festivity, you must bring out our lovely maidens for the guests to see – the pride of Burgundy![1] Where else could a man find delight, if not in pretty girls and fine-looking women? Have your sister appear before the company.' This advice was to the liking of many young warriors.

'I shall be pleased to do so,' replied the King, and all who heard it were deeply gratified. Thus Gunther sent to lady Uote and her beautiful daughter to summon them to court with their young ladies-in-waiting, whereupon bevies of handsome girls chose fine gowns from the coffers and attired themselves with care from stores of noble garments, of bracelets and galloons, which they found in Uote's chest.

Many youthful warriors cherished hopes this day that their looks might please the ladies – good fortune they would not have exchanged for a kingdom! They loved to gaze at women whom they had never seen before.

The noble King commanded a full hundred of his vassals, kinsmen of his and his sister's and members of the Burgundian household, to wait upon her and escort her, sword in hand. And now queenly Uote appeared with Kriemhild, having chosen for company a hundred fair ladies or more, magnificently gowned, while her daughter, too, was attended by a troop of comely maidens.

When these all came into view from their apartment, the knights surged forward with much jostling, in the hope of eyeing the maidens to their hearts' content, if that were possible.[2]

But now lovely Kriemhild emerged like the dawn from the dark clouds, freeing from much distress him who

1. Unmarried girls and young women of the nobility were kept in seclusion during the German Middle Ages. A year has passed, yet Siegfried has not set eyes on Kriemhild.
2. As later in England at the Court of St James, it was a sign of good breeding on the part of the gentlemen to respond vigorously to the charms of the ladies.

secretly cherished her and indeed long had done so. He saw
the adorable maiden stand there in all her splendour –
gems past counting gleamed from her robe, while her rosy
cheeks glowed bewitchingly; so that even if a man were to
have his heart's desire he could not claim to have seen any-
thing fairer. Kriemhild outshone many good ladies as the
moon the stars when its light shines clear from the sky, and
those gallant warriors' hearts rose within them as they gazed
on her.

Stately chamberlains preceded her, but the spirited
knights would not desist from pressing forward to where
they could glimpse the charming girl. As to Siegfried, he was
both glad and sad. 'How could it ever happen that I
should win your love?' he asked himself. 'This is a foolish
self-deception. But I would rather I were dead than shun
your company.' At these thoughts his colour came and
went.

Siegfried son of Siegmund stood there handsome as
though limned on parchment with all a master's skill (as
indeed it was admitted that none was his equal for looks).

Those who were escorting the ladies bade the knights
make way everywhere, and many of them complied. And
as they observed all these fine women with their well-bred
ways, the high aspirations in their hearts brought joy to
many men.

Then lord Gernot of Burgundy spoke. 'Gunther, dear
brother, you must make a like return in the presence of all
these warriors to the man who gave his services so kindly,
nor shall I ever blush for having counselled it. Present
Siegfried to my sister, so that the maiden may accord him
her greeting – we shall never cease to reap the benefit.
Although she has never addressed a knight before, let her
now bid Siegfried welcome. With this we shall attach this
splendid warrior to ourselves.'

Kinsmen of Gunther went over to where the hero of the
Netherlands was standing, and said: 'The King gives you
leave to enter his presence, for he wishes to honour you
with his sister's salutation.'

Lord Siegfried was delighted in his heart, which now nourished joy without sorrow, for he was to meet fair Uote's daughter. And indeed she greeted him becomingly.

When the proud man stood before her, she saw his face take fire. 'You are welcome lord Siegfried, noble knight,' said she. Siegfried's spirits soared at this greeting, and he bowed his devoted thanks. Then she took him by the hand, and how ardently did this lord walk beside the lady, exchanging tender looks with her in secret!

If a white hand were pressed there affectionately at the promptings of sweet love, then I was not told so; yet I cannot believe that it was not, for she had soon conveyed her liking; so that in days of summer or at the approach of May,[1] Siegfried had never had cause for such ecstasy as now, as he walked hand in hand with her whom he wished to wed.

'Ah, if only this had happened to me,' thought many a knight, 'that *I* should walk at her side as I have seen him do – or even lie beside her! I should not quarrel with that.' Yet no warrior served better to win a queen than Siegfried.

Whichever lands they were from, the guests had eyes for those two alone. Leave was granted for her to bestow a kiss on the handsome man,[2] and never in all his life had anything so pleasant befallen him.

'This most exalted kiss has been the cause of many a man's lying wounded from Siegfried's strong arm, as I know to my cost,' the King of Denmark interposed quickly. 'May God never permit him to enter my kingdom.'

The courtiers everywhere were ordered to fall back and make way for fair Kriemhild, and then a company of brave knights took her decorously to church. But, arriving there, handsome Siegfried was parted from her,[3] while she entered the minster with her train of ladies, making such a picture in all her finery that many knights picked her

1. The time associated in medieval poetry with love-making.
2. A ceremonial kiss exchanged by nobles of comparable rank.
3. As in most archaic churches, the women were separated from the men.

out to feast their eyes, nursing hopes as vain as they were lofty.

Siegfried could scarce wait till mass had been sung. He had reason to bless his good fortune that the young woman whom he cherished in his thoughts was so well-disposed towards him; and indeed there was no small reason why he should love the beautiful girl. When she came out of church, Siegfried was there in advance of her, and they asked the brave knight to rejoin her.

Only now did charming Kriemhild thank him for having fought so magnificently at the head of her kinsmen. 'May God reward you, lord Siegfried', said the lovely girl, 'for having earned from our knights such loyal devotion as I hear them speak of.'

'I shall always be at their service,' he answered, with a loving look at Kriemhild, 'and, unless death prevents me, I will never rest my head before I have done their pleasure. This I do to win your favour, my lady Kriemhild.'

Each day for the space of twelve, the excellent young woman was seen in Siegfried's company when she had to appear at court in the presence of her relatives, a compliment they paid him in the hope that it would give him much pleasure. And daily there was great merriment below Gunther's hall and the happy clamour, both outside and within, of a crowd of bold men jousting. Ortwin and Hagen performed great feats; for whatever pursuit anyone wished to follow these gay knights were ready for it with all their heart, so that they became well known to the guests, and the whole land reaped glory from it.

Those who had been wounded came outside and sought entertainment with the company at fencing under the shield and at javelin-throwing, and numerous strong men joined in with them.

The King regaled them all with the choicest viands at this feast; he had placed himself beyond all such reproach as kings may incur. Going up to his guests, he addressed them in friendly fashion. 'Before you leave you must accept my gifts, good knights,' he said, 'for it is my thought

that if you do not disdain them I shall be forever obliged.
I shall be heartily glad to share my wealth with you.'

'Before we ride home to our country,' answered the
Danes immediately, 'we wish to make peace with you
firmly; and not without good reason, since we have lost
many dear friends whom your knights have slain.' Though
Liudegast was now healed of his wounds and the lord of
the Saxons too had recovered from the hurts of battle,
they were leaving some few dead in Burgundy.

King Gunther went to Siegfried. 'Advise me what to do,'
he said. 'Our opponents wish to ride home tomorrow
morning, and are asking me and my vassals for a firm
treaty of peace. Now you must advise me, brave Siegfried,
which course you think the best. Let me tell you what these
lords are offering me. If I were to set them free, they
would be pleased to give me as much gold as can be
carried by five hundred sumpters.'

'That would be wrong,' said mighty Siegfried. 'You
must allow the noble warriors to go free of obligations on
the understanding that in future they must refrain from
invading your country. Let both give you this assurance
on their royal oaths.'

'I shall follow this advice.' Thereupon they left that place.
And it was announced to Gunther's enemies that nobody
wanted the gold which they had offered. (How their dear
relations at home longed to see these battleworn men!)

Shield after shield full of gold was carried in, and, on
Gernot's advice, Gunther doled it out copiously to his
friends in unweighed heaps of about five hundred marks, and
to some of them even more. Then, when they were on the
point of departing, all the guests took leave of the King and
they also appeared before Kriemhild, and before Queen
Uote's throne; and never were knights dismissed with
greater honour.

When they rode away, the guests' quarters were empty;
but the King remained at home in his magnificence to-
gether with his many noble kinsmen, who daily came to
wait on lady Kriemhild.

Then, in despair of achieving his purpose, Siegfried wished to take his leave, and it came to the King's ears that he was intending to depart. But youthful Giselher dissuaded him from going.

'Where did you intend to ride off to, most noble Siegfried? Do as I ask you and stay with us knights, with King Gunther and his vassals. There are many beautiful ladies here with whose acquaintance we shall be pleased to honour you.'

'Then do not fetch the horses,' mighty Siegfried commanded. 'I was meaning to ride away, but I shall not do so – and take our shields away! – I was planning to return to my country. But lord Giselher has turned me from my purpose in the loyal affection that he bears me.'

And so, to please his friends, the valiant man remained: nor was there another land anywhere in which he might have sojourned so agreeably; with the result that, now, he saw Kriemhild every day. It was her transcendent beauty that caused lord Siegfried to stay there.

They passed the time with all manner of amusements, except that, time and time again, he was tormented by the passion she aroused in him, thanks to which, in days to come, the hero met a pitiful end.

CHAPTER SIX

How Gunther sailed to Iceland for Brunhild

*

TIDINGS never heard before had crossed the Rhine, telling how, beyond it, there lived many lovely maidens. Good King Gunther conceived the idea of winning one, and his heart thrilled at the thought of it.

Over the sea there dwelt a queen whose like was never known, for she was of vast strength and surpassing beauty. With her love as the prize, she vied with brave warriors at throwing the javelin, and the noble lady also hurled the weight to a great distance and followed with a long leap; and whoever aspired to her love had, without fail, to win these three tests against her, or else, if he lost but one, he forfeited his head.

The maiden had competed in this way times out of number; and having heard this report in his kingdom on the Rhine, the handsome knight turned his thoughts to winning the lovely woman, for which brave warriors had to die in the end.

'Whatever fate is in store for me,' said the lord of the Rhenish land, 'I shall sail down to the sea and go to Brunhild. To win her love I mean to stake my life and indeed I shall lose it if I fail to make her mine.'

'I would advise against that,' said Siegfried. 'This queen has such terrible ways that it costs any man dear who woos her, so that truly you should forgo this journey.'

'In that case', interposed Hagen, 'I should advise you to ask Siegfried to share these perils with you, seeing that he is so knowledgeable about Brunhild's affairs.'

'Will you help me woo this handsome woman, noble Siegfried?' asked Gunther. 'If you do as I ask, and I win her for my love, I will stake my life and honour for you in turn.'

'I will do it, if you will give me your sister fair Kriem-
hild, the noble princess,' answered Siegfried, Siegmund's
son. 'I wish no other reward for my trouble.'

'I agree to that,' replied Gunther. 'Siegfried, here is my
hand on it! If fair Brunhild comes to this country I will
give you my sister to wife, and you can live in joy with the
lovely girl always.'

The exalted knights swore oaths on it; and this added
mightily to their toils, for great were the dangers they had
to face before they brought the lady to Burgundy.

They now made preparations for their voyage. Siegfried
would have to take with him the magic cloak which he had
won so manfully from the dwarf Alberich, and at such peril.
Wearing it, he gained the strength of twelve beyond that of
his own powerful frame. He wooed the splendid woman with
great subtlety, since the cloak was of such a kind that
without being seen any man could do as he pleased in it.
In this way he won Brunhild, though he had cause to rue
it later.

'Now tell me, Siegfried, brave knight, before I start on
my journey, must we take a retinue to Brunhild's land in
order to go to sea with full honours? Thirty thousand
knights can soon be mustered.'

'However great an army we take, the Queen has such
dreadful ways that they would all have to die through her
arrogance. Let me propose something better, good warrior.
Let us sail down the Rhine like soldiers of fortune, and let
me name those who are to form the party. We shall put to
sea four in all and so win the lady, whatever becomes of us
afterwards. Now, I shall be one of these companions, and
you be the second; let Hagen be the third, and brave
Dancwart the fourth. In this way we shall escape with
our lives, for a thousand others would not face us in battle!'

'Before we leave,' said King Gunther, 'I should very
much like to know what sort of clothes we must wear at
Brunhild's court – tell me that.'

'In Brunhild's land they always wear the very best
clothes you ever saw, and so we must appear splendidly

dressed at her court lest we be disgraced when the news of our arrival is brought.'

'Then I shall go to my dear mother,' answered the good knight, 'and see if I can obtain leave for those pretty girls of hers to help us to get ready such clothes as we can wear with distinction when we appear before noble Brunhild.'

'Why do you ask your mother for such services?' asked Hagen of Troneck in his lordly way. 'Tell your sister what you have in mind – her help will turn out well for you on this visit to Brunhild's court.'

Gunther accordingly sent a message to his sister to say that he and Siegfried wished to see her. But before this was done the lovely girl dressed herself exquisitely – it was only with mild regret that she viewed the warriors' coming! And now her train, too, were adorned becomingly. The two princes then entered; hearing which, Kriemhild rose from her seat and politely went to receive her noble visitor and her brother.

'You are welcome, brother, and your companion, too!' said the maiden. 'I should like to know what prompts you lords to seek my presence? Tell me, what brings you noble warriors here?'

'I will indeed, my lady,' answered King Gunther. 'Despite our gay aspirations we have grounds for anxiety too, since we intend to go travelling to distant lands in order to pay court to the ladies, and we need elegant clothes for our journey.'

'Be seated, dear brother,' said the princess, 'and tell me all about those ladies whose love you desire in other lands.' And she took the illustrious pair by the hand and led them to the sumptuous couch on which she had been sitting and whose covers, you may believe me, were embroidered in gold with fine pictures.

It was pleasant passing the time here with the ladies. As to Siegfried and Kriemhild, they had ample opportunity for kind looks and friendly glances. He cherished her in his heart, for she was as dear to him as life; and indeed in the end fair Kriemhild became strong Siegfried's wife.

'Dearest sister,' said the great King, 'we mean to pass the time in dalliance in Brunhild's country, and we need some fine clothes to wear before the ladies. But unless you help us this will not be possible.'

'I shall leave you in no doubt, dear brother, that I am ready to do anything within my power for you,' answered the young lady, 'and I should be very sorry if any other were to deny you. You must not ask so timidly but command me as my lord, since I am at your service for whatever you care to ask of me. I shall do it gladly,' the charming girl concluded.

'We wish to wear good clothes, sister, and you must help us to prepare them with your own noble hands. Let your girls complete the task, so that our clothes suit us well – for go on this journey we must!'

'Listen to me,' said the young lady. 'Silk I have myself; but you get your men to fetch us jewels by the shieldful, and then we shall stitch your clothes.' To this Gunther and Siegfried assented. 'But who are the companions that are to go to court with you in grand array?' continued the Princess.

'There are four of us all told,' he answered. 'Two of my men, Hagen and Dancwart, must accompany me to court. Now mark what I am telling you, my lady: we four are to wear three different sets of clothes a day for four days, and of such quality that we can quit Brunhild's land without disgrace.'

Their lordships withdrew after taking kind leave of Princess Kriemhild, who then summoned from her apartments thirty of her maidens that were gifted for such work. They threaded precious stones into snow-white silk from Arabia or into silk from Zazamanc[1] as green as clover, making fine robes, while noble Kriemhild cut the cloth herself. Whatever handsome linings they could lay hands on from the skins of strange water-beasts, wondrous to see, they covered with silk, just as the knights would wear

1. See Appendix 3, 'The Date of the Poem', p. 366.

them. And now hear some marvellous things about their dazzling clothes.

The ladies were well supplied with the best Moroccan and Libyan silk that a royal family ever acquired, and Kriemhild let it be seen clearly that these knights enjoyed her favour. And now that they had set their hearts on this voyage with its lofty goal, furs of ermine no longer seemed good enough: their linings were covered instead with coal-black brocades all spangled with brilliant stones set in Arabian gold such as would well become brave warriors on festive occasions today. The noble ladies had not been idle, since in the space of seven weeks they had finished the garments, by which time the good knights' armour, too, was ready. And now that their preparations were over, a stout bark that had been carefully built for them stood ready on the Rhine to carry them downstream to the open sea. The noble young ladies were spent with their toil; but they sent word to the knights to say that their work was done, and that the elegant clothes which they had wished to take with them were ready to their requirements.

Then the King and his men wished to tarry by the Rhine no longer, and he sent a messenger to the companions to ask them if they would like to see their new clothes and try them on. The clothes fitted them perfectly, and the warriors thanked the ladies. And all to whom they showed themselves had to admit never having seen anything better, so that they could wear them at court with pleasure. Theirs was the best of knightly apparel, and they thanked Kriemhild profusely.

Then these high-hearted warriors asked leave to depart with all knightly decorum, making bright eyes moist and dim with tears.

'Dearest brother,' Kriemhild said, 'if you would stay here, where your life would not be in such danger, and woo other ladies, I should say it was well done. You can find her equal nearer home.'

I imagine the ladies' hearts foretold them the outcome, since whatever anyone said to them they wept, one and all, so that the gold above their breasts was dulled by the copious tears they shed.

'Lord Siegfried,' said Kriemhild, 'let me commend my dear brother to your loyal protection so that no harm befalls him in Brunhild's land.'

The dauntless man gave Lady Kriemhild his hand and swore it. 'If I remain alive, madam,' he said, 'you shall be rid of all your cares. I shall bring him back here to the Rhine unscathed, rely on it!' The lovely maiden inclined her head in thanks.

Their shields that shone with gold were carried on to the river bank, and all their gear was brought. And now word was given for their chargers to be led out, for they were ready to go. At this fair ladies wept abundantly, while charming young girls thronged the windows.

A strong wind in the sail sent a shudder through the ship, and the proud companions embarked on the Rhine.

'Who will be captain?' said King Gunther.

'I,' answered Siegfried. 'I can pilot you over the deep, believe me, good warriors, for the right sea paths are well known to me.' Thus they were leaving Burgundy in good heart. Siegfried quickly seized a sweep and pushed off powerfully from the bank. King Gunther himself took an oar, and so these excellent knights put her out from land.

They had on board with them choice food and excellent wine, indeed the best Rhenish to be had; their horses were well stabled and they themselves were very comfortable; their craft sailed on an even keel, and they met nothing untoward; their stout halyards were hauled taut: and so before a good wind they sailed twenty miles down-stream by nightfall (though later these proud warriors were to rue their toil).

By the twelfth morning, so we are told, the winds had carried them far away to Isenstein in Brunhild's land, which none but Siegfried knew. Seeing so many walled cities and the broad domains, King Gunther swiftly said: 'Tell me, friend Siegfried, do you know whose cities and fine lands these are?'

'Indeed I do', answered Siegfried. 'They are Brunhild's land and people and the fortress of Isenstein, of which I told you; and before this day is out you shall see many lovely women there. But I would counsel you; knights, for it seems advisable to me, to be of one mind and all say the same thing, since when later today we enter Queen Brunhild's presence we must inevitably go in great fear of her. When we see the adorable woman with her retainers about her, noble warriors, you must abide by this one story – that Gunther is my overlord and I am his vassal. Then all his hopes will come true.'

They agreed to all that Siegfried bade them promise, and none refrained out of pride from saying whatever he wanted,[1] so that things went well with them when King Gunther met fair Brunhild.

'I undertake to do this not so much from affection for you as for the sake of your beautiful sister,' said Siegfried. 'I love her as my own life and soul, and I shall serve gladly to this end, that she shall marry me.'

1. This passage might also be rendered: 'and in their overweening pride not one of them refrained from saying . . .'. If this is what the poet meant, it would be one of several hints that in deceiving Brunhild the warriors were laying themselves open to their own destruction.

CHAPTER SEVEN

How Gunther won Brunhild

*

THEIR bark had now sailed near enough to the fortress for King Gunther to see troops of lovely maidens standing at the windows above, and he was sorry that none of them was known to him.

'Do you know anything about those girls looking down at us here on the water?' he asked his comrade Siegfried. 'Whatever the name of their lord, they look spirited young women.'

'Take secret stock of the young ladies,' replied lord Siegfried, 'and tell me which you would take, if you could choose.'

'I shall,' answered the bold knight. 'Now I can see one standing at the window there in a snow-white gown who is so beautiful that my eyes have singled her out, so that had I the power to choose I should assuredly make her my wife.'

'Your eyes have chosen very fittingly, for that lovely girl is noble Brunhild, to whom your whole being is so ardently drawn.' And indeed, Gunther liked everything about her.

Then the Queen told her superb young ladies to move away from the windows – they were not to stand there as a spectacle for strangers. They obediently did as they were told. But we have since learnt what these ladies did. They put on their finery to receive these unknown visitors, as comely women have always done, and, prompted by their curiosity, went up to the loopholes and through them took note of the warriors. Only four had entered their country.

Through their peep-holes those handsome women saw bold Siegfried lead a war-horse ashore, which to Gunther's way of thinking much enhanced his own importance. The horse was big and strong as it was handsome, and Siegfried

held the magnificent beast by its bridle till King Gunther
was seated in the saddle, such service did Siegfried render
him; though the time was to come when Gunther had
utterly forgotten it. Then Siegfried fetched his own horse
from the ship; but never had he done such duty before
as to hold a warrior's stirrup for him. All of this was seen
by those proud and comely women through the loop-
holes.

The horses and robes of this gay pair of knights were of
the very same dazzling snow-white hue; their fine shields
shone in their grasp; their gem-studded saddles and narrow
poitrels were hung with bells of lustrous red gold: thus
magnificently did they come riding up to Brunhild's hall.
These handsome knights arrived in her country, as their
high courage demanded, with newly ground spear-heads
and splendid swords that reached down to their spurs
and were both broad and sharp. Such weapons did they
wear, and none of this was lost on noble Brunhild.

With them came Dancwart and Hagen, and we are
told that these warriors wore rich clothes as black as the
raven, with fine great shields. You could see the Indian
jewels they were wearing on their robes move in gorgeous
ripples as they walked.

The good warriors had left their bark beside the sea
unguarded, and were riding up to the castle, within whose
walls they saw eighty-six towers, three great palaces and a
splendid hall of noble, grass-green marble, where Brunhild
waited with her court.

The fortress was opened and the gates were flung wide,
and Brunhild's vassals ran out to meet them and to welcome
them to their lady's country. Word was given to take their
horses and shields to be cared for. 'You must give us your
swords and bright corselets,' said one of the chamberlains.

'You shall not have them,' answered Hagen of Troneck.
'We will carry them ourselves.'

But Siegfried intervened to enlighten him. 'In this
castle, let me tell you, it is the custom that no guest shall
wear his armour. Now let them take yours away, that would

be the right thing to do.' Gunther's man Hagen complied, yet much against his will.

They ordered drink to be poured for the guests and gave them comfortable quarters. Many brave warriors in princely clothes were to be seen at court there, coming and going in all directions; yet the appearance of the bold strangers attracted great attention.

It was then reported to lady Brunhild that unknown knights clad in magnificent robes had arrived after a sea-voyage, and the good maiden began to ask questions. 'Tell me who these strange knights may be', said the fair Queen, 'that stand within my walls in such stately array, and for whose sake they have made the journey here.'

'I dare assert, my lady,' said one of her court, 'that I have never set eyes on any of them, save that one of them bears a likeness to Siegfried. I earnestly advise you to receive him kindly. The second of the companions has this distinction, that he could be a mighty king holding sway over great principalities, if they were his for the ruling; for he stands so majestically beside the others. The third, though of handsome appearance, mighty Queen, strikes terror with his vehement glances which he darts ceaselessly about him, so that I fancy his is a fierce humour. Of the youngest this can be said to his praise, that I saw the noble knight standing there as modest as a maid, excellent in his bearing and altogether charming; yet we should have cause to be afraid if anyone here provoked him, for however engaging his manners, and however handsome his looks, he has it in him to bereave many fair women, once his blood is up. He has the whole appearance of a fearless knight in all that goes to make one.'

'Bring me my robes,' said the Queen. 'If strong Siegfried has come it is at peril of his life, since I do not fear him so much that I should consent to marry him.'

Fair Brunhild was soon beautifully attired, and then, accompanied by bevies of pretty girls, a full hundred or more and all of them elegantly dressed, she went. For these comely ladies were curious to see the strangers. Brunhild's warriors, knights of Iceland to the number of five hundred or more, attended them sword in hand, a sight far from pleasing to the visitors, who nevertheless rose from their seats undismayed and undaunted. Now pray listen to what this maiden-queen said when she saw Siegfried. 'Welcome, Siegfried, to my country. I should very much like to know what brings you here.'

'You accord me too much favour, my lady Brunhild, magnanimous Queen, when you deign to salute me before this noble knight, who, as befits my lord, stands nearer to you than I – an honour I would gladly forgo! My liege is a prince of the Rhenish lands – what more need I tell you? – and we have voyaged here to win your love. For whatever the fate in store for him he means to make you his wife. Now consider this while there is time, since my lord means to hold you to your terms. His name is Gunther, and he is a king most high. If he were to win your love, he would have nothing left to wish for. The handsome warrior commanded me to sail here, but, had it been in my power to deny him, I would gladly have refrained.'

'If he is your lord and you are his liegeman, and provided he dares essay my sports (whose rules I shall lay down for him) and proves himself the winner, I shall wed him. Otherwise, if I win, it will cost you all your lives!'

'Madam, show us your formidable contests,' said Hagen of Troneck. 'It would have to go hard with my lord Gunther before he would own you had beaten him. He trusts himself to win a handsome young woman such as you.'

'He will have to cast the weight, follow through with a leap, and then throw the javelin with me. Do not be too hasty – you may well lose your lives and reputations here,' said the charming woman.[1] 'Consider it very closely.'

Brave Siegfried went up to the King and told him not to be afraid, but to speak his whole mind to the Queen. 'With the aid of my ruses I shall see that she does you no harm.'

'Most noble Queen,' replied King Gunther, 'lay down

1. There is always a touch of burlesque when Brunhild goes into action; cf. p. 88.

whatever rules you like. Even were there more to come, I would face them all for love of your fair person. If I fail to make you my wife, then let me lose my head!'

Having heard Gunther's words, the Queen commanded them make haste with the games, this being her good pleasure. She sent for a stout suit of armour, a corselet of ruddy gold, and a good shield. She drew on a silken gambeson beautifully fashioned from Libyan brocade that no weapon ever pierced in battle,[1] agleam with dazzling orfrays.

All this time the Burgundian knights were being threatened and taunted, so that Dancwart and Hagen were far from pleased and were troubled in their hearts how the King might fare. 'This journey of ours does not look too good for us,' they thought.

Meanwhile, before any could notice it, handsome Siegfried had returned to their ship to fetch his magic cloak from its hiding-place, and, quickly slipping into it, he was invisible to all. Hurrying back, he found many warriors assembled where the Queen was explaining her hazardous sports, and thanks to his magic wiles he rejoined them secretly and unseen.

The ring was marked out in which the games were to be witnessed by over seven hundred bold fighting-men that were seen there under arms and would declare who had won the contest.[2]

And now Brunhild had arrived, armed as though about to contend for all the kingdoms in the world and wearing many tiny bars of gold over her silk, against which her lovely face shone radiantly. Next came her retainers, bearing a great, broad shield of reddest gold, with braces

1. It is not clear whether this tunic had never been worn in battle before or whether it was of its nature impenetrable. Those who believe the latter also consider it to be a counterweight to Siegfried's impenetrable skin of horn, to equalize the contest.

2. The outward conditions are those of ancient Germanic judicial proceedings.

of hardest steel, under which the enchanting maiden meant to dispute the issue. For its baldrick her shield had a fine silk cord studded with grass-green gems whose variegated lustre vied with the gold of their settings. The man whom she would favour would have to be a very brave one: for this shield which the girl was to carry was (so we are told) a good three spans thick beneath the boss; it was resplendent with steel and with gold, and even with the help of three others her chamberlain could scarce raise it.

'What now, King Gunther?' stalwart Hagen of Troneck asked fiercely, on seeing the shield brought out. 'We are done for – the woman whose love you desire is a rib of the Devil himself!'

You must hear more about her attire, with which she was amply provided. The Queen wore a magnificent tabard of silk of Azagouc,[1] from which shone many precious stones, adding their lustre to hers.

They thereupon carried out for the lady a great spear, both sharp and heavy, which she was accustomed to throw – it was strong, and of huge proportions, and dreadfully keen at its edges. And now listen to this extraordinary thing about the weight of that spear: a good three-and-a-half ingots had gone into its forging, and three of Brunhild's men could scarcely lift it, so that noble Gunther was deeply alarmed. 'What will come of this?' he wondered. 'How could the Devil from Hell survive it? If I were safe and sound again in Burgundy, she would not be bothered by my wooing till Doomsday!'

'I heartily regret our visit to this court,' said bold Dancwart, Hagen's brother. 'We have always borne the name of heroes, but what a shameful way of dying if we are to perish at the hands of women! I bitterly rue ever having come to this country. But if my brother Hagen and I had our swords in our hands, all these vassals of Brunhild would have to tread gently with their arrogance. And know this for sure: they would do well to repress it,

1. See Appendix 3, 'The Date of the Poem', p. 366.

for had I sworn a thousand oaths to keep the peace, that bewitching young lady would have to lose her life before I would see my dear lord die!'

'If we had our battle gear and our trusty swords,' replied his brother Hagen, 'we should certainly leave this country as free men, and this amazon's proud spirit would be mollified.'

The noble maiden heard the warrior's words, and, looking over her shoulder, she said with a smile: 'Since he fancies himself to be so brave, bring these knights their armour, and give them their sharp swords too.'

When they had regained possession of their swords, as the maiden had commanded, bold Dancwart flushed with joy. 'Let them do what sports they like,' he said. 'Now that we have our swords, Gunther will remain unbeaten!'

Brunhild's strength was clearly tremendous, for they brought a heavy boulder to the ring for her, round, and of monstrous size – twelve lusty warriors could barely carry it! – and this she would always hurl after throwing her javelin. The Burgundians' fears rose high at the sight of it. 'Mercy on us!' said Hagen. 'What sort of a lover has the King got here? Rather should she be the Devil's drab in Hell!'

She furled her sleeves over her dazzling white arms, took a grip on her shield, snatched her spear aloft, and the contest was on! Gunther and Siegfried went in fear of her enmity, and she would have taken the King's life, had not Siegfried come to his aid. But Siegfried went up to him unseen and touched his hand, startling him with his magic powers. 'What was it that touched me?' the brave man wondered, looking all around him, yet finding no one there. 'It is I, your dear friend Siegfried,' said the other. 'You must not fear the Queen. Give me your shield, and let me bear it, and take careful note of what I say to you. Now, you go through the motions, and I shall do the deeds.' Gunther was relieved when he recognized him. 'Keep my wiles a secret,' continued Siegfried, 'and tell nobody about them, then the Queen will get little of the glory which she nevertheless hopes to win from you. Just see how coolly she faces you!'

Thereupon the noble maiden let fly with great power at the large, new shield which the son of Sieglind bore, so that sparks leapt up from the steel as though fanned by the wind, while the blade of the stout javelin tore clean through the shield, and a tongue of fire flared up from Gunther's mailshirt. Those strong men reeled under the shock, and, but for the magic cloak, they would have died there and then. Blood spurted from Siegfried's mouth, but he quickly rebounded, and, taking the spear which she had cast through his shield, the powerful warrior sent it back at her. 'I do not wish to wound or kill the lovely girl,' he thought, and reversing the spear so that its point was now behind him, he hurled the shaft with such manly vigour that it went straight through to her corselet with a mighty clang, and sent the sparks flying from the chain-mail as though driven by the wind. Siegmund's son put such lusty strength into his throw that, for all her might, she failed to keep her feet under its impact – an exploit, I swear, which King Gunther would never have accomplished.

But Brunhild swiftly leapt up again. 'My compliments on that throw, Gunther, noble knight!' said she, imagining that had Gunther achieved it with his own strength; but the man who was on her tracks was far mightier than he.

The noble maiden hastened up to the mark, for she was very angry now, and, raising the stone on high, flung it with great force a long stretch away from her, then followed her throw with a leap that set all her harness ringing. The boulder had fallen a good twenty-four yards away – but the fair maiden's leap exceeded it! Lord Siegfried went to where the great stone lay. Gunther took the strain of it, but it was brave Siegfried who did the throwing.

Siegfried was a valiant man. He was tall, and of powerful build. He hurled the boulder farther, and he surpassed it with his leap; and, thanks to his wonderful magic powers, he had the strength as he sprang to take King Gunther with him.

The leap was done, the stone had come to rest. None was to be seen other than doughty King Gunther, from whom Siegfried had warded off death. Fair Brunhild flushed red with anger. Seeing the warrior unscathed at his side of the ring, she said to her retainers in a voice not altogether quiet: 'Come forward at once, my kinsmen and vassals! You must do homage to King Gunther.' Then those brave men laid down their weapons and knelt before the great King Gunther of Burgundy in large numbers, in the belief that it was he who with his unaided strength had performed those feats.

Gunther saluted the illustrious maiden pleasantly, for he was a man of fine breeding. Then, clasping him by the hand, Brunhild gave him express authority to rule over her country, much to warlike Hagen's pleasure.

And now Brunhild desired the noble knight to go with her to her spacious palace, and when they arrived there the Burgundian warriors were shown all the greater courtesy,[1] so that Dancwart and Hagen had to put their anger by. As to brave Siegfried, he had the prudence to take his magic cloak and stow it away again, after which he returned to where the ladies were assembled.

'What are you waiting for, Sire?' the resourceful man asked the King, pretending he did not know, and thereby showing his sagacity. 'Why do you not begin the games, of which the Queen is setting so many for you? Let us soon see what they are like.'

'How did it happen, lord Siegfried,' asked the Queen, 'that you did not witness the games that Gunther won here?'

'You made us nervous, madam,' replied Hagen, 'and so while the Rhenish Prince was winning the games from you, Siegfried was down by our ship – that is why he does not know.'

'I am delighted to hear that your pride has been lowered in this way,' said brave Siegfried, 'and that there is someone alive who can master you. You must come to the Rhine with us now, noble maiden.'

'This cannot be done before my kinsmen and vassals are

1. For having been coldly received at first.

acquainted with it,' replied handsome Brunhild. 'You must know I cannot leave my country so lightly without first summoning those who are nearest me.' She then sent messengers riding in all directions to summon the kinsmen and vassals on whom she most relied, requesting them to come to Isenstein at once. And indeed, day by day, morning and evening, they came riding to Brunhild's fortress by companies.

'Good Heavens!' said Hagen. 'What have we done? This is asking for trouble, waiting here like this for fair Brunhild's men to arrive! Once they are here in force – we do not know the Queen's intentions – what if she be so furious that she is plotting our destruction? – the noble maiden may prove our undoing!'

'I shall prevent it,' said mighty Siegfried. 'I shall not let your fears come true. I shall bring rare warriors here to your aid whom you have never met before. Do not ask after me, for I shall sail away; and may God preserve your honour in the meantime! I shall return with all speed, bringing with me a thousand of the very best fighting-men I know.'

'Well, do not be too long,' replied the King. 'We are very glad of your help, and rightly so.'

'I shall return within a very few days. And tell Brunhild that it was you who dispatched me.'

CHAPTER EIGHT

How Siegfried sailed to fetch his vassals

*

HIDDEN in his magic cloak, Siegfried left by the gate that opened on to the shore. There he found a bark, and, boarding it unseen, sculled it swiftly away as though the wind were blowing it. None could see the helmsman, yet, propelled by Siegfried's huge strength, the little craft made such headway that people thought a gale must be blowing it. But no, it was being sculled by Siegfried, fair Sieglind's son.

After voyaging for the rest of that day and on into the night for upwards of a hundred miles, Siegfried thanks to his vast exertions reached a land that was named after the Nibelungs, of whose great treasure he was lord. Alone though he was, the dauntless warrior sailed to a large island in the river, quickly moored the bark, and made for a castle on a hill in quest of shelter, as is the way with travel-weary men.

Arriving before the gateway he found it barred, for those within were punctilious in discharge of their duty, as people still are today. The stranger fell to pounding on the gate, but the gate was well guarded – he saw standing inside a gigantic watchman, whose arms always lay near to hand.

'Who is that pounding on the gate so mightily?' asked the warden.

'A soldier of fortune! Come, throw open the portal!' answered lord Siegfried from the other side, disguising his voice. 'Before the day is out I shall rouse the fighting-spirit of some few out here who would prefer to lie snug and at ease!' The gatekeeper was annoyed to hear lord Siegfried say so.

In a trice the giant had donned his armour, put on his

helmet, snatched up his shield, and flung open the gate; and how ferociously the burly man rushed at Siegfried! How dare this visitor wake so many warriors! And he began to lay about him with his iron pole, forcing the noble stranger to seek cover under his shield, whose braces this watchman yet managed to shatter. This bought the hero into great peril, so that Siegfried was in no small fear of being killed by the mighty blows of this gatekeeper – a feat that much endeared the man to his liege lord Siegfried!

They fought so fiercely that the whole castle re-echoed and the din was heard in the hall of the Nibelungs. Yet Siegfried overcame the watchman and afterwards bound him, news of which went round all Nibelungland.

Far away through the cavern the fearless kobold Alberich, heard this savage fight, and, arming himself at once, rushed to where the noble stranger had laid the giant in bonds. Alberich was very strong and of ferocious temper; he wore a helmet, and chain-mail on his body, and wielded a scourge heavy with gold and on whose thongs seven massive balls were hung. Running at great speed towards Siegfried, he struck such bitter blows at the shield which the hero was gripping that large parts of it were smashed, and Siegfried feared for his life. Flinging his ruined shield aside, the handsome stranger thrust his long sword into its sheath, remembering his good breeding as decency required; for he was loath to slay his own treasurer. Thus, with only his strong hands to help him, he leapt at Alberich, seized the old man by his grey beard, and roughly dragged him to and fro till he shrieked at the top of his voice. This chastisement[1] by the young hero was a painful thing for Alberich.

'Let me live!' cried the dwarf, who was both brave and subtle. 'If I could be the bondman of any man except only that one warrior whose subject I swore to be, I would serve you, rather than die!'

---

1. There seems to be a double pun in the original, where *zuht* can mean (*a*) 'tugging', (*b*) 'chastisement', (*c*) 'good breeding' (which has just been referred to).

He bound Alberich as he had bound the giant before him, and much did Alberich suffer from his might.

'Who are you?' the dwarf managed to ask.

'I am Siegfried. I thought I was well known to you.'

'I am very glad to hear it!' replied Alberich. 'I have now made the acquaintance of your heroic handiwork and see that you are indeed fit to be a sovereign lord. If you let me live I shall do all that you command.'

'Go quickly, and bring me the best fighting-men we have, to the number of a thousand Nibelungs. They are to come and see me here.' But none heard him declare just why he wanted this done.

He loosed the giant's and Alberich's bonds, and the latter made haste and found the warriors. With fear still upon him, he roused the Nibelungs. 'Get up, you warriors!' he cried. 'You must go to Siegfried.' They jumped up from their beds with alacrity; and when a thousand brave knights had donned their fine clothes, they repaired to where Siegfried was standing, and gave him a warm welcome with formal show of their allegiance. Many candles were lit, and a spiced wine was poured for him. He thanked them for coming so promptly. 'You must sail away over the sea with me,' he told those good warriors, and he found them most willing to do so.

Three thousand knights had hastened there, of whom a thousand of the best were chosen. Their helmets and other harness were brought for them, since it was Siegfried's intention to take them to Brunhild's land.

'You good knights,' he said, 'listen to what I have to tell you. You must wear magnificent robes to court, since we are to appear before many beauties there – so adorn yourselves in fine clothes!'

Early one morning they put to sea. What gallant companions Siegfried had enlisted! – they had good mounts and splendid accoutrements on board with them and they arrived in Brunhild's country with much pomp. And there, standing on the battlements, were the lovely maidens.

'Does anyone know who those men are, whom I see

sailing far out at sea?' asked the Queen. 'They carry magnificent sails, whiter even than snow.'

'They are my men,' answered the King of the Rhineland. 'I left them near at hand as I sailed here. I sent for them, and now they have arrived, my lady.'

The noble strangers came in for very close scrutiny. Then Siegfried, splendidly attired, was seen standing forward in the ship in the company of many others.

'My lord King,' said the Queen, 'kindly tell me whether I am to receive these strangers or withhold my greeting from them.'

'You should go to meet them in front of the palace, so that they may know we are pleased to see them,' he replied. She did as he advised her, according Siegfried a separate greeting.[1] Lodgement was provided for them, and their gear was safely stored. So many foreigners had entered the country that they were thronging the place in crowds, here, there, and everywhere.

But now the brave knights wished to sail home to Burgundy.

'I should be obliged to anyone who could dole out my treasure of both silver and gold among my guests and the King's,' said the Queen.

'Let me take care of the keys, most noble Queen,' answered bold Giselher's vassal Dancwart. 'I vow I shall distribute it in such a way that any disgrace I incur will be entirely due to me.' The brave knight made it very plain that he was generously inclined.

When Hagen's brother had taken charge of the keys he lavished magnificent gifts; and if any asked for a mark he gave them so much that all who were poor and needy could live happily on it. Over and over again he bestowed

1. As the leader, Siegfried was received with marks of distinction. The other interpretation, that Brunhild receives Siegfried with lesser honours because he appears as Gunther's vassal, must be wrong, if only for the reason that the men from Nibelungenland appear as Gunther's vassals, too. The latter interpretation is of course inspired by the idea (suggested by parallel Norse sources) that there was a broken romance between Siegfried and Brunhild. See pp. 332 and 387.

a hundred pounds or more at a time; and many who had never worn such fine clothes in their lives walked past that hall arrayed in splendid robes. But when the Queen came to hear of it, believe me, she was piqued.

'My lord King,' said that proud lady, 'I could do without your treasurer's generosity, since he intends not to leave me a stitch and is frittering away all my gold. I should be eternally obliged to any who would put a stop to it. This knight is lavishing such gifts that he must fancy I am thinking of dying! But I mean to keep my money and I trust *myself* to squander my inheritance.' Never did a queen have so open-handed a treasurer!

'My lady,' said Hagen of Troneck, 'let me tell you that the King of the Rhenish lands has so much gold and so many clothes to bestow that there is no need for us to take any clothes of yours away with us.'

'I disagree,' replied the Queen. 'Do me the pleasure of letting me fill twenty trunks with silk and gold, so that I may give it away myself when we have crossed over to Gunther's land.' Her coffers were filled with precious stones but they were her own treasurers who had the charge of it, since (much to Gunther's and Hagen's amusement) she was loath to entrust it to Dancwart.

'To whom shall I make over my territories?' asked the Queen. 'Before we leave, you and I must duly appoint a governor.'

'Summon whomever you approve for the office, and we shall constitute him regent,' replied the noble King.

Close at hand the lady saw her maternal uncle, one of her most illustrious kinsmen. 'I hereby commend to you my fortresses and lands,' she told him, 'until such time as Gunther shall have jurisdiction here.' She then chose two thousand of her retainers to sail away with her to Burgundy, in addition to the thousand from Nibelungland. They made ready for the voyage and were seen riding down to the shore. She also took with her eighty-six ladies and at least a hundred maidens, all very comely. And now they lost no time, for they were eager to be gone. But of those whom they were leaving behind them, how many gave way to tears!

Kissing those of her nearest relations who were in attendance, Brunhild decorously left the land that was hers by sovereign right; and, taking a friendly farewell, they gained the open sea. However, the lady never came back to this, her father's country.

As they sailed on, much merrymaking was heard, for they were well supplied with all amusements while an excellent sea-breeze came to speed them on their course, so that it was with great elation that they left the land behind. But Brunhild did not wish to embrace her lord on the way, and so their pleasures were deferred till a high festivity, when, amidst great joy, they and their warriors arrived at Gunther's palace in the castle of Worms.[1]

1. According to medieval notions, once the consent of Brunhild's family had been given, she and Gunther were free to consummate their marriage.

CHAPTER NINE

How Siegfried was sent to Worms

*

WHEN they had voyaged for nine full days, Hagen of Troneck said, 'Listen to what I have to say. We are late with our news to Worms on the Rhine – your messengers should already be in Burgundy.'

'What you say is true,' answered King Gunther, 'and none would serve for the journey as well as yourself, friend Hagen. Now ride home to my country,[1] since none will tell our people better about our visit to the Queen.'

'I am not a good messenger. Let me look after the treasury. I wish to stay on board with the ladies and keep their wardrobe till we have brought them to Burgundy. Ask Siegfried to convey your message, he is the man to carry out this mission with courage and energy. And if he declines to make the journey for you, you must ask him courteously, as a friend, to do it for love of your sister.'

Gunther summoned the hero; and Siegfried came at once when they had found him. 'Since we are nearing home,' said Gunther, 'I should be sending messengers to my dear sister, and to my mother, too, to inform them of our approach. Now I ask you to do this, Siegfried. Carry out my wish and I shall be for ever obliged to you.' But bold Siegfried refused the good knight's request, till Gunther earnestly implored him. 'Please ride there for my sake,' he said, 'and for that of comely Kriemhild, so that the noble girl and I will be beholden to you!' Hearing this, brave Siegfried was willingness itself.

'Send whatever messages you please – I shall not fail to impart them. For the sake of the loveliest of maidens I shall gladly discharge your mission. For why should I deny

1. The company have evidently sighted land, and may even be sailing up the Rhine.

her whom I love so tenderly? Whatever you command in her name shall be done.'

'Then tell my mother Queen Uote that we are in great spirits as a result of our voyage. Inform my brothers of our achievements, and also tell the news to our friends. Do not omit to give my sister, my household and all my retainers a greeting from Brunhild and me, or to say how fully I have attained my heart's desire. And tell my dear nephew Ortwin to have high seats set up at Worms by the Rhine, and let my other kinsmen be advised that, together with Brunhild, I mean to hold a great festivity. Tell my sister further that as soon as she has heard that I have landed with my guests she is to welcome my beloved most attentively, to that I shall never cease to be grateful to her.'

Lord Siegfried with all due form quickly took leave of Brunhild and her suite, and rode towards the Rhenish lands; nor could you have found a better messenger. He rode into Worms accompanied by twenty-four warriors. But when it was announced that he had come without the King, the household were seized with dismay, for they feared that their lord had met his end in Iceland.

Siegfried and his men dismounted in jubilant mood, and were immediately joined by Giselher, the good young King, and his brother Gernot. But failing to see Gunther at Siegfried's side, the former quickly said: 'Welcome, Siegfried! Kindly tell me where you have left my brother the King. I fancy mighty Brunhild has taken him from us. If so, the pursuit of her exalted loves has been a cause of grievous loss to us.'

'You can put aside that fear. My comrade bade me give you and his kinsmen his compliments! I left him in excellent health, and he has sent me here to bring you news as his messenger. So please arrange at once for me to see the Queen and your sister, however you arrange it, since I am to tell them the message from Gunther and Brunhild, whose fortunes stand so high!'

'Go to her,' answered young Giselher. 'It would give her much pleasure. She, too, is very anxious on her brother's account, and will be glad to see you, take my word for it.'

'Whatever I can do to serve her', said lord Siegfried, 'will be done most willingly in all sincerity. But who will tell the ladies that I wish to call on them?'

Handsome Giselher himself went to deliver the message, and finding his mother and his sister, he announced: 'The warrior Siegfried of the Netherlands has arrived! My brother Gunther has sent him here to Burgundy to bring us news of how he has fared. Please allow him to present himself, and he will tell you trustworthy news from Iceland.'

Still a prey to great anxiety, the ladies ran for their robes, and having attired themselves, summoned Siegfried to their court. He willingly complied, since he was eager to see them.

'Welcome lord Siegfried, worthy knight!' said noble Kriemhild in kindly greeting. 'But where is my brother, the illustrious King Gunther? We fear that Brunhild's mighty strength may have taken him from us. Alas, that I, poor girl, was ever born!'

'Now give me my reward for good news![1] You are weeping for no cause, fair ladies. I tell you I left him in good health, and he and Brunhild have sent me to you both with the news. Most noble Queen, Gunther and his beloved send their affectionate greetings. Now let your weeping be, for they will soon be here.'

Not for a long, long time had Kriemhild heard such joyful news. Taking the hem of her snow-white gown, she dabbed at the tears in her pretty eyes; then she thanked the messenger for the news she had received, and her sadness and weeping were no more. She bade her courier be seated – an honour he gladly accepted – and the adorable young woman said to him: 'I should not mind it overmuch if I might give you of my treasure to requite you for your message, but you are too exalted. Instead I shall always be grateful to you.[2]

1. Originally by custom a loaf of bread, so it seems.
2. The expression used also means 'I shall always love you', and the *double entendre* is intentional.

'Though I in my one person were lord of thirty lands', he replied, 'I should gladly receive a gift from your hands.'

'Then it shall be done,' said the well-bred girl. And she told her treasurer to go and fetch her guerdon.

Kriemhild repaid her messenger with four-and-twenty bracelets inlaid with fine jewels, but having no mind to keep them the hero at once gave them to her intimates whom he saw there in the chamber.[1] Her mother thanked him most graciously.

'I have news to tell you,' said the warrior, 'of what Gunther would have you do when he arrives in Burgundy, and for which, my lady, if you do it, he will always be obliged to you. He asks you through me to give his noble guests a kindly welcome, and he begs you to favour him by riding out to meet him on the river bank by Worms. This, in the loyal affection he bears you, the King bids you do!'

'I shall do so most willingly,' said the enchanting girl, and she blushed for pleasure. 'I shall deny him nothing that I could do to serve him. His wishes shall be met with all my fond regard.'

No prince's emissary was ever better received. Had she dared kiss him, the lady would have done so.[2]

Siegfried very charmingly took leave of the ladies. The Burgundians did as he had asked them, so that Sindold, and Hunold, and warlike Rumold had to exert themselves mightily getting the seats erected by the river before Worms, while the King's stewards had their hands full. Ortwin and Gere did not delay in sending messengers to their friends in all directions to proclaim the festivity that was due to take place, in readiness for which troops of lovely girls were donning their finery.

The palace and its walls were hung all over with tapestries to greet the guests, and Gunther's great hall was filled with

1. The gesture of Kriemhild's gift meant everything to Siegfried, the objects nothing.

2. In the absence of her brother Gunther and of the ceremonial described on p. 49, the circumstances would have been too un-ambiguously intimate for a kiss.

tables and benches to accommodate the crowd of strangers. Thus this tremendous celebration began merrily, and, having been summoned to meet those who were returning, the three kings' relations were soon riding along the ways all over Burgundy, to which end many fine clothes had been taken from their chests.

When it was reported that Brunhild's party had been sighted in cavalcade[1] there was frantic activity in Burgundy on account of that vast concourse! What multitudes of bold warriors there were on either side!

'My young ladies who wish to attend me to the reception,' said fair Kriemhild, 'you must choose the best clothes from your coffers, if we are to earn the commendation of our guests.'

And now the Burgundian warriors were there, sending for splendid saddles worked with red gold on which the ladies were to ride from Worms to the Rhine, than which no harness could be better – for oh, the bright gold that shone from those palfreys while gems without number flashed from their bridles! Golden footstools for the ladies to mount by were brought and set upon dazzling silks – what gay young ladies they were! As I have said, their amblers were ready for them in the courtyard, parading narrow poitrels of the best silk anyone could name for you.

Eighty-six ladies, bewimpled and dazzlingly gowned, emerged from their apartment, and walked decorously up to Kriemhild, followed by a bevy of handsome girls from the best Burgundian families to the number of fifty-four, their fair hair encompassed by braids of gleaming silk. They had eagerly complied with the royal request.

The ladies wore magnificent brocades, the best obtainable, to display before the warriors and altogether many fine robes that became their great beauty to the full, so that a man who nursed ill will against any must have been a half-wit. There were innumerable cloaks both of sable and of ermine, and many an arm and hand was adorned with

1. The company had evidently disembarked somewhere lower down the Rhine.

bracelets over the silk they were wearing – nobody could describe to you what efforts they had gone to!

Many hands flung many fine long girdles most ingeniously fashioned from Arabian brocade over their bright apparel and round their costly robes of farandine. Those noble young ladies were in high spirits, and many a one was laced in[1] under her breast-clasp, making a charming picture. Those whose radiant complexions did not vie in lustre with their gowns would have been sorry for themselves, for indeed no royal family today has so lovely a following.

And now that these ravishing women were attired, the proud warriors who were to escort them immediately came on in great force, bearing a forest of ashen spears, together with their shields.

1. The text says 'sewn', which may have been literally the case. Women's gowns were held together at the front by a large ornamental brooch or clasp.

CHAPTER TEN

How Brunhild was received in Worms

*

ON the far side of the Rhine, the King and his guests, in company after company, could be seen riding towards the river bank with many maidens led by their escorts, while those who were there to welcome them were in all readiness.

When the Icelanders and Siegfried's men from Nibelungland had boarded the ferries, they plied their oars very actively and made haste to land where the King's friends and relations were assembled on the shore.

And now hear how the noble Queen Uote rode with her maidens from the castle to the river, where numerous knights and young ladies made acquaintance. Duke Gere led Kriemhild's palfrey only to the castle gate, after which it fell to bold Siegfried to escort her, a service for which the lovely girl repaid him well in days to come. Brave Ortwin rode beside Uote, and a host of knights and maidens rode in pairs – never, dare we assert, were so many ladies seen together and at so great a reception!

Many a magnificent bohort was ridden by illustrious knights under the eyes of fair Kriemhild as they progressed towards the boats – an honour which it would have been discourteous to deny her. Then all those well-favoured women were lifted down from their palfreys.

The King had now crossed over together with many noble guests, and what a cracking of stout lances there was to greet the ladies! Shields re-echoed as thrust on thrust was delivered at full tilt, and oh, the din of their fine bosses as these were clashed in the mêlée!

The charming ladies of Burgundy stood there by the harbour as Gunther, leading Brunhild by the hand in person, disembarked with his guests – a refulgence of vivid robes and sparkling gems, each vying with the other!

With great elegance and breeding Kriemhild paced towards Brunhild and her suite, and bade them welcome. They pushed back their fillets,[1] with their gleaming white hands and the two kissed each other as good manners required.

'Welcome to my mother and to me here in this country and to all the loyal friends we have,' said Kriemhild courteously. This Brunhild acknowledged with a bow. The ladies embraced and embraced again, and, indeed, you never heard of a welcome so affectionate as Queen Uote and her daughter extended to the bride, for they kissed her sweet mouth many, many times.

When Brunhild's ladies had all come ashore, handsome knights took fine women by the hand, beyond number, while fair maidens were presented to Brunhild – so that, what with much kissing of red lips, it was long before their greetings were over.

The noble Princesses were still standing together, a delight for the eyes of many worthy knights. And those who till then had only heard it asserted that they could never have seen anything so lovely as these two (how well this was proved by the event!) now had them under their scrutiny: and, truly, they detected no fraud in their appearances. Those who were good judges of the charms of the fair praised Gunther's wife for her beauty; but those critics who had looked more discerningly declared Kriemhild to have the advantage.

Women and girls moved forward to meet each other, and very many handsome figures were to be seen there, elegantly robed, against the background of silken tents and magnificent pavilions with which the whole meadow below Worms was filled. Gunther's kinsmen jostled their way through, and inviting Brunhild, Kriemhild, and all the ladies to go into the shade, conducted them to the tents.

But now all the strangers had arrived on their chargers,

1. Unmarried girls normally wore fillets and garlands, married women wimples.

and they rode many a glorious joust clean through their adversaries' shields, so that the dust began to rise from that plain as though the whole land were on fire. It soon became apparent who were brave warriors! This sport of the knights was watched by many young ladies, and I fancy lord Siegfried rode through the mêlée past the tents in both directions many times. He had brought a thousand fine Nibelungs to the field.

Then, at the King's request, Hagen of Troneck came to part the two sides and bring the bohort to a friendly conclusion lest the pretty girls be all covered with dust, and the guests good-naturedly complied.

'Rest your horses till it begins to grow cool,' said lord Gernot, 'and then let us go jousting up to the great palace in honour of fair ladies. Pray be ready when the King wishes to mount.'

Now that the bohort had ceased throughout the meadow, the knights went to the high pavilions to dally with the ladies in hopes of rare delight, and here they whiled away the time till they had to start for Worms.

At the approach of evening, when the sun was going down and the air was growing cooler, the men and women delayed no longer but repaired to the castle, while the knights' eyes lingered caressingly on the charms of numerous beauties.

And now, after the custom of the land, the good warriors rode their clothes to tatters,[1] all the way up to the palace, where the King dismounted, and then they handed the ladies down, as is ever the way of men of spirit, after which the young Queen and the Princess parted company. For Uote and her daughter entered a vast chamber, together with their suite, and everywhere a merry din arose. High seats were made ready, and the King desired to dine with his guests. Beside him stood fair Brunhild,

1. The bohort, conducted not in armour but in magnificent clothes, gave the knights an opportunity of displaying their talent for conspicuous waste.

crowned as a queen of Burgundy, and what a magnificent figure she made! Many benches had been set at fine, broad tables loaded with viands (so the story says), and there was no lack of what was wanted.

Numerous distinguished strangers were seen standing near the King. And now the royal chamberlains brought water for their hands in bowls of red gold, and it would be a waste of effort, since I should not believe it, if someone were to say that better service was given at any princely function. Before the King of the Rhineland dipped his hands, lord Siegfried reminded him, as he was well entitled to do, of the promise which Gunther had given him before he met Brunhild in Iceland.

'Remember what you swore to me,' he said, 'namely that when lady Brunhild came to this country you would give me your sister. What has become of your oaths? I went to great trouble on your voyage.'

'It is right that you should remind me,' said the King to his guest. 'I do not intend to forswear myself. I shall help you to achieve your object to the best of my power.'

Kriemhild was summoned before the King, and she appeared at the foot of the hall with her comely maidens in attendance: but at once Giselher leapt down the stair. 'Tell these girls to withdraw – only my sister is to remain with the King!' and so Kriemhild was ushered into the royal presence, where noble knights from many princedoms were standing in the spacious hall. These were bidden to stay where they were, though the lady Brunhild had reached the table.[1]

'Dearest sister,' said King Gunther, 'of your own goodness, redeem my royal oath for me! For I swore to give you to a warrior, and if he becomes your husband you will have done my will most loyally.'

1. Brunhild is not of the Burgundian blood and in any case is a woman, and so she takes no part in the legal proceedings of Kriemhild's marriage, which is conducted in the formal ring of warriors; see p. 209. Thus Brunhild is left standing at her place.

'Do not entreat me, dear brother,' was the noble maiden's answer. 'I shall always be as you wish, and do whatever you command. I shall gladly accept the man whom you give me for a husband, sir.'

Siegfried flushed as her sweet glance rested on him, and then he humbly thanked the lady Kriemhild. Thereupon they were told to stand in the ring together, and she was asked whether she would have the handsome man.

In her maiden modesty she was somewhat abashed, yet Siegfried's luck would have it that she did not reject him there and then, while for his part the noble King of the Netherlands accepted her as his wife.

And now that he had sworn to have her and she him, Siegfried at once took the sweet girl in his arms very tenderly, and kissed his lovely queen in the presence of the warriors.

The suites of both parties dispersed from the ring. Siegfried sat with Kriemhild opposite the King in the high seat of honour to which he had been escorted by a great number of his Nibelungs. The King and the maiden Brunhild now took their seats, and when the latter saw Kriemhild at Siegfried's side – never had she suffered such torment – she began to weep so that the hot tears fell down her radiant cheeks.

'My lady, what is the matter that you allow your bright eyes to be dimmed so?' the sovereign asked. 'You have every cause to rejoice, since my lands, cities, and many fine men are all at your command.'

'I have every cause to weep,' retorted the lovely maiden. 'It wounds me to the heart to see your sister sitting beside a liegeman,[1] and if she is to be degraded in this fashion I shall never cease to lament it!'

'Not another word now,' replied the King. 'I shall tell you some other time why I have given my sister to Siegfried. She has good reason to live happily with the warrior forever.'

'I shall never cease to regret her beauty and fine breeding. How gladly I should take refuge, if only I knew where,

1. See p. 332.

so as not to share your couch, unless you were to tell me why Kriemhild should be Siegfried's spouse.'

'I shall tell you plainly,' said the noble King. 'He has cities and broad lands quite as good as mine, for, rely on it, he is a mighty king! This is why I consent to his loving my fine young beauty.' But Brunhild's heart was troubled, whatever the King said to her.

Then a crowd of worthy knights dashed from the tables, and went at it so hard with their bohort that the whole castle resounded. But in the company of his guests time hung heavy on the King – he fancied it would be pleasanter beside his fair queen, for he was by no means without hope in his heart that she would bring him much delight, and he began to cast amorous glances at her.

The guests were asked to cease from their chivalric sport, since the King wished to retire with his lady. Kriemhild and Brunhild came together at the stairs below the hall, for as yet there was no enmity between them, and were at once joined by their retinues, while their resplendent chamberlains brought lights without delay. Thereupon the two kings' vassals parted company, and many knights escorted Siegfried away.

And now those two great lords had come to where they would lie, and each thought how he would wrest love's victory from his handsome wife, and was comforted in his heart.

Lord Siegfried's pastime was to his vast contentment, for as he lay with the young lady and inured her so tenderly to his noble loves, she became as dear to him as life, and he would not have exchanged her for a thousand others.

But I shall tell you no more of Siegfried's attentions to Kriemhild. Listen instead to how gallant Gunther lay with lady Brunhild – he had lain more pleasantly with other women many a time.

His attendants, both man and woman, had left him. The chamber was quickly barred, and he imagined that he was soon to enjoy her lovely body: but the time when Brunhild would become his wife was certainly not at hand! She went to the bed in a shift of fine white linen, and the noble knight thought to himself: 'Now I have everything here that I ever wished for.' And indeed there was great cause why her beauty should gratify him deeply. He dimmed the lights one after another with his own royal hands, and then, dauntless warrior, he went to the lady. He laid himself close beside her, and with a great rush of joy took the adorable woman in his arms.

He would have lavished caresses and endearments, had the Queen suffered him to do so, but she flew into a rage that deeply shocked him – he had hoped to meet with 'friend', yet what he met was 'foe'!

'Sir,' she said, 'you must give up the thing you have set your hopes on, for it will not come to pass. Take good note of this: I intend to stay a maiden till I have learned the truth about Siegfried.'

Gunther grew very angry with her. He tried to win her by force, and tumbled her shift for her, at which the haughty girl reached for the girdle of stout silk cord that she wore about her waist, and subjected him to great suffering and shame: for in return for being baulked of her sleep, she bound him hand and foot, carried him to a nail, and hung him on the wall. She had put a stop to his love-making! As to him, he all but died, such strength had she exerted.

And now he who had thought to be master began to entreat her. 'Loose my bonds, most noble Queen. I do not fancy I shall ever subdue you, lovely woman, and I shall never again lie so close to you.'

She did not care at all how he fared, since she was lying very snug. He had to stay hanging there the whole night through till dawn, when the bright morning shone through the windows.[1] If Gunther had ever been possessed of any strength, it had dwindled to nothing now.

'Tell me, lord Gunther,' said the handsome maiden, 'would you mind it if your chamberlains were to find you, bound by a woman's hand?'

1. There is an ironic allusion here to the fashionable genre of dawn songs, which presents a lovers' parting at daybreak after a night of love.

'It would turn out very ill for you,' answered the noble
knight, 'and I should have little honour from it. Now, of
your courtesy, let me come to you. Since you object to my
embraces so violently, I promise not to lay hands upon your
attire.'

The lady then promptly freed him and set him down on
his feet – and he then rejoined her in bed. But he lay down
at such a distance that he never so much as touched her
beautiful gown, nor did she mean to let him bother her.

Their attendants now entered, bringing them new
clothes, of which many had been got ready for that morning.
But though all were in festive mood, and despite the crown
he wore in honour of the day, the lord of the land was
dejected.

In fulfilment of the custom, which they dutifully ob-
served, Gunther and Brunhild delayed no longer but went
to the minster, where mass was sung. Siegfried appeared
there, too, and there was a great press about them.

In accordance with the royal rites, all that they needed
by way of crowns and robes had been prepared for their
arrival, and they were duly consecrated. This done, all
four stood crowned and happy there.

You must know that six hundred or more squires were
knighted there in honour of those kings, and great joy arose
throughout Burgundy, with much cracking of spear-shafts
in the hands of the novices. Comely young ladies were
sitting at the windows, and the splendour of many shields
shone bright before their eyes. But the King had gone
apart from his men and appeared to be in very low spirits,
whatever else others might be doing.

Gunther and Siegfried were in very different moods. The
latter had divined how the noble warrior felt, and, going up
to him, asked: 'Tell me, how did you fare last night?'

'I was utterly humiliated, for I have brought the foul
fiend home with me! When I was about to make love to her,
she bound me very tight, carried me to a nail, and sus-
pended me high on the wall; and there I hung the whole
night through till daybreak, while she lay at her ease –

only then did she untie me! I tell you of my misfortune in confidence, as friend to friend.'

'I am truly sorry,' answered mighty Siegfried, 'and I shall prove it, unless my plan offends you. I shall see to it that she lies so close to you tonight that she will never deny you her favours again.' After what he had been through, Gunther's spirits revived at these words. 'This will turn out well for you in the end,' continued lord Siegfried. 'I fancy things went differently for you and me last night; for your sister Kriemhild is dearer to me than life. But lady Brunhild will have to submit to you tonight. I shall enter your room in my magic cloak so secretly that none shall see through my wiles. Send your chamberlains to their quarters. As a sign that I am there and ready to help you I shall put out the lights which the pages will be holding, and then I shall tame your wife for you to enjoy her this night, or lose my life in the attempt.'

'I agree,' replied the King. 'Except that you must not make love to my dear lady in any way. Do anything else you like – even though you killed her, I should find it in my heart to pardon you – for she is a dreadful woman!'

'I promise on my word of honour,' said Siegfried, 'that I shall not make free with her at all. I prefer your lovely sister to any I have ever set eyes on.' And Gunther believed him when he said it.

The knights' sport gave rise to both pleasure and pain! But when the ladies were about to leave for the dining-hall, the bohort with all its uproar was brought to an end, and the chamberlains bade the people make way. Thus the courtyard was emptied of man, woman, and beast, and every lady was escorted to table into the king's presence by a bishop and was followed to the high seats by many stately men.

The King sat there full of happy expectations, with Siegfried's promise ever-present in his mind, so that this one day seemed as long as a month to him; for he could think of nothing else than the enjoyment of his lady. He could scarcely wait for the board to be raised. Then troops of

gallant knights appeared before the queens – fair Brunhild
and lady Kriemhild as well, to conduct them to their
chambers.

Lord Siegfried sat beside his lovely wife with great
affection and delight while her white hands fondled his –
when he vanished suddenly before her very eyes! Toying
with him thus and then no longer seeing him, the queen
said to her attendants: 'I am amazed! Where can the
King have gone? Who took his hands out of mine?' But
she did not pursue the matter.

Siegfried had gone to Gunther's chamber where many
attendants were standing with lights. These he extinguished
in their hands, and Gunther knew that Siegfried was
there. He was aware what Siegfried wanted, and dismissed
the ladies and maids. This done, the King quickly thrust
two stout bolts across, barred the door himself, and hid
the lights behind the bed-curtains.[1] And now mighty
Siegfried and the fair maiden began a game there was
no avoiding and one that gladdened yet saddened the
King.

Siegfried laid himself close by the young lady's side.
'Keep away, Gunther, unless you want a taste of the same
medicine!' And, indeed, the lady was soon to inflict
great hurt on bold Siegfried. But he held his tongue and
said not a word. And although Gunther could not see him,
he could plainly hear that no intimacies passed between
them, for to tell the truth they had very little ease in that
bed. Siegfried comported himself as if he were the great
King Gunther and clasped the illustrious maiden in his
arms – but she flung him out of the bed against a stool
nearby so that his head struck it with a mighty crack! Yet
the brave man rebounded powerfully, determined to have
another try, though when he set about subduing her it
cost him very dear – I am sure no woman will ever again so
defend herself.

Seeing that he would not desist, the maiden leapt to her

1. Evidently a different sort of light from those extinguished by
Siegfried. Perhaps a kind of night-light.

feet. 'Stop rumpling my beautiful white shift!' said the handsome girl. 'You are a very vulgar fellow and you shall pay for it dearly – I'll show you!' She locked the rare warrior in her arms and would have laid him in bonds, like the King, so that she might have the comfort of her bed. She took a tremendous revenge on him for having ruffled her clothes. What could his huge strength avail him? She showed him that her might was the greater, for she carried him with irresistible force and rammed him between the wall and a coffer.

'Alas,' thought the hero, 'if I now lose my life to a girl, the whole sex will grow uppish with their husbands for ever after, though they would otherwise never behave so.'

The King heard it all and was afraid for the man; but Siegfried was deeply ashamed and began to lose his temper, so that he fought back with huge strength and closed with Brunhild desperately. To the King it seemed an age before Siegfried overcame her. She gripped his hands so powerfully that the blood spurted from his nails and he was in agony; but it was not long before he forced the arrogant girl to recant the monstrous resolve which she had voiced the night before.[1] Meanwhile nothing was lost on the King, although Siegfried spoke no word. The latter now crushed her on to the bed so violently that she shrieked aloud, such pain did his might inflict on her. Then she groped for the girdle of silk round her waist with intent to bind him, but his hand fought off her attempt so fiercely that her joints cracked all over her body! This settled the issue, and she submitted to Gunther.

'Let me live, noble King!' said she. 'I shall make ample amends for all that I have done to you and shall never again repel your noble advances, since I have found to my cost that you know well how to master a woman.'

---

1. Although the poet knows that Brunhild is the victim of a deception which cannot fail to disturb her, he, as a child of his age, is shocked by her refusal to consummate the marriage, and marks her clearly as both arrogant and unwomanly.

Siegfried left the maiden lying there and stepped aside as though to remove his clothes and, without the noble Queen's noticing it, he drew a golden ring from her finger and then took her girdle, a splendid orphrey. I do not know whether it was his pride which made him do it.[1] Later he gave them to his wife, and well did he rue it!

And now Gunther and the lovely girl lay together, and he took his pleasure with her as was his due, so that she had to resign her maiden shame and anger. But from his intimacy she grew somewhat pale, for at love's coming her vast strength fled so that now she was no stronger than any other woman. Gunther had his delight of her lovely body, and had she renewed her resistance what good could it have done her? His loving had reduced her to this.

And now how very tenderly and amorously Brunhild lay beside him till the bright dawn!

Meanwhile Siegfried had gone from the chamber to where a charming lady welcomed him very kindly. He eluded the questions which she was meaning to ask him and long concealed what he had brought for her until she had been crowned in his country, then he did not fail to give what he was destined to bestow on her.

When morning came, the King was in far better spirits than on the day before, so that happiness reigned entire not only among the nobles whom he had invited to his palace and to whom every attention was paid, but also throughout the land.

The celebrations lasted for two full weeks, during which time the glad sound of all the varied pleasures in which the guests were asked to share was never stilled. The King's outlay was put at a very high sum; yet at his request his noble kinsmen made gifts in his honour to many a wandering entertainer of clothes, of red gold, horses, and silver, so that those who had claimed largesse departed in great contentment.

Siegfried, Prince of the Netherlands, together with his

1. The poet's ignorance is diplomatic: see pp. 298-9.

thousand men, doled out all the robes which they had brought to the Rhineland with them, and their horses with their saddles – they well knew how to lord it!

But before the magnificent gifts had all been squandered away, those who wished to go home grew impatient to leave. No guests were ever better cared for. And so this festivity ended, since King Gunther wished it thus.

CHAPTER ELEVEN

How Siegfried came home with his queen

*

WHEN the guests had all departed, Siegfried said to his followers: 'We, too, must make ready to go home.'

This was welcome news to his wife. 'When shall we leave?' she asked her husband. 'I do not wish to have to hurry overmuch, because my brothers must first share our lands with me.' This intention of Kriemhild's was unwelcome news to Siegfried.

The three kings came to him and said with one voice: 'Believe us, lord Siegfried, we shall always be ready to serve you truly till we die.' He bowed and thanked them for their kind assurance. 'Furthermore,' added youthful Giselher, 'we mean to share with you the lands and castles that are our sovereign possession, and, jointly with Kriemhild, you shall have your due part of the spacious realms that are subject to us.'[1]

Hearing what those princes had in mind and seeing that they meant it, Siegfried answered them: 'May your hereditary lands and their peoples rest for ever happy, in God's name! Truly, my dear wife can forgo the portion you wished to give her. In the country where she is to be Queen (if I live to see it) she will be richer in possessions than anyone alive. But in whatever else you command I am ready to serve you.'[2]

---

1. Brunhild is not named in this scene and is presumably absent. This, like other 'absences', may well be due to calculation by the poet, since had Brunhild been present, she would have seen from this statement and Siegfried's answer that he was scarcely Gunther's vassal. See p. 332.

2. Siegfried acts freely as Kriemhild's legal guardian without consulting her. But she reminds him that although he may renounce her inheritance in the form of property, the bonds of feudal allegiance are not to be broken so lightly.

'You may well renounce my inheritance,' said Lady Kriemhild, 'but it will not be so easy where knights of Burgundy are concerned. They are such as a king may gladly take home to his country and I request my dear brothers to make division of them with me.'

'Take whomever you please,' said lord Gernot. 'You will find many here who will be willing to ride away with you. Of three thousand knights we shall give you a thousand – let them form your household.'

Kriemhild then sent for Hagen of Troneck and Ortwin, to ask them if they and their kinsmen would be her liegemen. But Hagen was incensed. 'Everybody knows that it is not in Gunther's power to give us to anyone!' he cried. 'Let others of your retainers go with you, for the custom of those of Troneck is well known to you. We are bound to abide at court beside the Kings and shall continue to serve those whom we have followed hitherto!'

They let the matter rest[1] and made ready to leave. Kriemhild assembled a noble retinue for herself, of thirty-two maidens and five hundred vassals; and Count Eckewart, too, went with Siegfried. And now they all took their leave, knights and squires, ladies and maidens, as they were bound to do, and, parting at once with many kisses, cheerfully quitted King Gunther's realm.

Their kinsmen escorted them for a great distance along the roads, and orders were given everywhere throughout the King's territories for their night quarters to be set up at places to their liking. Then messengers were dispatched to Siegmund to inform him and Sieglind that their son and lady Uote's daughter were on their way from Worms beyond the Rhine, than which no news could be more welcome to them.

1. Although the magnificent figure of lord Hagen emerges from this passage clearly as a vassal bound to the service of his overlords, he successfully resists this legitimate attempt to transfer him. It is significant that the senior king, Gunther, remains uncommitted during these abortive transactions. Hagen's indignant refusal serves to underline his unquestioning identification of himself with the dynastic interests of Burgundy, a bond that will bear any weight.

'How fortunate I am,' cried Siegmund, 'that I shall have lived to see lovely Kriemhild go crowned in this country! What glory this confers on my inheritance! My noble son Siegfried will have to rule here as King in his own right.' And as reward for this news, Queen Sieglind gave the messenger many lengths of red samite, silver, and heavy gold, so pleased was she to hear it. Their household then attired themselves assiduously, as was fitting.

Learning who were accompanying their son to the Netherlands, the King and Queen at once had high seats erected, and to these, when he was crowned, King Siegfried would go in the presence of his friends.

King Siegmund's vassals rode out to meet Siegfried; and if anyone was ever better received than were those fine warriors in Siegmund's land I have not heard of it. Comely Sieglind rode out to meet Kriemhild with many fair ladies attended by gay knights for a whole day's march, to where the others came in sight. Then natives and strangers alike shared the discomforts of travel together, till they arrived at a great city called Xanten, where the two were afterwards crowned.

With smiling faces (their cares were now over) Siegmund and Sieglind showered affectionate kisses on Kriemhild and Siegfried and gave a hearty welcome to all their followers. The guests were conducted before Siegmund's hall, where the charming young ladies were handed from their palfreys, and there were men in plenty to wait upon these beauties most attentively.

However great the festivity at Worms was held to be, the warriors here in Xanten were given far better clothes than they had worn in all their days. Marvels could be told of the Netherlanders' wealth, as they sat in their glory and abundance. The sight of all the gussets agleam with gold which their followers wore, embroidered on golden wire with pearls and jewels – so well did noble Queen Sieglind care for them!

Then lord Siegmund spoke in the presence of his friends. 'I declare to all of Siegfried's kinsmen that he shall wear my crown, with all these warriors to witness!' – an announcement which delighted the Netherlanders. Then Siegmund made over to his son his crown, his judicature, and his kingdom. From now on Siegfried was their supreme lord. And when any brought a lawsuit before him, and it fell within his jurisdiction, justice was done in such fashion that the son of fair Sieglind was held in great dread.[1]

Siegfried lived thus magnificently and (to tell the truth) dispensed justice as a crowned sovereign until the tenth year, when the lovely lady had a son, thus fulfilling his family's expectations. These hastened to baptize him and gave him the name of Gunther after his maternal uncle, a name he need not be ashamed of.[2] Were he to take after his Burgundian kinsman, things would go well with him. They reared him with care, and had very good reason to do so.

Queen Sieglind died at this time, and Kriemhild now had the entire power which such great ladies are entitled to wield over their territories. Many there were who lamented it that death had taken Sieglind from them.

And (so we are told) fair Brunhild, too, had borne a son to mighty Gunther in Burgundy on the Rhine, and, from affection for the hero, they gave him the name of Siegfried.[3] Noble Gunther commanded that he be watched over most zealously and he appointed tutors who had all the qualities to make an excellent man of him. But – in the end – of how many friends and relations did misfortune rob him!

News was constantly being brought of the splendid life the gay knights were leading in Siegmund's land all this time, and so it was with Gunther and his illustrious family. The land of the Nibelungs was subject to Siegfried in Xanten, as were the warriors of Schilbung, and his and Nibelung's hoard, so that no member of Siegfried's kindred

1. In this age of precarious law and order, the poet is of course praising his hero.

2. Dramatic irony, for later Siegfried eats the poet's words for him (p. 132).

3. The names of the heirs would suggest that relations between the two royal families are cordial, despite Brunhild's unsolved problem concerning Siegfried's status.

ever had more power, a fact that made his spirits soar the higher. He possessed the greatest treasure ever won by hero, apart from its former owners, and he had gained it in battle at the foot of a mountain thanks to his own strength, slaying many gay knights to get it. He had all the glory that a man can wish for, and even if this had not been the case we should have had to admit that he was one of the best that ever sat on horseback. Many feared his strength of body, and how right they were to do so.

CHAPTER TWELVE

How Gunther invited Siegfried to the festival

*

Now Gunther's queen was thinking, all this time: 'How comes it that lady Kriemhild can carry her head so high while her husband Siegfried is our vassal? It is a long time since he rendered us any dues.'[1] Such were the thoughts which she nursed in her heart, keeping them well hidden, for it vexed her deeply that those two should hold aloof from her and she receive so little service from Siegfried's land; and she longed to know why that should be. Thus she tried to discover from the King whether it might be possible for her to see Kriemhild again and she made her wish known to him in confidence. But her lord did not think too well of her suggestion.

'How can we fetch them here all that way?' asked the mighty King. 'It would not be possible. They live too far away from us for me to venture to invite them.'

'Whatever heights of power a royal vassal might have reached he should not fail to do his sovereign's bidding,' was Brunhild's subtle reply. Gunther smiled at her words, since whenever he saw Siegfried he did not reckon it as homage.

'My dear lord,' she said, 'if you wish to please me, help me to get Siegfried and your sister to visit us – I assure you nothing could make me happier, for what delight it gives me to recall Kriemhild's elegant ways and courteous nature and how we sat together when I first became your wife! Brave Siegfried honours himself in loving her.'

And she kept on begging him, till at last the King

1. The fact that Siegfried has paid no tribute to Gunther is quoted by Kriemhild in her quarrel with Brunhild as self-evident proof that Siegfried was not Gunther's vassal, and rightly. See p. 112.

said: 'I never saw any guests so gladly as I should see them, believe me. I need very little persuading. I shall dispatch my messengers to them to invite them here to Burgundy.'

'Tell me when you intend to invite them,' said the Queen, 'and when our dear friends are expected here, and let me know whom you mean to send to them.'

'Yes indeed,' replied the King. 'I shall have thirty of my men ride there' – and he immediately summoned them and gave them a message to take to Siegfried's land. Brunhild gave them some very magnificent robes, so pleased was she.

'You warriors are to inform mighty Siegfried and my sister from me – and keep nothing back of what I say – that none could love them more. And ask them both to visit us in our kingdom on the Rhine so that we shall always be obliged to them. Before midsummer he and his followers shall see many here who will hold them in high honour. Give King Siegmund my humble respects, and tell him that my friends and I remain his well-wishers as ever. And ask my sister to be sure to visit her relations, for never was there a festivity that she could more fittingly attend.'

Brunhild and Uote and all the ladies present asked them to deliver their good wishes to the charming noblewomen and all the brave men in Siegfried's country; and with the assent of the royal privy council the messengers set out. They travelled well-equipped for their journey, and when their horses and gear had been brought for them, they quitted the land. Under the protection of the King's safe-conduct, they were in great haste to reach their destination.

After three weeks they rode into Norway,[1] the land to which they had been sent, and there at Nibelung's stronghold they found the warrior. Their horses were very weary from the long way they had come.

1. The poet has merged the Netherlands, Norway, and Nibelungland into one indeterminate northern realm ruled by Siegfried.

Siegfried and Kriemhild were informed that some knights had arrived wearing clothes after the Burgundian fashion, and the Queen at once rose to her feet from the couch where she was resting and sent a maid to the window. As they stood there in the courtyard, the girl recognized brave Gere and his companions who had been sent to them as messengers, and what glad news it was for Kriemhild's homesick heart!

'See, they are there in the courtyard!' she said to the King. 'Stalwart Gere and his companions, whom my brother Gunther has dispatched down the Rhine to us.'

'They are welcome,' said mighty Siegfried, and the household ran out to them, while each said the kindest things he knew to greet those messengers. Lord Siegmund, too, was very glad of their coming.

Gere and his men were lodged in their quarters and their horses were taken to stable. The envoys were then allowed to present themselves to lord Siegfried and Kriemhild as they sat there side by side, and they accordingly did so. The King and his queen rose immediately and received Gere warmly, together with his comrades, Gunther's men, and then Gere was asked to sit down.

'Allow us to discharge our mission before we take our seats – let your travel-weary visitors remain standing long enough to deliver the message which Gunther and Brunhild, Queen Uote, young Gilselher, lord Gernot and your dearest kinsmen convey to you through us. Their fortunes are flourishing, and they send you their humble compliments from Burgundy!'

'Heaven reward you,' answered Siegfried, 'I well believe their good will and sincerity, as one should where friends are concerned, and the same goes for their sister. Now declare your news and let us know whether our dear friends at home are in good spirits. Tell me, has anyone wronged my wife's relations since we left them? If so, I shall not cease to bear them loyal aid till their enemies have cause to regret my help.'

'They live with undiminished honour and are in excellent

spirits. They would be very glad to see you again, never doubt it, and they invite you to the Rhineland to a high festivity. They beg my lady Kriemhild to accompany you and expect you in the spring before midsummer.'

'That would not be easy,' answered mighty Siegfried.

'Your mother Uote, and Gernot and Giselher, have bidden me urge you not to refuse them,' rejoined Gere of Burgundy. 'I have heard them lamenting daily that you live so far away. If it were possible for you to come and see them, Brunhild and all her maidens would be overjoyed to learn it.' This message pleased lovely Kriemhild.

Gere was a near-relation of the Queen's, and the King asked him to be seated; and when Siegfried ordered wine to be poured out for his guests, this was promptly done.

And now Siegmund came and saw the messengers from Burgundy and spoke some friendly words to them. 'Welcome, you knights and vassals of King Gunther! Now that my son Siegfried has taken Kriemhild to wife we ought to see more of you, if you call yourselves our friends.' – To which they answered that they would be glad to come as often as he pleased.

The envoys' hosts banished their weariness with pleasant entertainment. They asked them to sit down, food was set before them, and Siegfried saw to it that his guests had their fill. He prevailed upon them to stay for nine whole days till at last those brave knights began to fret at not being allowed to ride home. Siegfried meanwhile had summoned his friends to ask whether they would advise them to go to the Rhineland or no.

'My good friend Gunther and his kinsmen have sent to invite me to a feast. Now were it not that his country is too far off, I should gladly visit him. They also wish Kriemhild to come with me. Now advise me, dear friends – how can she make the journey there? But had I myself been asked to go campaigning in thirty different countries I could not fail to lend them a helping hand.'

'If you have a mind to go and attend the festivity,' replied his knights, 'we shall tell you what you should do. You must ride to the Rhenish lands with a thousand warriors,[1] then you can stay in Burgundy with honour.'

'If you are going to the festivity why don't you inform *me*?' asked lord Siegmund of the Netherlands. 'I shall ride with you, if you have nothing against it. I shall take a hundred knights with me and so swell the ranks of your party.'

'I shall be glad if you are coming with us, dear father,' answered Siegfried. 'I shall be leaving in twelve days' time,' – and all who asked were given horses and clothes.

Now that the noble King had decided to make the journey the brave envoys were told to return. Through them, Siegfried sent a message to Burgundy informing his wife's relations that he would be delighted to join them at their feast. We are told that both Siegfried and Kriemhild bestowed so many gifts on the envoys that their mounts could not carry it all home, so wealthy a king was he – hence they jubilantly drove sturdy pack-horses away with them!

Siegfried and Siegmund furnished clothes for their followers, and Count Eckewart[2] at once had the whole land scoured for the finest ladies' gowns that could be got hold of anywhere. Saddles and shields were made ready, and the knights and ladies who were to accompany Siegfried and Kriemhild were given what they needed so that they should want for nothing. Siegfried was taking many distinguished guests to see his friends.

The envoys made great speed over the roads that took them homewards, and when at last brave Gere arrived in Burgundy and they all dismounted before Gunther's hall, he was very well received. Both young and old came to ask for news (as they always do), but the good knight said to them, 'You will hear it when I tell the King,' and went in with his companions to Gunther.

The King leapt up from his throne for sheer pleasure,

1. No doubt 'Nibelungs' from 'Nibelungland', but they are first referred to as such in Chapter 17, p. 136.

2. Eckewart has evidently become Kriemhild's chamberlain.

and fair Brunhild thanked them for having come so soon. 'How is Siegfried, who was so kind to me?' Gunther asked his envoys.

'Both he and your sister flushed red for joy. No man of any condition ever sent his friends such loyal greetings as lord Siegfried and his father have sent you.'

'Tell me, is Kriemhild coming?' the Queen asked the Margrave. 'Does she retain the elegant style that used to be all her own?'

'She is most assuredly coming to see you,' was Gere's answer.

Then Uote quickly summoned the messengers, and you could easily tell from the way she asked that she was eager to learn how Kriemhild was. Gere told Uote how he had found her, and said she would be coming soon.

Nor did the envoys fail to tell the court of the gifts that lord Siegfried had made them. Thus the gold and the robes were fetched so that they could be displayed before the three kings' vassals, earning grateful applause for Siegfried's and Kriemhild's munificence.

'It is easy for him to bestow gifts,' said Hagen. 'Were he to live for ever he could never squander all that he owns, for he holds the Nibelungs' hoard in his power. Ah me, if that were to come to Burgundy!'

The household lived in joyful expectation of their coming. Morning and evening the kings' retainers knew no rest as they erected countless seats, while bold Hunold and brave Sindold, aided by Ortwin, were busy directing butlers and stewards to set the benches up. For this Gunther thanked them all.

And how well Rumold, Lord of the Kitchen,[1] governed his subjects, the great cauldrons, pots and pans! What multitudes there were of them, as the viands were made ready for the guests!

1. See pp. 367–8.

CHAPTER THIRTEEN

How Siegfried went to the festival with his queen

*

LET us leave all their bustle and tell how Kriemhild and her maidens journeyed from the land of the Nibelungs and on towards the Rhine.

Numerous coffers were got ready for the sumpters to take the road, and no horses ever carried fine robes in such number. And now brave Siegfried and his queen set out with their friends for where they were expecting much joy, though it turned out to the great sorrow of them all.

Siegfried and Kriemhild left their little son at home, since there was nothing else they could do. Great trouble arose for him from their visit to Worms, for he never saw his parents again.

Lord Siegmund rode off with them, too. But had he realized how things were to fall out later at the festivity he would not have attended it, since no greater affliction could have befallen him through those who were so dear to him.

They sent messengers ahead of them to tell the Burgundians they were coming, and accordingly many of Uote's friends and Gunther's vassals rode out to meet them, a delightful company, while the King himself made strenuous preparations for receiving his guests.

Going to where Brunhild was sitting,[1] Gunther asked her: 'Do you remember how my sister welcomed you when you entered my country? Please receive Siegfried's queen with the same honours.'

1. Brunhild's inactivity, so much in contrast with the general stir at court, is due to her curiosity about Siegfried. For if Siegfried is Gunther's vassal, as she has been led to believe, it would not be necessary for them to ride out and meet him; yet within a few lines Gunther shows that he means to welcome Siegfried as an equal.

'I shall most willingly,' she answered, 'for I wish her well, as she deserves.'

'They will be arriving tomorrow morning. If you mean to give them a welcome you must bestir yourself so as not to receive them here in the castle, for never have I been visited by such very dear guests.'

Brunhild at once asked her ladies and maids to seek out the best clothes they had, to wear before their guests, and it goes without saying that they needed no prompting. Gunther's men, too, were quick to wait on them with their palfreys. Gunther then assembled all his warriors and the Queen rode out with great magnificence.

They received their dear guests with many salutations and indescribable joy, and people thought that even lady Kriemhild had not welcomed Queen Brunhild so warmly.

Those who had never seen Kriemhild before now learnt how beauty can fire a man. Meanwhile Siegfried had arrived with his men, and you could see them winding to and fro all over the meadow in vast companies,[1] so that there was no avoiding the press and the dust.

When the lord of the land saw Siegfried and Siegmund, he said affectionately: 'You are very welcome indeed to me and all my friends, and we are happy and proud at your coming.'

'May heaven repay you,' answered Siegmund, the ever-eager in pursuit of honour. 'Ever since my son Siegfried gained your friendship I have felt an urge to meet you.'

'I am very glad you came,' replied King Gunther.

With the courteous participation of Gernot and Giselher, Siegfried was welcomed with all the honours due to him and none bore him a grudge. I fancy no guests ever had better treatment.

The two Queens now approached each other, and many saddles were emptied as the knights lifted whole bevies of fine-looking women down on to the grass; for there was a great flurry about them of those who liked waiting on ladies.

1. As formerly in honour of Brunhild, they were now riding the bohort in honour of Kriemhild; cf. p. 84.

Thereupon that lovely pair went up to each other, and it was a joy to countless knights that they greeted each other so courteously. Warriors were standing there in crowds beside the Queens' maidens, and now the knights and the young ladies took one another's hands, and there was much elegant bowing and sweet kissing by those fair ones, a spectacle that delighted the men of both Gunther and Siegfried.

They delayed no longer but rode up to the town, and the King asked his people to make it plain to his guests that they were very glad to see them in Burgundy. Thus they rode many splendid jousts under the eyes of the young ladies. Here Hagen of Troneck and Ortwin showed their authority, since none dared flout their commands, and much honour was paid to the visitors – under the thrusts and charges countless shields resounded all the way up to the castle gate, and the King himself halted outside for a long time with his guests before he entered, so pleasantly did they while away the hour.

But now they rode up to the broad palace in high spirits, and, flowing down from fair ladies' saddles, many fine brocades, well cut and ingeniously woven, caught the eye on all sides. Gunther's attendants appeared at once, and he told them to take the guests to their chambers. Now and again Brunhild darted a glance at lady Kriemhild who looked so very lovely, the radiance of her fair face vying magnificently with its setting of gold.

The hubbub of Siegfried's retinue could be heard all over the city of Worms. Gunther asked his marshal Dancwart to see to their needs, and Dancwart accordingly set about finding agreeable quarters for them. He ordered food to be brought for them, both within and without the fortress, and visitors from abroad never received better attention: whatever they desired was given them – the King was so rich that nobody was denied anything and they were served with the utmost good will.

The King sat down with his guests. Siegfried was asked to sit at the same seat as before, and as he went to take it he was attended by many splendid knights. Fully twelve hundred warriors sat at table in his ring, and Queen Brunhild was thinking no liege man could ever be mightier. Her feeling towards him were still friendly enough for her to let him live.[1]

That evening, while the King sat and dined, many fine robes were splashed with wine as the butlers plied the tables – they served the guests eagerly and plentifully, as has long been the custom at feasts. The King gave orders for the ladies and maidens to be comfortably lodged: he wished to serve them wherever they came from, and they all had to receive his bounty as a sign of his esteem.

When the night came to an end and dawn appeared, the ladies opened their coffers, and the lustre of innumerable jewels shone out from the fine stuffs as their hands moved among them, choosing many splendid robes. But while it was not yet full daylight, a host of knights and squires arrived before the hall, and once again the tumult was heard as young warriors jousted so spiritedly that, before early matins were sung for the King, they had earned his commendation! The crack of many trumpets rang out loud and clear, and the sound of drums and flutes grew so great that spacious Worms re-echoed with it, a sign for proud warriors everywhere to leap into their saddles.

And now far and wide and in great number the good knights began a most noble sport: you could see many there whose youthful hearts fired them with great zest, all fine, gallant knights beneath their shields! Magnificent women and bevies of lovely girls adorned in all their finery sat in the windows watching the pastime of all those fearless men, till the King and his friends took the field. Thus they passed the time, which did not lie heavy on their hands, till the bells pealed from the minster. The Queens' and their ladies' palfreys were fetched and they all rode off, attended by troops of knights. When they arrived before the cathedral

1. There is a *double entendre* in the original here, the other sense being 'to let him be'. Since Brunhild will one day wish Siegfried to die, I have chosen the former. On the poet's hints as to how he wishes Brunhild to be understood, see p. 332.

they dismounted on the grass. Brunhild was as yet well disposed towards her guests, and they all entered together in their crowns. Nevertheless, as a result of a bitter quarrel their friendship was soon to be broken.

When they had heard mass they returned, and with much ceremony went happily to table. Nor did their joy at that high feast droop till the eleventh day.

CHAPTER FOURTEEN

How the queens railed at each other

*

BEFORE vespers one evening there arose in the courtyard a great turmoil of warriors pursuing their pleasure at their knightly sports, and a crowd of men and women ran up to watch.

The mighty Queens had sat down together, and their thoughts were on two splendid knights.

'I have a husband of such merit that he might rule over all the kingdoms of this region,' said fair Kriemhild.

'How could that be?' asked lady Brunhild. 'If there were no others alive but you and he, all these kingdoms might well subserve him, but as long as Gunther lives it could never come about.'

'See how magnificently he bears himself, and with what splendour he stands out from the other knights, like the moon against the stars,' rejoined Kriemhild. 'It is not for nothing that I am so happy.'

'However splendid and handsome and valiant your husband may be,' replied Brunhild, 'you must nevertheless give your noble brother the advantage. Let me tell you truly: Gunther must take precedence over all kings.'

'My husband is a man of such worth,' answered lady Kriemhild, 'that I have not praised him vainly. His honour stands high on very many counts. Believe me, Brunhild, he is fully Gunther's equal.'

'Now do not misunderstand me, Kriemhild, for I did not speak without cause. When I saw them for the first time[1]

---

1. In view of the hints of prior acquaintance between Brunhild and Siegfried (see pp. 58–62) this ought to mean 'saw Gunther and Siegfried together for the first time'. In 'subdued me to his will' the reference is to Gunther's spurious victory over Brunhild in her three contests (see p. 68), and to associated events in Iceland.

and the King subdued me to his will and won my love so gallantly, I heard them both declare – and Siegfried himself said so – that he was Gunther's vassal, and so I consider him to be my liegeman, having having heard him say so.'[1]

'It would be a sad thing for me if that were so,' retorted Kriemhild. 'How could my noble brothers have had a hand in my marrying a liegeman? I must ask you in all friendship, Brunhild, if you care for me, kindly to stop saying such things.'

'I cannot,' answered the Queen, 'for why should I renounce my claim to so many knights who owe us service through Siegfried?'

At this lovely Kriemhild lost her temper. 'You will have to renounce your claim to him and to his attending you with services of any kind! He ranks above my noble brother Gunther, and you must spare me such things as I have had to hear. I must say I find it very odd, since he is your liegeman and you have such power over us, that he has been sitting on his dues for so long![2] You should not bother me with your airs.'

'You are getting above yourself,' replied the Queen, 'and I should like to see whether you are held in such esteem as I.' The ladies were growing very angry.

'We shall very soon see!' said lady Kriemhild. 'Since you have declared my husband to be your liegeman, the two Kings' vassals must witness today whether I dare enter the minster before the Queen of the land.[3] You must see visible proof this day that I am a free noblewoman, and that my husband is a better man than yours. Nor do I intend for my part to be demeaned by what you say. You shall see this evening how your liegewoman will walk in state in Burgundy in sight of the warriors. I claim to be of

1. See pp. 63, 331.

2. This was a matter which had been troubling Brunhild greatly; see p. 100.

3. Kriemhild's language is reminiscent of set challenges between heroes of the older period, and it is to be noted that the presence of the warriors, which she invokes, will give her 'duel' with Brunhild a quasi juridical status.

higher station than was ever heard of concerning any Queen that wore a crown!' And now indeed fierce hate grew up between those ladies.

'If you deny you are a vassal, you and your ladies must withdraw from my suite when we enter the cathedral.'

'We certainly shall,' answered Kriemhild. 'Now dress yourselves well, my maidens,' she said to them, 'for I must not be put to shame. Let it appear beyond all doubt whether you have fine clothes or not. We must make Brunhild eat her words.'

They needed little persuading and fetched out their sumptuous robes. And when all the ladies and maidens were beautifully attired, Queen Kriemhild, herself exquisitely gowned, set out with her train of forty-three maids-in-waiting whom she had brought with her to Worms, all dressed in dazzling cloth-of-gold from Arabia.

And so those shapely girls arrived at the minster, before which Siegfried's men were waiting, so that people were wondering why it was that the Queens appeared separately and no longer went together as before. However, in the end, many brave knights had to suffer dearly for their division.

Gunther's Queen was already standing before the cathedral and all the knights were passing the time pleasantly taking note of her lovely women, when lady Kriemhild arrived with a great and splendid company. However fine the clothes ever worn by daughters of any noble knights, they were as nothing beside those of her suite: Kriemhild was so rich in possessions that thirty queens could not have found the wherewithal to do as she had done. Even if his wishes were to come true, no man could assert that he had ever seen such magnificent clothes paraded as Kriemhild's fair maidens were wearing, though she would not have demanded it except to spite Brunhild.

The two processions met before the minster and the lady of the land, prompted by great malice, harshly ordered Kriemhild to halt. 'A liegewoman may not enter before a Queen!'

'It would have been better for you if you could have

held your tongue,' said fair Kriemhild angrily, 'for you have brought dishonour on your own pretty head. How could a vassal's paramour ever wed a King?'

'Whom are you calling a paramour?' asked the Queen.

'I call you one,' answered Kriemhild. 'My dear husband Siegfried was the first to enjoy your lovely body, since it was not my brother who took your maidenhead. Where were your poor wits? – It was a vile trick. – Seeing that he is your vassal, why did you let him love you? Your complaints have no foundation.'

'I swear I shall tell Gunther of this,' replied Brunhild.

'What is that to me? Your arrogance has got the better of you. You used words that made me your servant, and, believe me, in all sincerity I shall always be sorry you did so. I can no longer keep your secrets.'

Brunhild began to weep, and Kriemhild delayed no more but, accompanied by her train, entered the cathedral before Gunther's queen. Thus great hatred arose and bright eyes grew very moist and dim from it.[1]

However pious the ministrations and the chanting, the service seemed to Brunhild as though it would never end, since she was troubled to the depths of her being. Many good warriors had to pay for it later. At last she went out with her ladies and took her stand before the minster thinking: 'Kriemhild must tell me more about this thing of which she accuses me so loudly, sharp-tongued woman that she is. If Siegfried has boasted of it, it will cost him his life!'

And now noble Kriemhild appeared, attended by many brave knights. 'Halt for one moment,' said lady Brunhild. 'You declared me to be a paramour – now prove it! Let me tell you, your remarks have offended me deeply.'

'You would do better not to stand in my way! I prove it with this gold ring on my finger here which my sweetheart brought me when he first slept with you.' Never had Brunhild known a day so fraught with pain.

1. One thinks of Brunhild's eyes during her impending humiliation, of Kriemhild's when Brunhild has been avenged, and of those of all the women whose men will be slain before the end.

'This noble ring was stolen and has long been maliciously withheld from me! But now I shall get to the bottom of this affair and discover who took it.' The two ladies were now very agitated.

'You shall not make me the thief who stole it! If you cared for your honour it would have been wise to hold your tongue. As proof that I am not lying, see this girdle which I have round me – you shared my Siegfried's bed!'

She was wearing a fine silk braid from Nineveh[1] adorned with precious stones, and Brunhild burst into tears when she saw it. She was resolved that Gunther should hear of this, together with the men of Burgundy. 'Ask the lord of the Rhenish lands to come here. I want to tell him how his sister has insulted me; for she openly declares me to be Siegfried's concubine.'

The King came with his warriors and saw his spouse in tears. 'Tell me, dear lady,' he said very tenderly, 'has anyone annoyed you?'

'I have cause enough to be unhappy. Your sister means to rob me of my honour. I accuse her before you of having said for all to hear that her husband made me his paramour!'

'She would have acted very ill if she had,' said King Gunther.[2]

'She is wearing the girdle that I lost and my ring of red gold. I shall regret the day that I was born unless you clear me of this monstrous infamy, Sire, and earn my eternal thanks!'

'Ask Siegfried to appear. The knight from the Netherlands must either tell us that he made this boast or deny it.' And Kriemhild's beloved husband was summoned at once.

When lord Siegfried saw the Queens' distress (he had no idea what was amiss) he quickly asked: 'Why are these ladies

1. See Appendix 3, 'The Date of the Poem', p. 366.
2. Gunther's extreme caution during this scene is due partly to his fear of exposure, partly to his fear of Siegfried, and partly to the fact that with Brunhild's formal accusation the proceedings have become judicial, with Gunther himself as judge.

weeping? I should very much like to know. Or why has the King sent for me?'

'I deeply regret this necessity,' said King Gunther, 'but my lady Brunhild tells me some tale of your having boasted you were the first to enjoy her lovely person – so your wife, lady Kriemhild, avers.'

'If she said this,' answered mighty Siegfried, 'she will regret it before I have finished with her. I am willing in the presence of your vassals to rebut with my most solemn oaths that I ever said this to her.'

'You must give us proof of that. If the oath you offer is duly sworn here I shall clear you of all treason.' And he commanded the proud Burgundians to stand in a ring. Brave Siegfried raised his hand to swear[1] but the mighty king said: 'Your great innocence is so well known to me that I acquit you of my sister's allegation and accept that you are not guilty of the deed.'

'If my wife were to go unpunished for having distressed Brunhild I should be extremely sorry, I assure you,' rejoined Siegfried, at which the good knights exchanged meaningful glances.[2] 'Women should be trained to avoid irresponsible chatter,' continued Siegfried. 'Forbid your wife to indulge in it, and I shall do the same with mine. I am truly ashamed at her unseemly behaviour.'

All those comely women parted in silence. But Brunhild was so dejected that Gunther's vassals could not but pity her. Then Hagen of Troneck came to his liege lady, and, finding her in tears, asked her what was vexing her. She told him what had happened, and he at once vowed that Kriemhild's man should pay for it, else Hagen, because of that insult, would never be happy again. Then Ortwin and Gernot arrived where the knights were plotting Siegfried's death and took part in their discussion. Noble

1. Some critics think that Siegfried swore the oath, others that Gunther did not let him go so far.
2. The 'knights' referred to are probably the bystanders, who are beginning to have their suspicions: but it is also possible that Gunther and Siegfried are reassuring each other that their secret is safe.

Uote's son Giselher came next, and, hearing their deliberations, he asked in his loyal-hearted fashion: 'Why are you doing this, good knights? Siegfried has never in any way deserved such hatred that he should die for it. Why, it is a trifle over which the women are quarrelling!'

'Are we to rear cuckoos?'[1] asked Hagen. 'That would bring small honour to such worthy knights. His boast that he enjoyed my dear lady shall cost him his life, or I shall die avenging it!'

'He has done us nothing but good,' interposed the King himself, 'and he has brought us honour. He must be allowed to live. To what purpose should I now turn against him? – He has always shown us heartfelt loyalty.'

'His great strength shall not avail him,' said brave Ortwin of Metz. 'If my lord will let me, I shall do him some harm!'

Thus those warriors declared themselves his enemies, though he had done them no wrong. Yet none followed Ortwin's proposal, except that Hagen kept putting it to Gunther that if Siegfried were no more, Gunther would be lord of many kingdoms,[2] at which Gunther grew very despondent.

There they let the matter rest and went to look at the sports. And what a forest of stout shafts was shattered before the minster and all the way up to the hall for Kriemhild to see![3] But, for their part, many of Gunther's men nursed feelings of resentment.

'Let your murderous anger be,' said the King. 'Siegfried was born for our honour and good fortune, and moreover

1. One interpretation is: 'Are we to tolerate in our midst one who fathers his children on us?' But in asking this, Hagen would imply his belief in the *substance* of Kriemhild's allegation. The sense of 'bastards' for 'cuckoos' has also been proposed, but this would imply an intention to murder Brunhild's son, born only recently (see p. 98), which is unthinkable. A third suggestion, that 'cuckoos' means 'usurpers' lacks linguistic support. Since none of these interpretations suits the context well, and the passage is couched in archaic rhymes, this saying of Hagen's must be regarded as a survival from an earlier version, too colourful to drop.

2. On Siegfried as a possible threat to Gunther see p. 321.

3. Kriemhild's men celebrate her triumph with a show of high spirits.

he is so terribly strong and so prodigiously brave that were he to get wind of it, none could dare oppose him.'

'He will not,' answered Hagen. 'You just say nothing at all, and I fancy I shall manage this so well in secret that he will repent of Brunhild's weeping. I declare that I, Hagen, shall always be his enemy!'

'How could the thing be done?' asked King Gunther.

'I will tell you,' replied Hagen. 'We shall send envoys to ourselves here in Burgundy to declare war on us publicly, men whom no one knows. Then you will announce in the hearing of your guests that you and your men plan to go campaigning, whereupon Siegfried will promise you his aid, and so he will lose his life. For in this way I shall learn the brave man's secret[1] from his wife.'

The King followed his vassal Hagen's advice, to evil effect, and those rare knights began to set afoot the great betrayal before any might discover it, so that, thanks to the wrangling of two women, countless warriors met their doom.

1. The location of Siegfried's one vulnerable spot, not mentioned by Hagen in his brief account of Siegfried's horny skin in Chapter 3, p. 28 (cf. p. 121).

CHAPTER FIFTEEN

How Siegfried was betrayed

*

FOUR days later, in the morning, thirty-two men were seen riding to court who were to tell mighty Gunther that war had been declared on him – a lie from which ladies were to reap the greatest sorrow.

The envoys received permission to go before the King and they announced that they were men of that same Liudeger whom in time past Siegfried had overcome and brought captive to Gunther's country. The King greeted them and bade them go and sit down, but one of their number replied: 'Sire, allow us to stand till we have delivered the message which has been sent to you; for you must know that you have many a mother's son for your enemy. Liudegast and Liudeger, on whom you once inflicted fearful hurt, declare themselves at war with you and intend to invade you with their army here in Burgundy.'

The King was incensed at this news and ordered these accomplices in treachery to their quarters. How could lord Siegfried or anyone else save himself from their plotting – plotting that fell out to their own torment in the end?

Gunther went conversing with his friends in whispers, and Hagen of Troneck would not let him rest – a number of the King's friends would have composed the affair even now at this late hour – but Hagen would not give up his plot.

One day, Siegfried found them with their heads together and asked them: 'Why are the King and his men so dejected? I shall always help to avenge him if anyone has wronged him.'

'I have good reason to be downcast,' answered lord Gunther, 'for Liudegast and Liudeger have declared war on me. They intend to invade me openly.'

'I, Siegfried, shall prevent it with all energy, as befits

your honour, and I will deal with them now as I dealt with them before. I shall lay waste their lands and castles before I have finished with them, let my head be your pledge for it! You and your warriors must stay at home and let me ride against them with the men that I have here. I shall show you how glad I am to help you. Believe me, I shall make your enemies suffer!'

'How your words hearten me,' answered the King, as though he were seriously pleased at Siegfried's help. And the faithless man in his perfidy thanked him with a low bow.

'Have no fear,' said lord Siegfried.

Then, in a way that Siegfried and his men were bound to see, they prepared for the expedition with their squires, and Siegfried in turn told his Netherlanders to make ready, and they accordingly fetched out their armour.

'My father Siegmund, please remain here. If Heaven proves kind we shall be returning to the Rhineland shortly. You stay here with the King and enjoy yourself.'

They tied on their standards as though about to leave, and there were many of Gunther's men who did not know the reason. A great crowd of followers could be seen about Siegfried and they bound their helmets and corselets on to their mounts as many strong knights prepared to quit Burgundy.

Then Hagen of Troneck went to Kriemhild and asked for leave to depart, saying they were going abroad.

'How fortunate I am,' she replied, 'that I have a husband who has the courage to protect my dear relations as my lord Siegfried does. This makes me very happy. My dear friend, Hagen,' continued the Queen, 'bear it in mind that I am always ready to serve you and have never borne you any ill will, so let me have the benefit of it where my dear husband is concerned – he must not be made to pay for any wrong that I may have done to Brunhild. I have since repented of my fault, and Siegfried has beaten me soundly and taken ample vengeance for my having said anything that vexed her.'

'You and she are bound to be reconciled as the days go by,' he answered. 'Now tell me, Kriemhild, dear lady, what can I do for you with regard to your husband Siegfried? I should do it willingly, since there is none towards whom I am better disposed than you, ma'am.'

'I should not be afraid of anyone killing him in battle,' replied the noble lady, 'if only he would not let his rashness get the better of him. Apart from that, the good warrior would never come to harm.'

'My lady,' said Hagen, 'if you have any apprehension that a weapon might wound him tell me by what means I can prevent it, and I shall always guard him, riding or walking.'

'You and I are of one blood, dear Hagen, and I earnestly commend my beloved spouse to you to guard him.' Then she divulged some matters that had better been left alone. 'My husband is very brave and very strong,' she said. 'When he slew the dragon at the foot of the mountain the gallant knight bathed in its blood, as a result of which no weapon has pierced him in battle ever since. Nevertheless, when he is at the wars in the midst of all the javelins that warriors hurl, I fear I may lose my dear husband. Alas, how often do I not suffer cruelly in my fear for Siegfried! Now I shall reveal this to you in confidence, dearest kinsman, so that you may keep faith with me, and I shall tell you, trusting utterly in you, where my dear husband can be harmed. When the hot blood flowed from the dragon's wound and the good knight was bathing in it, a broad leaf fell from the linden between his shoulder-blades. It is there that he can be wounded, and this is why I am so anxious.'

'Sew a little mark on his clothing so that I shall know where I must shield him in battle.' She fancied she was saving the hero, yet this was aimed at his death.

'I will take some fine silk and sew on a cross that none will notice,' she said, 'and there, knight, you must shield him when the battle is joined, and he faces his foes in the onrush.'

'I shall indeed, my dear lady.' – And she fondly imagined

that it was for Siegfried's good, though her husband was betrayed by it. Hagen took his leave and went away rejoicing.

The King's followers were all in great heart. I fancy no warrior will ever again perpetrate such treachery as Hagen contrived, when Queen Kriemhild put her trust in him.

The next morning, lord Siegfried set out happily with a thousand of his men, imagining he would avenge his friends' wrongs, while Hagen rode near enough to be able to survey his clothes. And when Hagen had observed the mark he secretly dispatched two of his men to report news of a different sort – that Liudeger had sent them to King Gunther to say that Burgundy would be left at peace. How loath Siegfried was to ride home again without striking a blow for his friends – Gunther's men could scarcely get him to turn about!

When Siegfried rode back to the King, the latter thanked him: 'May Heaven reward you for your good intentions, friend Siegfried, and for being so ready to meet my wishes. I shall always seek to repay you, as I am bound to do, and put my trust in you before all my friends. But now that we have been spared this campaign I intend to go hunting the bear and the boar in the forest of the Vosges, as I have so often done.' It was the traitor Hagen who had put him up to this.

'Announce it to all my guests that we shall ride out very early and that those who wish to hunt with me are to make their preparations, but that those others have my blessing who wish to stay and wait on the ladies.'

'If you are riding out hunting,' said lord Siegfried generously, 'I shall be glad to accompany you. If you will lend me a tracker and some hounds I will ride into the forest.'

'Do you wish to take only one?' asked the King immediately. 'If you like, I will lend you four that have intimate knowledge of the forest and of the paths which the game follows and who will not lose the scent and send you home empty-handed.'

Then gallant Siegfried rode off to his wife, and Hagen

quickly told the King how he planned to get the better of him.

Never should a man practise such monstrous treachery.

CHAPTER SIXTEEN

How Siegfried was slain

*

THE fearless warriors Gunther and Hagen treacherously proclaimed a hunt[1] in the forest where they wished to chase the boar, the bear, and the bison[2] – and what could be more daring? Siegfried rode with their party in magnificent style. They took all manner of food with them; and it was while drinking from a cool stream that the hero was to lose his life at the instigation of Brunhild, King Gunther's queen.

Bold Siegfried went to Kriemhild while his and his companions' hunting-gear was being loaded on to the sumpters in readiness to cross the Rhine, and she could not have been more afflicted. 'God grant that I may see you well again, my lady,' he said, kissing his dear wife, 'and that your eyes may see me too. Pass the time pleasantly with your relations who are so kind to you, since I cannot stay with you at home.'

Kriemhild thought of what she had told Hagen, but she dared not mention it and began to lament that she had ever been born. 'I dreamt last night – and an ill-omened dream it was –' said lord Siegfried's noble queen, weeping with unrestrained passion, 'that two boars chased you over the heath and the flowers were dyed with blood! How can I help weeping so? I stand in great dread of some attempt against your life. – What if we have offended any men who have the power to vent their malice on us? Stay away, my lord, I urge you.'

1. The last poet has superimposed a more or less fantastic and at times comical hunt, with some exotic and even unknown beasts, upon an older hunting scene. It serves to show Siegfried for the last time in all his guileless excellence. The comedy relaxes the tension before the tragedy for which the poet has so long prepared us.

2. The European bison or *wisent*, until recently surviving in eastern Europe.

'I shall return in a few days time, my darling. I know of no people here who bear me any hatred. Your kinsmen without exception wish me well, nor have I deserved otherwise of them.'

'It is not so, lord Siegfried. I fear you will come to grief. Last night I had a sinister dream of how two mountains fell upon you and hid you from my sight! I shall suffer cruelly if you go away and leave me.' But he clasped the noble woman in his arms and after kissing and caressing her fair person very tenderly, took his leave and went forthwith. Alas, she was never to see him alive again.

They rode away deep into the forest in pursuit of their sport. Gunther and his men were accompanied by numbers of brave knights, but Gernot and Giselher stayed at home. Ahead of the hunt many horses had crossed the Rhine laden with their bread, wine, meat, fish, and various other provisions such as a King of Gunther's wealth is bound to have with him.

The proud and intrepid hunters were told to set up their lodges on a spacious isle in the river on which they were to hunt, at the skirt of the greenwood over towards the spot where the game would have to break cover. Siegfried, too, had arrived there, and this was reported to the King. Thereupon the sportsmen everywhere manned their relays.

'Who is going to guide us through the forest to our quarry, brave warriors?' asked mighty Siegfried.

'Shall we split up before we start hunting here?' asked Hagen. 'Then my lords and I could tell who are the best hunters on this foray into the woods. Let us share the huntsmen and hounds between us and each take the direction he likes – and then all honour to him that hunts best!' At this, the hunters quickly dispersed.

'I do not need any hounds,' said lord Siegfried, 'except for one tracker so well fleshed that he recognizes the tracks which the game leave through the wood: then we shall not fail to find our quarry.'

An old huntsman took a good sleuth-hound and quickly led the lord to where there was game in abundance. The party chased everything that was roused from its lair, as good hunting-men still do today. Bold Siegfried of the Netherlands killed every beast that his hound started, for his hunter was so swift that nothing could elude him. Thus, versatile as he was, Siegfried outshone all the others in that hunt.

The very first kill was when he brought down a strong young tusker,[1] after which he soon chanced on an enormous lion. When his hound had roused it he laid a keen arrow to his bow and shot it so that it dropped in its tracks at the third bound. Siegfried's fellow-huntsmen acclaimed him for this shot. Next, in swift succession, he killed a wisent, an elk, four mighty aurochs, and a fierce and monstrous buck[2] – so well mounted was he that nothing, be it hart or hind, could evade him. His hound then came upon a great boar, and, as this turned to flee, the champion hunter at once blocked his path, bringing him to bay; and when in a trice the beast sprang at the hero in a fury, Siegfried slew him with his sword, a feat no other hunter could have performed with such ease. After the felling of this boar, the tracker was returned to his leash and Siegfried's splendid bag was made known to the Burgundians.

'If it is not asking too much, lord Seigfried,' said his companions of the chase, 'do leave some of the game alive for us. You are emptying the hills and woods for us today.' At this the brave knight had to smile.

There now arose a great shouting of men and clamour of hounds on all sides, and the tumult grew so great that the hills and the forest re-echoed with it – the huntsmen had unleashed no fewer than four and twenty packs! Thus, many beasts had to lose their lives there, since each of these hunters was hoping to bring it about that *he* should be given the high honours of the chase. But when mighty Siegfried appeared beside the camp fire there was no chance of that.

The hunt was over, yet not entirely so. Those who wished

1. The traditional interpretation, although the MSS vary.
2. 'Schelch': possibly a semi-mythical tragelaph.

to go to the fire brought the hides of innumerable beasts, and game in plenty – what loads of it they carried back to the kitchen to the royal retainers! And now the noble King had it announced to those fine hunters that he wished to take his repast, and there was one great blast of the horn to tell them that he was back in camp.

At this, one of Siegfried's huntsmen said: 'Sir, I have heard a horn-blast telling us to return to our lodges. – I shall answer it.' There was much blowing to summon the companions.

'Let us quit the forest, too,' said lord Siegfried. His mount carried him at an even pace, and the others hastened away with him but with the noise of their going they started a savage bear, a very fierce beast.

'I shall give our party some good entertainment,' he said over his shoulder. 'Loose the hound, for I can see a bear which will have to come back to our lodges with us. It will not be able to save itself unless it runs very fast.' The hound was unleashed, and the bear made off at speed. Siegfried meant to ride it down but soon found that his way was blocked and his intention thwarted, while the mighty beast fancied it would escape from its pursuer. But the proud knight leapt from his horse and started to chase it on foot, and the animal, quite off its guard, failed to elude him. And so he quickly caught and bound it, without having wounded it at all – nor could the beast use either claws or teeth on the man. Siegfried tied it to his saddle, mounted his horse, and in his high-spirited fashion led it to the camp-fire in order to amuse the good knights.

And in what magnificent style Siegfried rode! He bore a great spear, stout of shaft and broad of head; his handsome sword reached down to his spurs; and the fine horn which this lord carried was of the reddest gold. Nor have I ever heard tell of a better hunting outfit: he wore a surcoat of costly black silk and a splendid hat of sable, and you should have seen the gorgeous silken tassels on his quiver, which was covered in panther-skin for the sake of its fragrant odour!¹ He also bore a bow so strong that apart from Siegfried any who wished to span it would have had to use a rack. His hunting suit was all of otter-skin, varied throughout its length with furs of other kinds from whose shining hair clasps of gold gleamed out on either side of this daring lord of the hunt. The handsome sword that he wore was Balmung, a weapon so keen and with such excellent edges that it never failed to bite when swung against a helmet. No wonder this splendid hunter was proud and gay. And (since I am bound to tell you all) know that his quiver was full of good arrows with gold mountings and heads a span in width, so that any beast they pierced must inevitably soon die.

Thus the noble knight rode along, the very image of a hunting man. Gunther's attendants saw him coming and ran to meet him to take his horse – tied to whose saddle he led a mighty bear! On dismounting, he loosed the bonds from its muzzle and paws, whereupon all the hounds that saw it instantly gave tongue. The beast made for the forest and the people were seized with panic. Affrighted by the tumult, the bear strayed into the kitchen – and how the cooks scuttled from their fire at its approach! Many cauldrons were sent flying and many fires were scattered, while heaps of good food lay among the ashes. Lords and retainers leapt from their seats, the bear became infuriated, and the King ordered all the hounds on their leashes to be loosed – and if all had ended well they would have had a jolly day! Bows and spears were no longer left idle, for the brave ones ran towards the bear, yet there were so many hounds in the way that none dared shoot. With the whole mountain thundering with peoples' cries the bear took to flight before the hounds and none could keep up with it but Siegfried, who ran it down and then dispatched it with his sword. The bear was later carried to the camp-fire,

---

1. According to the imaginative zoology of the time, the hide of the live panther emitted an agreeable scent which lured other animals towards it, and our poet no doubt intended to transfer the panther's hunting advantage to his hero through his quiver.

and all who had witnessed this feat declared that Siegfried was a very powerful man.

The proud companions were then summoned to table. There were a great many seated in that meadow. Piles of sumptuous dishes were set before the noble huntsmen, but the butlers who were to pour their wine were very slow to appear. Yet knights could not be better cared for than they and if only no treachery had been lurking in their minds those warriors would have been above reproach.

'Seeing that we are being treated to such a variety of dishes from the kitchen,' said lord Siegfried, 'I fail to understand why the butlers bring us no wine. Unless we hunters are better looked after, I'll not be a companion of the hunt. I thought I had deserved better attention.'

'We shall be very glad to make amends to you for our present lack,' answered the perfidious King from his table. 'This is Hagen's fault – he wants us to die of thirst.'

'My very dear lord,' replied Hagen of Troneck, 'I thought the day's hunting would be away in the Spessart and so I sent the wine there. If we go without drink today I shall take good care that it does not happen again.'

'Damn those fellows!' said lord Siegfried. 'It was arranged that they were to bring along seven panniers of spiced wine and mead for me. Since that proved impossible, we should have been placed nearer the Rhine.'

'You brave and noble knights,' said Hagen of Troneck, 'I know a cool spring nearby – do not be offended! – let us go there.' – A proposal which (as it turned out) was to bring many knights into jeopardy.

Siegfried was tormented by thirst and ordered the board to be removed all the sooner in his eagerness to go to that spring at the foot of the hills. And now the knights put their treacherous plot into execution.

Word was given for the game which Siegfried had killed to be conveyed back to Worms on waggons, and all who saw it gave him great credit for it.

Hagen of Troneck broke his faith with Siegfried most grievously, for as they were leaving to go to the spreading lime-tree he said: 'I have often been told that no one can keep up with Lady Kriemhild's lord when he cares to show his speed. I wish he would show it us now.'

'You can easily put it to the test by racing me to the brook,' replied gallant Siegfried of the Netherlands. 'Then those who see it shall declare the winner.'

'I accept your challenge,' said Hagen.

'Then I will lie down in the grass at your feet, as a handicap,' replied brave Siegfried, much to Gunther's satisfaction. 'And I will tell you what more I shall do. I will carry all my equipment with me, my spear and my shield and all my hunting clothes.' And he quickly strapped on his quiver and sword. The two men took off their outer clothing and stood there in their white vests. Then they ran through the clover like a pair of wild panthers. Siegfried appeared first at the brook.

Gunther's magnificent guest who excelled so many men in all things quickly unstrapped his sword, took off his quiver, and after leaning his great spear against a branch of the lime, stood beside the rushing brook. Then he laid down his shield near the flowing water, and although he was very thirsty he most courteously refrained from drinking until the King had drunk. Gunther thanked him very ill for this.

The stream was cool, sweet, and clear. Gunther stooped to its running waters and after drinking stood up and stepped aside. Siegfried in turn would have liked to do the same, but he paid for his good manners. For now Hagen carried Siegfried's sword and bow beyond his reach, ran back for the spear, and searched for the sign on the brave man's tunic. Then, as Siegfried bent over the brook and drank, Hagen hurled the spear at the cross,[1] so that the hero's heart's blood leapt from the wound and splashed against Hagen's clothes. No warrior will ever do a darker deed. Leaving the spear fixed in Siegfried's heart, he fled in wild desperation, as he had never fled before from any man.

When lord Siegfried felt the great wound, maddened with rage he bounded back from the stream with the long shaft

1. See p. 304.

jutting from his heart. He was hoping to find either his bow or his sword, and, had he succeeded in doing so, Hagen would have had his pay. But finding no sword, the gravely wounded man had nothing but his shield. Snatching this from the bank he ran at Hagen, and King Gunther's vassal was unable to elude him. Siegfried was wounded to death, yet he struck so powerfully that he sent many precious stones whirling from the shield as it smashed to pieces. Gunther's noble guest would dearly have loved to avenge himself. Hagen fell reeling under the weight of the blow and the riverside echoed loudly. Had Siegfried had his sword in his hand it would have been the end of Hagen, so enraged was the wounded man, as indeed he had good cause to be.

The hero's face had lost its colour and he was no longer able to stand. His strength had ebbed away, for in the field of his bright countenance he now displayed Death's token. Soon many fair ladies would be weeping for him.

The lady Kriemhild's lord fell among the flowers, where you could see the blood surging from his wound. Then – and he had cause – he rebuked those who had plotted his foul murder. 'You vile cowards,' he said as he lay dying. 'What good has my service done me now that you have slain me? I was always loyal to you, but now I have paid for it. Alas, you have wronged your kinsmen so that all who are born in days to come will be dishonoured by your deed. You have cooled your anger on me beyond all measure. You will be held in contempt and stand apart from all good warriors.'

The knights all ran to where he lay wounded to death. It was a sad day for many of them. Those who were at all loyal-hearted mourned for him, and this, as a gay and valiant knight, he had well deserved.

The King of Burgundy too lamented Siegfried's death.

'There is no need for the doer of the deed to weep when the damage is done,' said the dying man. 'He should be held up to scorn. It would have been better left undone.'

'I do not know what you are grieving for,' said Hagen fiercely. 'All our cares and sorrows are over and done with.

We shall not find many who will dare oppose us now. I am glad I have put an end to his supremacy.'

'You may well exult,' said Siegfried. 'But had I known your murderous bent I should easily have guarded my life from you. I am sorry for none so much as my wife, the lady Kriemhild. May God have mercy on me for ever having got a son who in years to come will suffer the reproach that his kinsmen were murderers. If I had the strength I would have good reason to complain. But if you feel at all inclined to do a loyal deed for anyone, noble King,' continued the mortally wounded man, 'let me commend my dear sweetheart to your mercy. Let her profit from being your sister. By the virtue of all princes, stand by her loyally! No lady was ever more greatly wronged through her dear friend. As to my father and his vassals, they will have long to wait for me.'

The flowers everywhere were drenched with blood. Siegfried was at grips with Death, yet not for long, since Death's sword ever was too sharp. And now the warrior who had been so brave and gay could speak no more.

When those lords saw that the hero was dead they laid him on a shield that shone red with gold, and they plotted ways and means of concealing the fact that Hagen had done the deed. 'A disaster has befallen us,' many of them said. 'You must all hush it up and declare with one voice that Siegfried rode off hunting alone and was killed by robbers as he was passing through the forest.'

'I shall take him home,' said Hagen of Troneck. 'It is all one to me if the woman who made Brunhild so unhappy should come to know of it. It will trouble me very little, however much she weeps.'

CHAPTER SEVENTEEN

How Siegfried was lamented and buried

*

THEY waited for nightfall and crossed over the Rhine. Warriors could never have hunted to worse effect, for the beast they slew was lamented by noble maidens, and many a good fighting-man had to pay for it in the end.

Now learn of a deed of overweening pride and grisly vengeance. Hagen ordered the corpse of Siegfried of Nibelungland to be carried in secret to Kriemhild's apartment and set down on the threshold, so that she should find him there before daybreak when she went out to matins, an office she never overslept.

They pealed the bells as usual at the minster, and lovely Kriemhild waked her many maids and asked for a light and her attire. A chamberlain answered – and came upon Siegfried's body. He saw him red with gore, his clothes all drenched with blood, but he did not recognize his lord. And now this man, from whom Kriemhild was soon to hear dread news, bore the light into her chamber, and as she was leaving with her ladies for the minster, the chamberlain said: 'Stay here! There is a knight lying outside the door – he has been slain!' and in the instant Kriemhild broke out into boundless lamentation. Before she had ascertained that it was her husband she was already thinking of Hagen's question how he might shelter Siegfried, and now she rued it with a vengeance! From the moment she learned of Siegfried's death she was the sworn enemy of her own happiness. Lovely, unhappy lady, she sank speechless to the ground and lay there for a while, wretched beyond all measure till, reviving from her swoon, she uttered a shriek that set the whole room echoing.[1]

1. In more archaic and primitive versions this traditional shriek was heard by an exultant Brunhild.

'What if it be some stranger?' asked her attendants.

'It is Siegfried, my dear husband,' she replied, the blood spurting from her mouth, such anguish did she feel. 'It was Brunhild who urged it, Hagen did the deed!' The lady asked them to lead her to the warrior and with her white hand she raised his splendid head. And red though it was with blood she immediately knew him as the hero of Nibelungland as he lay there, a most tragic sight. 'Alas, the wrong that has been done me!' cried the gracious Queen, in deepest sorrow. 'Your shield remains unhacked by any sword – you have been foully murdered! If I knew who had done this, I should never cease to plot his death.'[1]

All her retinue joined their dear lady in cries and lamentations since they were deeply afflicted for the noble lord whom they had lost. Hagen had indeed taken a harsh vengeance for Brunhild's outraged feelings.

'You chamberlains must go and wake Siegfried's vassals with all speed,' said the wretched woman, 'and tell Siegmund, too, of my grief and ask him if he will help me to lament brave Siegfried.'

A messenger quickly ran to where Siegfried's warriors from Nibelungland lay sleeping, and robbed them of their happiness with his dreadful news, though they refused to believe it till they heard the women weeping. Then the messenger hastened to find King Siegmund, who lay unable to sleep (for I fancy his heart had divined his dear son's fate and that he would never see him alive again).

Wake up, lord Siegmund! My lady Kriemhild has sent me to you. She has suffered a grievous wrong that afflicts her above all wrongs and she bids you help her lament it since it very much concerns you.'

Siegmund sat up. 'Of what wrong to the fair Kriemhild are you telling me?' he asked.

'I cannot withhold it from you,' said the messenger, in tears. 'Brave Siegfried of the Netherlands has been slain!'

'Do not mock people with such terrible news, saying that

1. Kriemhild needs firm legal proof, which, in medieval eyes, she will soon obtain beside the bier; see p. 137.

he has been slain, I beg you, for I could never cease to lament him till my dying day.'

'If you do not believe what I have told you, you yourself must hear how Kriemhild and all her suite are lamenting his death.'

At this, Siegmund gave a violent start, and, truly, there was cause. He leapt from his couch, followed by his hundred vassals – they snatched up their long sharp swords and in their misery made haste towards the wailing, when they were joined by a thousand of brave Siegfried's men. Hearing the women lamenting so dolefully it occurred to some that they ought to have their clothes on. – So great was the suffering embedded in their hearts that they had quite forgotten themselves.[1]

When he came to Kriemhild, King Siegmund said to her: 'Alas for our journey to Burgundy! Who has robbed me of my son and you of your husband in this murderous fashion in the midst of such good friends?'

'Ah, if only I could discover who,' answered the noble woman. 'He would find no favour with me, but instead I should set such bitter things afoot as would give his friends something to weep for!'

Lord Siegmund clasped the noble prince to him and the laments of his friends mounted to such a pitch that the palace and the hall and indeed the whole city of Worms echoed mightily with their weeping. Siegfried's wife would not be consoled. They drew the clothes off his fair body, washed his wounds, and laid him on his bier, to the great harassment of his people.

'We shall always be ready to avenge him,' said Siegfried's warriors from Nibelungland. 'The guilty man is somewhere in the castle.' So saying, they all made haste to arm themselves, and returned with their shields eleven hundred strong, all of them excellent knights, under lord Siegmund's command. How dearly he wished to avenge his son's death, and small wonder!

They had no notion whom they should attack unless it

1. Gentlemen (and often ladies) dispensed with night attire.

were Gunther and his men, with whom Siegfried had ridden
out hunting; but Kriemhild was far from pleased to see
them under arms since despite her deep grief and great
distress she was so afraid of her brothers' men slaying the
Nibelungs[1] that she forbade it; so with kind words she put
them on their guard, as is the way among friends.

'My lord Siegmund,' said that sorrowful lady, 'what are
you about to undertake? You have no idea how things
stand. King Gunther has so many brave vassals that you
are bent on suicide if you attack them.' Raising their swords
aloft, they were athirst for battle; yet the noble Queen
first begged, then bade those gallant warriors to refrain,
and she was greatly troubled when they would not do so.
'Lord Siegmund,' she said, 'you must let the matter rest
till you have a better opportunity. I shall always be ready
to avenge my husband with you and if I ever obtain proof
who took him from me I shall have the life out of him.
There are many arrogant men here about the Rhine and
they are thirty to one against you, so I should not advise
you to start fighting. But may God let them prosper as
they have deserved of us! Please stay here and mourn with
me. As soon as it is daylight, you gallant knights, help me
lay my dear husband in his coffin.'

'It shall be done,' they answered.

None could tell in full the extraordinary lamentation of
those knights and ladies whose wailing was heard in the
town, with the result that the worthy burgesses came hurry-
ing along and added their laments to the guests', so dis-
tressed were they. Nobody had told them any reason why
Siegfried had to die. Thus the wives of the good citizens
were weeping there with the ladies.

Smiths were bidden to make haste and fashion a great,
stout coffin of silver and gold and to furnish it with good
steel braces. At which the thoughts of all grew very sad.

The night came to an end and they were told that it was
dawning, whereupon the noble lady gave orders for lord
Siegfried, her dearly beloved spouse, to be carried to the

1. Cf. pp. 104*n*., 192*n*.

cathedral; and all who were his friends were seen weeping as they went with him. On their arrival at the minster many bells were tolled and the clergy were chanting on all sides. And now King Gunther and his men, and fierce Hagen, too, joined the mourners.

'Dearest sister, what sorrow is yours!' said Gunther. 'How I regret that we could not be spared this great bereavement! We must lament the death of Siegfried always.'

'You have no cause to do so,' said the wretched woman. 'If you regretted it, it would never have happened. I was far from your thoughts, I dare declare, when my dear husband and I were sundered from one another. Would to God it had befallen me!'

They vigorously denied their guilt on oath but Kriemhild cut them short. 'Let the man who says he is innocent prove it, let him go up to the bier in sight of all the people and we shall very soon see the truth of it!'

Now it is a great marvel and frequently happens today[1] that whenever a blood-guilty murderer is seen beside the corpse the wounds begin to bleed. This is what happened now, and Hagen stood accused of the deed; for the wounds flowed anew as at the time of Siegfried's murder, so that those who were loudly wailing redoubled their cries of woe.

'I tell you he was killed by robbers,' asserted King Gunther. 'Hagen did not do it.'

'Those robbers are well known to me,' retorted Kriemhild. 'God grant that Siegfried's friends avenge it. Gunther and Hagen, it was you who did the deed!' Siegfried's warriors saw hopes of battle.

'Bear this sorrow with me,' Kriemhild told them.

And now her brother Gernot and young Giselher arrived beside the bier and loyally mourned with the others. They wept for Kriemhild's husband from the bottom of their hearts. Mass was due to be sung and everywhere people were streaming towards the minster, man, woman, and

1. See Appendix 3, 'The Date of the Poem', pp. 365f.

child. Even those scarce touched by his loss began to weep for Siegfried.

'Sister,' said Gernot and Giselher, 'be consoled after your bereavement, as indeed you must. We mean to help you over it as long as we live.' But none was able to comfort her at all.

Siegfried's coffin was ready towards noon and he was lifted from the bier on which he had been lying: but the Queen would not yet let them bury him so that all were put to great trouble. They wound the body in a magnificent pall, and I fancy there was not one who was not weeping. Noble Uote lamented handsome Siegfried from the bottom of her heart, together with all her court.

When people heard the mass being sung and learnt that he had been laid in his coffin they brought countless offerings for the good of his soul, since he had no lack of friends as well as enemies.

'Let those who wish him well and who have friendly feelings towards me submit to grief and austerities for my sake,' said poor Kriemhild to her chamberlains. 'Share out his gold for the benefit of his soul.' And there was no child so small which, if it had reached years of understanding, was not asked to go and make its offering. And before Siegfried was interred more than a hundred masses were sung there that day. There was a great press of his friends; but when the chanting was over, the people went away.

'You must not leave it to me alone to keep watch over the illustrious warrior, at whose death all my happiness was humbled. I shall let my dear husband rest here for three days and nights, until I have looked my fill on him. What if the Lord should ordain that death should take me too? – Then poor Kriemhild's sorrows would be over.'

The townsfolk returned to their quarters, but she asked the priests and monks and all of Siegfried's followers to remain and keep vigil over the hero. Thus they had irksome nights and very arduous days, for many denied themselves meat and drink though they were told that those who wanted it could have food in plenty which Siegmund had provided.[1] The Nibelungs subjected themselves to great hardship. During those three days, so we are told, those who were skilled at singing mass had to exert themselves greatly: but such a wealth of offerings was brought them that those who had been very indigent were now rich indeed. Poor people who had not the means were nevertheless told to go and make their offertory with gold from Siegfried's treasure-house. Since he was fated not to live, many thousand marks were bestowed for the good of his soul. Kriemhild distributed revenues in the lands around wherever there were convents and hospitals, to whose needy folk she gave ample clothes and silver, as a mark of the love she bore her husband.

On the third morning, at the hour of mass, the broad churchyard beside the minster was filled with the wailing of the Burgundians who were honouring him in death as a dear friend deserves. It has been reported that some thirty thousand marks or more were given to the poor for the good of his soul during those four days – but the life and great beauty of his body had come to naught.

When divine service had been sung many people were assailed by violent grief. Word was given to bear him from the minster to the grave, while those who missed him sorely wept and lamented. And so, with loud cries, people followed him away – not one of them was happy, man or woman. Before he was buried there were prayers and chants from the great concourse of clergy who were present at his funeral.

On her way to the graveside Siegfried's faithful Queen had been at grips with such grief that, time and time again, she had to be splashed with water from the stream. Her suffering was utterly beyond all measure and it is a marvel she survived it. She was assisted in her laments by many ladies.

'You men of Siegfried,' said the Queen, 'do me one favour, I beg you by your fealty. After all that I have suffered do me the small kindness of allowing me to gaze

1. A reference to the funeral feast customary at ancient wakes.

on his lovely head once more.' She entreated them so long in all the intensity of her grief that they had to break open his magnificent sarcophagus. Then the lady was led to where he lay and she raised his handsome head with her white hand and kissed the noble knight in death, while her bright eyes in their sorrow wept tears of blood.

The farewell was heartrending. They had to carry her from that place, for she was unable to walk – the splendid woman had fainted away. Lovely Kriemhild might well have died of grief.

Now that the noble lord was buried, all those who had accompanied him from Nibelungland were seized with boundless sorrow; nor did they ever find Siegmund in happy mood again.

There were some few who had neither eaten nor drunk for three days on end on account of their great mourning; but they could not utterly forsake their bodies: they took nourishment after their cares, as happens with many today.

CHAPTER EIGHTEEN

How Siegmund returned home

*

QUEEN KRIEMHILD's father-in-law went to her and said: 'Let us return to our own country. We are unwelcome guests here beside the Rhine, so it seems to me. Kriemhild, dearest lady, come home with me. You must not be made to suffer for our having been treacherously robbed of your noble husband here in Burgundy, since I shall cherish you for my son's sake, rely on it. And, madam, you shall wield all the power which brave Siegfried made known to you while he lived. The crown and realm shall be subject to you and Siegfried's men will serve you gladly.'

The squires were informed that Siegmund and his vassals were leaving, and there was a great race to fetch the horses, for they did not at all like to remain under the roof of their deadly enemies. The married ladies and maidens, too, were told to take out their travelling clothes.

When King Siegmund was ready and anxious to go, Kriemhild's kinsmen begged her to stay there with her mother.

'That can never be,' said that proud lady. 'How could I have the man who made me suffer so cruelly always before my eyes, wretched woman that I am?'

'Dearest sister,' answered young Giselher, 'I implore you by your family loyalty to stay with your mother. You can dispense with the services of those who have so distressed you. You can live from my private resources.'

'It is impossible,' she told the knight. 'It would kill me to have to see Hagen.'

'I shall save you from that, sweet sister. You must stay with me, your brother Giselher, who will console you for the loss of your husband.'

'How dearly I stand in need of it,' answered that forlorn lady.

When Giselher offered her such kind treatment, Uote and Gernot and others of her loyal relations joined with their entreaties, begging her to stay and arguing that she had no kinsmen among Siegfried's followers. 'They are all strangers to you,' said Gernot. 'Consider it, dear sister, and comfort your soul: there is none, however strong, but he must die. Remain here with your friends – it cannot fail to help you.' And so she promised Giselher to stay.

The horses had been led from the stable for Siegmund's knights in readiness for them to leave for Nibelungland and their gear was loaded on the sumpters. Lord Siegmund went and stood before Kriemhild.

'Siegfried's men await you by their horses,' he said, addressing the lady. 'Now let us ride away, since it irks me here in Burgundy.'

'The loyal friends that I have advise me to stay here, for there are none of my kin in Nibelungland.'

These words of Kriemhild's pained King Siegmund. 'You should not listen to that. You shall hold sway over all my kinsmen with undiminished powers. You shall not be made to suffer for our having lost Siegfried.[1] But come back with us, too, for the sake of your little son – you must not leave him an orphan. When he grows up he will console you. Meanwhile many brave warriors shall attend you.'

'Lord Siegmund,' she replied, 'I cannot ride away with you. I must remain here with my kinsfolk – they will help me to mourn, whatever betides me.'

The good warriors were much put out at what she said. 'If that were the case,' they answered with one voice, 'we dare assert that we have been wronged indeed! If you

1. Siegmund again assures Kriemhild that if she returns with him she will maintain her status as a ruling queen, which would not be the case if she remained at Worms. The usual view, that he is promising her she will not be the object of a blood-feud as a member of the murderer's family, is less likely to be true.

intend to stay here with our enemies, no knights will ever have gone visiting in such peril.'

'You shall travel without fear in God's keeping, for I shall see to it that you are escorted in safety to Siegmund's land. As to my dear son, you knights, I commend him to your kind protection.'

When Siegmund's men realized that she would not go with them they wept, one and all. And in what wretched state did lord Siegmund take leave of lady Kriemhild. 'Unhappy feast!' said the noble king in his anguish. 'Never again in days to come will a king and his kinsfolk suffer, as a result of a merrymaking, the fate which has overtaken us! We shall never be seen in Burgundy again.'

'We might well mount an expedition to this country,' objected Siegfried's men for any to hear who cared, 'when we have established who killed our lord. Among Siegfried's kinsmen the plotters have deadly enemies enough.'

Siegmund kissed Kriemhild and having convinced himself that she meant to stay behind addressed her mournfully: 'We ride back home bereft of all our happiness and only now do I know the full measure of my grief.'

The Nibelungs rode out without escort from Worms beside the Rhine, relying on their own high courage to defend them, should they be attacked. They asked none for leave to depart;[1] but those gallant warriors Gernot and Giselher went up to Siegmund affectionately and left him in no doubt of their sympathy regarding the loss that he had suffered.

'God in Heaven knows that I was guiltless of Siegfried's death, never even having heard who his enemy here might be,'[2] said Gernot courteously. 'I have just cause to lament him.'

Young Giselher provided an escort and with all care for

1. According to the medieval code, a hostile act. Had they been leaving on good terms they would have been bound to ask for their congé.

2. This does not accord with what was narrated at the time; see p. 117.

their safety conducted them out of the country and back to the Netherlands where there was not one of Siegfried's kinsmen who was not mourning.

Of how they fared after this I can tell you nothing. But here in Burgundy Kriemhild was heard lamenting at all times so bitterly that none could comfort her heart save good and faithful Giselher.

Brunhild sat enthroned in her pride, and however much Kriemhild wept it mattered nothing to her. Never again was she ready to extend loyal affection towards lady Kriemhild: and in days to come Kriemhild in turn inflicted mortal sorrow on her.

CHAPTER NINETEEN

How the Nibelung treasure was brought to Worms

*

Now that noble Kriemhild had thus been made a widow, Count Eckewart remained in Burgundy with her, together with his vassals. He was always at her service and helped his lady to mourn her lord unceasingly.

A magnificent house was built for her beside the minster at Worms. It was large and spacious, and here in joyless state she resided in the company of her household. She was devoted in her churchgoing and never neglected to visit her darling's grave but went there at all times sad at heart and praying to the good God to have Siegfried's soul in his keeping. How often did she not weep for that warrior in loyal affection.

Uote and her people were always comforting her, but her heart had been wounded so sorely that whatever consolation they offered her was all of no avail: she suffered the keenest regret for her companion that any woman ever knew for a beloved spouse, in which her great virtue was apparent. As long as she had life in her body she went on mourning him until the day when, fit mate for bold Siegfried, she took a brave revenge.

Thus she lived in her palace for fully three and a half years after the affliction of her husband's death, without speaking any word to Gunther or ever during all that time setting eyes on her enemy Hagen.

'If you could succeed in winning your sister's friendship,' said Hagen, the warrior of Troneck, 'we could bring Nibelung's treasure here to Burgundy. If only the Queen were well-disposed towards us you could possess yourselves of much of it.'

'We shall try,' replied Gunther. 'My brothers see her constantly. We shall ask them to try whether she will not be our friend and whether we cannot gain her consent.'

'I do not fancy that will ever happen,' was Hagen's answer.

Gunther then commanded Ortwin and the Margrave Gere to wait on lady Kriemhild, and next Gernot and young Giselher were conducted to court, whereupon they made friendly overtures to her.

'Madam, you have been mourning Siegfried's death overlong now,' said bold Gernot of Burgundy. 'Always you are heard passionately lamenting! Yet the King is willing to show in a court of law that it was not he at all that murdered Siegfried.'

'Nobody is accusing him of having done it,' the Queen retorted. 'It was Hagen who killed him. How could I imagine that Hagen was his enemy when he got me to tell him where Siegfried could be wounded? Otherwise I should have been sure not to betray my husband's fair body by any word of mine and should have no reason to weep now, wretch that I am! I shall never love those who did it'.

Then handsome Giselher begged and entreated her. And as soon as she had given the promise 'I will receive the King', Gunther appeared before her accompanied by his intimates. But Hagen dared not enter her presence, so conscious was he of his guilt and of the wrong that he had done her. And now that Kriemhild was ready to give up her feud with Gunther, and it was time for the King to kiss her in reconciliation, he would have felt more at ease had he had no hand in wronging her: then he could have gone to her holding his head high.

No peace-making among friends was ever effected amid such weeping, for Kriemhild was still a prey to her affliction. She made peace with them all save one, since none would have killed her husband had not Hagen done the deed.

It was not long before they got Kriemhild to have the treasure brought from Nibelungland and ferried over the Rhine – it was her nuptial dower and thus it was hers by right. Giselher and Gernot were sent there with eight thousand men under Kriemhild's orders to fetch it from the hiding-place where brave Alberich and his cronies guarded it.

When they saw the men from the Rhineland coming for the treasure, fearless Alberich said to his friends: 'We dare not withhold the treasure from the noble Queen since she claims it as her dower. But this would never have happened had we not lost our good magic cloak along with Siegfried so disastrously; for Kriemhild's handsome lover always had it with him. But now his robbing us of our cloak of invisibility and subduing the whole land, alas, has worked out very ill for him.' With this the Lord Treasurer went to fetch the keys.

Kriemhild's men were standing outside the cavern with a number of her relations. Orders were given to carry the treasure to the sea and aboard the little ships and it was then conveyed over the waves and up the river Rhine.

And now listen to some marvels concerning this treasure! It was as much as a dozen waggons fully loaded could carry away from the mountain in four days and nights coming and going thrice a day! It was entirely of gems and gold, and even if one had paid all the people in the world with it, it would not have lost a mark in value! It was not for nothing that Hagen had desired it. In among the rest lay the rarest gem of all, a tiny wand of gold, and if any had found its secret he could have been lord of all mankind!

Many of Alberich's kinsmen went away with Gernot. And when they stored the treasure away in Burgundy and it came into Queen Kriemhild's keeping, her rooms and towers were crammed with it – never at any time was such stupendous wealth reported! And yet, had there been a thousand times as much, Kriemhild would have gone empty-handed in order to be with lord Siegfried, could he but have lived, for no hero ever had a wife more loyal.

Now that Kriemhild had possession of the hoard she lured many foreign warriors to Burgundy, and indeed her fair hand lavished gifts with such bounty that the like has never been seen. Many were the fine qualities she showed, for which she received due credit. Kriemhild was now showering such largesse on rich and poor alike that Hagen declared that were she to live for any time she would recruit so many men that matters would go ill with the Burgundians.

'She is mistress of her person and property,' replied King Gunther. 'Why should I prevent her from doing whatever she likes with them? It was only with great difficulty that I succeeded in bringing her round to me. Let us not bother our heads as to where she bestows her treasure.'

'No man who is firm in his purpose should leave the treasure to a woman,' said Hagen. 'By means of her gifts she will bring things to the point where the brave sons of Burgundy will bitterly regret it.'

'I swore her an oath that I would wrong her no more,' replied King Gunther, 'and I mean to keep it henceforward. After all, she is my sister.'

'Let me take the blame,' answered Hagen. Then the oaths of a number of them[1] were forgotten; for they took that vast hoard from the widow, and Hagen secured all the keys. But when her brother Gernot came to hear of it he was very angry. Then –

'Hagen has greatly wronged my sister!' cried lord Giselher. 'I ought to put a stop to it. If he were not my kinsman it would cost him his life!' This brought fresh tears from Kriemhild.

'Rather than always be plagued with this gold let us have it sunk in the Rhine so that no one would have possession of it,' said Gernot. But Kriemhild went to her brother Giselher and stood most piteously before him.

'Dearest brother, remember me,' she said. 'You ought to be my protector with regard to both person and property.'

'It shall be done when we return,' he told the lady. 'We have a journey to make.' And indeed the King and his relations, together with the best they could find, quitted those parts with the sole exception of Hagen, who be-

1. As the sequel shows, the poet is here alluding darkly to the Burgundian kings.

cause of the grudge that he bore her remained with great good will.

In the interval before the great King's return Hagen took the entire treasure and sank it in the Rhine at Locheim imagining he would make use of it some day: but this was not destined to happen.

When the princes rode back with many in attendance, Kriemhild and her maids and ladies woefully complained of the great loss that she had suffered. The news of it vexed these lords, and Giselher especially would have liked to give proof of his affection.

'He has acted very badly,' they all agreed. Hagen kept well away from the princes' anger till he regained their favour. They let him go unpunished: but Kriemhild could not have borne him greater malice.

Before Hagen of Troneck hid the treasure in this way he and the princes[1] had confirmed with mighty oaths that its whereabouts should be hidden so long as any one of them lived: yet in the event they were unable to bestow any of it, either on themselves or on others.

Kriemhild's heart was burdened with sorrow that was ever fresh for the passing of her lord and the loss of all her treasure, and her laments never ceased until the day she died. To tell the truth, she lived in great pain at heart for thirteen years after Siegfried's death without ever being able to forget it. She held him in loyal remembrance, as all the world concedes.

1. The text says 'they'. Some critics, jealous of the reputations of Gernot and Giselher, consider that 'they' must refer only to Hagen and Gunther. This, however is untenable in view of Hagen's direct admission in Chapter 28: 'My lords commanded it to be sunk in the Rhine', pp. 216f.

CHAPTER TWENTY

How King Etzel sent to Burgundy for Kriemhild

*

AT the time when the lady Helche died and King Etzel desired to take another queen, his friends counselled him to woo a proud widow of Burgundy whose name was lady Kriemhild.[1] Now that lovely Helche was dead, 'If you wish to win the hand of a noble woman, the best and most exalted that any king ever had, then take this lady,' they urged him. 'Her husband was mighty Siegfried.'

'How could this ever come about?' asked the great king, 'seeing that I am a heathen and was never baptized, whereas the lady is a Christian and will therefore withhold her consent? Short of a miracle this could never happen.'

'But what if she would, nevertheless, for the sake of your fame and vast possessions? We must at least try to win the highborn lady – you would be glad to lie in the arms of such a beauty.'

'Who among you is acquainted with the Rhineland and its people?' asked the noble king.

'I have known the illustrious queen since childhood,' replied good Rüdiger of Pöchlarn. 'Each one of those noble knights Gunther, Gernot, and Giselher shows the utmost distinction in every deed, like all their line before them.'

'Tell me, my friend, whether she is fit to wear a crown in my country,' continued Etzel. 'For if she is as beautiful as they tell me, my privy councillors shall never regret it.'

'For looks she can well bear comparison with the Queen, my lady Helche. No royal consort anywhere could possibly

1. Some critics maintain with considerable justification that the poet's full-scale epic source for the second half of the poem (the older 'Nôt') began at this point. Were this the case, this re-introduction of Kriemhild would easily be accounted for. See pp. 390–3.

be more lovely. The man she swore to love would find all the solace he could wish for.'

'Then undertake this mission, Rüdiger, by the affection you bear me,' said Etzel. 'And if I ever lie with Kriemhild I shall reward you to the best of my power, for you will have done my will entirely. From my treasury you shall receive the means for yourself and your companions to live very pleasantly, and I shall see that you are given all the mounts and clothes you want for your embassage.'

'It would not be seemly to ask for anything of yours. I shall be happy to go to Burgundy as your envoy, using the means which – thanks to your generosity – I have already.'

'Now when do you intend to set out to woo the charming woman?' asked the mighty king. 'May God preserve your honour on the journey, and my lady's, too. May fortune be on my side and incline her to a gracious answer.'

'Before we leave the country we must see to our weapons and accoutrements so that they recommend us to princely eyes. I shall go to the Rhineland at the head of five hundred splendid warriors, resolved that wherever the Burgundians see us they will have to admit that no king ever sent so many men so far or better turned out than those whom you sent Rhinewards. And if you deem it no obstacle, mighty King, let me tell you that with her noble love she belonged to Siegfried, Siegmund's son, whom you once received at court here[1] and who may truly be accounted most illustrious.'

'If she was the wife of that noble and warlike prince,' replied King Etzel, 'he was of such merit that I have no cause to disdain his queen. Moreover, she pleases me well in virtue of her great beauty.'

'Then let me tell you that we shall set out from here within twenty-four days,' said the Margrave. 'I shall send a message to my dear wife Gotelind to tell her that I intend to go to Kriemhild as ambassador.'

1. The poet has invented Siegfried's visit to Etzel's court on the spur of the moment; it is not known from any other source.

Rüdiger sent his message to Pöchlarn telling the Margravine that he was to woo a wife for the King. This made her both sad and elated – affectionate thoughts of lovely Helche made her sad. Yes, when she heard the message she was not a little downcast and she found reason to weep as she pondered whether she might have another queen like the first. Whenever she thought of Helche it was with deep distress.

One week later Rüdiger rode out from Hungary, much to King Etzel's joy. In Vienna their clothes were made for them, after which Rüdiger had no cause to delay his journey. Gotelind was expecting him in Pöchlarn and his daughter the young margravine[1] was longing to see him and his men – comely maidens were waiting in fond anticipation! But before noble Rüdiger left Vienna for Pöchlarn their clothes had been safely packed on their sumpters down to the last stitch and their cavalcade was so ordered that nothing was stolen on the way.

When they arrived in the town of Pöchlarn lord Rüdiger invited them to their quarters most hospitably and saw to it that they were comfortable. Gotelind, wealthy lady, was pleased at her lord's coming and so was his darling daughter the young margravine – she was overjoyed. And how glad she was to see those warriors from Hungary!

'My father and his vassals are most welcome!' said the noble maiden, laughing happily. For this many a good knight thanked her warmly.

Gotelind was well aware of what occupied Rüdiger's thoughts and that night as she lay at his side she inquired of him in friendly terms where the King of Hungary had sent him.

'I shall tell you gladly, my lady Gotelind,' he answered. 'Now that fair Helche is no more I am to woo another wife for my lord. I shall ride to Burgundy to sue for Kriemhild, since it is intended that she shall rule as Queen here in Hungary.'

'I wish to Heaven it would happen,' cried Gotelind.

1. Rüdiger's daughter is not once named in the poem.

'Seeing that we hear so much to her credit she might well make good the loss of our lady in our declining years. We too should be pleased to see her crowned in Hungary.'

'My dear,' said the Margrave, 'you must make friendly gifts to those who are to ride to the Rhineland with me, for when knights ride in sumptuous style they go in good heart.'

'There is none to whom I shall not make a suitable gift, each man of them, if he will accept it, before you and they depart,' she promised.

'That is just as I would have it,' said the Margrave.

You should have seen the costly brocades most carefully lined with fur from neck to spur that were carried out from her storeroom and lavished on the noble knights whom Rüdiger had picked for his journey.

On the seventh morning his lordship rode out from Pöchlarn with his men and they conveyed their clothes and weapons through Bavaria safely without once being attacked by robbers on the road.

Before twelve days were out they arrived beside the Rhine. This event could not remain hidden, and it was reported to the King and his vassals that strangers were come. The King then asked whether anyone knew them – he wished to be informed. The strangers' sumpters were heavily laden and they were clearly very wealthy. These unknown lords were at once given quarters within the spacious city, and when they had been lodged they were the object of intense curiosity – the people of Worms were burning to know where they were from. The King summoned Hagen in order to learn whether they were known to him.

'I have not glimpsed one of them,' replied the warrior of Troneck, 'but when we see them shortly I shall have no difficulty in telling you where they come from. They would have to come from outlandish parts for me not to say at once who they are.'

The guests had taken up their quarters and the envoy and his comrades had donned some magnificent robes; and so they rode to court parading fine clothes of most ingenious cut.

'To my mind – not having seen this lord for many a day – I should say from their allure that this is Rüdiger, the proud warrior from Hungary.'

'How can I believe that the lord of Pöchlarn has come to visit us?' the King was quick to ask. But no sooner had he spoken than fearless Hagen espied good Rüdiger, whereupon he and his friends ran out to meet him. Five hundred Hunnish knights clad in robes of such magnificence as no messengers had ever worn dismounted from their chargers and were very well received.

'These knights are welcome in God's name, the lord of Pöchlarn and all his men,' cried Hagen in ringing tones. The brave Huns were received with all honour. Then the King's nearest relations went out to where Ortwin of Metz was telling Rüdiger 'On my word, we have never been so glad to see guests here!' – a greeting for which the strangers thanked the Burgundians one and all.

Thereupon, accompanied by their retinue, they entered the great hall where they found the King amid a throng of valiant knights. Of his great courtesy his majesty rose from his seat and most graciously advanced towards the envoy. Attended by Gernot, Gunther received their guest and his men with all the honour due to him. Then, taking him by the hand, he led good Rüdiger to the seat on which he sat himself. The cupbearers were bidden to pour excellent mead for the guests and the best Rhenish you could find thereabouts, and this they did with a will.

Hearing about these guests, Giselher, Gere, Dancwart, and Volker came to court and joyfully welcomed those excellent knights into the royal presence.

'We knights of Burgundy must always seek to repay the Margrave for his kindness to us,'[1] Hagen of Troneck reminded his King. 'Fair Gotelind's consort should receive his due reward.'

1. Hagen was once a hostage at Etzel's court; cf. p. 371.

'I cannot forbear asking how Etzel and Helche of Hungary are – tell me,' said King Gunther.

'With pleasure,' answered the Margrave. He stood up from the seat and all his men stood with him. 'By Your Majesty's leave,' he continued, addressing the King, 'I shall not withhold my message, but tell it willingly.'

'I shall allow you without first consulting my friends to deliver whatever message has been sent to us through you,' replied Gunther. 'Let me and my subjects hear it, since you have my full favour for the execution of your mission.' At this the worthy envoy began to speak:

'My great lord sends to you here in Burgundy together with all your friends his sincere respects, and indeed this embassy is undertaken in all good faith. The noble King has asked me to claim your sympathy for his affliction. His people are desolate, for my lady the Queen has died, mighty Helche, my master's consort, in whom many maidens have lost a mother, noble princes' daughters reared by her – the land is in a pitiful state, for, alas, they have none to care for them, so that I fear the King's anxiety will not be quickly allayed.'

'May God reward him for sending his respects both to me and to my friends with such goodwill,' answered Gunther. 'It was with pleasure that I heard his greeting here, and my kinsmen and vassals will be glad to show their gratitude.'

'The world will always have reason to lament the death of fair Helche because of her many excellences,' said Gernot, knight of Burgundy. And Hagen assented to what he had said, and many other warriors with him.

'Since I have your leave, Sire,' went on Rüdiger, the noble envoy, 'I will tell you more of my dear lord's message, seeing in what a wretched plight the death of Helche has left him. My sovereign was informed that lord Siegfried had died, leaving Kriemhild a widow. If that is how matters stand and if she may do it with your blessing, she shall go crowned before Etzel's warriors. This my lord bade me tell you.'

'If she is willing she shall hear my opinion,' was the mighty king's courteous reply, 'and I shall make it known to you within three days. For why should I refuse Etzel before I have learned her wishes?'[1]

Orders were meanwhile given to see to the comfort of the guests, and these received such attention that Rüdiger declared he had good friends among Gunther's vassals. Hagen in particular was pleased to wait on him, for in bygone days Rüdiger had done the like for him.

Rüdiger thus remained there till the third day. With his accustomed prudence the King summoned a family council to ascertain whether they thought it advisable that Kriemhild should marry King Etzel. All but Hagen were in favour of it.

'If you have any sense you will take care not to let it happen, even though she be willing,' he said to valiant Gunther.

'Why should I not consent?' asked the latter. 'I ought to wish her joy of any good thing that comes her way – after all, she is my sister. If it could bring her any honour we ourselves are bound to work for it.'

'Have no more to do with it,' rejoined Hagen. 'If you knew Etzel as I do and she were to wed him as you say, you would have trouble on your hands with a vengeance and all of your own making.'

'But why?' countered Gunther. 'I shall take good care not to come near enough for him to harm me if Kriemhild marries him.'

'I shall never give my assent to it,' was Hagen's answer.

Lord Gernot and lord Giselher were sent for[2] so that they could be asked whether they would approve of Kriemhild's marrying the great king. Hagen was still opposing it and remained alone in doing so.

1. As a widow, Kriemhild cannot be disposed of by her brother as freely as when she was a maiden. Cf. p. 54.
2. We must suppose Gernot and Giselher to have attended the family council and to have gone away, leaving Gunther in conversation with Hagen.

'Now you have a chance to show your decency, friend
Hagen,' said Giselher, knight of Burgundy. 'Make amends
for the harm that you have done her – you should let her
enjoy in peace any good fortune that befalls her. When I
think of it,' the spirited warrior confirmed, 'you have so
much wronged my sister that she has every cause to hate
you. Never did a man rob a woman of more joy.'

'I shall tell you what I plainly foresee,' retorted Hagen.
'If Etzel marries her and she lives long enough she will do us
some great harm yet, however she contrives it. When all is
said, she will have many fine men at her command.'

'Matters can rest as they are till both of them are dead
without our ever riding into Etzel's country,' was bold
Gernot's answer to Hagen. 'We ought to be loyal towards
her – that would stand to our credit.'

'No one can contradict me,' replied Hagen. 'I tell you, if
noble Kriemhild comes to wear Helche's crown she will
harm us, however she achieves it. You knights had far
better let it rest.'

'We should not all of us act like blackguards,' cried
Giselher, fair Uote's son, angrily. 'We should be glad of any
honour that befalls her. My affection bids me stand by her,
whatever you say, Hagen!'

Hagen was vexed at his words. But those proud and
worthy knights, Gernot and Giselher, together with mighty
Gunther, declared that if Kriemhild gave her assent, it
should have their blessing.

'I will tell her that she should let King Etzel find favour
in her eyes,' said lord Gere. 'So many warriors serve him
with reverence that he has it in his power to make good all
her sorrows.' And the brave knight went to find Kriemhild,
who received him kindly. He lost no time in addressing her.

'You have reason to be glad to see me and to reward me
as first with the news! Fortune is about to part you from all
your troubles! One of the best who ever won a kingdom
with all its glory or was ever fitted to wear a crown has sent
to woo your hand, my lady. His ambassadors are noble
knights. Your brother asked me to tell you.'

'God forbid that you and all my other kinsmen should make a mock of me, wretched woman,' said the doleful lady. 'What could I mean to any man that has known true happiness with a faithful wife?' Kriemhild refused it utterly. But then her brother Gernot arrived and with him young Giselher, too, and they affectionately entreated her to be of better cheer. If she would accept King Etzel, they told her, hers would be a truly happy lot. But none could quell the lady's resistance to marrying any man.

'Then at least deign to receive the envoy, if you will do nothing else,' the knights requested her.

'I will not deny that I shall be pleased to see Rüdiger for the sake of his many fine qualities,' answered the highborn lady. 'Had any other than he been sent I should not have admitted the ambassador, whoever he was. Tell him to come to my apartment tomorrow,' she continued, 'and I shall make my mind very plain to him myself.' And her laments broke out anew and ever fresh.

For his part, noble Rüdiger desired nothing more than to see the august queen. He knew himself to be so versed that if it came to a meeting she must submit to his persuasion.

Early next morning after mass had been sung the noble envoys who wished to go to court with Rüdiger arrived amid a great press, and to this end many fine men wore their robes of state. Kriemhild, proud sorrowful lady, awaited Rüdiger the good ambassador, who found her in her everyday clothes,[1] whereas her suite were splendidly attired. She came to the door to meet him and received Etzel's vassal very graciously. He entered her apartment with eleven others all told and they received every possible attention, for more exalted envoys had never called on them. They begged lord Rüdiger to be seated, together with his men. The two Margraves Eckewart and Gere stood before her; but in sympathy with their mistress, none of them there looked cheerful. They also saw many fair ladies seated in her presence. Kriemhild did nothing but weep – her dress where

1. Her widow's habit.

it covered her breast was wet with her hot tears. This did not escape the noble Margrave when he looked at her.

'Most noble Queen,' said the illustrious envoy, 'pray give me and my companions leave to stand before you and tell you our purpose in riding here.'

'You have my permission,' said the Queen. 'I am well disposed to hear whatever you wish to say, for you are a worthy ambassador.' But the others clearly heard her reluctance.

'The august monarch, Etzel, conveys to you here in Burgundy, my lady, his great and sincere affection. He has sent a host of good knights to ask your hand in marriage. He bids me speak to you from his heart of love untouched by sorrow. He offers you steadfast friendship as he did to lady Helche, who was very dear to his heart. Through many an unhappy day he has felt the loss of her virtuous person.'

'Margrave Rüdiger,' answered the Queen, 'if you knew the sharp pangs I suffer, you would not ask me yet to love another man. I lost one of the best that a woman ever had.'

'What else but tender affection can help one over one's sorrow?' asked the fearless man. 'If one finds a mate to one's liking who can bestow such affection? For mortal grief there is no remedy like it. And if it pleases you to accept my noble master you shall rule over twelve mighty kingdoms, to which he will add full thirty principalities, all subdued by his valiant arm. Moreover,' the knight continued, 'you shall be mistress over many worthy men who were subject to the lady Helche and of numerous ladies of princely rank who served her. Over and above all this, my sovereign bade me tell you that if you will consent to go crowned beside him you shall wield the utmost power that Helche ever had and rule over Etzel's vassals with might irresistible.'

'How could I ever desire to marry any warrior?' asked the Queen. 'Through one man, death has inflicted such suffering on me that I can never be happy again!'

'Mighty Queen,' answered the Huns, 'your life with Etzel will be so splendid, if matters go so far, that it will give you endless delight. The Great King has many proud knights, so that if Helche's young ladies and your maidens form one suite it will raise the spirits of the warriors. Be advised, my lady. You will be truly happy.'

'Let the matter rest till tomorrow morning,' she said with all the courtesy that was hers, 'and then come and see me here. I shall then give you an answer to your question.'

The good warriors had no recourse but to comply, and when they had all returned to their quarters the noble lady summoned Giselher and her mother and told the two of them that all she was fit for was mourning, and nothing else in the world.

'I have been told, and I willingly believe it, sister,' said her brother Giselher, 'that King Etzel will banish your sorrows if you take him for a husband. Whatever anyone else may say, I think it a wise thing to do. Etzel has it in his power to make good your loss to you, since from the Rhone to the Rhine and the Elbe to the sea, there is no king so mighty. You would have every cause to be happy, were he to take you to wife.'

'Why do you ask me to do this, dear brother?' she asked. 'For me, weeping and wailing will always be more seemly. How could I appear at court there under the eyes of the warriors? — If ever I had any beauty I have lost it quite.'

'Dear child,' said Queen Uote to her beloved daughter, 'do as your brothers counsel you. Take your kinsmen's advice, then things will turn out well for you. I have seen you grieving and lamenting for such a long time now.'

Kriemhild prayed to God again and again to vouchsafe to her the means of bestowing gifts of gold, silver, and fine clothes as she had done when her husband was alive, a time of such happiness as she was never again to experience. 'Were I to give myself to a heathen, though I am a Christian,' she mused, 'I should always be disgraced before the world. I shall never do it, no, not if he were to give me all the kingdoms in the world!' She let it rest at that. But all night long till daybreak the lady lay on her bed pondering many things; nor did her shining eyes grow dry again till she went out to mass in the morning.

The kings had arrived for the service and they went to work on their sister again, urging her to marry the King of Hungary. Yet none found the lady in the least bit gaily inclined.

Etzel's vassals were then summoned. They were impatient to be gone by Gunther's good leave, with or without success, whichever it was to be. Rüdiger came to court and he and his men agreed among themselves that they should sound the King's intentions and that the sooner they did so the better, since their way back home was a long one.

Rüdiger was ushered in to Kriemhild and he asked the noble Queen with much charm to make known to him what message she wished to send to Hungary; yet I fear he won nothing from her but denials that she would ever marry again.

'That would be very wrong – why let such beauty fade? You can still – and with great honour – be wife to a good husband.'

Their entreaties were all in vain till Rüdiger told the proud Queen in private that he would make amends to her for any wrong that should befall her[1], at which her great sorrow began somewhat to abate.

'Do not weep any more,' said he. 'If you had none but me in Hungary, and my trusty kinsmen and vassals, any man who had wronged you would have to pay very dearly for it.' And so her feelings were assuaged.

'Swear to me on oath that if anyone ever harms me you will be the first to avenge my wrongs!'

'I am ready to do so, my lady,' replied the Margrave. Rüdiger, together with all his vassals from Hungary thereupon swore to serve her loyally always and never to deny

1. An alternative rendering, neither obligatory in syntax nor suited to the context is: 'for anything that had ever been done to her'.

her anything, provided it was to her honour, and he gave her his hand on it.

'Now that I have won so many allies,' thought the faithful lady, 'poor wretch, I shall let people say what they like. For who knows whether my dear husband may not yet be avenged? Since Etzel has so many fighting-men,' she thought further, 'if I am to have command of them I shall achieve whatever I wish. Moreover, he is so very rich that I shall again have the means to attract warriors by gifts after being robbed of all I owned by Hagen, curse him!' Turning to Rüdiger she said: 'If I had not heard that Etzel is a heathen I should be pleased to come to wherever he wished and marry him.'

'Do not say so, my lady,' replied the Margrave. 'The King has so many Christian warriors that you will never be unhappy at his side. What if you were to deserve so well of him that he had himself baptized? – You might well be glad to become King Etzel's queen.'

'Give your consent, dear sister,' her brothers joined in again. 'Make an end of your mourning.' And they continued to entreat her till the sorrowful lady promised in the hearing of all those warriors that she would marry Etzel.

'I will take your advice, poor Queen that I am,' said she, 'and when it can be done, and provided I have friends who will escort me there, I shall go to the land of the Huns.' With the warriors to witness, fair Kriemhild gave her hand in pledge.

'If you can muster two men I have many more,' said the Margrave. 'It will be easy to escort you over the Rhine with full honours. My lady, you should delay no longer here in Burgundy! I have five hundred men, not to mention my kinsmen, and all shall do your bidding here and at home, whatever you require of them; and I shall do likewise, unless it should dishonour me[1], my lady, whenever you remind me of what was said here. Now see that your trappings are got ready for you – you will never regret my advice – and inform the young women whom you wish to

1. It was Rüdiger's tragedy that this normal saving clause in a feudal oath did not avail him in his moment of need. See pp. 268, 334.

take with you, not forgetting that we shall be met on the road by many excellent knights!'

The ladies still had the harness, studded with jewels and gold, which they had been wont to parade in Siegfried's days and with which Kriemhild, accompanied by her maidens, could ride out in state when she wished to go abroad – oh, what magnificent saddles they fetched for those young beauties! Whether or no they had ever worn fine robes before, many such were now made ready for their journey, since they had been told so much about King Etzel; with the result that only now did they open chests that had stayed well locked till then. For no less than four and a half days they were busy choosing from the coffers the things these contained in such abundance; and then, intending to lavish gifts on all Rüdiger's men, Kriemhild opened her treasury. She still had more of the gold from Nibelungland than a hundred pack-horses could carry[1] and she fancied that once she was in Hungary she would dole it out as largesse; but Hagen got to hear of her plans.

'Since Queen Kriemhild will never be reconciled with me,' he said, 'Siegfried's gold must stay here. Why should I yield so much wealth to my enemies? I know precisely what she will do with it. If she succeeds in conveying the treasure away, I do not doubt that it will be shared out to my harm. In any case, they have not the horses to carry it. Tell Kriemhild Hagen means to keep it.'

When Kriemhild learned this, fierce anger seized her. All three kings received news of it, too, and they wanted to prevent it. But since nothing of the sort was done, noble Rüdiger was more than pleased.

'Why do you lament your gold, mighty Queen?' he asked. 'King Etzel loves you so well that as soon as he sets eyes on you I swear he will give you more than you could ever squander away, my lady.'

---

1. A typical surprise, although it is not intended as such. It is probably a survival from 'Diu Nôt.' It has been suggested that the poet introduced what follows in order that Rüdiger might have ocular demonstration of how Hagen treats Kriemhild.

'Noble Rüdiger,' answered the Queen, 'no daughter of a king ever had such wealth as Hagen has taken from me.'

Kriemhild's brother Gernot came to the door of her Treasury and thrust the key into the door in the King's name. Her gold was handed out to the value of thirty-thousand marks or more and this he offered to the visitors, much to Gunther's pleasure.

'If my lady Kriemhild could have all the treasure that was ever fetched from Nibelungland neither she nor I would touch any of it,' answered the husband of wealthy Gotelind of Pöchlarn. 'Now have it all safely locked away again because I will have none of it, having brought so much of my own that we can easily do without it on the road and still afford to travel in splendour.' But while this was taking place, Kriemhild's young ladies had already filled twelve chests with the very finest gold and this was carried away with many feminine adornments which they would be needing for their journey.

Kriemhild thought fierce Hagen too despotic by far. She still had a thousand marks of gold set aside for offerings, and these she distributed for the good of her dear husband's soul, an act that impressed Rüdiger as one of deep attachment.

'Where are those friends of mine who will ride with me to Hungary and endure life in a strange land for my sake?' asked the lady ruefully. 'Let them take my treasure and purchase mounts and clothes.'

'Ever since the day I joined your household I have served you faithfully,' said Margrave Eckewart to the Queen, 'and I shall continue to do so till I die. I shall also take five hundred men with me and assign them to your service most loyally. You and I shall remain inseparable till death.' Kriemhild thanked him graciously, as well she might.

The sumpters were led before the palace, for the party was ready to start. This occasioned much weeping between friends. – Noble Uote and her many comely maidens showed by their demeanour that they would miss the lady Kriemhild.

How King Etzel sent to Burgundy for Kriemhild

The Queen took a hundred superb young ladies away with her – gowned in accordance with their station – causing the tears to tumble from their bright eyes. But later at Etzel's court Kriemhild was to know many pleasures.

As their high breeding demanded of them, lords Giselher and Gernot came at the head of their retinues as a guard of honour for their dear sister, numbering fully a thousand fine warriors. Brave Gere and Ortwin came; and Rumold, Lord of the Kitchen, had also to be one of their number. These established their night quarters for them all the way along to the Danube. Gunther on the other hand rode but a short way out from Worms.

Before setting out from Burgundy they had sent messengers ahead of them to Hungary post-haste to inform the King that Rüdiger had won for him the hand of the august Queen.

CHAPTER TWENTY-ONE

How Kriemhild journeyed to Hungary

*

LET the messengers ride on! – It is our purpose to tell you how Queen Kriemhild progressed from land to land and where Giselher and Gernot, having attended her as affection bade them, took their leave of her. They accompanied her as far as Pföring[1] on the Danube and, desiring to ride back to Burgundy, asked permission to depart. But this could not be done without weeping among good friends.

'If you should ever need me, madam, or suffer any annoyance, inform me of it, and I shall ride to your aid in Etzel's land,' brave Giselher promised his sister.

Her relations kissed her on the lips, the gallant Burgundians bade a kind farewell to Rüdiger's men, and she led her handsome maidens away, a hundred and four of them in all, magnificently attired in ornate brocades that were set off in turn by many a broad shield which their escorts bore beside them on the roads. A host of splendid knights now turned away from the Queen, while her party moved down through Bavaria. The news that a great number of foreigners were fast approaching reached the Bishop's town of Passau (where the Inn flows into the Danube and there is a monastery still standing)[2] and emptied the houses and the Prince-Bishop's palace, too; for everyone was hurrying up through Bavaria in the direction of the strangers, where Bishop Pilgrim soon met lovely Kriemhild. The warriors of this region were not sorry to see so many fine-looking girls in her train, all daughters of noble knights, and they paid ardent court to them with their eyes.

The strangers were comfortably quartered later. But now the Bishop rode to Passau with Kriemhild (who was his sister Uote's daughter), and when the merchants of the city

1. See p. 399.   2. See p. 397.

learned that their prince's niece had arrived they gave her a warm welcome. The Bishop was hoping they would stay with him, but lord Eckewart replied: 'Impossible. We must travel down to Rüdiger's lands, where we are expected by many knights who have all been told what is happening.'

Fair Gotelind had learnt the news and was getting herself and her noble daughter ready with great care, for Rüdiger had sent her a message saying he thought she ought to cheer the Queen's spirits by riding out to meet her with his vassals up-river as far as the Enns. And when she did so the roads everywhere were put to very hard use by those who went to meet the guests, both on horseback and on foot.

The Queen had now arrived in Eferding. Had certain lords of Bavaria[1] succeeded in robbing them on the roads in their usual style they might possibly have harmed the visitors, but the noble Margrave prevented it – he led a thousand men or more. Then his wife Gotelind joined them, too, bringing with her many noble knights in magnificent array.

When the strangers crossed over the Traun and into the plain before Enns they could see huts and pavilions being raised at hospitable Rüdiger's cost, for them to spend the night in. Fair Gotelind left this camp behind her, and fine horses past counting advanced over the roads to the music of their bridles! It was a very fine welcome and Rüdiger was highly gratified. And now a host of knights came riding in from both sides, performing splendid feats of horsemanship and jousting under the eyes of the young women, a tribute which the Queen, too, found not at all displeasing. As Rüdiger's men met the strangers you could see them send the splinters flying with their thrusts in truly knightly fashion – there was some magnificent riding in the presence of those ladies!

But now they made an end of their sport, and the men exchanged kindly greetings on both sides. Fair Gotelind was led away to Kriemhild and then ladies' men found little respite. The lord of Pöchlarn rode up to his wife, who was

1. See p. 362.

glad at his safe return from Burgundy; indeed she was much relieved. When she had welcomed him back he told her to dismount on to the grass with all her suite, a sign for many a nobleman to leap into activity – so assiduously did they attend to the ladies!

When she saw the Margravine standing there with her retinue, lady Kriemhild would not ride another step. She reined in her palfrey and asked at once to be lifted from the saddle. Thereupon the Bishop, assisted by Eckewart, was seen leading his niece towards Gotelind, and the crowd immediately fell back, while she – a stranger in a foreign land – kissed Gotelind.

'How happy I am, dear lady, that it has been granted to me to see your lovely person in this country with my own eyes,' said Rüdiger's wife very kindly 'Nothing could give me greater pleasure at this time.'

'May God reward you, most noble Gotelind,' answered Kriemhild. 'If Etzel[1] and I live for any time you may well benefit from having met me.' Neither had any foreboding of what was destined to happen.

The young ladies decorously approached on either side with knights in eager attendance. Their salutations done, they sat down on the grass, where many became acquainted who had been strangers until then.

Word was given to pour out drinks for the ladies. It was high noon, and the noble retainers tarried there no longer but rode to where the spacious lodges awaited their exalted guests, and saw to their every need.

They rested during that night till early the next morning, while those who had remained in Pöchlarn made ready to house this host of distinguished visitors, Rüdiger having made it his personal concern that they should want for nothing. They saw the casements in the walls of Pöchlarn open to greet them, and the castle-gates flung wide; and when these very welcome guests rode in, their illustrious host gave orders for them to be lodged in comfort.

Rüdiger's daughter went with her retinue and received

1. Text: *Boteluncs kint* = Botelung's son.

,the Queen most charmingly, and there, too, she found her mother the Margravine. Many young ladies-in-waiting were warmly welcomed there. Then knights and ladies took each other by the hand and entered the broad palace, a very handsome building past whose base the Danube flowed. Here they sat at the windows, where the air was freshest, and passed the time very pleasantly. But what else they did I cannot say, except that Kriemhild's men were heard complaining at the tiresome way their journey was dragging out. Oh, what a press of fine warriors rode out with her from Pöchlarn!

Rüdiger looked after them most amiably. The Queen gave Gotelind's daughter twelve bracelets of red gold and the finest cloth she had brought with her to Etzel's country. And although she had been deprived of her Nibelung treasure, she even now won the goodwill of all she met, thanks to the slender means that remained to her: her host's retainers were rewarded with great munificence. In return, lady Gotelind showed the visitors from Burgundy such friendly marks of esteem that you might scarcely have found one who was not wearing jewels or splendid clothes of her giving.

When they had taken their repast and it was time for them to go, Gotelind assured Etzel's queen of her loyal devotion. Kriemhild gave the lovely daughter of the house many an affectionate kiss and embrace, and the girl said to her: 'I know my dear father will gladly send me to you in Hungary, if it is your wish,'[1] from which Kriemhild clearly saw that she was much attached to her.

The horses had been harnessed and led before the walls of Pöchlarn, the noble Queen had taken leave of Rüdiger's wife and daughter, and now whole bevies of comely maidens said a ceremonious farewell to each other. Neither court was to see the other again in days to come.

When they reached Melk, magnificent gold goblets filled with wine were brought from the castle and handed to them on the road – Astolt, lord of that place, bade them welcome!

1. To finish her education: a compliment to Kriemhild.

He pointed out the way into Austria for them, down-Danube towards Mautern, where the mighty Queen was well served later. Here the Bishop took affectionate leave of his niece, urging her to be of good cheer and to acquire honour through liberality as Helche had done before her. And, indeed, great was the honour she won in the land of the Huns in days to come!

Thence the visitors were conducted to the Traisen and Rüdiger's men guarded them most sedulously till the Huns rode out over the country and paid the Queen high honour; for the King had a renowned and splendid fortress on the Traisen that went by the name of Traisenmauer.[1] Lady Helche had her seat there and lived a life full of excellence scarce ever to be repeated, unless it was achieved by Kriemhild, who gave largesse on such a scale that after all her suffering she knew the pleasure of being praised by Etzel's knights, having won their full esteem in later days.

Etzel's dominion was so widely known that the most fearless warriors that were ever heard of among Christians and heathen alike were always to be found at his court, all having joined him. And always – a thing that will hardly happen again – the Christian life and the heathen existed side by side. But whichever rite a man followed, the King's magnanimity saw to it that all were amply rewarded.

1. See p. 398.

CHAPTER TWENTY-TWO

How Kriemhild was received by Etzel

*

KRIEMHILD stayed at Traisenmauer till the fourth day, during which time the dust never settled on the highway but flew up in clouds while Etzel's men rode through Austria, as though there were fires everywhere.

And now the King, too, had been told in full in what magnificent state Kriemhild was passing through those regions, so that his sorrows vanished away at the mere thought of it and he set out in haste to meet his lovely queen. Ahead of him you could see numbers of bold knights of many different languages riding along the roads, great companies past counting of both Christians and heathens who were marching in splendid array to where they found their lady. Many men from Greece and Russia were riding there, and the good horses of Poles and Wallachians passed swiftly by as their riders spurred them with vigour, while they all freely comported themselves according to their native usage. From the land of Kiev, too, many a knight was riding there, not to mention wild Pechenegs who, laying the arrow to the bow at full stretch, shot at birds on the wing with zest.

There is a town in Austria on the Danube called Tulln, where Kriemhild saw many strange customs that she had never met before. Here she was received by various knights who were to suffer at her hands in days to come.

In advance of King Etzel there rode a retinue – magnificent men they were, both courtly and debonair – composed of four and twenty princes of lofty rank who desired nothing more than to see their queen. Duke Ramung of Wallachia galloped by with seven hundred men, and it was as though they sped past like birds in flight. Then King Gibech[1] came

1. Originally the father of Gunther, Gernot, and Giselher, replaced by Dancrat in the present poem. See pp. 371, 376.

with his splendid squadrons. Next brave Hornboge wheeled away from the King with fully a thousand men and approached the Queen: these Hunnish clansmen raised a confused din after the fashion of their country and rode some vehement jousts. Bold Haward of Denmark rode up, and Iring, the brave and true; and then Irnfrid of Thuringia, a fine figure of a man. At the head of their squadron of twelve hundred men these welcomed Kriemhild in a way that could not but do them credit. After them came Etzel's brother lord Bloedelin of Hungary, who rode past the Queen with three thousand men in splendid array.

Finally King Etzel appeared, accompanied by Dietrich and all his comrades, and here there were noble knights of great excellence and worth, so that the Queen's spirits rose at the sight of them.

'Madam,' said Rüdiger to the Queen, 'His Majesty desires to receive you here. Pray kiss whomever I tell you – you cannot possibly salute all of Etzel's vassals equally, regardless of their rank.'

The exalted Queen was handed down from her palfrey, and mighty Etzel delayed no longer but dismounted from his charger, followed by many gallant men, and joyfully advanced towards Kriemhild. We are told that a pair of noble princes walked behind the lady and carried her train for her as King Etzel paced towards her. She received the illustrious monarch kindly with a kiss, to bestow which she pushed back her wimple and revealed her lovely face all radiant amid the gold of her hair, so that many a man declared that Queen Helche had not been lovelier.

Close beside the King stood his brother Bloedelin, and the noble Margrave Rüdiger bade her kiss him, and then King Gibech and Dietrich, standing near. In all, Etzel's queen kissed twelve, after which she received many knights with the usual greeting.

Now during the whole time that Kriemhild stood beside Etzel the young blades were engaged on what they still do today – Christian and pagan warriors rode many fine jousts, each in his own style – and in what truly chivalrous fashion did Dietrich's vassals send shattered shafts flying over the shields with thrusts from their expert hands, while the guests from Germany punched many a shield full of holes! That field re-echoed with the splintering of lances. All the warriors of the land were now there, and the King's guests, too, a great assembly of noble men.

The great King, however, left that place with the lady Kriemhild. Nearby they saw a resplendent pavilion in a meadow crowded with huts in which all were meant to rest themselves when their exertions were ended, and into this knights conducted many well-favoured young women together with the Queen, who then sat down on a thròne covered with rich fabrics. It was the Margrave who had taken such care to provide her with so excellent a seat, much to the gratification of King Etzel.

I do not know what Etzel spoke of, though her white hand was resting in his. They sat together in all friendliness; but gallant Rüdiger would not permit the King to have any intimate dealings with her.[1]

Word was given to stop the bohort that was being ridden all over the field, and the clashing and shouting were brought to an end with honour to all concerned. Thereupon Etzel's men went to their huts and were given shelter everywhere, far and wide.

The day was now drawing to an end and they were taken to where they rested until they saw the bright dawn shine out on them again. Already many knights had mounted their chargers and oh, what sport they made in honour of the King!

Etzel asked the Huns to do things in grand style. They then rode out of Tulln to the city of Vienna, where they found crowds of ladies in gala dress who gave Kriemhild a glorious welcome. Here they were offered whatever they wanted in vast abundance. Many a gay knight looked

---

1. At the Burgundian court Rüdiger assumed legal guardianship over Kriemhild from Gunther, and he will continue to exercise it until it has been transferred to Etzel on consummation of the marriage in Vienna.

forward to joining that happy tumult! They made for their quarters as the King's wedding festivity went off to a jubilant start.

They could not lodge them all in the city, so Rüdiger asked the natives to find quarters in the country round about. I imagine lord Dietrich was in attendance on Queen Kriemhild at all times, with many another knight: they exchanged leisure for toil in their desire to cheer the guests, so that Rüdiger and his friends had excellent entertainment.

The festal day on which King Etzel and Kriemhild were wedded in the city of Vienna fell at Whitsuntide, and I do not think she gained so many vassals through her first husband. By means of her gifts she made herself known to people who had never before set eyes on her and many of them said to the visitors: 'We imagined lady Kriemhild had no means, instead of which she has performed marvels of generosity!'

The festivities continued for seventeen days, and I do not believe it can be said of any king that his wedding celebrations were on a vaster scale – no news of such has reached us. Why, all who attended it wore brand new clothes! And I do not fancy either that, rich in possessions though Siegfried was, he ever had so many noble heroes about him as Kriemhild saw with Etzel, nor did any man at his own wedding bestow so many gorgeous cloaks of ample cut or so many other fine clothes (of which they had abundance), as they all had done in honour of Queen Kriemhild. Their friends and the visitors had but a single thought – not to hold back anything they had, of any sort. Instead they freely gave whatever was asked of them, with the result that, thanks to his generosity, many a knight was left there with no clothes to stand up in!

Kriemhild was thinking of how she had dwelt beside the Rhine with her noble husband, and her eyes filled with tears; yet so well did she hide them that no one saw that she was weeping – such honour was being paid to her after her great grief.

Whatever feats of liberality were performed there, they

were as nothing compared with what Dietrich achieved, for everything that Etzel had given him he had now squandered away, while open-handed Rüdiger worked wonders too. Prince Bloedelin of Hungary had coffer upon coffer emptied of its silver and gold, which he gave away as largesse, and evidently the King's warriors were greatly enjoying themselves! As to the royal minstrels Werbel and Swemmel, each got a full thousand marks or more at that wedding feast, if you ask me, as lovely Kriemhild sat crowned beside Etzel.

On the morning of the eighteenth day they rode out of Vienna to the accompaniment of jousting, during which many shields were pierced by the spears which the knights wielded. Thus did Etzel come to Hungary.

They passed the night in Old Hainburg, and none could have said at a rough guess how many there were in that host or in what strength they traversed the country next morning – but oh, the crowds of pretty women they saw in Etzel's homeland! At the wealthy town of Wieselburg[1] they embarked on the Danube[2] in such numbers that the water was covered with men and horses as far as its course was visible, as if they were on dry land! The travel-weary ladies could now repose in comfort, for numbers of good barks had been lashed together lest the wash or the current harm them, whilst on deck many fine tents had been pitched as though they were still in the meadows.

News of their approach preceded them all the way to Etzelnburg,[3] and its men and women were delighted. (Indeed, the household whom Queen Helche had maintained there in times past were to know many a happy day with Kriemhild.) Noble young ladies who had been much distressed by Helche's death stood looking out to catch sight of them – Kriemhild found no less than seven royal princesses, the glory of all Hungary, who had stayed there to receive her. It was Herrat (Helche's niece on her mother's side, daughter of noble King Nantwin and betrothed to

1. The Hungarian Moson, not Wieselburg near Pöchlarn (see p. 398).
2. The 'Little Danube' is meant.
3. See Appendix 5, p. 396n. 2.

Dietrich) who kept up Helche's court. She would reap much honour later.[1] But now Herrat was eagerly looking forward to the arrival of the guests, towards which vast stores had been amassed.

Who could tell you in detail how the King fared since that day? – Suffice to say that never under any Queen did the Huns have a better life there.

While the King rode from the shore with his consort, the ladies were presented individually. For this they welcomed noble Kriemhild all the more, and great was the dominion she was to hold in Helche's place. She received many marks of loyal submission and made royal gifts of gold and silver, of fine stuffs and precious stones, insisting on giving away all that she had brought over the Rhine with her to Hungary. With the passage of time all the King's relations, too, and all his vassals became her devoted servitors, with the result that Queen Helche never wielded such power over them as Kriemhild enjoyed till she died.

The court and the whole country lived in such splendour that through the favour of the King and the bounty of the Queen they at all times sought their pleasures as each one felt inclined.

1. Other epics let it appear that Herrat was destined to return to Verona with Dietrich as his queen and reign with him.

CHAPTER TWENTY-THREE

How Kriemhild invited her brothers to the festival

*

ETZEL and Kriemhild lived together in great splendour, if the truth be known, until the seventh year, in the course of which time the Queen gave birth to a son, making the King as happy as he could possibly be. She insisted on Etzel's son being baptized, and amid rejoicing all over Hungary he was given the name of Ortlieb.

Lady Kriemhild strove unceasingly to acquire the high distinction that Queen Helche had attained, and in this she was instructed by poor Herrat who mourned bitterly in secret for Helche. Kriemhild was renowned among natives and foreigners alike, who declared that no queen had ever reigned in any kingdom more magnanimously or more successfully, a reputation she bore in Hungary till her thirteenth year. By this time she had ascertained that there was none who dared cross her will (as courtiers are still apt to do where a princely consort is concerned) and never did she fail to see a dozen kings in attendance. She brooded on the many wrongs that had been done to her at home and all the honours that had been hers in Nibelungland, but of which Hagen had stripped her by murdering Siegfried, and she wondered whether she could ever make him rue it. 'If I could get him to this country it could be done,' she mused. Then she dreamt that she was walking with her brother Giselher, hand in hand, repeatedly, and that she kissed him time and time again as she lay gently sleeping. (As things turned out, they were all to know much suffering).

If you ask me, it was the foul fiend who prompted Kriemhild to break with Gunther, whom she had kissed in the land of Burgundy in token of reconciliation.[1] Thus the hot tears began to soil her gown once more. Night and day she was oppressed by the memory of how through no fault of her own she had been brought to the point of having to wed a heathen and that it was Hagen and Gunther who had brought her to this pass. 'I have such wealth and power that I shall yet do my enemies some harm,' she thought, 'and most gladly would I do it to Hagen of Troneck.' Most tenaciously did she nurse this intention within her. 'My heart pines for those who are loyal to me,' she continued. 'But if I could be with those who have wronged me I would avenge my darling to the full – how I yearn for that moment!'

All the King's vassals, warriors of Kriemhild, held her in affection, and well they might: for Eckewart had charge of her treasury, and with it he won many friends for her. Nor was there anyone who could thwart her plans. She would ask the King to do her the favour of inviting her relations to Hungary – this was her constant thought, though none guessed her foul intention. So, one night, as the high-born lady lay beside the King and he held her in his arms and caressed her as was his wont (for she was as dear to him as life) she was thinking of her enemies.

'My dear lord,' she said to the King, 'if I may do so with your favour and have in any way deserved it I should very much like you to show me whether you love my kinsmen at all.'

'I shall convince you that I cannot fail to be pleased by any good fortune that betides them,' answered the mighty king, who was a loyal-hearted person, 'since I never gained better relations through love of any woman.'

'As you are well aware, I have many illustrious kinsmen,' replied the Queen, 'and I am very sorry they so seldom

1. The poet probably means us to believe this for the moment, despite his having shown how all three kings dishonoured the reconciliation (see pp. 148, 327). He is beginning to shift his ground here, and 'cover' himself for the dire events he will relate.

think of coming to see me here, with the result that people say that I am a friendless foreigner.'

'My dearest lady,' rejoined King Etzel, 'if those whom you wish to see do not think the way too far I shall invite them to cross the Rhine and visit us here in my country.'

Having learnt the King's will in the matter, the Queen was greatly cheered. 'If you mean to keep faith with me, my lord,' she said, 'you will dispatch messengers over the Rhine to Worms. I can then make my wishes known to my relations, and a host of noble knights will come to visit us.'

'If that is your wish then let it be done,' said he. 'The sight of your kinsmen could not give you the pleasure that it would give me, for it troubles me greatly that the sons of noble Uote hold aloof from us so long. If it meets with your favour, dearest madam, I should like to send my two fiddlers to your friends in Burgundy.' And he at once summoned the good minstrels, and they hastened to where he was sitting beside the Queen.

Etzel told them that they were to go as his envoys to Burgundy, and he commanded splendid clothes to be made for them, and clothes were also made for four-and-twenty warriors. The King told them his message and in what terms they should invite Gunther and his men, and then the lady Kriemhild had a private conversation with them.

'I shall tell you what you have to do,' said the great King. 'I send to my friends through you my esteem and every good wish and I invite them to be so gracious as to make the journey here to my kingdom. I have never known any who would be such welcome guests. And if lady Kriemhild's kinsmen feel at all inclined to humour me, they must be sure to come to my summer festival this year – for much of my joy in the season will depend on my brothers-in-law.'

'In order that I may tell your kinsmen: *when* is your festival to take place here?' asked proud Swemmel the fiddler.

'This coming midsummer,' answered King Etzel.

'We shall carry out all your commands,' said Werbel.

The Queen had them secretly brought to her appartment, and there she had a conversation with them from which, in the event, many warriors were to have small joy.

'Now do exactly as I ask,' she said to the two messengers, 'Tell them my message there at home and you will earn a great reward. If you do this, I shall make you very rich and give you splendid clothes. And whomever of my kinsmen you should meet in Worms beside the Rhine, you must never let them know that you once saw me sorrowing. Give the brave knights my humble respects and ask them to do as the King says in his message and so part me from all my troubles – for the Huns are persuaded I have no friends or relations! And tell them that were I a knight I should come among them some time or other.[1] Assure my noble brother Gernot that there is no one in the world who could love him more than I, and ask him to bring our most intimate friends to see me here so that we are all honoured by it. And tell Giselher to bear it well in mind that I was never made to suffer through any fault of his, so that I should be very glad to see him again and long to have him with me because of the great love he bears me. Further, tell my mother of the exalted life I lead. And, if Hagen of Troneck should wish to stay at home, who would guide them then from one country to another? – he has known the roads here to Hungary since childhood days.'[2]

The messengers had no idea why they should not let Hagen of Troneck remain in the Rhenish lands, and they came to rue it, later, for when war was declared on Hagen, cruel death took not only him but many other warriors with him. The fiddlers received their letters and message, and Etzel and his fair queen dismissed them. Their persons were beautifully attired, they had ample means for their journey and the wherewithal to live in style.

1. A *double entendre* in the original: (i) if Kriemhild could travel freely like a man she would visit her relations; (ii) if she were an armed man she would 'get at' Hagen and Gunther.

2. According to the epic of Walter of Aquitaine, Hagen had once been a hostage at Etzel's court, cf. p. 371.

CHAPTER TWENTY-FOUR

*How Werbel and Swemmel accomplished their
sovereign's embassy*

*

WHEN Etzel had dispatched his envoys Rhinewards the
news of it flew from land to land, for he sent his invitations
to his festival by fast messenger, requesting here, summon-
ing there – for which many were to die later.

His envoys rode out from Hungary towards Burgundy
where they had been sent to ask three noble kings and their
vassals to come and stay with Etzel, and they made great
speed on their errand.

On riding into Pöchlarn they had to submit to much
willing attention. Rüdiger, Gotelind, and their dear
daughter sent their humble duty through them to the lords
of the Rhinelands, but they did not let Etzel's men go
without making them presents for the way. Rüdiger then
gave them a message for Queen Uote and her sons, saying
they had no Margrave who wished them better than he,
and he gave them a message for Brunhild, too, assuring her
of their loyal devotion and readiness to serve her. Having
listened to this the envoys were impatient to be gone, and
the Margravine commended them to God.

Before they had fully traversed Bavaria, bold Werbel
called on good Bishop Pilgrim. I do not know what message
he sent his kinsmen on the Rhine, but he bestowed gifts of
red gold on these messengers in token of his friendship and
when he allowed them to go he said: 'It would give me
much pleasure to see my nephews here, since I can never
come to Burgundy to visit them.'

I am unable to tell you through which regions they
passed on their way towards the Rhine, but nobody robbed
them of their silver or their baggage, such fear did their

lord's anger inspire, for he was a very mighty man. Before twelve days were out, Werbel and Swemmel arrived at the Rhine in the neighbourhood of Worms, and the news that messengers were come from abroad was reported to the kings and their vassals.

'Who is going to tell us from which country these strangers have ridden here?' enquired Gunther, lord of the Rhinelands. But nobody knew until Hagen of Troneck saw them.

'There is some great news for us, I do declare!' he told Gunther. 'They are Etzel's fiddlers whom I saw out there, and it is your sister who has sent them to Burgundy. For their master's sake we must give them a very warm welcome.'

They were already riding past the palace, nor did royal minstrels ever proceed in finer style. The King's retainers lost no time in receiving them but took them to their quarters and had their belongings stored away. The envoys' travelling clothes were rich and of such elegance that they could have gone before the King in them with honour, yet they did not wish to wear them any longer at court and so they asked whoever would accept them to say so.[1] People were soon found on these terms who were very glad to have them and the clothes were duly sent to them. Then the visitors donned other attire that was far superior, such as is fitting for envoys to wear in state.

Etzel's retainers were now admitted to the royal presence and the courtiers gazed at them with pleasure. Hagen politely ran to meet the messengers and warmly welcomed them, and Etzel's servants thanked him for his courtesy. Eager to learn their news, Hagen asked after Etzel and his men.

'The country was never in better shape nor the people so contented, know it for a fact.' The strangers went through the crowded palace to the King, and were received with the gracious welcome to which all who visit foreign kingdoms

1. Apart from this one occasion when they can behave with the munificence of great lords, the role of the two minstrels is humbly to receive, not to bestow largess.

are entitled. Werbel saw many warriors grouped around King Gunther, who greeted them thus courteously:

'Welcome to you both, you minstrels from Hungary, and also to your comrades! Has mighty Etzel sent you here to Burgundy?'

They bowed their thanks to the King, and Werbel answered: 'My dear lord and your sister Kriemhild send you their loyal respects from distant Hungary and they have dispatched us to you warriors relying on your good faith.'

'This news gives me pleasure,' replied the mighty King. 'How are Etzel and my sister Kriemhild of Hungary?'

'I shall tell you,' said the fiddler. 'Rest assured that no people were ever in better spirits than they and all their knights, both kinsmen and vassals. When we left they were pleased at our journey.'

'I thank Etzel for his good wishes, and my sister too, since he and his men are happy; for I confess I asked your news with some misgiving.'

And now the two young kings arrived, only just having heard the news. Young Giselher was glad to see the messengers for the love he bore his sister. 'You envoys are very welcome,' he said, addressing them affably. 'If you came to the Rhineland more often you would find such friends here as you would be happy to see. You will suffer no annoyance in this country.'

'We do not doubt that honour inspires your every act,' answered Swemmel. 'I have not the wit to express the truly friendly spirit in which Etzel and your noble sister, whose fortunes stand so high, send you their salutation. The Queen bids you remember the love and good will between you, and how you were always devoted to her, body and soul. But first and foremost we have been sent to Your Majesty to ask you to favour us by riding to the land of mighty Etzel, who most urgently commanded us to invite you all by this message and to say that if you will not visit your sister he would like to know how he has offended you, that you should avoid him and his country in this way. Even if the Queen were an utter stranger to you he feels that he himself might merit a gracious visit from you, and indeed he would be very much gratified if this should come to pass.'

'I shall let you know the outcome of my deliberations with my privy councillors within a week from now,' answered King Gunther. 'Meanwhile, go to your quarters and rest yourselves well.'

'Would it be possible for us to see my lady, the great Queen Uote, before we go to our lodgings?' asked Werbel.

'If you wish to call on her no one shall prevent you,' said noble Giselher courteously. 'You would be doing the very thing she wanted. She would be glad to see you for my sister lady Kriemhild's sake. You will be welcome there.' And he led them to Lady Uote's apartments. She was pleased to see the messengers from Hungary and gave them a friendly greeting as her noble nature prompted her. Then, versed in courtly usage as they were, those worthy envoys told her their message.

'My lady sends you her duty and loyal affection,' began Swemmel. 'And if it were possible for her to see you often, rely on it, there is nothing on earth could make her happier.'

'That is not possible,' answered the Queen. 'However pleased I should be to see my darling daughter, she, as noble Etzel's consort, alas, lives too far away. May she and Etzel always be blessed with happiness! Before you leave this country you must tell me when you intend to return, for it is a very long time since I saw messengers with such pleasure as I see you.' These royal servitors from Hungary promised her that they would do so and then went away to their quarters.

Meanwhile, noble Gunther, mighty King, had summoned his intimates and was asking them how the matter appealed to them. A great many said that he might well ride to Etzel's country, indeed the best among them advised it with the sole exception of Hagen. Hagen was fiercely opposed to it.

'You are bent on your own destruction,' he said to the King in private. 'You know what we have done. – We must always go in fear of Kriemhild, for I killed her husband with my own hand. How then should we ever dare to ride into Etzel's country?'

'My sister has put her anger by,' said the great King. 'Before she rode away she renounced her feud against us with the kiss of reconciliation, forgiving all that we had ever done to her, save that her quarrel with you alone, Hagen, remains open.'

'Do not deceive yourselves,' replied Hagen, 'whatever these messengers from Hungary say. If you are resolved on visiting Kriemhild you may well lose your honour and your lives there, for in matters of revenge King Etzel's queen has a long memory.'

'Granted you have cause to fear death in the Hunnish kingdoms,' said King Gernot, adding his opinion to the discussion, 'it would be very wrong of *us* to leave seeing our sister for that reason.'

'Since you are so conscious of your guilt, Uncle Hagen,' said King Giselher to that warrior, 'you stay here in safety and let *those that dare* come with us to see my sister.'

'I would not want you to take anyone on your journey who dared ride to court with greater courage,' retorted Hagen angrily, 'and since you are set on going I shall prove it!'

'Why not entertain us, natives and strangers alike, according to your royal pleasure? You have the means to do so,' asked Sir Rumold, Lord of the Kitchen. 'As far as I know, Hagen has never betrayed you. But if you will not follow his advice, let your most humble and loyal servant Rumold counsel you to stay here, and leave King Etzel there with Kriemhild. What life more full of ease could you lead? You have nothing to fear from your enemies – deck yourselves out in fine clothes, drink the best wine, and make love to pretty women! In addition you will be given the best food any king ever had in the world! But even if that were not possible, you ought to remain for the sake of your beautiful wife, rather than hazard your life in this childish fashion. And so I advise you to stay. Your territories are very rich and we can ransom you here far better than in Hungary – for who knows how matters stand there? Stay at home, my lords: that is Rumold's advice.'

'We have no intention of remaining,' answered Gernot, 'considering the friendly message that my sister and mighty Etzel have sent us. Why should we refrain? Those who are unwilling to go are free to stay at home.'

'Do not take offence at what I am going to say,' replied Hagen, 'however things turn out for you. I counsel you in all sincerity that if you mean to uphold your honour you must go heavily armed to Hungary. Since you are not to be dissuaded, summon your vassals, the very best you have, and I will pick a thousand good knights from among them; then you will suffer no harm from the designs of vengeful Kriemhild.'

'I willingly assent to that,' was the King's prompt answer. And he commanded his messengers to ride through the length of his realm. Of his warriors three thousand or more were assembled, but little did they dream what great hurt they would be reaping, for it was with joy that they came riding into Gunther's lands. Orders were given to equip all who were to set out from Burgundy with mounts and gear, and in this way the King won many willing men. Hagen of Troneck told his brother Dancwart to bring eighty of their own men to Worms, and these valiant knights came in splendid array to Gunther's domains, bringing their armour and other equipment. Then bold Volker, a gentleman-musician, arrived for the State visit with thirty of his vassals, all attired in such robes as a king might wear, and he had Gunther informed of his wish to go to Hungary. Let me tell you who this Volker was. He was a noble lord and he had as his vassals many good warriors of Burgundy; and because he could play the viol he was nicknamed 'the Minstrel'![1]

Hagen chose a thousand whom he knew to be dependable, having witnessed many of their exploits in mighty

1. The poet's explanation is necessary (see pp. 337f.). Volker is introduced here as though for the first time; but see Chapter 1, p. 18.

battles. One could not say otherwise of them than that they were brave.

Kriemhild's messengers were growing very impatient to be gone, since they dreaded their sovereign's anger. They asked daily for their dismissal, but Hagen would not grant it, and this was from shrewd calculation.

'We must take good care not to let them go before we ourselves leave for Hungary in a week's time from now,' he told his lord. 'Then, if anyone bears us a grudge, it will be revealed to us all the more clearly. If we take this course Kriemhild can make no preparations for inciting anyone to harm us. But if she intends to do so things will go ill with her, since we are taking so many picked men with us.'

Shields and saddles and all the gear they were planning to take with them to Etzel's country were now fully ready for this host of valiant men, and Kriemhild's envoys were then summoned before Gunther.

When they arrived, Gernot addressed them. 'The King will comply with Etzel's invitation. We shall be glad to come to his feast and see our sister, rest assured of it.'

'Can you tell us when the festival will take place or by when we are expected to arrive?' asked Gunther.

'It is fixed for this coming midsummer,' answered Swemmel.

They had yet to visit Queen Brunhild, and the King gave them leave to wait on her, should they wish to do so. – But (much to her satisfaction) Volker put a stop to it.

'My lady Brunhild is not in the humour to receive a visit from you,' said the good knight. 'Wait until tomorrow, then you will be allowed to see her.' But when next they were hoping to see her there was something else to prevent them.

Then of his own high excellence the mighty King, who was well-disposed towards the envoys, had some of his abundant gold carried out to them on broad shields, and his kinsmen also gave them splendid gifts: Giselher and Gernot, Gere and Ortwin, gave ample proof that they, too, were open-handed, such rich presents did they offer them.

Yet, out of consideration for their master's prestige, the messengers dared not accept them.

'Sire,' said Werbel the envoy, 'permit your gifts to remain here at home, since we cannot take them with us. My lord forbade us to accept presents and indeed we have little need of them.'

The lord of the Rhinelands was deeply angered that they should decline the wealth of so powerful a king as himself and in the end they had no recourse but to accept his gold and precious cloth which they subsequently took back with them to Etzel's country.

The minstrels wished to see Uote before leaving, and brave Giselher took them into his mother's presence. She gave them the message that she was glad at all the honour paid to Kriemhild. She then told her chamberlains to bestow gold and silken cords on the minstrels for her darling Kriemhild's sake, and also for King Etzel's. These presents they were able to accept readily, since they were tokens of affection.

And now the envoys had taken their leave of man and woman alike and they rode happily into Swabia, whither Gernot had told his knights to conduct them lest anyone molest them. But when their escorts parted company with them Etzel's power and prestige afforded them protection on every road, so that nobody robbed them either of mounts or gear. They made great speed towards Etzel's land and wherever they knew they had friends they informed them that the Burgundians would soon be coming to Hungary from the Rhinelands, which news was also announced to Bishop Pilgrim. And as they spurred down the road past Pöchlarn, Rüdiger was duly told of it, and the Margravine Gotelind, too. She was delighted that they were to see them.

The minstrels hastened on with their news till they found King Etzel in his city of Gran[1] where they gave him all the many greetings that had been sent to him, so that he flushed red with joy. And when the Queen had ascertained that her brothers intended to visit Hungary her spirits

1. Esztergom. See Appendix 5, p. 396

rose within her and she lavished rewards on those minstrels and enhanced her good name in doing so.

'Tell me, Werbel and Swemmel, the pair of you,' she said. 'Of my closest relations whom we have invited here, which mean to attend the festival? And tell me, what did Hagen say when he learned the message?'

'He joined their deliberations early one morning and had nothing good to say on the matter. And when they decided in favour of coming, fierce Hagen thought it tantamount to death. All three of your royal brothers will be coming, in magnificent spirits, but what others will accompany them I cannot know in full, except that bold Volker the Minstrel has promised to ride with them.'

'I could easily dispense with ever seeing Volker here,' observed the Queen, 'but I am very well-inclined towards Hagen, for he is a worthy knight. I am glad we are to see *him* here.' And she went straight to the King and asked him most engagingly: 'How does the news please you, my dear lord? The wish I have cherished all this long time is about to be accomplished.'

'To do your wishes is my good pleasure,' answered the King. 'I was never so truly happy when my own kinsmen were due to visit me. This pleasant prospect of seeing your relations has banished all my cares.'

The King's officers had the hall and palace provided with seats in anticipation of the dear guests they would receive, though, in the event, these were to rob him of untold joy.

CHAPTER TWENTY-FIVE

How the Nibelungs journeyed to Hungary

*

Now let us leave those of Hungary to their own devices.

Prouder warriors than the Burgundians[1] never marched to any kingdom in greater splendour. They had all the weapons and gear they wanted. The lord of the Rhenish lands (as I learned) found clothes to wear at the festival for a thousand and sixty of his vassals, and for his squires to the number of nine thousand. But those whom they left behind lived to mourn it later.

As their baggage was carried over the courtyard, the old Bishop of Spires remarked to fair Uote: 'Our kinsmen are making preparations to go to Etzel's festival – God preserve their honour!'

'Stay at home, good warriors,' noble Uote implored her sons. 'Last night I had a dreadful dream that all the birds of this land were dead!'

'Those who set store by dreams cannot rightly know where their whole honour lies,' interposed Hagen. 'I would urge my lord to ask the Queen's leave to depart. By all means let us ride to Etzel's country where, since there is nothing for it but to attend Kriemhild's festival, the sword-arms of stout fighting-men may render kings good service.' Hagen spoke in favour of the journey, though later he regretted it. Yet he would have advised against it had not Gernot treated him with such gross discourtesy as to taunt him with Siegfried, lady Kriemhild's husband, adding:

'That is why Hagen is not coming on our great visit of state.'

---

1. It is in this chapter that the Burgundians are first called 'Nibelungs' (see pp. 301f.). The Burgundians are not named as such in the second sentence above; I have had to supply the name in order to avoid a confusion with the Huns. The next mention of the Burgundians (closely followed by the mention of Nibelung) is as it stands in the original.

'It is not fear that makes me say so,' retorted Hagen of Troneck. 'If such is your wish, knights, then set things moving! There can be no doubt that I shall gladly accompany you to Etzel's country.' And indeed, in days to come, Hagen gashed many a shield and helmet.

The ferries were made ready and all the clothes of that great company were taken aboard; and very busy they were till darkness fell, when they jubilantly set out from home. On the grassy farther shore of the Rhine they pitched tents and huts. This done, the King asked his lovely queen to linger there, and, when night came, she solaced his handsome person with amorous caresses.

Early next morning there was a blowing of trumpets and flutes as a sign that they must leave, and they accordingly bestirred themselves. Whoever held his love in his arms consoled her tenderly. But King Etzel's queen parted many such pairs in sorrow, in days to come.

Fair Uote's sons had a vassal who was both brave and loyal, and when they were about to leave he took the King aside and told him what he thought. 'I cannot help being sad that you are going on this visit,' said he. (His name was Rumold,[1] and he was a doughty warrior.) 'To whom will you entrust your land and people?' he then asked. 'Alas, that none can turn you from your purpose! I did not like Kriemhild's message from first to last.'

'I entrust my land and little son to you. Attend well to the needs of the ladies – such is my desire. Comfort any whom you see weeping.[2] Yet I am convinced we shall suffer no harm from Etzel's wife.'

The horses stood ready for the three kings and their men, and many who were in the best of spirits said good-bye with affectionate embraces (though many a fine woman was to rue it in after days). As the brave knights went to their horses you could see numerous ladies standing there, their

1. On this reintroduction of Rumold (a rather different Rumold) as though he were not known, see pp. 367f.

2. Many ladies, from Uote and Brunhild downwards, will be without their natural protectors.

heads bowed down with sadness. – No doubt they knew by instinct that their separation would be a long one and that ruin and loss lay ahead, such as always harass the spirit.

The brave Burgundians set out on their journey, and there was a great stir in the land. On both sides of the mountains men and women were weeping but, unconcerned at their people's doings, those knights rode gaily away. Nibelung's[1] warriors accompanied them in a thousand haubercs, leaving many fair ladies at home who never saw them again: for Siegfried's wounds were still tormenting Kriemhild.

Gunther's men directed their march towards the Main up through East Franconia with Hagen as their guide, since he was well acquainted with the country, while Dancwart, warrior of Burgundy, acted as their marshal. And as those excellent knights, the princes and their kinsmen, rode from East Franconia towards Schwanenfeld[2] they could be seen comporting themselves as great noblemen do.

On the twelfth morning the King arrived on the Danube. Bold Hagen of Troneck, Protector of the Nibelungs,[3] who was riding at the head of the column, now alighted on the shore and losing no time tethered his horse to a tree. The river had overflowed its banks, the ferries had been hidden, and the Nibelungs were in great anxiety about how they would cross, for the flood was too wide for them and all those gay knights had to dismount.

'Misfortune may overtake you here, my lord of Burgundy,' said Hagen. 'You can see for yourself that the river has risen mightily and overflowed its banks. If you ask me, we are going to lose many men before the day is done.'

1. See p. 27n. 3. Nibelung here is the eponymous ancestor of the Nibelungs. Nibelung's warriors were really Siegfried's vassals, and thus enemies of the Burgundians (see pp. 72, 136, 302).

2. Once a district between Nuremberg and the Danube, earlier Swalefelt. The MSS have *Swanvelde, Salvelde,* even *Swaben.* See Appendix 5, p. 396.

3. It is from this point that 'Nibelungs' become synonymous with 'Burgundians' (see pp. 301f.), and it is significant that Hagen is here referred to by an expression derived from an ancient kenning.

'Why do you reproach me, Hagen?' asked the august King. 'I conjure you, as you are a good knight, not to dishearten us further, but to go and find us the ford that leads to the other side so that we can get our mounts and gear away.'

'My life is not such a burden,' answered Hagen, 'that I should wish to drown myself in this broad torrent. Before that, many men must be slain by me in Etzel's country, as I am firmly resolved. You stay beside the river, proud knights, while I search the shore for a ferryman who will ship us over to Gelpfrat's lands.' So saying, burly Hagen laid hold of his good shield.

Hagen was well armed. He carried his shield as he went, his bright helmet was strapped on his head, and suspended over his ring-mail he wore a broad sword whose edges were terribly keen. He searched for the ferrymen up and down the river bank. Hearing the plashing of water in a fair spring he listened intently. The sound was made by water-fairies endowed with second sight who were bathing there to cool themselves.

Hagen grew aware of them and silently stole in their direction, yet, perceiving his approach, they fled and were glad to elude him. The warrior took only their garments and did them no other harm.

'Hagen, noble knight,' said one of the nixies, who was called Hadeburg, 'if you will give us back our clothes we shall tell you how your visit to Hungary will turn out for you.' They floated on the waves before him like water-fowl, and this led him to think that they were gifted with second sight, so that he more readily believed whatever they told him. And indeed they told him all that he wished to know of them.

'You can ride with confidence to Etzel's country,' said Hadeburg. 'I pledge you my word of honour that no warriors ever travelled to any kingdom to win such glory, rest assured of it.'

Her words pleased Hagen in his heart. He delayed no longer but gave them back their clothes. And when they had donned their marvellous garments,[1] they told him the whole truth about the Burgundians' expedition to Hungary.

'Let me warn you, Hagen, son of Aldrian,'[2] said the second water sprite, whose name was Sieglind. 'My cousin lied to you for the sake of her clothes. If you ever get to Hungary you will be sadly disappointed. Turn back – there is still time! For, bold knights, you have been invited to Etzel's country in order that you shall die there! All who ride to that land have linked their hands with Death!'

'It is in vain that you try to deceive me,' answered Hagen. 'How is it possible that we should all fall there as the result of anyone's malice?'

Then they told him in greater detail.

'It is fated that not one of you shall survive there apart from the King's chaplain,' said a nixie, 'as is well known to us. Only he will get back to Burgundy alive.'

'It would be vexatious news to have to tell my lords that we were all doomed to die in Hungary,' said Hagen grimly. 'But now, most knowing of fairies, show us the way over the water.'

'Since you will not abandon your journey,' she answered, 'let me tell you that at the riverside upstream there is a house where a ferryman lives and no other anywhere.' At this, Hagen abstained from further questions.

'Stay awhile, lord Hagen,' one of them called after that disgruntled warrior, 'you are in too great a hurry. You must hear more about your landing on the other shore. The margrave there is called Else, and his brother is the warrior Gelpfrat, a lord of Bavaria. If you mean to pass through his frontiers you will have trouble on your hands. Be very much on your guard and handle the ferryman discreetly, for he is of so ferocious a turn that he will not suffer you to live unless you give him good treatment. You must pay him his due if you want him to ship you across.

---

1. Possibly some sort of feather robe, since these nixies rather resemble swan-maidens.

2. Again, it is only from this chapter onwards that Hagen's father Aldrian is named (see pp. 376, 386).

He stands guard over this region and owes homage to
Gelpfrat. If he does not come promptly, shout across the
river and say your name is Amelrich – he was a good
warrior who left this land owing to a feud. When he hears
his name, the ferryman will come.'

Hagen bowed his thanks to the fairies but said not
another word. He went farther up-river along the sandy
shore till he saw a dwelling on the other bank. 'Come and
fetch me, ferryman,' the good knight bawled across the
water, 'and I will give you a torque of red gold for your
hire! I tell you, I have urgent need to make this crossing!'

The ferryman was of such standing[1] that it was unfitting
for him to render services, so that he never accepted pay-
ment from anyone, and his underlings, too, were very
haughty. Thus Hagen had to stand and wait on his side of
the flood. But then he shouted with such force that the
whole river re-echoed with it, for he was a very powerful
man. 'Now come and fetch me, I am Amelrich, Else's man,
who fled abroad through a bitter quarrel!' On the tip of his
uplifted sword he offered him a bracelet, fair and gleaming
with red gold, as the price for being ferried to Gelpfrat's
land.

The proud ferryman seized an oar himself, for he was
newly married: yet lust for pelf comes to a bad end. – He
was hoping to earn Hagen's gold that shone so red, but what
he in fact received from him was cruel death at the sword's
edge.

The ferryman sculled lustily over to the hither shore and
not finding the man who had been named to him flew into
a towering rage. Catching sight of Hagen, he addressed that
warrior in a fury. 'For all I know your name may be
Amelrich, but you don't at all resemble the man I expected
to find here. He was my brother by the same mother and
father. Since you have deceived me, you will have to stay
over here.'

'No, by God Almighty!' cried Hagen. 'I am a knight in

---

1. He is a ministerialis, or 'unfree' knight, entrusted by his overlord
with guarding his frontier.

a foreign land and have warriors in my care. Now kindly accept my hire for ferrying me over today and I shall be deeply obliged to you.'

'That can never be,' replied the ferryman. 'My dear lords have their enemies and so I shall take no strangers over into this territory. As you value your life, step out on to the shore – and quickly!'

'Do not refuse,' answered Hagen, 'for I am not feeling very gay. Take this good gold of mine in amicable settlement and ship us across, a thousand of us, together with our beasts.'

'Never!' said the bloodthirsty ferryman. And raising his huge, stout oar he struck Hagen such a blow as brought him to his knees amidships, much to his dismay. Never had the lord of Troneck met so savage a ferryman! The latter meant further to provoke the haughty stranger since, exerting his great strength, he hit Hagen on the head so hard with a pole that it smashed to pieces. But this was the undoing of Else's ferryman, for in fierce rage Hagen seized his sheath and drawing no mean sword[1] struck off his head and threw it to the bottom.

The news of these events was soon to reach the Burgundians. At that same instant in which Hagen struck the shipman the ferry floated downstream, much to his annoyance, and he was growing very tired when he at last retrieved it. King Gunther's man pulled mightily at the oars; he turned the craft with lightning strokes till the stout oar shivered in his hands. The intruder was hoping to disembark at a sandy beach and rejoin the knights, but there was no other oar. – Then with what speed did he lash that oar together with a fine shield-sling of corded silk! Steering for a wood lower down he saw his lord standing on the shore, where a crowd of stately knights came to welcome him with friendly salutations; but at once they saw the blood steaming in the ship from the great wound that he had dealt the ferryman, and they plied him with many questions.

1. The famous sword Balmung, of which Hagen had despoiled Siegfried after murdering him.

Seeing the hot blood swimming amidships, King Gunther promptly said: 'Now tell me, lord Hagen, what has become of the ferryman? I fancy your manly strength has proved the death of him.'

Hagen denied it. 'Finding the ship beside a wild willow, I unmoored it,' he said. 'I have seen no ferryman today, nor has anyone hereabouts come to any harm through me.'

'I am in great fear now for the death of dear friends,' lamented lord Gernot of Burgundy. 'It troubles me that there are no shipmen here to take us over.'

'Lay the harness and baggage on the grass!' bellowed Hagen. 'I recall that I was the best ferryman of all in the Rhineland and I trust I shall get you over to Gelpfrat's country.'

They drove their horses into the water with blows so that they should cross the better, and the beasts swam very well; for the strong current did not take a single one, though as a result of their tiring some drifted far downstream. Then they carried their gold and clothes to the ship, since this crossing had to be made. Hagen took charge and ferried a host of splendid fighting-men over to alien territory, taking first a thousand proud knights and then his own warriors. But still there were more to come, for he took nine thousand squires to land. That day the bold lord of Troneck was not idle![1]

Having got them safely over, the good warrior was reminded of the strange revelations which the wild nixies had made to him, whereupon the royal chaplain all but lost his life. Hagen found that priest beside the chapel baggage, resting his hand on the sacred utensils. But this helped him not at all; for as soon as Hagen saw him the wretched cleric had to suffer misery. In a trice Hagen had flung him overboard! 'Fish him out, sir, fish him out!' they cried in chorus. Young Giselher was indignant, but Hagen would not give up before doing the chaplain some injury.

'What good will the priest's death do you, Hagen?' asked lord Gernot of Burgundy. 'If anyone else were to do

1. See p. 306.

so, you would be offended. What has the chaplain done to earn your enmity?'

The priest made great efforts to keep himself afloat, thinking to save his life if only someone would help him. This, however, was ruled out, for mighty Hagen vehemently thrust him to the bottom, to the scandal of everyone there. Seeing no aid forthcoming, the miserable cleric turned back to the shore to his great discomfort, and although he could not swim he was succoured by the hand of the Lord and reached dry land in safety. Standing up, he shook his cassock, and this brought it home to Hagen that there would be no escaping the fate which the wild nixies had foretold. 'These knights are doomed to die,' thought he.

When they had unloaded the ship and carried off all the gear that the three kings had in her, Hagen smashed her and threw the pieces in the river, to the good warriors' great amazement.[1]

'Why do you do that, brother?' asked Dancwart. 'How shall we cross when we ride back from Hungary to Burgundy?'

'I do it,' answered the knight of Troneck, 'in anticipation that if there is some craven among us that wished to run away, he must die a shameful death in this torrent.'

Among those whom they brought with them from Burgundy there was a redoubtable warrior called Volker. He voiced his opinions shrewdly, and whatever Hagen did, the Fiddler always approved.[2]

Their mounts were harnessed, the sumpters were laden. They had as yet sustained no hurt to annoy them on the journey, save for the royal chaplain. He had to foot it back to Burgundy.

1. See p. 339.
2. Volker is reintroduced, for the second time; see p. 338.

CHAPTER TWENTY-SIX

How Gelpfrat was slain by Dancwart

*

WHEN they had all landed on the shore the King asked: 'Who will show us the right paths through this country so that we do not lose our way?'

'I and no other shall see to it,' answered mighty Volker.

'Now hold still, knights and squires,' said Hagen. 'You must be advised by your friends, I think that only right. I am going to tell you news that will shock you. We shall never get back to Burgundy! Two water-fairies told me this morning that we shall never return. Now here is what I counsel you to do. – Arm yourselves, warriors, and be much on your guard! We have powerful enemies here – we must proceed with caution! I thought I should catch the nixies lying when they declared that not one of us would get back to Burgundy alive – bar the chaplain. That is why I tried so hard to drown him.'

The news flew round from company to company, and brave warriors blenched with anguish as they brooded on the harsh death looming ahead on their visit to the Hunnish court, as indeed they well might.

They had crossed the river at Mehring,[1] and it was here that Else's ferryman had been slain. 'Since I have acquired some enemies on the road,' resumed Hagen, 'we are sure to be attacked. I *did* kill that ferryman this morning, and the news is bound to have reached them. Make yourselves ready at once, so that if Gelpfrat and Else attack our column today it will go ill with them! I know them to be so resolute that they will not refrain. Let the horses pace more leisurely, lest it be thought that we are fleeing along the roads.'

'I shall do as you advise,' said the warrior Giselher. 'But who is to guide our troop across country?'

1. See pp. 379, 398.

'Let brave Volker the Minstrel do it,' they all answered. 'He knows the paths and ways here.' And before they had finished asking him the gallant Fiddler stood there fully armed. His battle-dress was of a magnificent hue; he laced his helmet on and affixed a red pennant to his lance. Later he was to come into dire straits, together with his kings.

Firm news of the killing of his ferryman had now reached Gelpfrat, and mighty Else had learned of it, too. Both were incensed to hear it, and they summoned their fighting-men. These were soon ready, and in a brief space (I would have you know) the Burgundians saw warriors riding towards them who had wrought havoc in mighty battles ere now and dealt many ugly wounds. Of these, seven hundred or more had now joined Gelpfrat, and when they set off in pursuit of their fierce enemies their lords were riding at their head. But in their eagerness to vent their anger they were rather too quick off the mark in following the brave intruders, as a result of which (as things turned out) many of their masters' allies were lost.

Hagen of Troneck in his great sagacity – what warrior could better guard his kinsmen? – had so arranged it that he had charge of the rearguard with his vassals and his brother Dancwart. The day had drawn to a close and the light was beginning to fail. Hagen feared grief and pain for his friends as they rode through Bavaria under cover of their shields, and, truly, it was not long before they were assailed. On both sides of the road and hard behind them they heard the clatter of hooves. But their pursuers were too impatient, for 'They are going to attack us here!' called Dancwart. 'Lace on your helmets – that would be best!' The Burgundians halted their march, since there was no alternative. And now in the gloom they saw bright shields flashing. Hagen was unwilling to keep silent any longer. 'Who is pursuing us on the highway?' he demanded an answer from Gelpfrat.

'We are looking for our enemies and have chased after them this way,' answered the Bavarian margrave. 'I have no idea who killed my ferryman this morning – he was a very formidable warrior. I am heartily displeased.'

'Was the ferryman your vassal?' asked Hagen of Troneck. 'He refused to take us over. I am the guilty party, for it was I who killed the knight. But, believe me, I was forced to do so, since he came near to killing me. Good warrior, I offered him gold and precious stuffs if he would ferry us over to your territory, but he went so far in his rage as to strike me with a stout pole, and I grew very angry. I found my sword and put a stop to his fury with a mighty wound that finished him. I will make you amends as you think fit.' But it came to a fight nevertheless – the Bavarians were not men to yield.

'When Gunther and his retinue rode past,' said Gelpfrat, 'I was convinced Hagen would do us some wrong. But he shall not escape! He must pay for my ferryman's death with his life!'

Burning to have at each other, Gelpfrat and Hagen lowered their spears over their shields to aim their thrusts, and Else and Dancwart too rode splendidly to try each other's mettle. Fierce fighting ensued.

How could warriors ever test each other more keenly? – From a powerful joust by Gelpfrat bold Hagen flew over the cruppers and took a seat on the ground – his horse's poitrel had broken, and the woes of battle were brought home to him! But, to the cracking of their retainers' lances, Hagen meanwhile recovered himself after being thrust on to the grass, and I fancy they were no gentle feelings that he harboured towards Gelpfrat. I do not know who held their chargers for them, but both Hagen and Gelpfrat had dismounted on to the sand and were attacking each other on foot while their comrades saw to it that all were drawn into the fray. Yet although Hagen sprang at Gelpfrat with great ferocity the noble margrave hacked off a piece of his shield so that a shower of sparks leapt from it and King Gunther's bold liegeman but narrowly escaped his end.

'Help, dear brother!' he called to Dancwart. 'A most

redoubtable warrior has fronted me and is bent on having my life!'

'I will be your umpire,' replied bold Dancwart, and he leapt in and struck Gelpfrat such a blow with his keen sword that it stretched him dead. Else burned for instant revenge, yet he and his retainers withdrew after having had the worst of it, for his brother had been slain and he himself was wounded, while at least eighty of his knights lay on the field of battle struck down by pitiless death. Thus this lord had to turn away from Gunther's men and take to flight.

As the Bavarians withdrew you could hear terrible blows re-echoing behind them while the men of Troneck chased their enemies, who, for their part, hoping to escape the penalty, were all making off at speed.

'We must now turn back to our path,' said Dancwart as the others fled, 'and let them ride away, all drenched in blood as they are. Let us hasten back to our friends, that is my advice.'

When they returned to the scene of havoc, Hagen of Troneck said: 'Knights, you must ascertain who is missing or whom we have lost in this skirmish as a result of Gelpfrat's fury.' They had to resign themselves to the loss of four. But these had been well paid for, since on the other count a hundred or more Bavarians had been slain, whence the shields of those of Troneck were dulled and wet with blood. Then, as the gleam of the bright moon peeped above the clouds, Hagen said: 'Nobody is to tell my dear lords what we have done here. Let them stay free of care till sunrise.'

When those who had been fighting caught up with the others, they were far gone with fatigue. 'How long do we go on riding?' asked many a man. 'We cannot bivouac,' answered bold Dancwart. 'You must all keep riding till daybreak.' Then brave Volker, who had charge of the baggage-train, sent to ask the Marshal: 'What place shall we come to tonight where our horses and my dear lords can rest?' 'I do not know,' answered Dancwart. 'But we cannot rest before dawn. Then as soon as we find an opportunity let us lie down in the grass.' When they heard this, how disgruntled some few of them were! That they were dyed red with the hot blood remained undivulged till the sun sent its bright rays over the hills to greet the morning, when, seeing that they had been fighting, the King angrily asked:

'How now, friend Hagen, it seems that you set little store on my being with you when your chain-mail was drenched with blood.[1] – Who did this?'

'It was Else,' Hagen answered. 'He engaged us during the night. We were attacked because of his ferryman. My brother killed Gelpfrat. Coming into great danger, Else had no choice but to run away from us. A hundred of theirs to four of ours fell there.'

We cannot tell you where they camped, but all the people thereabouts got wind of it that the sons of noble Uote were on their way to Etzel's court, and before long these were well received in Passau. For Bishop Pilgrim, the noble kings' uncle on their mother's side, was more than pleased when his nephews rode into his territory with such a host of warriors, and it was soon brought home to them that he wished them well. Already on the road they were welcomed warmly by their friends, yet they could not be lodged in Passau but had to cross the river[2] to a meadow, and here they pitched their camp.

They were prevailed upon to stay in Passau for a whole day and night – and how excellently they were cared for! They then had to set out for Rüdiger's domain, who for his part soon learned of their coming. And when those travel-weary men had rested and were approaching his lands they found a man asleep at the frontier. – Hagen of Troneck at once took his stout sword.[3]

This worthy knight's name was Eckewart,[4] and he was very woebegone at having lost his weapon at the approach

1. The king reproaches Hagen for having left him out of the fighting.
2. The Inn.
3. This episode is an ancient one, which survives here divorced from its original function (see p. 393). Nevertheless, it serves to foreshadow Hagen's chivalry towards Rüdiger (p. 271).
4. See Chapter 11, p. 96, and Appendix 6, under 'Eckewart'.

of these warriors who had found Rüdiger's marches so ill guarded.

'Alas, I am disgraced!' cried Eckewart. 'How bitterly I rue the coming of you Burgundians! All my happiness vanished on the day when I lost Siegfried! Shame on me, lord Rüdiger, how I have wronged you!'

As he listened, Hagen could not mistake the noble warrior's anguish. He gave him back his sword and six bracelets of red gold into the bargain.

'Accept these, knight, as amends and as token of our friendship. You are a fearless warrior, lying all alone at the frontier though you do.'

'Heaven reward you for your bracelets,' replied Eckewart. 'Yet I much regret your visit to Hungary, for you killed Siegfried, and people hate you here. I advise you in all sincerity – be on your guard!'

'May the Lord preserve us,' answered Hagen. 'But these knights, both the kings and their vassals, have no other care than where we can find quarters for the night. Our horses are jaded from the long ways that we have come, our provisions have run out, and we can find none for sale anywhere. We are in need of a patron who of his courtesy will give us his bread this evening.'

'I will find you such a host that nowhere in any land will you ever have come to a house so hospitable as his, if only you brave knights will go to Rüdiger,' answered Eckewart. 'His residence is just off the road, and he is the best host that ever gained a home. His heart blossoms in fine qualities like sweet May with flowers in the greensward! He is always in a merry mood when he can wait upon warriors!'

'Will you be my messenger to my dear friend Rüdiger, to ask him whether he will take my kinsmen and our vassals under his roof?' asked King Gunther. 'I shall always strive to repay him as well as I can.'

'I shall gladly be that messenger,' answered Eckewart. And he set out on his way with great good will and repeated the message to Rüdiger, who had not received such glad news for a long time.

How Gelpfrat was slain by Dancwart

A knight was seen hastening in to Pöchlarn, and it was
Rüdiger who saw and recognized him. 'Kriemhild's liege-
man Eckewart is spurring along the road here!' he exclaim-
ed, imagining he had been wronged by his enemies. He
went outside and met the messenger, but the latter ungirt
his sword and laid it by:[1] nor did he keep back from his
lordship and his friends the news which he had brought, but
told it them promptly.

'Gunther, lord of Burgundy, and his brothers Giselher
and Gernot, have bidden me come to you,' he announced to
the Margrave. 'They each send you their respects, as do
Hagen and Volker most devotedly. And I will tell you
further that the Royal Marshal sent you this message by me:
"The good squires are in need of your shelter."'

'How glad I am to hear that the noble kings deign to ask
my services,' exclaimed Rüdiger with a happy smile. 'They
shall not be refused. I shall be delighted if they enter my
house.'

'Dancwart the Marshal asked me to tell you whom else
you would have here with the kings: sixty picked warriors,
a thousand good knights, and nine thousand squires and
grooms.'

'How fortunate I am to have these guests,' answered
Rüdiger, 'and to be visited by such noble warriors whom I
have never yet served in any way! Now ride out to meet
them, my kinsmen and my vassals!'

Knights and squires accordingly hastened to their horses,
fully approving of their lord's commands, and thus gave
their service with all the more alacrity. But the lady Gote-
lind, sitting in her chamber, as yet knew nothing of these
things.

1. A sign that the news is peaceful.

CHAPTER TWENTY-SEVEN

How they came to Pöchlarn

*

THE Margrave went to find the ladies, that is his wife and daughter, and lost no time in telling them the pleasant news which he had learned – that they were to have their mistress's brothers as their guests.

'My dearest spouse,' said Rüdiger, 'I want you to give these exalted kings a warm welcome when they present themselves with their retinue, and you must also give Gunther's vassal Hagen a fair greeting. With them comes a lord called Dancwart and another by the name of Volker, both very well-bred men. These six you and my daughter must receive with a kiss and you must offer them such friendly company as good manners require.'

The ladies assented willingly and from their coffers chose splendid gowns to wear when they went to meet the warriors, and altogether fair ladies were very busy at their toilet. Nevertheless no lady's complexion owed anything to false arts and, believe me, they wore costly fillets gleaming with gold on their heads lest the winds tousle their beautiful hair.

But let us leave the ladies to their flurry. Outside, Rüdiger's people galloped across country till they met the princes, and they received them kindly into their lord's territory. And when brave Rüdiger the Margrave saw them approaching, 'Welcome, my lords, to this domain,' he said with great good humour, 'and your vassals, too. It gives me much pleasure to see you here.'

The warriors bowed and thanked him from their hearts, and he left them in no doubt that he wished to please them. To Hagen he gave an especial greeting, having known him in former days, and also to Volker of Burgundy.

When he welcomed Dancwart, that bold knight asked:

'Since you are going to look after us, who will care for our retinue?'

'You and all your train shall have a good night,' replied the Margrave. 'I shall set such a guard on all the beasts and gear you have brought here that you shall not lose so much as a single spur! – Pitch the tents in the meadow, men! – I shall stand surety for anything you lose here. Remove your horses' bridles, and let them roam.' No host had ever welcomed them like this, and they were very pleased. These arrangements made, the gentlemen rode off and their attendants everywhere lay down at ease on the grass; and I fancy that never during their journey did they find such comfort as here.

The noble Margravine went before the castle with her lovely daughter, and you could see standing beside them charming ladies and numerous comely maidens, whose arms covered with bracelets and who were draped in gorgeous robes worked with precious stones that cast their lustre far and wide as they shone from the costly fabric – what fine-looking women they were!

But now the guests had come and they at once dismounted – and oh the marvellous good breeding the Burgundians displayed! Thirty-six young ladies and many other women of exquisite figure advanced to meet them accompanied by many brave knights, after which those noblewomen received the guests becomingly.

The young Margravine kissed all three kings, as did her mother. Hagen was standing close at hand, and her father bade her kiss him. She took a look at Hagen and found him of so fearsome an aspect that she would gladly have refrained: yet, as her colour came and went, she had to do the master's bidding. She also kissed Dancwart, and then the Minstrel, who was thus greeted for his personal courage.[1] And now the young Margravine took Giselher, the warrior of Burgundy, by the hand, while her mother took brave Gunther, and they gaily led them away. His lordship conducted Gernot into a spacious hall, where the knights and ladies

1. See pp. 337f.

took their seats. The servants were bidden quickly to pour good wine for the guests – scarce ever can knights have known better treatment!

They all gazed at Rüdiger's daughter with enamoured eyes, so handsome was she. And indeed many a good knight indulged in tender thoughts of her, and these she richly deserved, for she was a spirited young beauty. But however they let their fancies roam nothing could come of it. Many glances, too, swept the ranks of the ladies and young women who sat there in such numbers. The noble Fiddler warmed to his host.

The knights and ladies separated as custom prescribes and withdrew to different rooms. In the broad hall, tables were set up and the visitors from abroad were regaled in lordly fashion. As a favour to the guests the noble Margravine joined them at table, but she left her daughter with the young ladies where she belonged. However, failing to see her, the visitors were truly vexed.

When they had all partaken of food and drink, the fair were shown into the hall again and there was a free exchange of quips and sallies – not least by bold, gay Sir Volker.

'Noble Margrave,' said he, so that all could hear, 'God has treated you very graciously, having given you a wife of great beauty and a very delightful existence. If I were a great prince and wore a crown,' continued the Minstrel, 'I should wish to have your lovely daughter to wife – that is what my heart would desire for me. She is so enchanting to look at, and is of noble birth and disposition as well.

'How could it ever come about that a king should want my daughter?' asked the Margrave. 'My wife and I both live in exile here. What advantage could great beauty bring the good young lady?'

'If I were to have a dear wife as I would wish her I should be eternally glad of one such as she,' answered Gernot urbanely.[1]

1. Just how embarrassing this public and apparently haphazard matchmaking is for Rüdiger's family is hard to assess; but the allusion to

'Now my lord Giselher ought to be getting married,' interposed Hagen benignly. 'The young Margravine is of such high lineage that his vassals and I would gladly serve her were she to go crowned in Burgundy.'

Rüdiger and Gotelind were well pleased with these words, indeed they were inwardly delighted. Following this, the Burgundian warriors arranged things so that noble Giselher took her to wife in a manner befitting a king.

Who can thwart the workings of destiny? The young lady was sent for, and they solemnly promised to give him the entrancing woman, while he for his part vowed to cherish her adorable person. The Burgundians allotted castles and lands to her for her nuptial dower, and the noble King and Gernot confirmed with oaths that this pledge would be fulfilled.

'Since I have no castles,'[1] said the Margrave, 'I shall be your sincere and devoted friend always. And to go with my daughter, I will give you as much silver and gold as a hundred sumpters, fully laden, can carry so that the young knight's kinsmen may rest content that honour has been done.'

Then the two were told to stand in the ring according to the custom. Numbers of young men stood opposite her in the highest of spirits and they indulged in the same idle fancies as young men do today.

When they asked the lovely girl whether she would have the warrior she was somewhat averse, though she meant to take the handsome fellow! – Like many another young woman she found the question embarrassing. Her father Rüdiger urged her to say 'yes' and to accept him willingly – and at once noble Giselher was there to take her with his white hands and kiss her – small joy though she was to have of him.

Gernot's urbanity at this point encourages the thought that he is, with a tactful remark, easing a delicate situation into which Volker has got them. All ends well: but there are no signs that the Burgundians had agreed beforehand to Giselher's marrying the young Margravine.

1. Rüdiger presumably means castles which he can transfer to a foreign power, since he in fact holds many from Etzel (see p. 265).

'You illustrious kings,' said the Margrave, 'when you ride back to Burgundy I will give you my daughter, so that you may escort her home with you in the time-honoured way.' And to this they all assented.

Sounds of merrymaking rose on the air, but at length they had to make an end. The young lady was sent back to her apartment and the guests were invited to retire and rest themselves till the morrow.

Breakfast was prepared in the morning, and their host attended kindly to their needs. When they had partaken of their meal, they said they would set out for Hungary.

'I shall see to it that you do not,' said their most noble host. 'You must stay here; for never did I have guests that were so welcome!'

'But this is out of the question,' replied Dancwart. 'Where would you find all the food and bread and wine which you would need tonight for so many warriors?'

'No more of that, if you please!' answered Rüdiger when he heard it. 'My dear lords, do not refuse me. I could feed you for a fortnight together with all your following, since King Etzel has never yet laid me under any contribution.'[1]

However much they tried to defend themselves they had to remain till the fourth morning, when his lordship performed such feats – bestowing on his guests both horses and clothes – that it was spoken of far and wide. But now it could go on no longer, and they simply had to go. Yet it was not in Rüdiger's nature to let anything escape his generosity: he denied to no man whatever he wished to take – they all had to give way to him!

Their noble squires led droves of horses before the gate ready saddled and were then joined by the many foreign knights, all carrying their shields; for they were bound for Etzel's country.

Rüdiger made presents to all his noble guests before they

---

1. As Rüdiger's benefactor and overlord, Etzel could expect him to make any outlay necessary for the maintenance of his margraviate.

left the hall and his munificent style won him great renown. To Giselher he had given his lovely daughter. To the excellent warrior Gunther he gave a suit of armour which the illustrious king wore with honour, unused though he was to accepting gifts, and he thanked the noble donor with a bow. Then Rüdiger gave Gernot a sword of no mean quality which he later carried in battle with much glory and which the Margravine was very far from grudging him (though as things turned out her husband was to lose his life from it).

Since his king had accepted, it was fitting for Gotelind to offer Hagen a friendly gift lest he go to the festivity without some mark of her favour, yet he declined it.

'Of all that I have seen,' said Hagen, 'there is nothing I should wish to take away save that shield hanging on the wall there. I should very much like to take that to Etzel's country.'

Hearing Hagen's words, the Margravine was reminded of her old grief, and the tears could not fail to come. She was thinking with deep anguish of the death of Nuodung whom, to her bitter sorrow, Witege slew.[1]

'I will give you that shield,' she told the warrior. 'Would to God that he who used to wear it were still alive! He was killed in battle and I, wretched woman, shall always have cause to weep for him!' And the noble Margravine went from her seat, took the shield in her white hands, and carried it to Hagen, and he received it. – The gift was one that brought him great honour! Over the gem-studded colours of its blazon there lay a cover of shining brocade: the sun never illumined a better shield, and if anyone had wanted to buy it, it was worth a thousand marks.

Hagen had the shield carried away for him, and Dancwart came to present himself. The Margrave's daughter bestowed some sumptuous clothes on him which he wore in Hungary to magnificent effect.

Not one of these knights would have accepted any of the gifts they received but for their wish to please their host who had entertained them so well – yet the time would come

1. See Appendix 6, p. 403, under 'Nuodung'; also p. 380.

when they grew so hostile towards him that they had no recourse but to slay him.

Then brave Volker went and stood before Gotelind very decorously with his viol and he sang her a song to his own tuneful accompaniment. This was his farewell on leaving Pöchlarn. The Margravine for her part had a chest brought in, and – now you shall hear of a lady's guerdon! – from it she took a dozen bracelets and fastened them round his arm.[1] 'Please take these with you to Etzel's country and wear them to court for my sake so that I can be told on your return how you served me at the festivity.' And indeed, in the event, Volker carried out the lady's wishes to the full.

'So that you may travel in greater ease I shall myself escort you and see to it that you are well guarded lest anyone harm you on the road,' the host told his guests. His lordship's pack-horses were promptly laden and he and five hundred of his men were amply furnished with mounts and clothes; and he took these men away with him to the festival in great good spirits. Yet not one of them got back alive to Pöchlarn.

Rüdiger took his leave with affectionate kisses, and Giselher's noble nature prompted him to do likewise. The knights of Pöchlarn took fair women into their arms and embraced them tenderly (though in the outcome many young ladies had cause to lament this parting). And now the casements were opened everywhere as their lord and his men turned towards their horses, and many ladies and pretty girls wept there, for I fancy their hearts foretold them what

1. The situation is to be viewed in terms of the convention of 'Minnesang', which was at its peak in Germany at the time when the *Nibelungenlied* was being written. According to this cult, a knight would address love-songs of his own composition to a high-born lady who was ostensibly beyond his reach, in expectation of her 'reward', a highly ambiguous term that could mean all or nothing. In the present scene everything is unambiguous – Volker pays Gotelind a public compliment, and she repays him in good metal – and it may be (did we but know) that the situations of the ardent and sometimes impudent lyrics that have come down to us were normally as innocent as this, in real life. A knight might also joust as a form of service to his lady, and there is a reference to this too in our passage.

great sorrows lay ahead. Many of them felt bitter longing for dear friends whom they were never to see in Pöchlarn again: yet these were now riding happily on the sandy shore of the Danube, down-river and out into Hungary.

'We must not keep the news to ourselves that we are coming to the Hunnish lands,' said that happy knight Rüdiger to the Burgundians. 'King Etzel never heard anything that pleased him so well.' – His messenger galloped down through Austria telling the people everywhere that the warriors were arriving from Worms beyond the Rhine, and no news could be more welcome to the King's retainers. But now numbers of messengers were racing ahead of them to announce that the Nibelungs were in Hungary.

'Pray receive them well, lady Kriemhild. Your dear brothers are coming with much honour to visit you.'

Kriemhild took her stand at a window. She was looking out for her relations, as friends do for their dear ones. She saw a host of men from her native land. King Etzel also learned of this, and beamed with pleasure.

'How happy am I!' said Kriemhild. 'My kinsmen are bringing new shields and dazzling hauberks here in plenty.[1] Whoever is willing to take gold, let him remember my grief and I shall always show myself grateful!'

1. See p. 393.

CHAPTER TWENTY-EIGHT

How the Burgundians arrived in Hungary

*

WHEN the Burgundians arrived in Hungary, old Hilde-brand came to hear of it and he told his master lord Diet-rich,[1] who was very sorry to learn it; but he asked him to give the gallant knights a warm welcome. Bold Wolfhart had their horses fetched, and a host of stout warriors rode out with Dietrich to the meadows where he meant to greet the visitors.

Here the Burgundians had just packed their splendid pavilions on to their sumpters, and when Hagen saw the others riding far afield he courteously told his lords: 'You brave knights must rise from your seats and go to meet these men, whose intention it is to welcome you. The company riding this way is one that I know well – they are the doughty warriors of Amelungland. Their leader is the lord of Verona, and they are men of spirit. You must not look askance at any service they may render you.'

And now numerous knights and squires dismounted with Dietrich, as the occasion demanded, went up to the visitors from Burgundy, and amicably saluted them. And hear what lord Dietrich said to Uote's sons as he saw them advancing towards him, for he regretted their coming and fondly imagined that Rüdiger knew the facts and had already told them.

'Welcome, you lords, Gunther and Giselher, Gernot and Hagen, and lord Volker and valiant Dancwart, too! Are you

---

1. Dietrich, lord of the Amelungs, better known as Theoderic the Goth, was the hero of a whole cycle of epics. His trusty follower Hilde-brand was the hero of the magnificent 'Lay of Hildebrand' (*c.* A.D. 650). These two characters were introduced rather late into the story of the Nibelungs. See p. 392.

not aware that Kriemhild still weeps bitterly for the hero of Nibelungland?'[1]

'She has good reason for her long mourning,' answered Hagen, 'but he was killed many years past. She ought to love the King of the Huns now, for Siegfried will never come back – he was buried long ago.'

'Let us speak no more of Siegfried's death-blow,' said lord Dietrich of Verona. 'But as long as lady Kriemhild lives, harm can still be done. Be on your guard, protector of the Nibelungs!'[2]

'Why should I be on my guard?' asked the noble King. 'Etzel sent us his envoys to invite us here, and my sister Kriemhild, too, sent urgent messages. What further assurance do I need?'

'Let me give you good advice,' rejoined Hagen. 'Ask lord Dietrich and his worthy knights to go on with what they were saying and unfold lady Kriemhild's designs to you.'

Then the three kings, Gunther, Gernot, and lord Dietrich went aside to confer in private. 'Tell us what you know of the Queen's mind, noble knight of Verona.'

'What is there more to tell you,' replied the lord of Verona, 'than that every morning I hear Etzel's queen piteously weeping and lamenting the death of Siegfried to Almighty God in heaven?'

'The things we have been told of will happen irremediably,' said bold Volker the Fiddler. 'Let us ride to court and see what can happen to us fearless men in Hungary.'

So, nothing daunted, the Burgundians went to court, riding in splendid style according to the custom of their land, and many a brave man among the Huns was most

1. Dietrich warns Gunther and Hagen because legend had it that he, as an exile, and Hagen, as a hostage, were comrades at Etzel's court.

2. The archaic title has shifted from Hagen (see p. 192) to Gunther, who has a better claim to it, according to ancient Germanic notions, since it was always applied to kings. It is ironic that Hagen is more kingly than Gunther in his powers of leadership.

curious to know what Hagen of Troneck looked like. Because of all the many tales told about his slaying of Kriemhild's husband Siegfried of the Netherlands, the strongest of all warriors, numerous questions were asked at court regarding Hagen.

To tell the truth, the hero was well-grown, being broad-chested and long-legged. His hair was flecked with grey, and his gaze was terrible. His carriage was majestic.

Orders were given to lodge the Burgundian knights; but at the instigation of the Queen (who bore him great ill will) Gunther's train were taken elsewhere, as a result of which these squires were later butchered in their quarters. Hagen's brother Dancwart was Marshal, and the Burgundian king entrusted these followers to him and urged him to take good care of them and satisfy their needs, so concerned for their welfare was he.

Fair Kriemhild went with her suite and with perfidy in her heart she welcomed them. Giselher alone did she kiss, after which she took him by the hand. This was not lost on Hagen, who laced his helmet tighter.

'After such a welcome,' said he, 'brave warriors may well bethink themselves. They have one greeting here for the kings, and another for their vassals. It was no good journey that brought us to this festival.'

'Welcome to whomever you are welcome!' she said. 'But *I* shall not greet you for any love between you and me. Tell me what you bring me from Worms beyond the Rhine, that you should be so very welcome to me.'

'Had I but known that knights were meant to bring you gifts,' he replied, 'I am not so poor that I could not have brought you some present here – had I given it more thought.'

'Tell me further: what have you done with the treasure of the Nibelungs? – It was mine, as you well know. *That* is what you should bring me here to Etzel's country!'

'Truly, my lady Kriemhild, it is many a day since I had charge of the treasure of the Nibelungs. My lords commanded it to be sunk in the Rhine,[1] and there it must stay till the end of time!'

'This is just as I thought: not one piece have you brought me, though it was my lawful property and I once had it in my power, so that now I shall spend my days in never-ending sorrow.'

'I have brought you nothing and be damned to you!' retorted Hagen. 'My shield, my corselet, and my bright helmet are burden enough for me. As to this sword in my hand, it is not for you that I bring it.'[2]

'It is forbidden to carry weapons in the King's hall,' said the Queen to the warriors on all sides. 'You knights must surrender them to me and I will have them lodged in safety.'

'Indeed,' said Hagen, 'that shall never happen. I do not aspire to this honour, that you, the gracious mistress of a great prince, should carry my shield or any other of my weapons to my quarters – after all, you are a queen! That is a thing my father did not teach me. I intend to be my own chamberlain.'

'Alas,' cried lady Kriemhild, 'why will my brother and Hagen not let their shields be placed in safety? Someone must have warned them! If I knew who it was he would surely die!'

'It was I that warned the illustrious kings of Burgundy and their vassal, fearless Hagen,' replied King Dietrich angrily. 'Now come on, you she-devil,[3] you must not let me go unpunished!'

Etzel's queen was in great confusion, for she went in bitter fear of Dietrich. She turned away from him at once without another word, except that she darted baleful glances in the direction of her enemies. Then two warriors, lord Dietrich and Hagen, took each other by the hand, and the one lusty warrior said with all courtesy: 'In view of

1. Hagen thus exposes the deception narrated in Chapter 19, but (for all that we can tell) Kriemhild overlooks it (see p. 148).
2. The sword in question is Balmung, Siegfried's sword.
3. See p. 319.

what the Queen has said I am truly sorry you have come to Hungary.' 'Things will right themselves,' replied Hagen of Troneck. Such was the conversation between two brave men. And King Etzel, seeing them talking, began to ask questions.

'I should very much like to know,' said the mighty King, 'who that knight is whom lord Dietrich is welcoming so warmly and who bears himself so proudly. Whoever his father may be, I judge him to be a fine warrior.'

One of Kriemhild's men gave the King this answer: 'He is of the line of Troneck, and his father's name was Aldrian; and however good-humouredly he comports himself here, he is a ferocious man, and I shall convince you through your own eyes that what I say is true.'

'How can I tell that he is so fierce?' – Etzel was still in ignorance of the many foul wiles that Kriemhild was to practise against her kinsmen, with the result that she allowed not one to leave Hungary alive. 'I knew Aldrian well, he was a vassal of mine,' continued Etzel, 'and he won great honour here with me. I made him a knight and gave him presents of my gold, and faithful Helche, too, had a deep affection for him. Thus I know all about Hagen from those days. There were two fine boys that came to be my hostages, he and Walter of Spain, and they grew up to manhood here. Hagen I sent home, but Walter ran away with Hildegund.'[1]

Etzel was recalling events long past. And now he had recognized his friend of Troneck who in his youth had rendered him diverse mighty services, though he was to slay many a dear friend of his, now that he was old.

1. See Appendix 6, p. 404, under 'Walter of Spain'.

CHAPTER TWENTY-NINE

How Kriemhild upbraided Hagen and he did not rise to greet her

*

THE two excellent warriors, Hagen of Troneck and lord Dietrich, now parted company, and Gunther's liegeman looked over his shoulder for a comrade-in-arms. Nor was he long in finding one, for he saw Volker standing beside Giselher and he asked the skilful Fiddler to accompany him in full knowledge of his fierce courage – Volker was altogether a brave and worthy knight.

The Kings were left standing in the courtyard[1] while Hagen and Volker alone crossed over to a spacious palace away on the far side, fearing no man's enmity like the rare warriors they were. It was in fact Kriemhild's palace, and they sat down in front of it with their backs to the great hall, and as their magnificent armour shone on their bodies many who saw it would gladly have known who they were. Indeed, the Huns' retainers stared at the proud warriors as though they were strange beasts, while Kriemhild, too, espying them through a window, was downcast for the second time. It reminded her of her grief and she began to weep, so that Etzel's men were greatly puzzled as to what had weighed her down so suddenly.

'It is Hagen who has done so, you brave warriors,' she answered.

'But how did that happen?' they asked the lady. 'It was only recently we saw you so happy. If anyone has wronged you, and you tell us to avenge it, it shall cost him his life, be he never so daring.'

'I should be forever obliged to whoever avenged my wrongs and would gladly give him all that he asked for.

1. See p. 304f.

I kneel before you and beg you,' said Etzel's queen. –
'Avenge me and kill Hagen!'

Sixty brave men armed themselves, bent thus treacher-
ously on slaying Hagen, the most valiant knight, in order
to gratify Kreimhild, and with him the Fiddler, too. But
seeing how few of them there were, she said fiercely to those
warriors:

'Abandon your high hopes – so meagre a band as yours
could never take on Hagen. For however strong and brave
Hagen of Troneck may be, Volker the Fiddler – the man
sitting beside him – is far mightier, he is an ugly man to
deal with. You must not attack these warriors at such
unfavourable odds.'

Hearing this, more of them made ready to the number of
four hundred knights, so obsessed was she with doing the
pair some harm (and, indeed, the two came into grave
peril, later).

When the Queen saw that her retainers were well armed
she said to the valorous warriors: 'You stay here and
wait a while. I intend to go to my enemies wearing my
crown and you shall hear the wrongs with which I shall
upbraid Gunther's liegeman, Hagen of Troneck. I know him
to be of so arrogant a temper that he will not deny them to
my face. Then I shall not care what vengeance overtakes
him.'

The bold Fiddler caught sight of the noble Queen
descending a stair that led down from the palace, and, see-
ing it, valiant Volker addressed his comrade thus:

'Look, friend Hagen, the woman who invited us here
so treacherously is coming this way. I have never seen so
many men escort a queen in such warlike array with
drawn swords in their hands. Do you know if they bear you
any grudge, my friend? I would advise you to guard your
life and honour all the more for it, that would be a wise
thing to do. To my mind they are in an angry mood, and
some of them, too, are so broad in the chest that anyone
who means to defend himself should lose no time in doing
so; for I fancy they are wearing their bright mail-shirts

beneath their silken robes, yet whom they have in mind
with it I cannot say.'

'I have no doubt whatever that it is all aimed at me,'
said brave Hagen wrathfully, 'with their gleaming swords
in their hands. But they are not the men to stop me from
riding back to Burgundy! Tell me, Volker my friend, will
you stand by me if Kriemhild's men attack me? Let me
hear your answer, by the love you bear me, and I shall be
deeply bound to you till the end of my days.'

'You can count on my aid for sure,' replied the Minstrel,
'even if I were to see the King making for us with all his
warriors. Fear shall not make me desert you by yielding so
much as one foot as long as I remain alive!'

'God in Heaven reward you, noble Volker! If they
attack me what more shall I need? Since you are going to
stand by me, as I have heard you say, those warriors had
better come warily.'

'Now let us rise from our seats as she passes,' said the
Minstrel, 'for she is a queen, you know. Let us show her
the courtesy that is due to a noble lady. Doing so, we shall
enhance our own good names.'

'No, by the affection you bear me!' answered Hagen.
'If I were to make any step in her direction those knights
would think that fear prompted me. I shall not rise from
this bench to suit any of them. It is seemlier for the two of us
to refrain. Why should I honour one who is my mortal
enemy? This I shall never do as long as there is life in my
body! However much Kriemhild hates me, it leaves me
quite unmoved.'

So saying, Hagen provocatively laid across his knees a
dazzling sword from whose pommel there shone a brilliant
jasper, greener than grass, and Kriemhild knew it at once
for Siegfried's and, recognizing it, was inevitably distressed.
Its hilt was of gold, its sheath a scarlet orphrey. The sight
of it revived her sorrow and she began to weep; and this,
I fancy, was why Hagen did it.

Brave Volker drew towards him on the bench a mighty
fiddle-bow that you would have said was a sword – for it

was broad and very keen! And thus the pair sat there, serene and unafraid. And so lordly did they think themselves that they declined to rise from their seat in fear of anyone, and the noble Queen therefore went up to them and offered them a hostile greeting.

'Tell me, lord Hagen,' she said, 'who sent for you who have made so bold as to come here, knowing full well how you have wronged me? If you had any sense you would never have done so.'

'Nobody sent for me,' answered Hagen. 'Three warriors were invited to Hungary. They are accounted my overlords and accordingly I am their liegeman. I have never yet stayed behind while they went to a foreign court.'

'Tell me further,' she said. 'Why did you do the deed for which you have earned my hatred? – You slew Siegfried, my dear husband, for which I shall have cause to weep till the end of my days!'

'Enough has been said, why continue?' he asked. 'I am that same Hagen who slew Siegfried the doughty warrior! How dearly he had to pay for lady Kriemhild's maligning of fair Brunhild! There is no denying it, mighty Queen, I bear the entire guilt of your ruinous loss. Now let anyone who likes avenge it, be he man or woman. Unless I were minded to lie to you, I must admit that I have wronged you greatly!'

'Do you hear, you knights?' she cried, 'He does not deny that he is the cause of all my sorrows. Whatever fate were to overtake him in consequence, it would not trouble me.' But her fire-eaters looked at one another; and if anyone had started fighting, such deeds would have been done that the two comrades would have taken the honours, for they had proved themselves in battle time and time again. Thus the others were forced by fear to abandon their foolhardy enterprise.

'Why do you look at me?' asked one of Kriemhild's knights. 'I take back what I promised – I do not wish to die in exchange for anyone's gifts. Cannot you see that King Etzel's queen is luring us to our doom?'

'That is just what I think,' chimed in another. 'I would not face this Fiddler, not if I were given whole dungeons full of good red gold – such wild glances have I seen in his eyes! Besides, I know Hagen from the days of his youth – I do not need to be told about him. I have seen him in action in more than a score of battles in which he brought mortal grief to women without number. He and Walter of Spain marched on many an expedition together and fought many a battle hereabouts in Etzel's service and to the honour of our King, so that we must concede in all fairness that Hagen has won great glory. Moreover he was still a boy in years – how grey they have all grown, those who were young then! But now he has reached full maturity and he is a bloodthirsty man. Add to that, he carries Balmung, which he came by very evilly.'

This settled it that there was to be no fighting, to the Queen's heartfelt sorrow. Fearing death from the Fiddler, her valorous knights turned back – and they assuredly had reason to do so!

'We have clearly seen that we shall find enemies here, as was foretold to us,' said the Fiddler. 'Let us join the Kings at court, then none will dare attack our lords.'

How often men abandon their plans from fear when one friend stands by another in the loyal way he ought, so that if they are men of sense their enemies take no action! – Widespread harm can be prevented by the use of good sense.

'I will do as you say,' answered Hagen. Thus they went and joined the handsome knights where they were standing in the courtyard in the press of those who were welcoming them.

'How long do you mean to stand there and be jostled?'[1] bold Volker asked his lords very audibly. 'You must go to court and learn from the King what he intends.'

At this, the good warriors paired off, the Prince of Verona

---

1. Courtesy demanded that the natives should crowd round the guests and try to elbow their way in to have a look at them: but Volker fears that an attempt might be made on their lives.

taking mighty Gunther of Burgundy by the hand, and Irnfrid bold Gernot, while Rüdiger went to court with Giselher. But whoever went to court with whom, Volker and Hagen remained inseparable till a great battle ended their lives. Before long noble ladies were bitterly to rue their partnership.

In the company of the kings the bystanders saw a thousand brave retainers go to court and, over and above these, sixty picked warriors who had come with them to Hungary and whom bold Hagen had taken from his domain. Two men of rare excellence, Hawart and Iring by name, were walking companionably beside the kings; and Dancwart and Wolfhart, a most distinguished knight, outdid all others with the fine manners they displayed.

When the lord of the Rhinelands entered the palace mighty Etzel saw him come in and at once sprang up from his throne – never did a king salute his guests with such fine ceremony!

'Welcome, lord Gunther, and also lord Gernot, and your brother Giselher too! I sent you my humble respects in Worms across the Rhine in all sincerity and affection! All your followers, too, are welcome to me. And you are very welcome here, brave Volker and Hagen, both to me and my lady, who sent you many messages to the Rhine.'

'So I have heard repeatedly,' said Hagen of Troneck. 'Had I not come to Hungary for love of my lords I should have ridden here in your honour.'

Their illustrious host took his dear guests by the hand and led them to the throne on which he himself had been sitting. Then with great alacrity the butlers poured mead, and wine of grape and mulberry for them in broad drinking cups of gold, and the strangers were pledged very warmly.

'I assure you that nothing could give me greater pleasure in the world than this your coming here to visit me, you warriors,' said King Etzel, 'and it has also greatly cheered the Queen. But when I consider all the high-born guests whom I have had here, I am at a loss to know what I have done that you have never cared to come and see us. But now that I see you here this affords me pleasure!'

'And you may well be pleased to see them,' said proud Rüdiger, 'for the affection that my lady's kinsmen entertain towards you is good and true, and they have brought with them under your roof crowds of splendid knights!'

It was on Midsummer's Eve that their lordships had arrived at the court of mighty Etzel, and seldom if ever has one heard of such lofty marks of respect as those with which he received them. But now it was time for their repast, and the King went with them to table; and never did a host sit among his guests so festively. They were given meat and drink in abundance and their every wish was attended to, for great prodigies had been told of those heroes.

CHAPTER THIRTY

How Hagen and Volker kept watch

*

THE day drew to its end, the night came on, and the travel-weary knights wondered anxiously when they could go to bed and rest themselves. Hagen mentioned this to Etzel, and he at once gave his people the sign.

'God bless you,' said Gunther to his host, 'we should like to go to bed! Please give us leave to retire. We shall come again tomorrow morning if that is your pleasure.'

As happy as could be, Etzel left his guests, and they were then hemmed in by a jostling throng. 'How dare you clutter the feet of these warriors?' cried bold Volker to the Huns. 'If you do not stop, something will happen to you! I shall strike one or other of you such a thwack with my fiddle-bow that if anyone loves him he will have reason to lament it. Now make room for us to pass – you would be well advised! They insist on being called "knights", but they are not knights at heart!'

Hearing the Fiddler speak so angrily, brave Hagen looked over his shoulder and said: 'It is good advice the brave Minstrel gives you, you men of Kriemhild. You ought to go to your quarters. I doubt whether any will bring off what you have a mind to do. But if you are spoiling for a fight, then come tomorrow morning, but let us wanderers rest in comfort now. I thought that was the way true warriors always agreed to do things.'

The guests were conducted into a spacious hall which they found to be provided for them over its whole extent with magnificent, roomy beds: yet lady Kriemhild was plotting bitterest pain for them. There were many elaborate quilts there, made from shimmering brocades of Arras, and the finest coverlets of Arabian silk, trimmed with dazzling borders. There were also very many bedcovers of

226

ermine, and of black sable too, under which they were to find their ease that night, till the bright dawn – never did a king lie with his retinue in such magnificence!

'Alas for the night that we must pass here,' cried Young Giselher, 'and alas for my friends who have accompanied us! Although my sister has treated us so kindly I fear we shall have to die through her contriving!'

'Now abandon your cares,' said Hagen the warrior, 'for I intend to stand guard myself tonight, and I trust myself to keep us safe till daybreak, have no fear of that. Then each man for himself.'

They all thanked him with a bow and went to their beds; nor was it long before those splendid men had lain down. But meanwhile bold Hagen armed himself.

'If you have no objection, Hagen,' said Sir Volker the Fiddler, 'I should like to keep watch with you tonight till morning.'

Hagen thanked Volker most affectionately. 'God in Heaven reward you, dear Volker. If ever I were in peril I could wish for no other than you alone to share my troubles. I shall repay you well, unless death prevents me.'

And so the two together drew on their shining armour and then each laid hold of his shield, went outside the building, took his stand before the door, and loyally kept watch over the guests.

Brave Volker leant his good shield against the palace wall and went to fetch his fiddle, whereupon in a way that was all his own he entertained his friends. He sat down on the threshold below the great door of the hall – never was there a bolder fiddler – and he brought such sweet notes from the strings that those proud knights so far from home all applauded him. And now the strings were sounding so that the whole palace re-echoed with it, for Volker was very accomplished as well as very brave and strong. Then he played ever more softly and sweetly till he lulled many a careworn man to sleep who lay there in his bed. And when he saw that they were slumbering, the warrior took up his shield again, went out of the hall, took his stand before the door, and guarded the visitors from Kriemhild's men.

In the middle of the night – I doubt whether it was earlier – bold Volker saw the gleam of a helmet far out in the darkness somewhere. – Kriemhild's vassals would dearly have loved to harm the guests!

'Friend Hagen,' said the Fiddler, 'this trouble should be borne by us together. I can see some armed men standing in front of this hall. To my mind they are going to attack us.'

'Then say no more,' replied Hagen, 'and let them come nearer. Before they know that we are here we shall knock their helmets askew for them with some blows from our two swords and send them back to Kriemhild all the worse for it!'

But one of the Hunnish knights was quick to see that the door was guarded and promptly said: 'We cannot carry out our plan. I see the Fiddler standing sentinel there. On his head he wears a flashing helmet, hard, burnished, strong, and unscarred, while his chain-mail darts flames like fire. At his side stands Hagen – the foreigners are well guarded.' The Huns turned back without more ado.

Seeing this, Volker said angrily to his comrade: 'Let me leave the building and join those knights of Kriemhild's – I should like to have a word with them.'

'No, do not, for my sake,' answered Hagen. 'If you leave the palace those valorous knights might perhaps get you into such straits that I should have to come to your aid even though it meant the death of my kinsmen. Were we both to become involved in the fighting, two or four of them could quickly run into the palace and do us such harm among the sleepers as we should never cease to lament.'

'Then let us at least make it known to Kriemhild's men that I saw them, lest they have grounds for denying that they were bent on a treacherous deed.' And he at once called out to them: 'Why do you go armed like this, valorous knights? Are you off on a plundering expedition? If so, you must take me and my comrade to help you there!'

But nobody answered him. 'Fie, you vile cowards!' shouted the trusty warrior angrily. 'Would you have murdered us in our sleep? The like has never happened yet to good fighting men such as we are!'

The Queen was told in all detail how her emissaries had failed in their purpose and, understandably, she was deeply vexed. Nevertheless in her fierce hatred she devised other means, thanks to which brave warriors had to perish in the end.

CHAPTER THIRTY-ONE

How they went to church

*

'My chain-mail has grown so cool on me,' said Volker, 'that I fancy the night cannot last much longer. I sense from the breeze that it will soon be daylight.' And so they woke many men who still lay sleeping. And now indeed the bright morning sent its rays into the hall to light the guests, while Hagen roused the knights everywhere, asking whether they wished to go to mass in the cathedral, for there was a great pealing of bells in keeping with the Christian rite. But Christians and heathen sang mass differently, as was very evident – they were at variance in this.[1] Gunther's men *did* wish to go to church and they had immediately risen from their beds and were lacing themselves into clothes of such quality that no knights ever brought better into any realm.

But this was not to Hagen's liking. 'You warriors must wear other clothes than these. Surely you all know how things stand? Now that we are well acquainted with vile Kriemhild's plans you should be carrying swords, not roses; wearing good, bright helmets, not gem-encrusted chaplets! I tell you we shall be forced to fight today, so you should not have silken shirts but hauberks; not luxurious cloaks but broad, stout shields: so that if anyone comes to blows with you, you can give a good account of yourselves. My most dear lords, my kinsmen and our vassals, you should go to church with willing heart and pray to Almighty God to look with mercy on your fears and perils, since I would have you know for certain that death is

1. The medieval Europeans imagined pagan rites to be much like their own, with a difference. Their ignorance concerning the religious practices and general outlook of others was matched only by the ignorance of these others concerning theirs.

drawing near. Do not forget your sins, and stand with rapt devotion in the presence of the Lord. Illustrious warriors, I wish to warn you of this: unless God in Heaven wills it, you will never hear mass again!'

And so the kings and their men went to the minster, and Hagen told them to halt within the sacred precincts and not lose touch with one another. 'No one has any idea as yet what the Huns may do to us,' said he. 'Therefore, my friends, lay your shields at your feet and pay back any incivilities with deep wounds that let the life out, then you will be known for worthy warriors. This is my advice.' Then those two, Volker and Hagen, went and stood before the door of the spacious minster, and they did this because they had an idea that the vengeful Queen might have to jostle past them.

And now the lord of the land and his fair consort arrived. The persons of the brave knights who escorted them were adorned with splendid robes, and you could see clouds of dust rising high on the air at the approach of Kriemhild's squadrons.

Observing the kings and their followers thus armed, the mighty lord of the Huns was quick to ask: 'How is it that I see my friends with their helmets on? I protest I am very sorry if anyone has wronged them. I shall be glad to make amends to them in whatever way they please, if someone has vexed their spirits. I shall find a way to convince them that I regret it deeply. I am willing to do whatever they command.'

'Nobody has wronged us,' answered Hagen. 'It is my lords' custom to go armed for three whole days at all festivities. We should certainly tell Etzel if anyone offended us.'

Kriemhild heard all that Hagen said and with what savage enmity did she look him in the eyes! Nevertheless she was loath to divulge the true usage of Burgundy for all her long acquaintance with it. However great and fierce her hatred for the Burgundians, Etzel would have forestalled what happened later had anyone told him the position, but so haughty were they all that not one of them informed him.

A great press of people accompanied the Queen to church, but Hagen and Volker declined to stand aside as much as two hand breadths, to the great annoyance of the Huns who were thus forced to jostle with the gay warriors. Etzel's chamberlains did not like it and, believe me, they would have roused the others to fury, only they dared not do so in the King's presence. Thus there was much pushing and shoving, yet nothing more.

When the service was over and they were all leaving, crowds of Huns mounted their chargers. There were many comely maidens in Kriemhild's train and no less than seven thousand knights rode with her. She did mighty Etzel the pleasure of joining him at the windows with her ladies, for they all wished to see those vivacious knights show their horsemanship – and oh what numbers of exotic warriors rode in the courtyard before them!

Bold Dancwart, the Marshal, had also come with the squires (his sovereign's train from Burgundy) and so their mounts stood ready saddled for the Nibelungs. And when the kings and their men were up, burly Volker suggested they should ride the bohort[1] in their native style, and this was followed by some magnificent riding, for Volker's proposal was far from displeasing them! The bohort with all its din grew very intense. Many men assembled in that vast courtyard, and Etzel and Kriemhild began to watch it, too.

Six hundred of Dietrich's knights rode to the bohort to meet the visitors from Burgundy, in the hope of finding some sport with them, and if their lord had allowed it they would gladly have joined in. What troops of fine warriors rode after them! But this was reported to Dietrich, and he forbade them to joust with Gunther's vassals, and beyond doubt it was right of him to do so, since he had fears for his men.

When those of Verona had left the field, Rüdiger's men from Pöchlarn to the number of five hundred came riding

1. See p. 21n.

past the hall with their shields held ready for the fray; but the Margrave would rather they had not done so. He therefore wisely rode to his knights through the formation, and asked them whether they could not see that Gunther's men were in an ugly mood – so that he would be glad if they would give up the bohort.

And when those spirited warriors had left the visitors we are told that the Thuringians arrived and also a full thousand Danes, causing the splinters to fly up in clouds under their lance thrusts!

Irnfrit and Hawart,[1] whom the Rhinelanders proudly awaited, now rode into the bohort. The latter delivered many jousts against the Thuringians and countless fine shields were riddled by their thrusts.

Now lord Bloedelin came on with three thousand men. Etzel and Kriemhild saw him arrive, since all this knightly sport was taking place before their eyes. The Queen watched it with pleasure in the hope that the Burgundians might come to harm. And now Schrutan, Gibech, Ramung, and Hornboge entered the bohort after the Hunnish fashion and paused opposite the Burgundians – then the splinters were sent twirling high over the King's hall! But whatever they did there it was but harmless noise, with the palace and hall resounding loudly, as Gunther's men struck the shields and covered themselves with glory.

Their sport had become so fast and furious that the glistening sweat flowed through the housings of the good chargers they bestrode, as with lofty disdain the Burgundians tried conclusions with the Huns.

'I doubt if these knights dare stand up to us,' said bold Sir Volker the Minstrel, 'but I have always heard it said that they detested us. Now there could never be a better opportunity! – Take our mounts to stable, squires!' he continued. 'And then let us ride again towards evening, at the proper time. What if the Queen were to declare us the winners!'

They then saw a man riding up to them with such

1. The leaders of the Thuringians and the Danes respectively.

bravado that no other Hun could have equalled him – he may well have had a darling mistress at this time and he was decked out in his finery like a young wife of the nobility.

'How can I let this pass?' rejoined Volker. 'This lady's pet must take a hard knock! No one shall deter me but it shall cost him his life! What do I care if it angers Kriemhild?'

'No, for my sake, don't,' interposed King Gunther. 'If we attack them first we shall earn the blame. Let the Huns start it, that would be far better.'

Meanwhile Etzel still sat beside his Queen.

'I shall join in the bohort,' announced Hagen. 'Let us show the knights and ladies our skill on horseback – that would be a good move, for they do not concede knightly prowess to any of King Gunther's men.'

Volker wheeled round to renew the bohort, and this gave many ladies untold sorrow in days to come, for he thrust his spear clean through the body of that gorgeously turned-out Hun,[1] a blow that was to be lamented by women and maidens alike. Hagen at once spurred to the scene of the joust with sixty of his men at full gallop to cover the Fiddler while Etzel and Kriemhild looked on, noting every detail. Nor did the three kings wish to leave their Minstrel amidst their enemies unsupported, and so a thousand knights rode up in intricate formation and haughtily imposed their will.

When the richly decked Hun was killed the cries of his kindred complaining rose loud on the air. 'Who did it?' 'It was Fiddler Volker, the bold Minstrel!' At once the dead margrave's Hunnish clansmen called for swords and shields with the intention of killing Volker, while King Etzel left his window and raced out to the field. A great clamour arose from the concourse on all sides as the

---

1. The rules of the bohort required all lances to be blunted; thus, since there is no evidence that Volker cheated in this respect, this feat must be ascribed to his uncommon strength and skill. He further seems to have used some guile to mask the blow, because Etzel is convinced that it was due to an accident.

Burgundian kings and their followers alighted before the hall and thrust their mounts behind them. Then King Etzel arrived and at once proceeded to settle the matter. Tearing a mighty sword from the hand of one of the dead Hun's relations, Etzel beat them all back, for he was in a towering rage. 'How I should have failed in my duty as host towards these warriors if you were to kill this Minstrel whilst he is a guest of mine!' said King Etzel. 'That would be disgraceful. I saw very clearly how he was riding when he ran our compatriot through and that it happened accidentally as a result of his horse's stumbling. I command you to leave my guests in peace!' And he himself escorted them. Their chargers were led away to their stables, for they had many squires in attendance who saw to their every need.

The King went into his palace with his friends and allowed no further outbreaks of anger. The tables were set up and water was served for their hands. The Rhenish knights had mighty enemies enough about them! But it was a long time before their lordships took their seats, for Kriemhild's griefs would not leave her any peace.

'Prince of Verona,' she said, 'I need your counsel, help, and protection in my affairs, which are in a parlous state.'

'Whoever attacks the Nibelungs for the sake of whatever treasure,' broke in doughty Hildebrand, 'will do so without me! He might well regret it – those fine warriors have not been downed yet!'

'Do not ask this thing, great Queen,' said Dietrich with all the courtesy that was his. 'Your kinsmen have not done me such wrong that I should wish to do battle with the valiant knights. Queen of an illustrious King, your request does you little honour with its plotting against the lives of your kindred, who came here in good faith. Siegfried will not be avenged by Dietrich.'

Finding no treachery in the lord of Verona, she at once swore to give Bloedelin some broad march-lands formerly held by Nuodung: but Bloedelin was later slain by Dancwart, with the result that he forgot the gift.

'Pray help me, lord Bloedelin,' she said. 'My enemies,

the murderers of my dear husband Siegfried, are within these walls, and I shall be forever devoted to whoever helps me avenge him!'

'My lady, let me tell you that I dare not make any attempt on them for fear of Etzel, since he is very glad to see your kinsmen, madam. If I were to do them any harm, the King would not condone it.'

'Do not say so, lord Bloedelin. *I* shall always be your friend, and I will reward you with gold and silver and a lovely girl – Nuodung's destined bride – with whose entrancing person you would be glad to take your pleasure. I will give you castles, and lands to match, so that were you to become lord of the marches where Nuodung held sway you could live happily, noble knight, all your life. I shall faithfully carry out what I have promised you today.'

Hearing what the reward was to be (the lady was very acceptable to him by virtue of her good looks) Bloedelin fancied he would win the charming woman by force of arms. But in fact, as a result, he had to lose his life.

'Go back to the hall,' he said to the Queen, 'before anyone gets wind of it, and then I shall start an uproar. I shall make Hagen pay dearly for what he did to you: I shall deliver him to you in bonds, King Gunther's vassal or no. Now, all my men, to arms!' cried Bloedelin. 'We are going to attack our enemies in their quarters – Etzel's queen insists on my doing so and we knights shall have to risk our lives.'

Leaving Bloedelin resolved on battle, the Queen went to table with King Etzel and his men. She had laid a deadly plot against their guests.

Kriemhild's old grief was embedded deep in her heart. Since there was no beginning the fighting in any other way, she had Etzel's son carried to the board. (How could a woman ever do a more dreadful thing in pursuance of her revenge?)[1] Four of Etzel's followers went immediately and returned bearing the young Prince Ortlieb to the King's

1. See pp. 302f. for an explanation of this whole passage.

table, where Hagen, too, was seated, owing to whose murderous hate the boy must needs soon die.

Seeing his son there, the mighty king kindly observed to his wife's relations: 'Look, my friends, this is your sister's and my only son. This could serve you well one day; for if he takes after his relations he will grow up a valiant man – mighty, high-born, handsome, and strong! And if I live for any time I shall make over a dozen lands to him. Thus young Ortlieb could render you great service. I therefore have pleasure in asking you, when you ride home to the Rhinelands, to take your nephew with you and treat him with signal favour by rearing him to a life of honour until he reaches manhood. Then, being fully grown, if anyone has wronged you in the countries around you he will help you to avenge it.' Etzel's consort Kriemhild also heard these words.

'Were he to grow to manhood,' said Hagen, 'these warriors might well rely on him: but the young Prince has an ill-fated look. You will never see me ride to court to wait on Ortlieb.'

King Etzel looked at Hagen, deeply pained at his words; and although that serene monarch did not refer to it, it saddened his heart and weighed upon his spirit. Nor had Hagen meant it as a joke. Moreover, what he had said about their King's son wounded all his great lords with him too, and they chafed at having to suffer it in silence. They had no inkling of the deed that Hagen was to do.

CHAPTER THIRTY-TWO

How Dancwart slew Bloedelin

*

BLOEDELIN's stalwarts were all in readiness and they set out with a thousand hauberks and came to where Dancwart sat at table with the squires, and there the bitterest of battles broke out among those warriors.

When lord Bloedelin went up to the board, Dancwart the Marshal received him with every attention. 'Welcome to our quarters, my lord Bloedelin! I wonder what it is that brings you here?'

'You have no cause to bid me welcome,' replied Bloedelin. 'My coming means the end of you – your brother Hagen murdered Siegfried! You and many other knights will have to pay for this in Hungary.'

'Do not say so, lord Bloedelin,' answered Dancwart, 'otherwise we shall dearly regret our visit here. I myself was a little child when Siegfried lost his life,[1] so I cannot imagine what King Etzel's queen has to reproach me with.'

'I can tell you no more than this: it was your kinsmen Gunther and Hagen that did the deed. Defend yourselves, you wretched foreigners – nothing can save you now. You must stand forfeit to Kriemhild with your lives!'

'Then you mean to go through with it?' asked Dancwart. 'In that case I am sorry I ever appealed to you. It would have been better had I refrained.' And the valiant warrior leapt up from the table, drew his great sharp sword and struck Bloedelin such a violent blow that – in a trice! – his head lay at his feet. 'Let that[2] be your nuptial gift to Nuodung's betrothed, whose loves you were hoping to

1. On the contrary, Dancwart was one of four picked men on the wooing expedition to Iceland. See p. 54.
2. Bloedelin's head.

enjoy! They can affiance her to another man tomorrow: if he wants the bridal gift[1], the same will happen to him.' (A loyal-hearted Hun had told him that the Queen was plotting great ills for them).

Seeing their lord dead on the ground, Bloedelin's men would no longer stand it from the strangers. Raising their swords aloft, they sprang at the boys in a fury (though many were to rue it later).

'You see for yourselves, noble squires, which way things are going,' shouted Dancwart to his retinue. 'Now defend yourselves here in this foreign land – I swear you have great need to do so, despite the sweet messages which noble Kriemhild sent us.'

Those who had no swords to hand groped below the benches and lifted from under their feet diverse long foot-rests – the squires of Burgundy were not going to take it lying down! – and wielding these heavy stools they inflicted scores of great bruises through the helmets. How fiercely those forlorn youngsters defended themselves! They eventually drove the armed men from the building, though not before five hundred or more of these had fallen, while the squires themselves ran red with blood.

The startling news that Bloedelin and many of his men had been slain by Hagen's brother and the squires was then reported to Etzel's warriors, and deeply did it grieve them. And before the King came to hear of it two thousand Huns or more armed themselves in their frenzy, sought out the squires and – what was to happen had to happen – left not one of them alive. Those traitors brought a vast army to that building from which the young foreigners offered a spirited defence – but what did their courage avail them? They had to die, and from this was soon to arise a gruesome tragedy, for hear this monstrous thing: nine thousand

---

1. The *brûtmiete* of the original, recording the only instance of this word, ought to mean 'bride-price', which in medieval times may have been converted into a gift for the bride. 'Bride-price' would afford an inaccurate metaphor in this context.

squires lay dead there, and over and above that a dozen knights of Dancwart's following! As to Dancwart himself, he stood amid his enemies all alone!

The din of battle was silenced, the clash of arms had died away, and Dancwart looked over his shoulder. 'Alas for the friends whom I have lost!' he cried. 'Now to my sorrow I must stand alone among my enemies!' Sword blows thick and fast fell on his one body. But many a fighter's widow had to weep for that in the end, for, lowering the grip of his shield so that he could hold it the higher, he made the blood flow in streams through corselet after corselet.

'Alas for this sad mischief,' said the son of Aldrian. 'Make way, you Hunnish knights! Let me get to the open air so that the breezes may cool me, battle-weary man.' And they saw the hero come forward with majestic stride. But when the tired warrior leapt out from the building fresh swords clanged on his helmet with redoubled force, since those who had not witnessed his marvellous feats sprang forward to meet the man from Burgundy.

'I would to God I had a messenger who would tell my brother Hagen what peril I am in as I stand and face these warriors!' said Dancwart. 'He would either help me out or die fighting beside me.'

'You will have to be the messenger,' said some Hunnish warriors. 'When we carry your dead body to your brother, only then will he know from the sight what sorrow is! What great harm you have done here to King Etzel!'

'Leave your threats and move aside, or I will make the corselets of some few of you run with blood! I intend to take my news to court myself and make complaint to my lords of my great troubles in person!'

Dancwart made himself so hateful to Etzel's vassals that they dared not oppose him with their swords; instead they hurled so many spears into his shield that the sheer weight of it made him drop it. And now that he was shieldless they imagined they would get the better of him: but you should have seen the deep wounds that he dealt them through their helmets, reaping high honour thereby! They attacked him from both sides – but more than one entered the fray too precipitately! He stood at bay before his enemies like a wild boar before the hounds in the forest – what greater courage could he have shown? He constantly renewed his progress with fresh streams of hot blood – no lone warrior could ever put up a better fight against his enemies than he had done. Thus gloriously did Hagen's brother make his way to court!

Hearing the clang of swords, numerous stewards and butlers flung down the food and drink they were carrying to the royal table, and a new throng of sturdy enemies beset Dancwart below the stair.

'How now, you stewards?' cried the weary knight. 'You should be attending to the guests in friendly fashion and serving good food for your masters, leaving me to report to my dear lords.'

If any were impelled by their valour to run and meet him from the stair he struck one or other of them such a heavy sword-blow that they had to fall back again in fear.

Dancwart had performed mighty prodigies of high courage.

CHAPTER THIRTY-THREE

How the Burgundians fought with the Huns

*

WHEN bold Dancwart entered at the door, his armour all streaming with blood and his strong sword naked in his hand, he told Etzel's men to stand back.

'You have been sitting here too long, brother Hagen!' he shouted. 'I cry out our injury to you and God in Heaven: our knights and squires have been butchered in their quarters!'

'Who did this deed?' Hagen called over to him.

'Lord Bloedelin and his men! And I tell you, he has dearly paid for it, since I cut off his head with my own hands.'

'It is but a minor misfortune when it is related of a warrior that his life was taken by a hero: comely women should bewail him all the less for that. But tell me, brother Dancwart, why are you so red with gore? I fear you must be badly wounded. If the man who did this is anywhere in the country it will cost him his life, unless the foul fiend save him.'

'You see me sound in wind and limb, it is only my covering that is bloody. It comes from the wounds of other men, of whom I have slain so many today that were I put on oath I could not name the number.'

'Then guard the door for us, brother Dancwart,' Hagen answered, 'and do not let a Hun out through it. Meanwhile I will have a word with these knights as our predicament demands of us. They have struck down our squires without provocation on our part.'

'If I am to stand usher,' answered the valiant man, 'I shall know how to give excellent service to such mighty kings. I shall take charge of the stair in a way that shall earn me some praise.' There was nothing Kriemhild's knights could have wanted less.

'I wonder what the Hunnish knights have to whisper about here in the hall,' rejoined Hagen. 'I fancy they would rather be quit of the doorkeeper and of the court-gossip he has told the Burgundians. I have long heard tell how Kriemhild would not forgo her grievance: therefore let us now drink to the dead[1] and so repay the King's wine – with the young lord of the Huns as the first.' And Hagen the doughty warrior struck Ortlieb so that the blood washed along the sword to his hands and the boy's head fell into the Queen's lap, unleashing a vast and savage slaughter among warriors. Next he deal the tutor who had charge of the boy a vehement two-handed blow so that in an instant his head lay on the floor by the table – such pitiful wages did he mete out to that pedagogue. Hagen then caught sight of a minstrel standing by Etzel's table and in his fury he made straight for him and struck off his right hand as it lay upon his fiddle. – 'Take that for your embassy to Burgundy!'

'Alas, for my hand!' cried Werbel the Minstrel. 'What wrong have I done you, lord Hagen of Troneck? I came to your master's country in all good faith. How shall I set the strings a-sounding now that I have lost my hand?'

Little did Hagen care whether he ever played again. Instead he began to deal raging death-wounds among Etzel's warriors and to slay them one after another. Great was their number whom he sent to their deaths in that hall.

Valiant Volker leapt up from the table and, wielding his fiddle bow, made loud music; Gunther's Minstrel played some very rough tunes – and what scores of enemies this earned him among the fearless Huns!

The three noble kings also sprang up from the board in the hope of arranging a settlement before more damage was done; but for all their shrewdness they were unable to put a stop to it now that Volker and Hagen were roused. Then,

---

1. A reference to an ancient Germanic custom of drinking in memory of the dead. Hagen may already number Ortlieb among them; or is this a grim allusion to Siegfried's death, the subject of Krienhild's 'grievance'? Cf. the *Thiðrekssaga*, p. 382.

seeing that the conflict was not to be composed, the lord of the Rhinelands himself hacked gaping wounds a-plenty through his enemies' bright chain-mail, giving ample proof that he, too, was a doughty fighting-man. Next, mighty Gernot entered the fray, slaying many a Hunnish warrior with the keen sword Rüdiger had given him and doing much hurt to Etzel's knights. Lastly, the young son of lady Uote leapt into battle, and his sword went clanging gloriously through the helmets of Etzel's Huns, so that brave Giselher achieved great marvels there. However gallant the kings and their men all were, it was Giselher who stood foremost fronting the enemey: he was an excellent warrior, and with the wounds which he inflicted he toppled many into the blood.

Etzel's men defended themselves stoutly; but the visitors traversed the King's hall from end to end, slashing with their bright swords like boars, whereupon a great sound of wailing met the ear from all sides. And now those who were outside wished to join their friends within but they made little headway at the door, while those who were within would dearly have liked to leave: yet Dancwart allowed none to pass either up or down the stair. Nevertheless, such a mighty press arose before the door and there was such a loud ringing of helmets under the sword-blows that bold Dancwart came into great difficulties; but, prompted by the love he bore him, his brother took care of that.

'Can you see my brother over there, comrade, at grips with Hunnish warriors under a rain of blows?' he bawled across to Volker. 'Rescue my brother, friend, before we lose him.'

'Rely on me,' replied the Minstrel. And he began to fiddle his way through the palace, making his hard sword ring out as he swung it time and time again, and earning the Rhenish warriors' warm applause.

'You have endured great hardship today,' said Volker to Dancwart, 'and your brother has asked me to help you. If you would like to go outside I will take my stand within.' And so brave Dancwart stood beyond the door and barred the stairs to all who presented themselves, following which you could hear swords ringing high and clear in the warriors' hands, while Volker of Burgundy did likewise on the inside.

'The hall is well and truly closed, lord Hagen my good friend,' cried the bold Fiddler over the mêlée. 'I tell you it is firmly barred – the sword-arms of two warriors have slid a thousand bolts across it!'

Seeing the door so well secured, Hagen of Troneck, like the splendid fighting-man he was, jerked his shield on to his back, and only now did he begin in earnest to avenge the wrongs which he had suffered so that his foes abandoned all hope of living.

When he observed how mighty Hagen was breaking so many helmets, the lord of Verona and King of the Amelungs leapt on to a bench and cried: 'Hagen is pouring us the worst of all drink!'

Meanwhile the monarch of that region was in great fear, and this was only natural, for he barely escaped his enemies – and what numbers of dear friends were taken from him before his very eyes! He sat there in great jeopardy – what did it profit him that he was King?

'Help me to get away alive, noble knight,' cried Kriemhild to Dietrich, 'by the honour of all the princes of Amelungland! For if Hagen reaches me, death will take me.'

'How can I help you, noble Queen?' answered lord Dietrich. 'I go in fear for my own life. Gunther's men are in such a passion that at present I can assure no one's safety.'

'Do not say so, lord Dietrich, worthy, noble knight! Give us proof of your fine breeding today by helping me out, I implore you, otherwise I shall die here.' Indeed Kriemhild had the best possible grounds for her fears.

'I will see if I can help you. But never over many years have I seen so many good knights so bitterly roused, with the blood spurting up through helmets under the sword-blows.' And the illustrious warrior began to shout with might and main so that his voice resounded like a wisent-horn and the whole castle – such was Dietrich's vast strength! – rang with it far and wide.

In the thick of the battle Gunther heard this man calling and he began to hearken. 'The voice of Dietrich has reached my ears,' said he. 'I suppose our knights have killed one or other of his men. I can see him on the table, and he is making a sign with his hand. My friends and kinsmen of Burgundy, hold your hands from battle! Let us listen and see what my men have done to that knight!'

In obedience to Gunther's command they put up their swords in the direst distress of battle, and it argued great control that none struck a further blow there. Then he swiftly asked the lord of Verona what he wanted.

'Noble Dietrich,' he said, 'what harm have you suffered here at the hands of my friends? I am willing to make it good to you and settle the affair. I should be very sorry if anyone has wronged you.'

'Nobody has wronged me,' answered Dietrich. 'Allow me to go from this fierce encounter and out of the hall together with my retainers under your safe-conduct, and you can rely on it that I shall always be obliged to you.'

'Why are you so quick with your entreaties?' asked Wolfhart. 'I declare the Fiddler has not barred the door so firmly that we cannot open it wide enough to pass!'

'Silence!' said lord Dietrich. 'A devil of a lot you have done!'

'I will permit you to take from this palace,' said King Gunther, 'as few or as many as you please, save for my enemies – they must stay within, for they have wronged me so utterly here in Hungary.'

At these words, Dietrich put one arm round the noble Queen – she was in a state of great apprehension – and with the other led Etzel away, while six hundred fine men accompanied him.

'Let us know whether any others who wish you well are to leave the palace,' said noble Rüdiger the Margrave, 'for among good friends firm peace should reign.'

'You shall have peace and a settlement from us,' replied

Giselher of Burgundy, 'since you and your men are trusty and true. You shall leave this place without fear in the company of your friends.'

When lord Rüdiger left the hall he was followed on all sides by his kinsmen and vassals of Pöchlarn to the number of five hundred or more, from whom, however, Gunther was to suffer much harm in the event.

One of the Hunnish knights saw Etzel walking at Dietrich's side, and would gladly have taken shelter with him, but the Fiddler dealt him such a blow that his head lay at Etzel's feet in a trice. When the lord of Hungary arrived outside the palace he turned and, looking at Volker, he said: 'Alas that I ever had such guests! Matters have reached a grim pass that all my knights are to lie slain at their feet! Out on this cursed festivity!' cried the noble King. 'There is a man in there called Volker who fights like a wild boar, and he is a minstrel, too. I bless my good fortune that I eluded the fiend! His lays grate on the ear, his fiddle-bow draws red, and his tunes fell warriors past counting. I do not know what this Minstrel has against us, only I have never had so dreadful a guest!'

They had now let out those whom they wished to let out of the hall, and at once a great clamour arose within, for the visitors were avenging the wrongs they had endured. As to the helmets bold Volker smashed, they are past all telling.

'Hagen, can you hear the tunes which Volker is playing to the Huns that venture to the door?' asked noble King Gunther, turning in the direction of the din. 'It is a red rosin that he uses for his bow.'

'I infinitely regret that I sat above the knight in this hall,'[1] said Hagen. 'I was his companion, and he mine, and if we ever return home we shall remain so in all affection. now see how devotedly Volker serves you, noble King! He is earning your gold and silver with a right good will. His fiddle-bow slices its way through tough steel and he

1. Hagen had sat at the kings' high table. For this oblique reference to Volker's status, see p. 337.

shatters the gleaming crests on the helmets. I never saw a fiddler cut such a splendid figure as Sir Volker has done today. His lays go ringing through shields and helmets: he has every right to ride good horses and wear magnificent clothes.'

However many of the Hunnish kindred there had been in that hall, not one of them was left alive now. Thus the clamour of the battle against them died away, and the bold, gay knights of Burgundy laid their swords aside.

CHAPTER THIRTY-FOUR

How they threw the corpses from the hall

*

THEIR lordships sat down after their exertions, while Volker and Hagen went outside; and there, leaning on their shields, the haughty pair conversed together with much shrewdness.

Then Sir Giselher of Burgundy spoke up. 'Believe me, dear friends, you cannot rest yet. You must carry the dead from the palace. Take my word for it, we shall be attacked again. These corpses must lie under our feet no longer. Before the Huns get the better of us in battle we shall inflict such a wound on them as will warm the cockles of my heart! On this I am firmly resolved.'

'What fortune to have such a master!' cried Hagen. 'From no other than a true hero could this counsel have come which my young lord has given us today, and you Burgundians may all rejoice in it!'

They followed this advice and carried seven thousand bodies to the door and threw them out. These fell at the foot of the stair before the hall, and their relations raised a most pitiful clamour at the sight of it; for some of those thrown out were not so seriously wounded that careful nursing could not have healed them, but they were nevertheless killed by the fall, and it was this that their kinsmen were lamenting, as well they might!

'I can see that what I have been told is true,' said Fiddler Volker, the sprightly warrior. 'The Huns are cowards and they weep like women when they should be tending the seriously wounded!'

A certain Hunnish margrave thought Volker had said this with kindly intent and, espying a kinsmen of his lying in his blood, he put his arms round him and was about to carry him away when the valiant Minstrel killed him with a javelin-throw as he was bending over the body. Seeing this, the others took to flight and they all began to curse the Minstrel, who then snatched a hard, keen spear that had been flung up at him and hurled it powerfully to a great distance over their heads from one end of the fortress to the other, thus inviting the Huns to seek quarters farther away from the hall. The people everywhere went in dread of his vast strength.

There were thousands upon thousands of men standing outside the palace, and Volker and Hagen began to tell King Etzel all that they had on their mind, though in the outcome it brought the good warriors into jeopardy.

'It would well grace the people's Protector[1] were he and his great nobles to fight foremost of all,' said Hagen, 'as does each of my lords here: for they hack through helmets and draw streams of blood after their swords.'

Etzel was a very brave man and he laid hold of his shield. 'Now take care,' said lady Kriemhild, 'and be sure to offer your warriors gold by the heaped-up shieldful, for if Hagen reaches you there, die you surely must!'

The King was a very brave man, and he would not be dissuaded (a thing that seldom happens now with such mighty princes) and they had to pull him back by his shield-strap. Then fierce Hagen returned to taunting him.

'It was a very distant relationship that Etzel and Siegfried shared!'[2] said the knight. 'He had his pleasure of Kriemhild long before she met you! So why, you dastardly King, do you plot against my life?'

Hearing these words, the queen of that noble monarch was incensed that Hagen should dare to abuse her within

1. Etzel is meant. The old kenning is now turned to the advantage of the Burgundian kings at Etzel's expense. See p. 215n. 2

2. Hagen means that Etzel is not a member of Siegfried's kindred and thus is not obliged to seek revenge in a blood-feud on that score; though of course Etzel was bound to seek revenge for his son Ortlieb. Hagen, however, refers to Etzel's invitation to Burgundy, doubting his good faith.

hearing of Etzel's men, and so she went to work again for the destruction of the foreigners.

'If anyone would kill Hagen of Troneck for me and bring me his head,' said she, 'I would pile Etzel's shield with red gold and give him many fine castles and lands for his pains.'

'I do not know what they are waiting for,' observed the Minstrel. 'When such big rewards were offered I never saw heroes stand around so bashfully! Etzel should never show them favour again. I can see them here in crowds shaking at the knees, those who eat their Prince's bread so disgracefully and now leave him in the lurch in his hour of greatest need, though they give themselves the airs of stalwarts! They will never live down the shame of it.'

CHAPTER THIRTY-FIVE

How Iring was slain

*

'I HAVE long abandoned myself to the pursuit of honour,' said Margrave Iring of Denmark, 'and have done outstanding deeds in battles between nations! Now bring me my weapons: I am resolved on fighting Hagen.'

'I would not advise it,' replied Hagen. 'But if you insist, tell the Hunnish knights to move back. For if two or three of you run into the hall I shall send them downstairs again in a very unhealthy condition.'

'I shall not let that deter me,' retorted Iring. 'This is not the first time that I have attempted matters every bit as dangerous. I shall take you on with the sword single-handed, so where will your boasting get you?'

Sir Iring was quickly armed, and also Irnfried of Thuringia, a brave young stalwart, and stout Hawart too, with fully a thousand men, since they were all going to stand by Iring whatever he took in hand. But seeing this armed host accompanying Iring with many a fine helmet laced on for the fray, Volker the bold Fiddler was highly incensed.

'Friend Hagen, can you see Iring approaching there, the man who said he would fight a duel with you? Should a hero lie? I consider it a disgrace – there are a thousand or more warriors with him, fully armed.'

'Don't make me out to be a liar,' replied Hawart's man. 'I shall gladly do as I have promised, I shall not go back on my word for any fear whatever. I shall face Hagen single-handed, be he never so frightful.' And Iring begged his kinsmen on bended knee to allow him to face Hagen alone, but this they were very loath to do, for arrogant Hagen of Burgundy was very well known to them. Yet Iring implored them so long that finally the thing was done. – Seeing that his whole heart was set on winning

honour his household let him go, with the result that a
fierce battle broke out between them.

Iring of Denmark poised his spear high above his head
and, covering himself with his shield, the excellent warrior
raced up the stairs towards Hagen before the hall, and the
two together at once set up a tremendous din. They hurled
their spears with all their strength through each other's
stout shields on to their shining armour so that the shafts
rebounded, twirling high in the air, then the fierce pair
snatched their swords. Bold Hagen was a man of mighty
courage, and Iring for his part hammered away at him so
that the whole building reverberated; indeed under the
weight of their blows the palace and towers rang and rang
again.

Failing to wound Hagen, Iring left him and hastened
towards the Fiddler, imagining that he would vanquish
him with powerful strokes of his sword. But the stately
warrior parried them in masterly fashion and then struck
some blows that sent the braces whirling over Iring's
shield! Thus, finding him to be such an ugly man to deal
with, Iring let him be and ran to attack Gunther of Bur-
gundy. They were both very stout fighting-men, yet for all
the blows they exchanged they did not set the blood flowing,
since their tough armour prevented it. So Iring left Gunther
to attack Gernot. And now he began to hew sparks from
Gernot's chain-mail, but a moment came when Gernot all
but killed him. So, nimble man, he skipped away from that
prince. And now in swift succession Iring slew four noble
members of the household from Worms, rousing Giselher to
the peak of fury.

'By Heaven, lord Iring,' said Young Giselher, 'you will
have to repay me for those whom you have laid low here –
and promptly!' And he ran at the Dane and felled him on
the spot. – As Giselher followed through, Iring pitched into
the blood and left them all thinking that he would never
strike another blow in battle! Yet Iring lay at Giselher's
feet unscathed; he had only been dazed by the clang of the
sword and the mighty buzz inside his helmet, and had

altogether lost count of himself – thus much had lusty Giselher achieved.

When the dizziness which Iring had suffered from the great blow began to leave his head, he thought: 'I am alive and unwounded. I have made the acquaintance of Giselher's fighting spirit to my cost!' He could hear his enemies on either side of him, and had they known the truth, worse would have befallen him. He also heard Giselher beside him, and he pondered how he might elude them. Then suddenly he leapt up from the gore like mad and, thanks to his fleetness of foot, ran out of the hall back to where Hagen was and struck him some savage blows with his doughty sword arm.

'You will have to die,' thought Hagen, 'you are lost unless the foul fiend shields you.' Nevertheless, Iring wounded Hagen through his helmet with his excellent sword Waske, and when Hagen felt the wound, his sword began to thresh so wildly that Hawart's man had to give ground as Hagen pursued him down the steps. Valiant Iring swung his shield over his head, and if the stair had been three times as long, Hagen would never have let him strike a blow – and oh, the fiery sparks that rained down upon his helmet!

Iring returned to his people safe and sound, and the news of his prowess against Hagen was faithfully reported to Queen Kriemhild, who thanked him most profusely.

'God reward you, Iring, illustrious warrior. What balm you have given to my heart, now that I see Hagen's corselet stained with blood!' And in her joy she herself relieved him of his shield.

'You should not thank him overmuch,' interposed Hagen. 'If he were to have another try he would be a stout fellow, and if he got back safely I should call him a brave man. The wound that I had from him will do you little good. Your having seen my corselet bloody from my wound whets my appetite for killing – only now am I really angry with Hawart's man, lord Iring, who has done me little harm as yet.'

Having removed his helmet, Iring stood in his chain-mail to cool himself in the breeze, and all were saying what a spirited man he was, praise which made the Margrave feel gloriously elated.

'My friends,' said he, 'I would have you know that you must arm me quickly because I am going to try again whether I cannot subdue that overbearing man!' His shield had been badly hacked about, and he was according-ly given a better one, and he was swiftly equipped with better weapons. In his fury he took a very stout spear, with which he intended to face Hagen for the second time.

Bent on his destruction, warrior Hagen kept a fierce watch. Indeed he could not wait for Iring, but ran down to meet him to the very foot of the stair with javelin-casts and sword-blows; and so enraged was Hagen that Iring's strength was of little use to him. They struck through the shields so that showers of sparks shot out in blasts of fiery red. And then through his shield and corselet Hawart's man took a great wound from Hagen's sword, from which he never recovered. Feeling the stab of the wound, Iring the warrior shifted his shield over his helmet-strap, deeming the hurt he had sustained quite enough: but Gunther's liegeman Hagen had not finished with him yet. He found a spear lying at his feet and this he flung at Iring, transfixing him so that the shaft stood jutting out of his head. Hagen had made a grim end of him.

Thus Iring had to retire towards the Danes. But before they took off his helmet they plucked the spear from his head, bringing death closer, much to the sorrow of his kinsmen, who had every reason to weep. The Queen came and stood over stout Iring and, breaking out into lamen-tations, she wept for his wounds that caused her bitter grief. But, with his relations to witness, the gallant warrior said:

'Do not lament, most noble lady – what good can your tears do now? I shall certainly die from my wounds. Death will not let me serve you and Etzel any longer.' Then, turning to the Danes and Thuringians: 'None of you

must accept the Queen's gifts of bright red gold, since if
you fight against Hagen you must die!'

The colour had left his face, and most valiant Iring wore
Death's token, to the deep sorrow of his friends. It was all
over with Hawart's liegeman, and nothing would hold the
men of Denmark back from battle.

Irnfried and Hawart ran towards the hall with fully a
thousand warriors, and an unholy din burst on the ear on
all sides as they hurled showers of keen javelins at the
Burgundians. Brave Irnfried fronted the Minstrel and
sustained great damage in return, for in a fury the noble
Fiddler struck the Landgrave[1] through his stout helmet,
and although lord Irnfried replied by dealing brave Volker
a blow that burst the mesh of his chain-mail and sent a
mantle of fiery sparks on to his corselet, yet the Landgrave
dropped dead at his feet. And now Hawart and Hagen
had clashed, and anyone who had witnessed it could have
seen miracles performed – the swords in those warriors'
hands fell in blow upon blow. But in the end Hawart had to
die, vanquished by the knight from Burgundy.

When the Danes and the Thuringians saw that their
lords were dead, there was a ghastly struggle in front of the
hall before they could fight their way to the door, during
which time many shields and helmets were shattered.

'Fall back and let them in,' counselled Volker. 'Other-
wise they will never have their way. Once inside, they will
be killed off in no time. They will buy the Queen's gifts with
their lives.'

When those rash men had gained the inside of the hall,
the vicious strokes of the Burgundians bowed the heads of
many so low that, willy-nilly, they died. Bold Gernot
fought a good fight, and so did Giselher.

A thousand and four had come into that hall and there
was a deadly flashing and swishing of swords till at length
all the knights who had entered were slain there. – Great
were the marvels that could be told of the Burgundians!

1. The first mention of Irnfried's rank: but contemporaries would
have known that the lord of the Thuringians must be a landgrave.

Then, after the clamour had died down, there was silence. The blood from the corpses was flowing away everywhere through the water-spouts into the gutters. This the great fighting-spirit of the Rhinelanders had achieved.

Once again the men of Burgundy laid aside their shields and swords; they sat down to rest. But the bold Fiddler still stood before the door, keeping watch for any who might yet wish to come and fight them.

King Etzel lamented bitterly, and with him his queen, while ladies and maidens tormented themselves. I fancy death had sworn to destroy them: for many more warriors yet were to perish at the hands of these strangers.

CHAPTER THIRTY-SIX

How the Queen had the hall burned down

*

'TAKE off your helmets,' said Hagen. 'My comrade and I will look after you so that if Etzel's men make another attempt on us I shall warn my lords with the utmost speed.'

Numerous worthy knights thus bared their heads of armour and squatted upon the bodies which, thanks to the wounds they had dealt them, had fallen into the blood; for the comfort of the noble guests had been shockingly neglected.

Before evening came, the King and Queen made dispositions for the Hunnish warriors to try their fortunes again, and fully twenty thousand assembled before them and were ordered into battle, whereupon a fierce assault was launched against the visitors. Hagen's brother, valiant Dancwart, rushed past his lords and out through the door to meet the enemy, and they feared that he was lost; but he returned to the portal unharmed. This bitter struggle lasted till darkness stopped the fighting. The foreigners had defended themselves from Etzel's vassals in a manner befitting good warriors through a livelong summer's day! What never-ending numbers of brave knights perished at their feet!

It was at midsummer when this great slaughter took place and lady Kriemhild avenged her mortal wrongs on her nearest kinsmen and on many others, so that King Etzel never knew happiness again.

The day had ebbed away, and the Burgundians had good reason to be alarmed. They were thinking that a swift death would suit them better than this long-drawn agony in the hall, with unspeakable torment to come, and so the proud, gay knights asked for a truce, requesting that

King Etzel be brought along to them. Those heroes, the three noble kings, stained with blood and rust, stepped from the hall not knowing to whom to make complaint of the measureless hurt they had sustained.

And now Etzel and Kriemhild came, to whom the land belonged; and numberless were their men who kept arriving.

'Tell me, what do you want of me?' the King asked the strangers. 'You hope to gain a truce? After such vast loss as you have inflicted on me that could never be. If I go on living you shall have no mercy! What of my son, whom you butchered, and many of my kinsmen? You shall never have a truce and settlement!'

'We were driven by dire necessity,' answered Gunther. 'Your heroes massacred my squires in their quarters! What had I done to deserve it? I came to visit you in good faith, imagining you wished me well.'

'You surviving warriors of Etzel,' interposed young Giselher, 'of what crime do you accuse me? How have I wronged you? I came riding to this country as a friend.'

'This whole castle and the country are so full of your loving-kindness as to be grief-stricken,' they replied. 'We should not have minded had you never come from Worms beyond the Rhine. – You and your brothers have made this a land of orphans.'

'It would be to our mutual advantage if you would compose this bitter feud with us warriors from afar,' said Gunther in a great passion, 'since there are no grounds for what Etzel is doing to us.'

'The wrongs that you and I have suffered do not bear comparison,' said the lord of Hungary in answer to the foreigners. 'In view of the great misery, the damage and insult that I have endured here, not one of you shall get away alive!'

'In that case, may Heaven prompt you to do us this kindness,' said stalwart Gernot to the King. 'First let us come down to you in the open, and then make an end of us wretches. That would do you honour. Let whatever is in store for us take its course swiftly. You have so many able-bodied men that if they dared face us, spent in battle as we are, they could finish us off. How long are we to continue in this torment?'

Etzel's warriors were on the point of complying when Kriemhild came to hear of it. She was deeply angered at this news, and so the truce was withdrawn from the strangers before it was ever granted.

'No, no, you Hunnish warriors, I earnestly advise you not to carry out your intention of letting them out of the hall, thirsting for bloody revenge! If you do, your kinsmen will go hurtling to their deaths! For if Uote's sons, my noble brothers, alone survived and were to gain the fresh air to cool their corselets you would all be lost – more valiant knights were never born.'

'It was to my undoing, my handsome sister, that I trusted you when you invited me over the Rhine into this great peril,' cried young Giselher. 'What have I done to merit death here from the Huns? I was always loyal to you and never plotted any wrong against you. I rode to court here, noble sister, firmly believing that you loved me. Think whether you cannot show us mercy – there is nothing else for it!'

'I cannot show you mercy – my heart has none to show!' said Etzel's queen. 'Hagen of Troneck has done me such wrong that there can be no reconciliation as long as I live! You must all pay for it together. Yet if you will give me Hagen alone as my prisoner I will not deny that I may let you live – for are you not my brothers, and sons of the same mother? – and I will discuss the matter of a settlement with these warriors standing here.'

'God in Heaven forbid!' replied Gernot. 'If we were a thousand men of your family we would all die before we should give you one of us as a prisoner. – That will never happen!'

'We have to die some time or other,' said Giselher, 'and no one shall prevent us from defending ourselves like knights. If anyone wishes to fight with us, here we are, at his disposal! I have never broken faith with a friend.'

It was only right that Dancwart should speak up. 'My brother Hagen does not stand alone,' said he. 'Those who are refusing a truce here may yet regret it – we shall convince you of that, rest assured of it.'

'You gallant warriors,' said the Queen, 'close in on the stairs and avenge my wrongs, and I shall always seek to reward you, as indeed I should be bound. I shall pay back Hagen's arrogance in full. Do not let a man leave the building anywhere, while I have the hall fired at all four corners. Thus shall all my sorrows be utterly avenged!'

Etzel's men were soon ready. They drove those who were still outside back into the hall with javelin-casts and blows, and raised a mighty din: but the kings and their vassals were resolved never to part company, they would not break the bonds of allegiance that bound them one to another. And now Etzel's spouse gave word for the hall to be kindled and they harassed those warriors with fire – which, fanned by the wind, soon had the whole palace in flames: and it is my opinion that no body of fighting-men were ever in a more parlous plight.

'Alas, alas! – We had far rather be killed fighting,' a number of them cried. 'God have mercy on us! – We are lost! This is monstrous vengeance that the Queen is taking on us!'

'It is all over with us,' said another of those within. 'Of what use to us is the friendly welcome we had from the King? This fierce heat has given me such a terrible thirst that I fear I shall soon expire amid all these perils.'

'You worthy knights,' cried Hagen, 'if any of you are plagued with thirst let them drink the blood here – in such heat it will be better than wine! In present circumstances it is the best that can be done.'

One of the warriors then went over to a corpse and, removing his helmet and kneeling over a wound, began to drink the blood that oozed from it and, little used to it though he was, he thought it very good. 'Heaven reward you, lord Hagen,' said the weary man, 'for having taught me such an excellent beverage! I have never had better wine poured for me. If I live for any time, I shall always have a friendly regard for you.' When the others heard that he judged it excellent, many more drank blood, and their bodies were greatly strengthened by it, as a result of which many fine women were to pay for it through the loss of their dear friends.

Burning brands were raining down upon them in the hall, so they deflected them to the ground with their shields; but the smoke and heat caused them agonies, and I doubt whether warriors will ever again suffer such misery.

'Stand close in to the walls,' shouted Hagen of Troneck, 'and don't let the brands fall on to your helmet-straps! Tread them deeper underfoot into the blood! – What a foul feast the Queen is giving us!'

Amid such hardships their night nevertheless drew to an end, and still the bold Minstrel and his comrade Hagen stood before the palace, resting on their shields as they kept watch for any further harm which the Huns might do them.

'Let us go into the hall,' said the Fiddler, 'so that the Huns think we have all succumbed to the torment they have inflicted on us – they will then discover that we shall attack them, whoever they are!'

'I fancy it will soon be dawning, for a cool breeze has sprung up,' said young Giselher of Burgundy. 'May God grant us a better time of it – it is a vile banquet my sister Kriemhild has been giving us.'

'I can see first light,' said another. 'Since there is no mending matters, arm yourselves, warriors, have a care for your lives. King Etzel's queen will soon be after us.'

The lord of Hungary was persuaded that the visitors must have perished from the toil of battle and the harassment of the flames, yet within that hall six hundred still survived, men of such mettle that no king ever had better. And the Huns sent to keep watch on the forlorn band had marked that both lords and vassals lived despite all that had been done to distress them – they could be seen standing in the hall in excellent shape.

Queen Kriemhild was informed that many were still alive, but she replied that it was not possible for any to have survived the fire. – 'I think they are more likely to be dead,' said she.

The Burgundian kings and their vassals would have been glad to escape their fate if any had wished to show them mercy, but they found no pity among the Huns and so it was with great goodwill that they avenged their deaths in advance.

That day, towards morning, the heroes were greeted with a stiff assault that reduced them to dire straits – showers of stout spears were hurled at them – and they defended themselves like the brave, noble knights they were. Etzel's retainers were deeply roused, since they hoped to earn Kriemhild's wealth and also do their king's bidding, for which reason many of them soon had to die. But of gifts and promises marvels might be related, for Kriemhild had the red gold carried there shieldwise and she gave it to any that wanted it or cared to accept it: never was there such a hiring of men against one's enemies!

A great force of such warriors now approached under arms.

'Here we are, as before,' cried bold Volker. 'I have never seen men go to battle more gladly than these who have received the King's gold as the price of our destruction.' And many of the Burgundians shouted: 'Come closer, you knights, so that we may do what has to be done and do it quickly! Only those who are doomed to die will fall.' And immediately their shields had loads of javelins sticking in them.

What more can I tell you? No less than twelve hundred men made a most determined attempt on them, now advancing, now retreating; but the strangers cooled their ardour for them with the wounds which they dealt them. None could resolve the conflict,[1] and so the blood had to

1. This short phrase looks forward to the unbridgeable gulf between the two groups, a gulf on both sides of which stands Rüdiger, the hero of the next chapter.

flow. Many death-wounds were given there, and you could hear them, one and all, lamenting the loss of their friends. In the end all those trusty men died for their august king, leaving their fond kinsmen with great longing for them in their hearts.

CHAPTER THIRTY-SEVEN

How Rüdiger was slain

*

THE strangers had acquitted themselves well during the early part of the day, when Gotelind's dear spouse came to court. Seeing the tremendous hurt that both sides had taken, faithful Rüdiger wept from the bottom of his heart.

'Alas, wretched man, that I was ever born!' the warrior cried. 'Can no one halt this calamity? However gladly I would compose this feud, the King will not do so, for he sees the sorrows of his people mount and mount.' And good Rüdiger sent to Dietrich to ask if they could not avert the disaster threatening the noble kings, but the lord of Verona replied with this message: 'Who can halt it? King Etzel will allow no one to settle it.'

At this point a Hunnish warrior noticed Rüdiger standing there with tears in his eyes – Rüdiger had been weeping copiously – and he said to the Queen: 'Just look at Rüdiger, the way he stands there, the man who has the greatest power here under Etzel, and to whom lands and people owe allegiance! Think of the castles that have been made over to him and in what numbers he has received them from the King! Yet in all these battles he has not struck an honourable blow! In my opinion he does not care what goes on here, since he has abundance of all that he can wish for. They say he is fabulously brave, but amid all these perils there has been shockingly little sign of it!'

With sadness in his heart the faithful warrior looked at the man who had spoken, thinking: 'You shall pay for this! You say I am a coward? You have said your piece at court too audibly!' And clenching his fist he ran at him and struck him such a blow that the Hun dropped dead at his feet, thereby adding to Etzel's sorrows. 'Away with you, infamous dastard!' cried Rüdiger. 'Have I not enough grief and pain? Why should you rebuke me for not fighting here? It goes without saying that I should be hostile to the foreigners, and for very good cause, and would have done all that I could to harm them, but for my having conducted them here – I was their escort into my lord's country, and therefore, wretch that I am, I may not fight them!'[1]

'Is that what you call helping us?' the august King asked the Margrave. 'We have so many dead in the land that we do not need any more. You have acted very badly.'

'He offended me,' replied the noble knight, 'and taunted me with the wealth and honours you have showered on me, and the traducer has been paid in some measure!'

The Queen, too, had witnessed how the Hun had fared as a result of the hero's anger and, coming up to them, she broke out into wild laments.

'What have we done to deserve that you should add to my sufferings and the King's?' she asked with tears in her eyes. 'Now you have told us all along, noble Rüdiger, that you would hazard your position and your life for us,[2] and I have heard many warriors acclaim you as far and away the best. And so, illustrious knight, I remind you of the aid you swore to bear me when you urged me to marry Etzel, saying you would serve me till one or the other of us died. – Poor woman, I was never in such need of that aid as now.'

'There is no denying it, noble lady, that I swore to risk my life and position for you: but that I would lose my soul I never swore! – Remember it was I who brought those high-born kings to the festival here.'

'Think, Rüdiger, of your great debt of loyalty and constancy,' she said, 'and of the oaths, too, by which you swore you would always avenge my wrongs and any harm that befell me.'

'I have never refused you anything,' answered the

1. Rüdiger's role of guide and escort bound him in honour to the Burgundians.
2. Although a few lines later Rüdiger admits that he promised this, he did not use this form of words during the wooing scene in Chapter 20.

Margrave. And now mighty Etzel began to entreat him, and both he and his queen knelt before their liegeman. The noble Margrave stood there in despair. 'Alas,' cried that most faithful knight from the depths of his anguish, 'that I have lived to know this, Godforsaken man that I am! I must sacrifice all the esteem, the integrity, and breeding that by the grace of God were mine! Ah, God in Heaven, that death does not avert this from me! Whichever course I leave in order to follow the other, I shall have acted basely and infamously – and if I refrain from both, they will all upbraid me! May He that summoned me to life afford me counsel!'

The King and his spouse begged and implored him, so that warriors had to lose their lives for it later at Rüdiger's hands in that same place where he, too, met his end. And now listen to his most lamentable acts.

Rüdiger knew that he would suffer hurt and boundless grief, and he would gladly have refused both King and Queen, dreading to be detested by all were he to slay one of the Burgundians.

'Sire,' said the hero to his King, 'take back all that I have received from you, my lands together with the castles! Let none of them remain to me. On my own feet I will go into exile.'

'But who would aid me then?' asked King Etzel. 'I will give you your lands and castles outright, Rüdiger, if you will avenge me on my enemies, and you shall rule as a sovereign beside me.'

'How shall I ever begin?' rejoined Rüdiger. 'I invited them to my own home and offered them meat and drink with friendly mien, and I also bestowed gifts upon them[1] – how shall I now conspire to kill them? People might come to think that I was turning craven. There is no service I have denied those illustrious kings and their vassals, and the thought of the family ties into which I have entered with them fills me with sorrow. I have given my daughter to Sir Giselher, nor could she be better bestowed anywhere in the

1. These hospitable acts of Rüdiger's were as binding on him as his escorting of the Burgundians to Etzel's court (see pp. 334f.).

world in respect of breeding, rank, personal integrity, or wealth, since I have never seen a king so young who was endowed with such excellent qualities.'

'Most noble Rüdiger,' pleaded the Queen once more, 'have pity for the King's and my sufferings, and bear it well in mind that no host ever had such terrible guests.'

'I, Rüdiger, must repay today all the kindness which you and my lord have shown me,' said the Margrave to the noble lady. 'For that I must lay down my life – this can go on no longer. I know full well that thanks to some Burgundian sword-arm my lands and castles must inevitably fall vacant and revert to you, and so I commend my wife and children to your gracious protection, and all the many exiles at Pöchlarn.'

'Heaven reward you, Rüdiger,' answered the King. He and the Queen were now well pleased. 'Your people shall enjoy my full protection, but I also trust to my good fortune to see you emerge unscathed.'

Rüdiger was ready to hazard both his body and his soul, and Etzel's queen began to weep. 'I must discharge my oaths to you,' said Rüdiger. 'Alas for those friends of mine, whom I attack so much against my will!' And he left the King most dolefully and came upon his warriors near at hand. 'Arm yourselves, all my men,' he said. 'To my sorrow I must cross swords with the bold men of Burgundy.'

They told their squires to run and fetch their armour with all speed, and these brought it along for them, shield and helmet, so that later the proud strangers came to hear bad news. And now Rüdiger was armed, together with five hundred men, and over and above these he gained the help of twelve stout knights who desired to win renown in battle. They had no inkling how death was drawing near to them.

As Rüdiger advanced in his helmet with his men holding their keen swords and broad bright shields ready for action, the Fiddler espied them, to his great sorrow. Young Giselher, too, saw his father-in-law with his helmet laced for battle – and how could he explain his intentions in any other than a favourable way? Thus the noble king was greatly cheered.

'Happy me, that I have friends like those whom we won on the way to Hungary!' cried Giselher the warrior. 'My wife is to be of much benefit to us. How truly glad I am that this wedding took place.'

'I do not know where you take your consolation from,' retorted the Fiddler. 'When did you ever see so many warriors come to talk peace sword in hand and with their helmets set for battle? Rüdiger means to earn his lands and castles from us.'

Scarce had the Minstrel finished speaking when Rüdiger appeared before the palace. Of necessity withholding from his friends all compliments and greetings, he planted his good shield in front of him.

'You bold Nibelungs,' the noble Margrave shouted into the hall, 'defend yourselves everywhere! You ought to profit from me, but instead I shall make you pay dearly. Till now we have been friends, but I wish to be quit of our ties!'

This declaration deeply shocked those hard-pressed men, since none derived any pleasure from the prospect of being attacked by a man they loved – they had endured much hardship from their foes as it was.

'God in Heaven forbid that you should set aside your goodwill towards us and the intimate bonds we were intending,' said Gunther. 'I cannot believe you would ever do such a thing.'

'It is quite impossible for me to refrain,' answered the brave man. 'I *must* fight you, since I am bound by oath. Now as you value your lives, you bold heroes, be on your guard! King Etzel's consort held me to my word.'

'It is too late for you to break with us,' said the august King.[1] 'May God requite you, illustrious Rüdiger, for the love and affection you have shown us, if it is your wish to let things end in more friendly fashion. My kinsmen and I would be forever obliged to you for all that you have given

1. Gunther intends to overlook this solemn act of 'defiance' as long as possible, in order to continue the parley. He treats it as invalid because 'too late' to be honourable, and he and his brothers seek to persuade Rüdiger in the strongest terms.

us, if you would only let us live. Think of the lordly gifts you made us, noble Rüdiger, when in good faith you escorted us to Hungary!'

'I should be happy for your sakes, could I lavish my gifts on you as freely as I was hoping!' cried Rüdiger. 'None would upbraid me for it then.'

'Abandon your intention, noble Rüdiger,' said Gernot, 'for no host ever entertained his guests in such truly delightful fashion as you entertained us,[1] and if we remain alive you shall be amply repaid for it.'

'Would to God you were back on the Rhine, most noble Gernot,' answered Rüdiger, 'and I were dead with some modicum of honour, seeing that I must attack you! Heroes were never worse treated by their friends.'

'May God reward you for your magnificent gift, lord Rüdiger,' answered Gernot. 'If so noble a nature as yours must perish with you, I shall lament your passing. Look, I am wearing the sword you gave me, good knight! Amid all these dangers it has never failed me, and beneath its edges many knights have fallen. It is firm and dazzling bright – a splendid, trusty weapon – and I doubt whether a warrior will ever make so rich a gift again. And if you will not forgo your intention of attacking us, and you kill any of the friends that are left to me in this hall, I shall take your life with your own sword; and then, Rüdiger, I shall mourn for you and your noble lady.'

'Would to God that what you are all desiring[2] had come to pass, lord Gernot, and that your friends had emerged unharmed! My wife and daughter must put their full trust in you.'

'Why do you act thus, lord Rüdiger?' asked fair Uote's son of Burgundy. 'Those who accompanied me here all wish you well. It is a bad thing on which you are embarking: you are bent on widowing your lovely child before she was ever a wife. If you and your knights attack me, how little you let it appear with such utterly loveless behaviour that I

1. See p. 267n.
2. In Rüdiger's eyes his own death.

place more trust in you than in all other men, to the point of having wed your daughter!'

'Should God deliver you from here, remember your plighted word, most illustrious king,' replied Rüdiger. 'Do not let the young lady suffer for any act of mine but by your own noble nature, condescend to treat her graciously.'

'It would only be right if I did so,' said Young Giselher. 'But if these illustrious kinsmen of mine who still remain in this hall are to die through you, the bonds of alliance with you and your daughter must be severed.'

'Then God have mercy on us!' said the valiant man. Hereupon they raised their shields as though about to move forward and fight with the strangers in Kriemhild's hall, but Hagen shouted down from the stair.

'Stay a while, most noble Rüdiger,' said he. 'Constrained by the plight in which we find ourselves, my lords and I would say more. How can the death of us outcasts serve Etzel? As to me,' he went on, 'I am in great anxiety, because the shield which my lady Gotelind gave me to carry has been hacked to pieces by the Huns, above my grip. It was as a friend that I brought it to Etzel's land. If only God in Heaven would grant me to carry another shield as good as the one you bear, most noble Rüdiger, I should need nothing else to guard me in the fray!'

'I would gladly help you with my shield if I dared give it you, standing as I do to Kriemhild. – Yet take it, Hagen, and wield it! What joy, if you were to bear it back to Burgundy!'

When Rüdiger proffered his shield so willingly to Hagen, the eyes of some few grew red with hot tears. It was the last gift that Rüdiger of Pöchlarn offered any knight. However fierce and harsh he was, Hagen was deeply moved by the present the good knight had made him so near to his own end, and many other knights shared his sadness.

'May God in Heaven reward you, most noble Rüdiger. Your like will never be seen again to make such lordly gifts to warriors far from home. God grant that your fine qualities abide on earth for ever! But out on this sorry business! – We have trouble enough to bear as it is. If we are to fight our friends, I must raise my voice to high Heaven in protest!'

'It cuts me to the heart,' answered the Margrave.

'Now let me repay you for your gift, most noble Rüdiger, in that, however these knights behave towards you, I myself shall never touch you in battle, no, not if you were to dispatch all the men from Burgundy!'

Good Rüdiger acknowledged this with a polite bow, and then they all wept because none could compose this heart-rending agony – theirs was a terrible plight. And indeed in Rüdiger's person the father of all knightly excellence was soon to be laid low.

'Since my comrade Hagen has set peace between you and him,' Volker the Minstrel called down from the hall, 'I will guarantee you the same with me, for you well deserved it when we came to this country. Most noble Margrave, be my messenger! The Margravine gave me these bracelets of red gold to wear here at the high feast – see them for yourself and be my witness that I did so.'

'I wish to God that the Margravine could give you more! I shall be glad to tell this to my dear spouse if I live to see her again, rest assured of it.'

Having promised him this, Rüdiger raised his shield. The noble Margrave's fighting blood was up, and he delayed no longer, but charged at the strangers like the true warrior he was, raining down deadly blows on them. Volker and Hagen moved aside, for this the doughty pair had promised him; but Rüdiger found standing beside the doors many another of equal mettle, so that he began the fight facing great perils. Thirsting for blood and vengeance heroic Gunther and Gernot let him into the hall, but Giselher fell back. And, truly, Giselher did not like it at all: he still had hopes of surviving, and so he kept clear of Rüdiger. And now the Margrave's vassals leapt at the enemy and they could be seen following their lord like true fighting men with their keen swords in their hands, so that numerous helmets and fine shields were shattered there, while the thrice-weary Burgundians struck back many bitter blows at those of

Pöchlarn, blows that sailed through the air and sank deep through the shining chain-mail and on to the springs of life. – What glorious deeds they did in that combat!

Rüdiger's noble retainers had now made their way right into the hall and Volker and Hagen sprang forward with great alacrity, giving quarter to none but that one man, while the blood ran down through helmets under the blows they dealt. With what a truly savage din did all those swords ring out as shield-braces flew from their housing with the gems dropping smashed into the blood! They fought with such ferocity that men will never fight so again.

The lord of Pöchlarn cut a path forward and then another path back, like one well used to playing a man's part in battle. On that day Rüdiger gave every proof in action that he was a bold and illustrious hero!

Gunther and Gernot stood there slaying warrior after warrior in the encounter, while with the greatest unconcern Giselher and Dancwart dispatched crowds to the Last Judgement. Rüdiger was giving ample demonstration how very strong, brave, and well-armed he was by the great numbers of stalwarts he was slaying, when one of the Burgundians – he was no other than mighty Gernot – took note of it and flew into a rage, from which moment Death began to dog noble Rüdiger.

Hailing the Margrave, Gernot said: 'You do not intend to let any of my men live, most noble Rüdiger, and this vexes me beyond measure. I cannot bear to go on watching it. Since you have taken so many of my friends from me, your gift may well be your undoing. Turn this way, illustrious hero, and I shall try to deserve your present to the utmost of my power.'

Before the Margrave fully succeeded in reaching him, dazzling shirts of ring-mail had to be tarnished with blood. Then, athirst for glory, the two sprang at each other, each shielding his vital parts; for their swords were so keen that nothing could withstand them. Soon Rüdiger struck Gernot through his rock-like helmet so that the blood streamed down; but the gallant knight paid it back to him forthwith.

Mortally wounded though he was, Gernot raised Rüdiger's gift-sword on high and struck him a blow clean through his good shield and on to his helmet-strap, with the result that fair Gotelind's spouse yielded up his life there. Never will so rich a gift be worse rewarded! In one and the same moment Gernot and Rüdiger fell in battle, each slain by the other.

Seeing this great ruin, Hagen was at last truly roused to fury. 'Things have taken an ugly turn for us,' said the warrior of Troneck. 'We have suffered such loss in those two as their lands and peoples will never surmount. Rüdiger's warriors shall stand forfeit to us outcasts!'

'Alas for my brother who has just been killed here! What harrowing news reaches me incessantly. I shall always mourn for noble Rüdiger, too – this vast loss and pain affect both sides.[1]

When lord Giselher saw his brother fall, those within were put to the last extremity – Death was very busy seeking those who were to join his retinue, so that soon not one of the men of Pöchlarn was left alive.

The good warriors Gunther and Giselher, Hagen, Dancwart, and Volker went to where the two men lay and they began to shed tears of grief.

'Death has robbed us mightily,' said Young Giselher. 'Now leave your weeping and let us go out into the air so that, battle-weary men, we may cool our armour. I fear God will not grant us longer life here.'

You could see numerous knights there, this man sitting, another reclining. They were at rest again, for Rüdiger's men were slain. The din had died away, and silence reigned so long that it became too much for Etzel.

'What sort of vassalage is this?' asked the Queen. 'Rüdiger and his men are not so constant in their duty that he will make our enemies suffer for it – he means to take them back to Burgundy! What was the use of our sharing

1. It seems best to ascribe this speech to Gunther and not to Giselher, first because Gunther as supreme king would regularly receive reports on the fighting, second because Giselher's reaction to Gernot's death is dealt with next.

with him all that he wished, King Etzel? The knight has done amiss, because he is working for a settlement, though it is he who should avenge us.'

'What you say is unfortunately not so, Queen of a most noble King,' interposed Volker, splendid knight. 'If I dared accuse so august a person of lying, I should say you had lied diabolically concerning Rüdiger, for he and his warriors got nothing from the "settlement"! He did the King's bidding with such a will that he and his retainers lie dead here. Look about you, Kriemhild, for any others you may now wish to muster! Heroic Rüdiger gave you loyal service till the end, and if you do not believe it, you shall be shown!' And they proceeded to do so for the mortal anguish it would cause her. They carried out the much-wounded warrior to where the King could see him – and never had Etzel's knights experienced such affliction! When they saw the Margrave's body borne out no scribe could formally set down or make report of all the wild lamentation which men and women evinced there under the stress of deepest grief, while the sorrow of mighty King Etzel was so great that, giving vent to the pain in his heart, he roared as with the voice of a lion, as also did his consort. They all lamented Rüdiger's passing with a vehemence beyond measure.

CHAPTER THIRTY-EIGHT

How Dietrich's warriors were slain to a man

*

SUCH great lamentation met the ear everywhere that the palace and the towers re-echoed with the doleful sound. A vassal of Dietrich of Verona heard it and he made great haste to bring the harsh momentous tidings.

'Listen, my lord Dietrich,' he said to that prince. 'Never in my life have I known lamenting beyond all human bounds such as I have just heard! I fancy King Etzel himself has met with disaster – how else could they all be so distressed? Either the King or Kriemhild – one or the other – lies dead through the spite of the bold strangers, since gallant knights in great numbers are weeping without restraint.'

'My beloved vassals,' said the hero of Verona, 'do not be over-hasty. Whatever the foreign warriors have done here, they were under great constraint. Let them profit from my pledge not to attack them.'

'I will go there and inquire what they have done, my dear lord,' said valiant Wolfhart, 'and then report my findings on what the wailing is about.'

'If someone asks a rough question where he expects an angry response, warriors may soon lose their composure,' answered lord Dietrich. 'I do not want *you* to make inquiries, Wolfhart.' Instead, he dispatched Helpfrich with orders to discover what had happened there by asking Etzel's men or the strangers.

Such great sorrow had never been seen. 'What happened here?' asked the emissary.

'All the joy that was ours in Hungary has vanished away!' said one of the crowd. 'Rüdiger lies there, slain by the Burgundians. And of those who entered the hall with him not one is now alive!' Nothing could have saddened

Helpfrich more, and never did he tell news more reluctantly. Shedding abundant tears he made his way back to Dietrich.

'What have you discovered for us?' Dietrich asked his messenger. 'Why are you weeping so, Sir Helpfrich?'

'I have good reason for passionate laments,' replied the noble warrior. 'The Burgundians have slain good Rüdiger!'

'God forbid!' cried the hero of Verona. 'That would be terrible vengeance and a diabolical mockery of all that is right; for how could Rüdiger have deserved it of them? – I am well aware of his friendship for the strangers.'

'If they have done this they shall all die for it,' broke in Wolfhart. 'If we were to take this lying down from them we should be disgraced – think of the great services good Rüdiger has rendered us!'[1]

The lord of the Amelungs commanded further inquiries to be made. Sitting at a window in a mood of saddest yearning, he bade Hildebrand go to the visitors and learn from them what had happened. And he, the intrepid warrior and Dietrich's Master-at-Arms, wishing to go to them civilly, took neither shield nor sword, but was rebuked for it by his nephew.

'If you go there unarmed,' said fierce Wolfhart, 'you are bound to be insulted, and then you must make a shameful retreat. But if you go there armed, some will stay their hands, if I know them!'

And so the old campaigner took the advice of the young hothead and donned his armour; and before he was aware of it, all Dietrich's knights were in their battle-dress and had their swords in their hands – much to his annoyance, since he would gladly have forestalled it. He asked them where they were going.

'We are going to the hall with you. Perhaps Hagen of

1. One such service, known from the 'Rabenschlacht', a poem in the Dietrich Cycle of epics, was Rüdiger's mediation between Etzel and Dietrich when the latter returned from battle without Etzel's sons, for whose safety he had assumed responsibility but who (owing to unforeseen events) had nevertheless been killed.

Troneck will find less courage to deride you, as is his way.'
Hearing this, Hildebrand gave them leave.

Bold Volker saw the knights of Verona approaching well-caparisoned. They had their swords girt on and were carrying their shields in their hands, all of which he reported to his Burgundian lord. 'I can see Dietrich's men advancing this way in a most hostile manner, armed and with their helmets on. They are going to attack. I fear events are about to take a fateful turn for us here in this foreign land.'

And at that same moment Hildebrand arrived there. He planted his shield before him and questioned Gunther's men. 'Alas, you good knights, what wrong had Rüdiger done you? My lord Dietrich has sent me to tell you that if any of you has slain the noble Margrave, as we have been informed, we could never surmount the anguish it would cause us.'

'What you have been told is true,' replied Hagen of Troneck. 'How glad I should be for you, from the love that I bear Rüdiger, if your messenger had deceived you, and he were still alive whom men and women must ever mourn!'

When they heard reliably that Rüdiger was dead, Dietrich's warriors lamented his loss as befitted their loyal regard for him – you could see the tears flowing down their beards and chins, for they had suffered a cruel loss.

'It is over and done with, the good life that Rüdiger gave us after our unhappy time!'[1] cried Sigestap, Duke of Verona. 'The joy of all exiled fighting men lies slain by you, doughty warriors!'

'If I were to see my own father dead today I could not be more grief-stricken than for Rüdiger,' said Sir Wolfwin of the Amelungs. 'Alas, who will console the good Margravine now?'

'Who will now lead the warriors on the many expeditions, as the Margrave has done so often?' asked Sir Wolfhart angrily. 'Alas, most noble Rüdiger, that we have lost you in

1. According to heroic legend (but at odds with history) the 'unhappy time' was the time between Dietrich's flight into exile from Odoacer (later from Ermenrich) and his friendly reception at Etzel's court.

this way!' And Wolfbrand and Helpfrich and Helmnot, too, lamented his death, together with all their kinsmen. Hildebrand was so overcome with sighs that he could question them no further.

'Now you warriors,' said he, 'do what my lord has sent me for: hand him to us from the hall, dead as he is,[1] the man in whom, to our desolation, our whole happiness lies ruined; and let us repay him for having always treated us and many others with supreme affection. Like valiant Rüdiger, we too are wretched exiles. Why do you keep us waiting? Let us carry him away so that we may render thanks to the man in death. Better it would have been had we done so while he lived.'

'No homage is as good as that which friend pays to friend when one of them has died,' said King Gunther. 'When a man finds the way to do so, I call it abiding love. It is fitting that you should requite Rüdiger, for he has been your benefactor.'

'How long are we to go on begging?' asked Sir Wolfhart. 'Since you have slain our staunchest ally and alas, we must now do without him, let us carry him away to bury him.'

'No one is going to *give* him to you,' replied Volker. 'Come and get him in this hall where, thanks to his great death-wounds, he fell into the blood. Then the homage you pay Rüdiger will be homage indeed!'

'By God, Sir Minstrel,' said bold Wolfhart, 'having wronged us so already, you do not need to provoke us! Were it not for my fear of my lord, things would go hard with you! But we shall have to let it be, since he has forbidden us to fight here.'

'There is too much fear when a man is ready to abstain from all that is forbidden him,' retorted the Fiddler. 'I cannot recall that a truly manly spirit.' Hagen approved of these words which his comrade-in-arms had spoken.

'Do not ask for it,' rejoined Wolfhart. 'I will jangle your fiddle for you so that you have something to talk about when you ride back to the Rhine! I cannot, without dishonour, let your swagger pass.'

1. Here Hildebrand is exceeding his orders.

279

'If you rob my strings of their sweet sound,' said the Fiddler, 'I shall take the shine out of your helmet, whether or not I ride back to Burgundy.'

At this Wolfhart would have leapt at him had not his uncle Hildebrand prevented it by hugging him tight. 'One would think you had taken leave of your senses, you tetchy young hothead! You would have lost my lord's favour for ever!'

'Let loose the ramping lion, Master!' said Volker the good knight. 'But let him come my way and I shall strike him to such effect that even though he had killed all the warriors in the world he would have no chance to tell the tale!'

This roused the men of Verona to fury. Snatching up his shield, Wolfhart the bold knight sprang forward like a wild lion, whilst his friends followed swiftly at his heels: yet however great the bounds that took Wolfhart to the palace wall, old Hildebrand – loath to let him enter the fray before him – beat him to the foot of the stair. They were soon to find what they were seeking from the strangers.

Master Hildebrand sprang at Hagen, and their swords rang clear as showers of fiery sparks fanned out from them, for as events were to show, those two were highly enraged. Nevertheless, in the turmoil of battle they were parted by the men of Verona exerting their great strength, and Hildebrand at once abandoned Hagen, while mighty Wolfhart charged at Volker, striking the Fiddler on his good helmet so that the sword's edge entered as far as the brace-bands; but the brave Minstrel repaid it with vigour, and sent the sparks from Wolfhart in clouds, so hard and fast did he strike him. Thus, inspired by mutual enmity, they hewed fire enough from each other's chain-mail; but they were finally parted by Sir Wolfwin, a deed none but a hero could have done.

The warrior Gunther received the proud heroes from the land of the Amelungs with a welcoming hand, and lord Giselher made many a bright helmet red and wet with blood. The feats which that fierce man Dancwart, Aldrian's son, had performed against Etzel's knights were as nothing to the frenzy of his fighting now, while on the other side Ritschart, Gerbart, Helpfrich, and Wichart were bringing it home to Gunther's men that they had never spared themselves in the many actions they had fought and Wolfbrand strode through the mêlée in splendid style.

Old Hildebrand was fighting as though he had gone berserk, and numerous good knights were doomed by Wolfhart's sword-blows to fall dying into the blood. Thus did those gallant warriors wreak vengeance for Rüdiger. Dietrich's nephew lord Sigestap acquitted himself as his courage urged him, and oh, the good helmets he carved up for his foes during that engagement! Never in any great battle could Sigestap do better than here. And when mighty Volker saw how bold Sigestap was hewing a river of blood from the hard rings, he was enraged, and leapt to meet him, with the outcome that Sigestap soon lost his life to the Fiddler, who gave him such a sample of his artistry that he died without a chance beneath his sword. But, impelled by his manly spirit, old Hildebrand avenged it.

'Alas for a dear lord who lies slain here at Volker's hands!' cried the Master-at-Arms. 'The Fiddler shall live no longer!' How could brave Hildebrand ever reach a higher pitch of fury? He struck Volker such a blow that the braces of the bold Minstrel's helmet and shield were smashed to atoms that wafted in clouds against the palace walls on all sides, and this proved the end of mighty Volker. Dietrich's men now pressed forward into the fray and dealt the Burgundians blows that sent the rings of their chain-mail spinning a great way off, whilst their sword-tips soared on the air as they drew hot springs from helmets.

When Hagen of Troneck saw that Volker was dead it was the most agonizing loss that he had suffered at that feast in the person of any kinsman or vassal, and how remorselessly the hero set about avenging him!

'Old Hildebrand shall not live to enjoy it! My helpmate, the best comrade-in-arms I ever had, lies slain at that warrior's hands!' And he shifted his shield up higher and went off slashing like a boar.

Sturdy Helpfrich slew Dancwart, and great was the sorrow of Gunther and Giselher when they saw him fall in the thick of it; yet he had paid well for his death in advance. Meanwhile Wolfhart was cutting his way to and fro through the hall, mowing down Gunther's men the whole time, and he had now completed his third traverse, with knight after knight going down.

'Wretched me, ever to have had so fierce an enemy!' lord Giselher called to Wolfhart. 'Now turn towards me, bold knight! I will do my share in making an end of it all – it cannot last much longer.'

Wolfhart turned and made for Giselher through the press, and each dealt the other many gaping wounds – with such impetuosity did Wolfhart thrust his way to the King that the blood underfoot spurted high over his head. Fair Uote's son received the bold knight with fierce and deadly blows, and however strong Wolfhart was, he was doomed, for no king so young as Giselher could be more formidable. He struck Wolfhart through his good corselet and brought the blood streaming from the wound: he had wounded Dietrich's vassal mortally, and no other than he could have done so. Feeling the wound, brave Wolfhart let go his shield and, swinging his stout keen blade the higher, brought it down on Giselher through helmet and chainmail. Each had wrought cruel death for the other.

And now not one of Dietrich's men was left[1]; and Gunther's men were all dead, too. Old Hildebrand saw Wolfhart fall, and I fancy he never endured such grief till his dying day. He went to where his nephew had fallen into the blood and took the good stalwart in his arms with the intention of carrying him from the palace; but Wolfhart was too heavy, and Hildebrand had to let him lie. Then the dying man looked up through the blood and saw how gladly his uncle would have got him away.

'My beloved uncle,' said the mortally wounded man 'there is nothing you can do for me now. I would advise you

---

1. Hildebrand is evidently too senior a man to be named as one of a crowd, though like the others he was Dietrich's vassal.

to guard against Hagen, he bears such savage hatred in his heart. And if my kinsmen wish to lament me when I am dead, tell those who are nearest and dearest not to weep for me, there is no need. I die a magnificent death, slain at the hands of a king! Furthermore, I have paid for my death in this hall in such coin that the wives of good knights may well bewail it. And should anyone ask, you may boldly assert that a hundred lie slain here by me and me alone!'

But Hagen was brooding over the Minstrel, whose life brave Hildebrand had taken. 'You shall pay for what you have done to me. You have begrudged us the lives of many a gay warrior here.' And as he struck out at Hildebrand you could not mistake the roar of Balmung which he had taken from Siegfried when he murdered him. The old man defended himself – he was not wanting in courage – and he hacked at the knight of Troneck with a broad sword that also cut very deep. Nevertheless he failed to wound Hagen, whereas Hagen dealt him a wound through his handsome corselet, and, feeling this, old Hildebrand was afraid he might receive further hurt from him, so he flung his shield over his back and, Dietrich's man or no, he fled from Hagen, carrying his great wound with him.

Of all the Burgundian warriors none was now left alive save that solitary pair: Gunther and Hagen. And now with the blood running down all over him, old Hildebrand went to Dietrich and brought him terrible news. He saw him sitting there disconsolately enough, but now the prince was to receive a far greater load of sorrow. He in turn saw Hildebrand in his bloody shirt of mail, and, full of foreboding, asked him for his news.

'Tell me, Master Hildebrand, why are you so drenched in life-blood? Who did this to you? I presume you have been fighting with the visitors in the hall? I forbade it you so urgently that in decency you ought to have refrained!'

'It was Hagen,' he told his lord. 'He gave me this wound in the hall just as I was turning away from him. I scarce escaped the demon with my life.'

'It serves you right for breaking the peace which I

promised those warriors when you heard me declare that we were friends,' said the lord of Verona. 'But for the fact that it would disgrace me for ever, you should die for it!'

'Do not be so angry, my lord Dietrich. – The damage I and my companions have suffered is too great. We were hoping to carry Rüdiger away, but King Gunther's men would not let us.'

'Unhappy wretch that I am! Then Rüdiger is really dead! This surpasses all my other griefs! Noble Gotelind is my cousin on my father's side – alas for the poor orphans at Pöchlarn!' Rüdiger's death woke thoughts of affection and grief in him, and the hero began to weep passionately, and indeed he had good cause. 'Alas for the trusty ally I have lost! Never, never shall I be consoled for the death of Etzel's man! Can you tell me for sure, Master Hildebrand, who it was that slew him?'

'It was mighty Gernot, exerting his great strength,' he answered, 'and he in turn was laid low by Rüdiger.'

'Tell my men to arm themselves at once,' Dietrich commanded Hildebrand, 'for I intend to go to the hall. And have my dazzling chain-mail fetched! I shall question those Burgundian warriors myself.'

'Who should there be to join you?' asked Master Hildebrand. 'You can see all the men whom you still have alive standing here beside you – myself and no other in the whole wide world! The others are no more.'

This news shocked Dietrich to the core, and well it might, since he had never in his life suffered such disaster. 'If all my vassals are dead,' said he, 'God has forsaken me, wretched Dietrich, once a lofty king of great power and dominion! How could it come about,' he continued, 'that all my excellent fighting-men were slain by those battle-weary knights, who, when all is said, were in such dire straits? But for my luckless destiny, death would still be a stranger to them.[1] Since my ill fortune would not forgo this, tell me, has any one of the visitors come through?'

1. Such was the mystique of Kingship that it was believed that an ill-starred King dragged his people down to ruin with him.

'None, save Hagen and noble King Gunther, in Heaven's name,' answered Master Hildebrand.

'Alas, if I have lost you, dear Wolfhart, I shall utterly regret that I was ever born! – And Sigestap and Wolfwin, and Wolfbrand, too! Who will help me now in the land of the Amelungs?[1] If most valiant Helpfrich has been killed, and Gerbart and Wichart, how shall I ever cease to mourn them? This is the doomsday of my joy! Oh, that no man can die of grief!'

1. According to heroic legend, Dietrich finally returned to Italy and won back his kingdom.

CHAPTER THIRTY-NINE

How Dietrich did battle with Gunther and Hagen

*

LORD DIETRICH went to fetch his armour himself, and Master Hildebrand helped him on with it. And now the mighty man lamented so loudly that the palace thundered with his cries.

Dietrich soon recovered his manly spirit, so that now the good warrior was armed in all fierceness. He seized a sturdy shield, and he and Hildebrand set out with speed.

'I see lord Dietrich coming,' said Hagen of Troneck. 'He intends to attack us in revenge for the great sorrow he suffered here. We shall see today who shall be accounted best. However fierce and strong lord Dietrich thinks he is, if he seeks vengeance on us for what has befallen him, I most certainly dare face him.'

Dietrich and Hildebrand heard what Hagen said. Dietrich went to where the two Burgundian warriors stood leaning against the palace wall and set his good shield on the ground. 'Gunther, mighty King,' he said with aching heart, 'why did you do this to me, wretched exile that I am? What have I done to you? I stand robbed of all that were my refuge.[1] When you slew our gallant Rüdiger you did not think it calamity enough, so you have now taken all my men from me. Indeed, noble warrior, I had done you no such wrong. Consider yourselves and your own misery, and whether the death of your friends and the toil of battle have not vexed your spirits. Alas, how cruelly Rüdiger's death afflicts me! No more grievous fate ever befell any man! Little thought did you have for my sufferings and yours. All the solace I ever had lies slain by you. The time will never come when I shall cease to lament my kinsmen.'

1. An ancient kenning survives here: a lord and his retainers were mutually each other's 'hope' or 'refuge'. Cf. p. 192n.3 and p. 215n.2.

'But we are not so much to blame,' answered Hagen. 'Your knights came to this hall fully armed with a great company. I do not think you can have been told the truth.'

'What more do I need to know? Hildebrand told me that when my stalwarts from the land of the Amelungs asked you to hand Rüdiger down from the hall you did nothing but mock them.'

'They said they wanted to fetch Rüdiger,' answered the Rhenish king. 'But in order to spite Etzel, not your vassals, I told my men to deny them Rüdiger's body; then Wolfhart grew abusive.'

'It was fated to happen thus: Gunther, noble King, I beg you of your courtesy to make good to me the losses I have suffered through you and to settle this affair in such terms as I may openly accept of you. Surrender yourself to me together with your vassal and to the best of my power I will see to it that none here in Hungary does you any harm. You will receive from me only loyal and kindly treatment.

'God in Heaven forbid,' interposed Hagen, 'that two knights should ever give themselves up to you while they stand armed before you and still so full of fight, and move so freely in the face of their enemies!'

'You must not reject my offer, Gunther and Hagen,' answered Dietrich. 'You have grieved my soul so deeply that in all justice you ought to make amends. I give you my hand on it that I will ride home with you to your country and escort you as honour requires, or die in the attempt. For your sake I will overlook my great affliction.'

'Do not urge this any further,' replied Hagen. 'The report that two such valiant men as we are had surrendered to you would disgrace us, for I see no one at your side apart from Hildebrand.'

'God knows, lord Hagen,' cried Hildebrand, 'the time will come when you would be glad to accept if someone offered to make peace with you. You could well assent to my lord's terms.'

'Indeed, I would accept them,' rejoined Hagen, 'before I would run from a hall as shamefully as you did here,

Master Hildebrand. I thought you could stand up to your enemies better!'

'Why do you reproach me with that?' replied Hildebrand. 'Who sat on his shield below the Waskenstein while Walter of Spain slew so many of his friends?[1] You yourself are far from being above reproach!'

'It ill becomes warriors to bandy insults like old women,' said lord Dietrich. 'I forbid you, Hildebrand, to say another word. Outcast warrior that I am, the sorrows that assail me are great enough. Now tell me, Hagen, what you two knights were saying when you saw me coming under arms,' continued Dietrich. 'Did you not declare that you would take me on in single combat?'

'No one will deny that I mean to put matters to the test with mighty blows so long as Nibelung's sword does not break in my hand,' said Hagen. 'It angers me that we two have been asked to surrender.'

When Dietrich heard Hagen's fierce intent the brave knight snatched up his shield, and how swiftly Hagen leapt from the stair to meet him! Nibelung's good sword rang clear on Dietrich's armour and he knew that the valiant man was in a ferocious mood, so the lord of Verona covered himself with his shield against Hagen's murderous blows. Well did he know Hagen and what a fine warrior he was, and he went in fear of that stout sword Balmung, too. But from time to time Dietrich struck back like the master he was till, despite all, he overcame Hagen with a long, deep wound. 'You have fought yourself to a standstill,' he reflected, 'and I shall earn little credit were you to lie slain by me. I will see if I can overpower you and take you prisoner.' He went about it not without anxiety.

Now Dietrich was very strong. Dropping his shield, he locked Hagen of Troneck in his arms, and so the dauntless man was overcome, much to noble Gunther's sorrow.

Dietrich bound Hagen, led him into the Queen's presence and delivered into her hands the boldest warrior that ever bore sword. After her great suffering, Etzel's queen was

1. See p. 371.

happy now. 'May you be blessed eternally!' she said to
Dietrich, bowing her joyful thanks. 'You have made ample
amends to me for all that I have endured and I shall always
try to deserve it, if death does not forestall me.'

'You should let him live, noble Queen,' replied lord
Dietrich, 'and if you do, what amends he will make for the
wrong that he has done you! He should not be made to
suffer for standing bound before you.'

Kriemhild commanded Hagen to be led to a cheerless
dungeon in which he was locked from sight. Meanwhile Gun-
ther was calling, 'Where did the Knight of Verona go? He
has done me a great wrong.' Lord Dietrich went to meet him.

Now Gunther's courage was much to be praised, for he
delayed no longer but ran out from the hall, and their
swords raised a mighty clatter. Although Dietrich's renown
was great and of long standing, Gunther was frenzied with
anger, for his great loss had made him Dietrich's deadly
enemy. It is still accounted a marvel that Dietrich escaped
with his life.

Great were their strength and courage. Palace and towers
resounded with their blows as they hewed with their swords
at the good helmets. King Gunther was in magnificent
spirits. Nevertheless, the lord of Verona eventually subdued
him, just as had happened with Hagen. You could see the
blood flowing through the hero's chain-mail from a wound
by the keen sword Dietrich wielded. Gunther had defended
himself very honourably despite his battle-weariness.

And now lord Gunther was bound by Dietrich. For al-
though kings ought never to suffer such bonds, Dietrich
thought that, had he let the king and his vassal go free, they
would have slain all who crossed their path. Dietrich took
Gunther and led him bound to Kriemhild. Thanks to
Gunther's misfortune many of her own cares left her. 'Wel-
come, Gunther of Burgundy,' she said.

'I would salute and thank you, dearest sister,' he ans-
wered, 'if your greeting were more gracious. But I know you
to be so angry that you will give Hagen and me scant wel-
come.'

'Queen of a most noble king,' said Dietrich, 'no knights as worthy as I have given you now were ever taken prisoner. Allow these wretched lords to profit from my entreaties.'

She declared she would gladly do so, and lord Dietrich left the heroes with tears in his eyes. But Etzel's queen was soon to exact fierce vengeance, for she robbed those matchless warriors of their lives, the one and the other. She kept them apart to add to their sufferings, and neither set eyes on the other again till she went in to Hagen with her brother's head. Kriemhild took ample vengeance on them both.

The Queen then went to visit Hagen and addressed that warrior with fierce hostility. 'If you will give me back what you have robbed me of, you may still return to Burgundy alive!'

'Your words are wasted, most noble Queen,' answered Hagen grimly. 'I have sworn as long as any of my lords remains alive never to reveal the treasure or yield it to anyone!'

'I shall make an end!' cried the noble lady, and she commanded them to take her brother's life. They struck off his head, and she carried it to Hagen by the hair. Great was the grief it gave him.

When the unhappy warrior saw his lord's head, he said to Kriemhild: 'You have made an end as you desired, and things have run their course as I imagined. The noble King of Burgundy is dead, young Giselher and lord Gernot, too. Now none knows of the treasure but God and I! You she-devil, it shall stay hidden from you for ever!'

'You have repaid me in base coin,' she said, 'but Siegfried's sword I shall have and hold! My fair lover was wearing it when last I saw him, through whom I suffered mortal sorrow at your hands.' She drew it from its sheath – he was powerless to prevent it – and bent her thoughts to robbing him of life. She raised it in both hands – and struck off his head! King Etzel saw this, and great was the grief it gave him.

'Alas!' cried this prince, 'that the best knight who ever

bore shield to battle should now lie slain by a woman! Although I was his enemy, great is the grief it gives me!'

'She shall not go scot-free for having dared to kill him, whatever becomes of me!' shouted old Hildebrand. 'Although he put me in deadly peril, I shall avenge the death of the brave lord of Troneck!' He leapt at Kriemhild in fury and struck the Queen with a heavy swing of his sword. She winced in dread of Hildebrand – but what could her loud shrieks avail her?

There lay the bodies of all that were doomed to die. The noble lady was hewn in pieces. Dietrich and Etzel began to weep, and deeply they lamented both kinsmen and vassals.

Their great pride lay dead there. The people, one and all, were given up to grief and mourning. The King's high festival had ended in sorrow, as joy must ever turn to sorrow in the end.

I cannot tell you what happened after this, except that knights and ladies, yes, and noble squires, too, were seen weeping there for the death of dear friends.

This story ends here:
such was
The Nibelungs'
Last Stand

AN INTRODUCTION TO A SECOND READING

*

THE POET, THE TIME, THE PLACE, AND THE PATRON

IN the absence of documentary evidence no precise answers can be given to the questions 'Who was the poet?', 'When and where did he write?', and 'For whom?'. Yet the possibilities can be narrowed down by inference.

The anonymous poet was probably one of the better sort of professional entertainers who in addition to their varied talents had learned to read and write after some measure of clerical education and who despite their official plebeian status might even be settled on a fief.[1]

The time when the poet was writing was somewhere between A.D. 1195 and 1205, a period during which other masterpieces of medieval German literature, both great and small, were being written, with yet others to follow.[2]

Under the conditions of medieval travel and patronage the questions 'Where?' and 'For whom?' are virtually the same. All are agreed that the court or courts for which our poem was composed must have lain on or near the Danube somewhere between Vienna and Passau. Beyond this, agreement ends. Nevertheless it can be shown from the text that the poet did not regard himself as a Bavarian writing for Bavarians, since he twice refers to the dangers of highway robbery in their territory.[3] Thus our poet and his patron must be sought in the Duchy of Austria, whose jurisdiction at this time had yet to be consolidated in the area between the Enns and the Hausruck well to the east of Passau,[4] for which city insistent claims have been urged. The suggestion that the poet wrote for the celebrated court of Vienna has nothing tangible to recommend it beyond his considerable

1. See Appendix 1, 'On the Status of the Poet' pp. 354–7.

2. See Appendix 3, 'On the Date of the Nibelungenlied', pp. 365–9.

3. See Appendix 2, 'The Manuscript Tradition, Bishop Wolfger of Passau, and the Homeland of the Poet', pp. 358–64.

4. This rejection of Passau tallies with the view, which I support, that the strophes concerned with Passau and its Bishop are interpolations of a recension hitherto called *B, and derive from an elegiac poem called *Diu klage*. See Appendix 2.

personal culture and the description of a great wedding in Vienna (p. 174). Another suggestion which has been revived recently is that the poet's patrons were members of the old Austro-Bavarian family of the Aribones who claimed descent from the Burgundian royal dynasty and to whom, in his time, the Bishop Pilgrim of our poem was related. There is evidence that families of the older nobility cultivated heroic legends whose leading characters they claimed as their ancestors, somewhat in the manner of ancient lineages in post-Mycenaean Greece, and the Aribones appear to be among them. The Aribones might have raised a good claim to the Margrave Rüdiger, for their great seat at Burg Peilstein lay near Rüdiger's seat at Pöchlarn and they are known to have revered his memory, but at a later date than that of our poem. Yet here, too, suggestive though the circumstances are, the case is not compelling. We are left, then, with the general inference, with which the last proposal does not conflict, that the poet and his patron were Austrians probably living east of the Enns within the consolidated region of the old Margraviate of Austria.

The anonymity of the author, by far the greatest heroic poet of medieval German literature, requires a word to itself. His anonymity was deliberate, in obedience to the ancient convention that as preservers, renewers, and interpreters of the poetic traditions of famous deeds believed really to have taken place, they should not name themselves as the 'authors' of their poems.

THE ACTION

The plot of the *Nibelungenlied* is single-stranded. But this does not mean that it is simple and straightforward. Each of the five characters named above in the bare gist of the plot (p. 7) – Kriemhild, Siegfried, Gunther, Brunhild, and Hagen – is indispensable to its unfolding; and it is the interplay of their wills and passions in shifting combinations that produces the final catastrophe. This interplay, moreover, is not always fully or frankly reported by the poet.

The action falls into two parts which are linked by a bridge. The first part ends with the murder and burial of Siegfried and the return home of his father (ch. 1–18), the second with Kriemhild's revenge and death (ch. 20–39). They have roughly parallel elements in wooing expeditions, weddings, pauses, and then invitations preceding the crises. In the bridge that links them (the only symmetrical chapter in the poem), Kriemhild (so it seems) allows herself to be reconciled with Gunther for the past, but, through Hagen's sinking her treasure in the Rhine, suffers further cause for vengeance in the future (ch. 19). Here, at the hinge of the poem, we find Kriemhild and Hagen at daggers drawn and manoeuvring for advantage. This is all there is to say on the structure of the poem.

The action is knotted in the fourteenth chapter, 'How the Queens railed against each other'. The murder of Siegfried, which it provokes, is narrated in the seventeenth. This in turn gives rise to the annihilation of the Burgundians, spread over eight chapters culminating in the thirty-ninth and last.

On what does the poet spend one third of his epic before arriving at the quarrel of the queens which first provides the makings of a tragedy? And with what degree of inevitability does the tragedy follow from there, as our poet tells the story? By gripping his poem thus by the throat we shall learn the truth about his art more speedily than by other more elaborate means.

In his first thirteen chapters the poet introduces Kriemhild and King Gunther's court of Burgundy, and he then presents Siegfried, who has come to woo the maiden. He tells of their growing love, though Siegfried has neither seen nor conversed with her, and how Siegfried wins the esteem of the Burgundians by defeating their enemies in battle, after which he is allowed to meet Kriemhild. Gunther now wishes to woo Brunhild of Iceland, whom he, likewise, has never seen, although to win her he must vanquish her in contests far beyond his powers. Hagen, however, rightly judges that Siegfried can achieve the adventure, with the result that Gunther and Siegfried strike a bargain: Kriemhild shall be given for Brunhild. And so it comes about, but not before Brunhild has been twice deceived: first, she is led to believe that Siegfried, of whom she has prior knowledge or acquaintance, is Gunther's vassal; second, she is vanquished in the contests by an invisible Siegfried while Gunther goes through the motions. As the Icelanders flock to court, Siegfried sails to Nibelungland for reinforcements, since the warriors from Worms are but four. Back in Worms there is a double wedding, and a banquet at which Brunhild weeps to see Kriemhild sitting beside Gunther's supposed vassal Siegfried. That night, Brunhild carries out her threat to deny Gunther her bed until she learns why Kriemhild should have married Siegfried, for she binds him with her girdle and leaves him hanging from a nail till sunrise. The following night, however, Brunhild is deceived for the third time, for

Siegfried enters the nuptial chamber in his cloak of invisibility and tames her to the point where Gunther can deflower her and so rob her of her fabulous strength. Just before leaving her to her lord, Siegfried takes her ring and girdle, which he will later hand to Kriemhild; but the only motive the poet can give for this strange deed is something between 'pride' and *'joie de vivre'*. Does he intend us to believe that Siegfried takes the ring and girdle in the flush of victory, as trophies of his hardest wrestling-match? Is he hinting that pride goes before a fall? Whatever the answer, Siegfried now takes Kriemhild to his country, from which they are invited back after an interval of ten years at the suggestion of Brunhild, who longs to know why the wife of a presumed vassal can hold her head so high.

Two of these episodes might be considered excessive. The long episode in which Siegfried defeats Liudegast and Liudeger (ch. 4); and Siegfried's quest for the Nibelung warriors (ch. 8).

The former might be interpreted as 'love-service' for Kriemhild, in keeping with the poet's endeavour to show Siegfried in love; but Siegfried has neither seen Kriemhild nor been admitted as her 'knight'. On the other hand, Kriemhild is as pleased to hear of Siegfried's prowess as if she *were* his 'lady'; and if Siegfried's exploits are indeed to be read as love-service they do something to raise Kriemhild from a mere chattel at the disposal of men. The episode also shows Siegfried in action, making himself valued by the Burgundians. But again, we have been told by Hagen in his thumbnail sketch of Siegfried on the latter's arrival at Worms that Siegfried had killed a dragon and hardened his skin in its blood, so that we can take his victory over the Saxons as read. All in all, the plot gains very little from this lengthy and ambiguous episode.

As to Siegfried's voyage to fetch his Nibelungs, this, surely, was scarcely necessary? There was no need in the first place for two kings to expose themselves by taking only two vassals to Iceland – or so the innocent reader might think.[1] A poet has only to wave his pen to obtain a fleet of ships crammed with fighting men, and this he could have done at Worms as easily as in Nibelungish waters. As with the Saxon war, so in this episode, the poet had other considerations in mind than economy of plot. He wished to provide Siegfried with a brilliant retinue for his wedding at Worms; he considered that he might reveal what the mysterious Nibelungland was like, and that Siegfried might in part re-enact

1. See p. 306

how he had mastered its denizens, an incident hitherto only reported; and in having Siegfried take a thousand Nibelungs to Burgundy he would at least associate (though not merge) these Northern Nibelungs with the Burgundians, who were to bear the name in the second part (p. 190*n*.). Yet these gains are dearly bought.

In my résumé of the first thirteen chapters I drew attention to the curious motive alleged for Siegfried's purloining of Brunhild's ring and girdle as she lay exhausted on her couch. The causes of the queens' quarrel, so closely linked with this, are equally strange and ambiguous.

When Siegfried and Kriemhild arrive at Worms after accepting the Burgundians' invitation, the pace begins to quicken. The queens are shown watching their men at the tournament (ch. 14). It is disconcerting that Brunhild, thrice deceived and suspicious, does not follow up her initiative, however covertly, but instead leaves it to Kriemhild to draw odious comparisons, and even then returns a soft answer. As the quarrel develops, Brunhild claims that she has heard Siegfried himself say that he was Gunther's vassal, and this she is entitled to do. Since Kriemhild is unaware of Siegfried's pretence of vassalage, she for her part is entitled to be incredulous, although her tone is unnecessarily scathing.[1] Up to this point, then, the women are innocent, and it is the men who bear the blame for striking an infamous bargain and for using deceit to accomplish it. The women's dispute now turns on the question of precedence, with Kriemhild challenging Brunhild to put it to the test whether Kriemhild, an alleged vassal-woman, would dare enter the cathedral in procession before Brunhild, Queen of the land. Arrayed in clothes of overpowering richness and splendour, Kriemhild is halted at the cathedral door by Brunhild, and she replies with the terrible question (p. 114): 'How could a vassal's paramour ever wed a king?' After varying the allegation she sweeps past Brunhild into church. The women meet again outside; and once more challenged by Brunhild, Kriemhild produces her trumps, Brunhild's ring and girdle, as proof that Siegfried was Brunhild's first man – that same girdle which Gunther could not loosen and by which he was hung on the wall. Gunther is now called, and he in turn summons Siegfried.

Gunther, of course, knows all the facts (of which not the least significant are Siegfried's mighty strength and horn-hard skin)

1. A sagacious critic has pointed out that the women become embroiled unwittingly because Kriemhild has Siegfried's natural qualities in mind, whereas Brunhild is thinking in terms of feudal hierarchy.

and what Gunther fears most is that he will be revealed as less than the man he was taken for by both his wife and his people. And so – whatever a woman's ring and maiden-girdle may have stood for in medieval society – the issue which Gunther takes up is whether Siegfried had ever boasted of enjoying Brunhild's body. Siegfried is fully entitled to offer an oath denying it, and either this offer to swear or his oath[1] settles the matter. Gunther clears him without question, Siegfried says they must discipline their wives, and we are told that the gallant knights looked at one another. But *which* knights? – All those who had witnessed the strange scene, because they were suspicious? Or Gunther and Siegfried, in token of their dire secret? Once again, the poet leaves us guessing. By a very narrow margin an ugly case of slander with more to it than meets the eye has swiftly been disposed of. We are not told what became of the exhibits. They disappear from the story and are never heard of again. Nobody has any interest in them, least of all the poet. Yet because of their silent language, and for no other reason now, Siegfried will have to die at Hagen's hands, and Kriemhild will bring the whole house of Burgundy down with Hagen. A ring and a maiden's girdle, we must learn, have more powerful utterance than words of law in a case of slander, just as in our own day the black cap of a judge is more eloquent by far than his verdict. In the more archaic version of this episode in the Norse *Thiðrekssaga* the men do not waste words on a lawsuit after Grimhild has flaunted the ring. The ring has spoken, all can read the token. Nothing remains but to plan the murder (p. 377).

Our poet has given us a powerful scene, most subtly constructed, and complete with costume and décor – yet at a price. He tries to pull the wool over our eyes in the most brazen fashion. Brunhild, Kriemhild, Hagen, and the bystanders all know what the ring and girdle signify, as did the poet's audience; all know it, it seems, except Siegfried, the man who purloined them – or he does not care. He took them, the poet suggests, in some freak of high spirits:

... and, without the noble Queen's noticing it, he drew a golden ring from her finger and then took her girdle, a splendid orphrey. I do not know whether it was his pride which made him do it ... (p. 93).

Even if there were no parallel version of this episode to confirm it,[2] we could be absolutely certain that our poet was here re-

1. The text is obscure at this point. See p. 116*n* 1.
2. In the *Thiðrekssaga*, already referred to, with Gunther's permission Sigurð deflowers Brunhild before leaving her to Gunther.

An Introduction to a Second Reading

fashioning an incident in which Siegfried deflowered Brunhild because that is what taking a ring and a girdle means in ancient poetic language. The phrase 'I do not know whether . . .' occurs elsewhere in medieval German literature precisely when a poet who is engaged in toning down an inherited crudity in the interests of a new decorum attempts to silence the diehards who have known the raw version all their lives. 'Do not ask me why,' he says, lying diplomatically to forestall their objections, 'for I do not know . . .' The situation of a medieval poet was much like that of a story-teller in the nursery: most tales were traditional and well known, and the audience were their part-owners, resenting wanton deviations. By the time of the *Nibelungenlied*, however, there was a breath of 'modernity' in the air. Courtly ladies had come to be judges of propriety and might influence poets directly or through their patrons. In keeping with the more refined and romantic expectations of a younger generation, our poet had set himself the task of presenting Siegfried in a more polished and chivalrous guise than that of the Siegfried of his sources. It had become unthinkable for many of his listeners that Siegfried should deflower his brother-in-law's wife, in order to oblige him, at the time of his nuptials with his own beloved Kriemhild:

'I promise on my word of honour,' said Siegfried, 'that I shall not make free with her at all. I prefer your lovely sister to any I have ever set eyes on.' (p. 90).

And so the poet has to weave his devious way past young and old by 'blinding' the motif before our eyes. In doing so, he reveals his limitations as an artist, although what he does in retrieving this lapse by way of consequential changes in the scene of the queens' quarrel shows to what heights he could rise. Yet this verdict needs charitable revision. Few poets at this time were free agents. Who knows what debates, arguments, and expressions of severe displeasure there were before the poet was browbeaten into this shifty compromise? Or, if not, what unpleasantness he shrewdly forestalled? Never was the saying truer than then: '*Kunst geht nach Brot*'.[1]

It is time to assess what we have learnt from this exploration. The author is a great epic-dramatic poet. He is nevertheless not entirely his own master. Not only must he pay more attention to his patron and public than most modern writers of integrity, but he also stands before a public more divided by the rift between

1. 'Artists must look to their bread'.

generations than is usual. To meet this situation, when reshaping traditional material, he will with a better or worse conscience compromise on issues that affect the heart of his poem. If need be, he will prevaricate or conceal. This accords well with a penchant for dráma, in which deeds, not explanations, count most. If one is lucky, as in the present instance, one can catch him at his task of recasting; failing that, there are parallel sources for the *Nibelungenlied* such as are largely lacking for the *Iliad*, and they allow us to delve beneath the surface. Another fact that emerges from this reconnaissance is that the poet is ready to invent entire episodes with very little excuse of plot (ch. 4, 8). Here reference to the genesis of the poem assures us that it is mainly in the first half that he descends to padding out a shorter source in order to raise it to the proportions of the second, which was based on a longer poem.

Most readers will rightly be interested in the *Nibelungenlied* as a self-contained work of art, and the remainder of this Introduction is for them. Some (certainly not wrongly) will be curious to know about the earlier stages of the Nibelung tradition and the growth of the present poem. For these I have provided an appendix.[1]

THE POEM AS AN ENTITY

Criticism of the *Nibelungenlied* has sometimes been unbalanced in the lands that lay claim to it, while elsewhere, with some notable exceptions, critics have tended to lean too heavily on what has been written in German. Modernizations of the *Nibelungenlied* and learned studies during the nineteenth century all speak of affection for the poem and of an awareness of a great heritage: but either the work was misinterpreted romantically or it was used for theoretical reconstructions which implied its fragmentation. The reaction was long in coming, but when it came it was just as painful. The extreme modern position is the super-aesthetic one of regarding the *Nibelungenlied* as a perfect and self-sufficient entity without a past. Faced with self-contradictions, lapses, or incongruities in the use of epithets, one declares them to be merely apparent, and bangs one's head on one's desk till illumination should come. This reaction against neglect of poetry in the interest of learned theorizing is healthy, and the pan-aesthetic approach is no doubt the best for countless literary masterpieces. The method can be profitable when applied to our poem within

1. See Appendix 4, 'The Genesis of the Poem', pp. 370–95.

reason – but reason draws a very firm line. I have shown above that although the poet wrote on parchment, he was not composing in a vacuum, whether social or aesthetic, but, instead, he was writing and then reciting under the pressure of live and far from unanimous audiences who somehow had to be appeased. This is a situation well known to students of traditional poetry.

The *Nibelungenlied* is not 'a perfect work of art' and of its nature could never have become one, yet it is none the less a powerful poem. In order totally to exclude the application of a critical approach suited to another age I shall enumerate its most alarming blemishes, assuring the reader that this is not undertaken in the spirit of a pedant who lists, say, the self-contradictions of a Jane Austen, but because the nature of these faults reveals the poem as belonging to a type of literature peculiarly its own. It is one thing when we are told that a character in an Edgar Wallace thriller, last heard of in Cape Town, suddenly reappears in Tierra del Fuego because the novelist's charwoman has knocked a flag from his wall-map, and southern capes are all one to her. It is quite another thing when we find that a poet of Homer's genius 'nods', as it must be conceded he does. That even Homer nods is a warning that we are dealing with a type of poetry different from our own, poetry with its own laws that bear mightily on the poet, whoever he may be.

INCONSISTENCIES, OBSCURITIES, PREVARICATIONS

With some strain on our gallantry, though helped by memories of Penelope, we may suppose Kriemhild to have kept her radiant looks at thirty-eight, when she married King Etzel, and we may concede her a son seven years later. Nevertheless we feel that time – even epic time, the most elastic – has been stretched to its limits. But when we turn to her contemporaries Giselher and Dancwart we find that time has snapped. For Giselher retains the description of 'boy' or 'youth' for thirty-six years,[1] and Dancwart, who went to Iceland to woo Brunhild as one of four tough men, claims shortly before his death in the second part to have been a 'tiny child' when Siegfried was killed. Of all names in the *Nibelungenlied*, the plural 'Nibelungs' is used in two senses. Up to the end of Chapter 18, when Siegfried's father returns home after burying him, it is applied either to members of King Nibelung's dynasty

1. I have rather desperately converted this into the sobriquet 'Young Giselher' and, I fear, made an 'old boy' of him.

or (more frequently) to the latters' vassals and men, whereas from Chapter 25 onwards till the end it is applied to the Burgundian warriors, except in the phrase 'the land of the Nibelungs'. Here it might seem possible to argue that the Burgundians have taken the name together with the Nibelung treasure; but this will not do, since there is no intimate symbolic link between the Burgundians and the treasure, either in the form of a curse or in any other way than by tenacious possession.[1] (The acquisition of the Nibelung treasure was in no wise a turning-point in the lives of the Burgundians, even though Kriemhild, in our author's ambiguous fashion, seems to make it a matter of Hagen's life or death at the end.)[2] Moreover there are still Nibelungs in Nibelungland who are the deadly enemies of the Burgundians, the murderers of their lord Siegfried. It is therefore not surprising that the poet succeeded in confusing himself in his use of the name of 'Nibelung' on one occasion.[3]

The common measure of all these faults is lack of harmony between the two halves of the epic, and it is only a step farther in thought to suppose that this lack of harmony was due to imperfect harmonization by a poet who was welding two not entirely congruous plots together, a supposition which has been triumphantly vindicated by comparison with parallel versions.[4]

A strange *non sequitur* occurs just before the fighting breaks out in Etzel's hall. We are told:

> Kriemhild's old grief was embedded deep in her heart. Since there was no beginning the fighting in any other way, she had Etzel's son carried to the board. (How could a woman ever do a more dreadful thing in pursuance of her revenge?) (p. 236)

The boy is fetched, but nothing happens. Hagen allows himself the offensive remark that the young prince has 'an ill-fated look', and that is all. The slaughter begins only when Dancwart, sole Burgundian survivor of a bloody battle in the squires' quarters, appears at the door, blood-stained and sword in hand. At his news, Hagen starts the fighting by beheading the young prince.

1. It is fatal to approach the *Nibelungenlied* from Wagner. The reader must make an entirely new start.
2. See p. 290. The motive of the treasure is entirely subordinated to that of revenge.
3. See p. 192 (= Strophe 1523,1).
4. See Appendix 4.

Next he dealt the tutor who had charge of the boy a vehement two-handed blow so that in an instant his head lay on the floor by the table — such pitiful wages did he mete out to that pedagogue. (p. 243)

The poet quite fails to tell us how Kriemhild's decision to fetch her son caused the fighting to break out, or why his tutor should be punished so ruthlessly. Actually, he has made the fighting in the hall inevitable with the slaughter of the Burgundian squires, and it would not matter whether Kriemhild's son were there or not. The words 'since there was no beginning the fighting in any other way' are meaningless in this situation and are beyond rescue by any purely aesthetic or logical method of interpretation. Recourse to the parallel version of the *Thiðrekssaga*, however, furnishes a complete explanation, though it leaves us wondering how our poet could be so clumsy. In this Norse compilation, Grimhild says to her son, who is appreciably older here:

... if you have the courage go up to Hogni (Hagen) ... clench your fist and buffet him on the cheek with all your might ...[1]

This the boy does, and Hogni strikes off his head for his pains. Now the meaningless phrase 'since there was no beginning the fighting in any other way' takes on a pregnant meaning, now we understand the words 'how could a woman ever do a more dreadful thing in pursuit of her revenge', and now we understand why the boy's tutor must be punished. As with the defloration of Brunhild, so with Kriemhild's sacrifice of her child to her revenge; when dealing with this passage in his source, the poet judged that the younger generation would not tolerate it as it stood; indeed, his notable elaboration of the massacre of the pages was largely in order to free Kriemhild from the need to sacrifice her offspring. Yet whilst removing the child's provocation he retained all that led up to it, even an expression of indignation at a deed no longer done. When the reader has read this epic, he will be in no doubt that the author was a great poet: nevertheless, he is capable of such shoddy, even stupid work as this! We have found him compromising again, attempting to please the moderns and yet giving the ancients as much of the old version as he dared.[2]

1. Cf. p. 382.
2. When such judgements are made, it must nevertheless always be borne in mind that a revisor has intervened between the poet and us, so that we can never be absolutely sure of the poet's text.

An Introduction to a Second Reading

When Gunther wins Brunhild by fraud at the games, she duly makes him sovereign of Iceland there and then (p. 68); but at the end of this episode and of the next, she can take no decisions until her kinsmen have assembled from far and wide. If we look below the surface we find that the reason for this assembly is to provide a motive for Siegfried to sail to Nibelungland to fetch his Nibelungs, some of whom he afterwards took to Worms on two occasions, first to the wedding, and then on his fatal visit to Gunther and Brunhild. In this way the poet not only provided a chapter which showed Siegfried's Nibelungs at home but he also caused them and the Burgundian Nibelungs to mingle, suggesting (however implausibly) some sort of continuity.

In the scenes in which Hagen tricks Kriemhild into revealing the position of Siegfried's vulnerable spot, the poet is again very careless. Playing on Kriemhild's inordinate love for her husband, which indeed is her own vulnerable spot, Hagen pretends that war is at hand and prevails upon her to mark the place on Siegfried's battle gear with a cross so that he may 'guard' it in the fray. He then calls off the war and calls on a hunt, for which Siegfried expressly takes magnificent hunting-clothes. Now, while Siegfried had his battle dress on, the poet had said: '. . . when Hagen had observed the *mark* . . .' (p. 122). It would have been easy for him later at the stream, over which Siegfried was bending, to have made Hagen 'aim at his mark', that is, at the remembered position. Instead he writes: '. . . Hagen hurled the spear at the *cross* . . .' (p. 130) – which was not there. When we recall *why* the poet has introduced this motif we are astonished at the contradictions of his art; for he contrived this scene in order to involve Kriemhild in her darling's death as a victim of her deadly enemy Hagen. There is nothing to contradict the notion that this fine conception was all our poet's own: and yet (if it really be he) he can be so slipshod. The moral surely is that – true to his dramatic genius – he was far more interested in confrontations of character than in the machinery by which he achieved them, or, as has been well observed by another writer, the poet is less concerned with 'why' than with 'how'. Chapter 29, in which he confronts Hagen and Kriemhild immediately on the Burgundians' arrival in Hungary, well illustrates this moral. The scene is an afterthought of the poet's, and a very fine one, which he obtains at the expense of leaving the Burgundian kings engulfed in a crowd in the courtyard, waiting to be received by Etzel, politest of monarchs. Only when Hagen returns from his tense scene with Kriemhild can the royal guests detach themselves and move on into the palace!

It would be futile to attempt an exhaustive treatment of the poet's more venial shortcomings in logical development and in the attribution of motives, whether he be too abrupt, obscure, ambiguous, or disingenuous; for this is no place in which to celebrate the triumph of the card index over a poet who little dreamt of us. Yet a bare selection must be given both for what it will tell us about him and his art and in order to alert the reader. It may perhaps encourage the latter, if he knows that others long familiar with the text can be as puzzled and irritated as he by the surprises that are sprung on us. The criterion of these shortcomings is in any case not given by the mass of scholarship that has accumulated about the poem, but by the poet's own great gifts, which challenge us to come to terms with both his lapses and his taciturnities. These can sometimes be questioned with profit, and our first example might be a case in point.

Before the wooing party leaves for Iceland and on its arrival there, it appears that Siegfried and Brunhild have prior knowledge or acquaintance of each other; but nothing is ever divulged. Are we meant to feel that something is going wrong, that this semi-mythic pair were perhaps destined for each other? The poet leaves us with our questions, and we remember that such is the pattern of life. In harmony with this effect there is Brunhild's obsession with Siegfried's status – was he a sovereign, or vassal to Gunther? In Worms she has ample occasion to satisfy herself of the truth, both during the wedding festivities and Siegfried's visit ten years later. Such things were known at great courts and were fittingly enshrined in ceremonial. Brunhild, however, clings to her memory of how Siegfried took second place to Gunther in Iceland, and she surely notes Gunther's evasiveness when he is taxed with it (p. 86). She had harboured some expectation of Siegfried; but what it was we are never clearly told.[1] She assumed that Siegfried had come to woo her, but was confident of her power to frustrate him. Here, then, the poet's silences, though disturbing, have some positive features.

The next two examples are of a sort met with elsewhere in heroic epic. Ancient elements of the story are preserved unchanged,

1. Recourse to parallel versions in Icelandic (see p. 372) tempts us to make various guesses. But no such version is known from Upper Germany, and so it is not legitimate to suppose that our poet was counting on his listeners to eke out his silence by recalling it.

though preceded and followed by modern elements, thus making an incongruous effect.

On their voyage to Iceland, Gunther, Siegfried, Hagen, and Dancwart, four men all told, and two of them kings, set sail and man the oars. If the smallness of the party was intended to underline their heroism, the effect is marred later by Siegfried's sailing for his Nibelungs. Similarly, on the way to Hungary, Hagen ferries an army of more than ten thousand men across the Danube. Again the change in texture is gross, and we know that a contemporary objected.[1] Since the former example occurs in the first, and the latter in the second half of the work, it would be idle to declare that the poet had yet to learn his trade. Rather did he bow too low to tradition, judging that the diehards would insist on their version, the second of which has its humorous aspects.

If Brunhild appears to remain morbidly uncertain whether Kriemhild is wife to a liegeman, Kriemhild (as the story is told) does not *know* whether Brunhild had been possessed by Siegfried. Each takes her stand by the symbolic act that she has witnessed. Brunhild has seen Siegfried hold Gunther's horse for him to mount (pp. 61f.); Kriemhild has been given the tokens of Brunhild's virginity (p. 93). The issue whether the symbols lie is never raised, fatal insults are exchanged on the strength of them, events march past the truth, the blind rush to their destruction. It is permissible for a poet to leave his characters in the dark, should he choose to do so; but it is unusual, whether in epic or in drama, to leave the audience in the dark too. We know that Siegfried was not Gunther's vassal, and we know that Siegfried did not deflower Brunhild: but we are unable to assess how far the queens believe the charges which they hurl at one another. This brings us very near to life; but the question whether the poet was consciously striving after dramatic realism must be deferred (pp. 338ff.).

If the poet is sometimes thrifty in his use of motive, on other occasions he moves fitfully among several. Hagen alleges two grounds for murdering Siegfried, and Kriemhild has two for killing Hagen. Hagen swears that Siegfried must die for having boasted he was Brunhild's lover, for with him, too, the symbol reigns supreme. Making little headway with this argument, Hagen puts the proposition to Gunther that if Siegfried were dead, Gunther would be lord of many lands. The idea that Siegfried's power is a threat to Gunther receives no support from the poem;

1. For the comment of the *C redactor see Appendix 2, pp. 363f.

for on the contrary, Siegfried saved Gunther from invasion.[1] When Hagen has murdered Siegfried he exults at having ended his dominion. Thus, if we are to believe Hagen, he made away with Siegfried both in order to redeem his queen's honour and to increase the power of his king, though this motive, as we saw, is hollow. Kriemhild pursues Hagen over the years with unrelenting thoughts of revenge, but when she at last has him at her mercy she makes the immediate point at issue the loss of Siegfried's treasure, with a prospect (feigned or otherwise) of Hagen's being spared if he returns it. This is a scene, be it noted, in which Hagen wins a great moral victory over Kriemhild even though the gold which he refuses to yield was ill-gotten, and it is only when the much-wronged woman draws Siegfried's sword from Hagen's side to make an end of him that the motive of revenge for ruined love returns. This vacillation between two motives is not due to deep calculation. The welding together of the two halves of the poem was based on Kriemhild's passion to avenge the murder of her husband: yet no requirement either of logic or of sentiment could dislodge the magnificent scene in which, since early times, Gunther and Hagen were faced with the alternatives of giving up the treasure or dying. Our poet thus has to shift from one motive to the other, as the plot requires him to do.

Here it would be wrong to speak of contradictions, since neither Hagen's nor Kriemhild's double motives are incompatible. Despite the plausible 'mock-ups' which barristers, psychologists, and novelists offer us, it is never possible in life to disentangle the motives for people's actions, be they saintly or devilish or merely human, and rarely will a deed have been prompted by one un-alloyed impulse. As a matter of literary history, however, it is possible to account for Hagen's and Kriemhild's shifting motives in terms of corresponding elements of plot which the poet decided to adopt, together with all that follows from them. This is no isolated phenomenon in the history of heroic poetry. The story of Patroclus requires a 'blind' Achilles who sends his friend to his death and thus brings on his own: but the story of Achilles himself requires a clear-sighted hero who makes a conscious choice between fame with early death and long life with obscurity. These two Achilles come and go in the *Iliad*, but the fact that they are combined into a figure of absorbing interest does not deceive us as

1. In Chapter 8, which, it will be remembered, was invented by the poet.

to their origins. There is no lack of other examples, either in the *Iliad* or the *Nibelungenlied*. The existence of divergent motives and characteristics attendant on additions or modifications of plot offered a challenge to the poets concerned. According to their skill and insight they made more or less of their chances. Here it must be admitted that, although he offers no contradiction, the Nibelung poet visibly shifts his ground.

As last examples of the poet's unconcern for clarity I will cite the two scenes in which the Burgundian leaders first plot the death of Siegfried and then sink his Nibelung treasure.

In the former case, Hagen (who was absent from the queens' quarrel) obtains the story from Brunhild and swears to take vengeance on Siegfried. Next, some warriors, whom we can only *infer* to be Hagen and Gunther, plot the death of Siegfried and are joined by Ortwin and Gernot, and then by Giselher, who, true to his role, objects. Hagen now utters his colourful 'Are we to rear cuckoos?' which, whatever its precise meaning,[1] must refer to the theme of adultery. To this, Gunther replies that Siegfried has always treated them well. Hagen then attacks from another quarter with the argument that if Siegfried were out of the way many kingdoms would subserve Gunther, a thought that saddens that feckless monarch. There is an interval during which Siegfried's knights appear to celebrate their queen's victory over Brunhild with jousting, while Gunther's are downcast. And then, without transition – the effect is like that of a nagging dream – Gunther and Hagen are in counsel again. This time Gunther takes our breath away by asking how the thing can be done, and, reassured by the technical excellence of Hagen's plan, he assents to it. Gernot and Giselher had presumably blown out from the conspiracy as airily as they had blown in, for they assert their complete innocence later. They act as though they had an alibi; yet the poet has taken no pains to establish it. But, after all, they knew that something was afoot and quite failed to warn their 'dear sister'. To thinking men they are revealed as hypocrites – but did the poet intend it? We are even more in the dark about Gunther. We could argue – but argument will not get us far with this poet – that Gunther declined to have Siegfried killed in revenge for adultery not because he knew of Siegfried's innocence but because such revenge would have implied the truth of the charge; so that his reminder of Siegfried's loyalty will have proceeded from cunning rather than from the better side of his weak nature. His quickening

1. See p. 117*n* 1.

interest in the means by which Siegfried could be safely removed is compatible with either interpretation, and so we are left guessing once more.

In the episode of the sinking of the treasure this impression of murky complicity among the privy council at Worms is heightened. It is Hagen who first suggests a reconciliation between Kriemhild and her brothers as a means of gaining possession of her treasure. The plan succeeds outwardly, though naturally Hagen was not received back into favour. (Whether Kriemhild was sincere on her part is yet another question which, for lack of assistance from the poet, we cannot answer.) The poet now hurries us past the point at which the Burgundians prevail upon Kriemhild to send for the treasure without telling us what was said (p. 146). Whether or not Kriemhild foresaw the possibility from the outset, she now employs her treasure to enlist warriors, whereupon Hagen decides to deny her the use of it. Gunther reminds him either weakly or cunningly but in any case fulsomely of the reconciliation, and at Hagen's shrewd offer to take the blame he allows his sister to be deprived of the hoard. Falling into his role, Giselher protests that were Hagen not his kinsman he would die, and Gernot then offers the compromise which brings the poet to his objective, namely the sinking of the treasure in the Rhine. Kriemhild goes piteously to Giselher, who promises to protect her – *when* they came back from abroad! All three brothers quit Worms, leaving Hagen to do the deed. On their return, they blame Hagen severely: but that this is all make-believe invented for the purpose of an alibi emerges from our poet's statement that before Hagen sank the treasure they had sworn to keep it secret as long as one remained alive. The reason why the poet 'blows' the alibi this time is that he has no choice: without the oath of secrecy there can be no final scene in which Hagen defies Kriemhild over the treasure. All three brothers, but Giselher most of all because of his show of tender feeling towards his sister – one of his stock roles – are revealed as nauseating hypocrites beside whom Machiavelli is a man of charm. Did the poet intend this? If he did, how long did he wish us to retain this impression? Upwards of twelve years later Kriemhild will dream that she is kissing 'Young' Giselher. And not long after that she will be sacrificing him, with many another, to her revenge.

The poet's treatment of time is unusual. On the one hand, he punctuates the various actions with intervals of such size that if we accept them at their face value they threaten to tear the characters apart; though, if we take our stand by the characters, these intervals tend to become nominal, suggesting 'a long time', in keeping with the poet's weak sense of numbers. On the other hand, the poet's thoughts are always flying to the final catastrophe towards which events are inevitably leading, thus bracing his sprawling tracts of time; but here the time in which he deals is a moral rather than chronological medium, time that knows a fulness, time that brings dark deeds to payment. These two different aspects of time merge in Kriemhild who is *lancræche* – 'tenacious in the pursuit of revenge long harboured'. She is the blind and also conscious instrument of retribution on the Burgundians, whether of Fate or of Divine Justice (p. 343), a conception that will have had much to do in deciding the poet to adopt an elongated time scheme when combining the two sources of his epic, rather than bringing them together as closely in time as possible. The longest interval in the unified epic need have been no longer than it took to dry the widow's tears: and the poet rightly judged that it must be a 'long' time, if ever.[1] But the other long intervals, Kriemhild's wedded bliss with Siegfried (some ten or eleven years), and her quiescent years in Hungary (twelve years), wantonly long as they are, lessen the effect of her protracted widowhood. Had the poet told us just enough to imagine Kriemhild as an old woman (he tells us nothing at all) he might have bought all these years at some profit and have added to the intensity of her revenge. As it is, Kriemhild's imperishable beauty, and the quarter of a century during which she nurses revenge, war against each other, with a 'Young' Giselher of fifty further to confuse the poet's meaning, and a Dancwart who was both a child and a man in the first part, or an awful liar in the second. It was, therefore, a characteristic of this poet's art not to worry too much about time, in the belief that time would surely come into its own – 'in the end'.[2]

As a result of the cross-relations in time which the poet gives us – they are mostly of a forward-looking nature – our interest is never quite absorbed in present actions: rather does he teach us to view them in the shadow of future events. And, from the opening scene, he has spanned these minor arches of anticipation with a lovely vault reaching out far beyond the loss of Siegfried into Kriemhild's

1. Dietrich tells the Burgundians on their arrival at Etzel's court that Kriemhild is still weeping for the loss of Siegfried. See pp. 214–15.
2. The poet's attitude to time, which he was not forced to adopt by the style of the heroic epic, speaks more for a 'superior minstrel' than a cleric or a clerically educated knight.

great sorrow, in which she nurses her plans for revenge – the maiden dream in which she is shown all that matters of her future life in condensed symbolic language:

> In disen hohen eren   troumte Kriemhilde,
> wie si züge einen valken,   starc, scœne und wilde,
> den ir zwene arn erkrummen.   daz si daz muoste sehen:
> ir enkunde in dirre werlde   leider nimmer gescehen.

(In the midst of such magnificence Kriemhild dreamt she reared a falcon, strong, handsome, and wild, but that two eagles rent it while she perforce looked on, the most grievous thing that could ever befall her).

She takes her dream to her mother, who tells her that the falcon is a noble man and that unless God preserves him he will soon be taken from her. Certainty as to who the two eagles will be grows as the first part unfolds. The poet's contemporaries of course knew from the beginning.

The poet never tires of directing our attention to the signs of calamity to come. Yet his hints of what will happen remain dark. Never is the future made so precise as to detract from the immediacy of the present. Only in dreams and in a fairy prophecy does the future break in upon us more clearly, and this is just as it should be. Although his characters are touched lightly by time, the poet himself does not make light of time. He is as far from playing with time as from weaving entrancing patterns with it, as in the *Odyssey.* He respects its logical order, abandoning it only on few occasions. His flight from the present is as brilliant and admirable in one instance as it is shifty and disturbing in another. Various poems about Siegfried's younger and wilder days must have been circulating in Germany at the end of the twelfth century, but they could not be encompassed in a poem that was to be held together by the love and hate of Kriemhild. Yet the plot of the *Nibelungenlied* turns on several attributes of Siegfried that were acquired in his wilder days.[1] It turns on his owning a cloak of invisibility, on his skin hardened in dragon's blood, and to a lesser degree on his Nibelung treasure. The poet gives us this essential information in a vignette. We are invited to peep through a casement opening on the hero's mythic past. For when Siegfried arrives at Worms, Hagen, most knowledgeable of Burgundians, looks out on the stranger through a window, concludes that it can only be he, and gives the court a thumbnail sketch of him (p. 26).

1. This 'wildness' of Siegfried comes to an end in the earlier chapters of the poem as he grows tame to Kriemhild's love.

A second flight from the present is one with which we are familiar. After overpowering Brunhild, Siegfried took her ring and girdle. 'Later he gave them to his wife ...' (p. 93). The poet says that Siegfried handed over the tokens 'later' so as to avoid the necessity of narrating the scene in full in its due position in time; for in such a scene Siegfried would have to say something, and why should he say anything but the truth? And if he told the truth, could Kriemhild still humiliate Brunhild? And, if not, could there be a murder and revenge?[1]

The poet's lack of concern with surprise does not mean that he does not build up tension. All knew that Kriemhild must humble Brunhild by flaunting her ring and girdle; that bloody fighting must break out in Etzel's hall; that, like a fury, Kriemhild must kill Hagen with her own hands. The question was *how*?

The poet breaks up the clash between the queens into three stages of rising intensity: at the tournament, and at the cathedral door, first before, then after mass. Confrontations, taunts, half-hearted attacks, demonstrations of force, pushing and shoving and threatening, and other provocations and counter-provocations mount and mount, with the blissful unawareness of Etzel as background – unawareness on the part of the one man who could have halted the downward march of events – till the dramatic appearance of Dancwart prompts Hagen to his fatalistic atrocity and so unleashes the battle. At the end, Kriemhild questions her captive Hagen on the subject of the treasure and is defeated in the traditional way, when her eye falls on his sword and she remembers the young lover Hagen took from her.

We have come very near to discussing the dramatic aspects of the poem. But this theme is best approached through the characters.

THE ART OF CHARACTERIZATION

As I have pointed out in the Introduction to my translation of the *Tristan*,[2] there is a tendency even in so 'literary' a poet as Gottfried to make the episode the unit of characterization thanks to the contradictory demands of the foreign plot, which he respected.

---

1. A minor deviation from strict chronology is Siegfried's chastisement of Kriemhild. For reasons of delicacy towards the ladies, no doubt, the poet refers to the beating as having already happened (see p. 120).

2. *Gottfried von Strassburg, Tristan. Translated entire for the first time, with the surviving fragments of the Tristran of Thomas, newly translated. With an Introduction by A. T. Hatto.* Penguin Classics, L 98 (1960), p. 22.

An Introduction to a Second Reading

How much more must this be the case with the less independent poet of the *Nibelungenlied*, who was not only concerned with strong native traditions but also committed to harmonizing for the first time two distinct plots which, despite incongruities in their behaviour, shared some leading characters. What, for instance was the poet going to do with a king who dishonestly married a queen beyond his own wooing and who then connived at the murder of his brother-in-law, but who afterwards fought and died as a hero? What would he do with a murderer who (in spite of his bad case) rises to the heights of fortitude in adversity? Or with a young woman of more than usual spirit who reappears as an implacable she-devil? We have already learned enough to know that the poet will say as little as possible about his characters' motives and keep explicit contradiction to a minimum. 'Character' will be commensurate with the deed in hand. The human psyche is in any case still largely inscrutable (as honest analysts have readily admitted), and the souls of kings are even more so – why say more than one knows? Crude though some aspects of our poet's art may be in the eyes of the modern reader, this aspect of his art is virile and mature, especially if one remembers how certain of our contemporaries go grubbing for motives in the dustbin of the mind.

The key to the problem is contained in the aphorism 'die Rolle prägt den Kopf',[1] and it has been wittily said that the central figures – the oldest in the Nibelung tradition – 'must not be weighed down by too much *soul*'; whereas Rüdiger, one of the more recent figures, himself lays claim to having one (p. 266).[2] Because the poet has narrated so many deeds, and such stark ones, he has surrendered some of his freedom to reveal his characters' motives or to place them in their best light. To understand his position one need only ask how much of the nobler Greeks' characters Homer could have left unchanged had he gone on to relate the pillage, atrocity, sacrilege, and rape that attended the fall of Troy.

It is therefore true as a general rule that the later a figure was introduced into the Nibelung tradition the more harmoniously are its actions motived – which is far from saying 'the greater is its impact on the imagination'. Knowledge of the genesis of the poem helps to account for fluctuations in character as the figures rise from or sink back into the older strata of the story. Thus it is hazardous, if not futile, to try to bridge the 'faults' by psychologizing

1. 'The role decides the soul.'
2. We have to modify Rüdiger's claim, however; see p. 334.

the characters.[1] Despite their fluctuations, the characters were no doubt continuous in the poet's imagination, but he did not expound this to the reader. He did not reduce his figures to a mechanism, however refined. To him his characters were *the people who did those deeds*. He has greater insight into human nature than he puts explicitly into words, and to find it we must read between the lines, adding nothing of our own. His characters' actions are mostly so incisive that although we cannot always show their continuity we sense it and accept it. Are Kriemhild the fulfilled young wife and Kriemhild the widow who forsook her child one and the same person? Why did she not return to the Netherlands to mother the pledge of Siegfried's love? One shudders to think what deep motives could be found by relating her failure to do so with other of her acts. What 'complex' or perversity does it argue when a woman dotes on her husband but abandons their offspring? Was this warped emotion also responsible for her carelessness with her second son at Etzel's banquet? Should we remember here that she once dreamt that she was kissing her brother? Or (worst of all) ought we to take note that she was tenacious of her gold? This is *not* the way to approach the problem. The truth is that by giving Siegfried such a definite background as the Netherlands, Norway, and Nibelungland, by making him ruler there and by giving him a son in concern for whose good name the hero finds moving words as he lies dying (p. 132), the poet has created for Kriemhild a centre of interest away from Worms, whereas the continuation of the story demands that she remain there. By keeping her in Worms he inevitably casts a shadow on her motherhood. Either he has invented her son or he has retained him from an unknown source, and, being unprepared to sacrifice him and his father's fine words, he decides to debit Kriemhild's character with the consequences, in view of her future ruthlessness. If he means us to understand that every human feeling died in Kriemhild when she buried Siegfried, he does not say so. The way he tells it is this. Kriemhild's kinsmen, and more particularly Giselher, entreat her to remain in Worms, but she answers that she cannot, for how could she bear the sight of her enemies? And now her mother Uote and her brother Gernot add their entreaties, pleading that she has few blood-relations in the Netherlands – a very powerful argument in itself but in shocking bad taste in the

1. See the Introduction to my *Tristan*, pp. 21ff., where my reasons are similar but not identical.

circumstances.[1] Siegmund, for his part, thinks it necessary to re-assure her that she would not be made to 'pay' for the loss of Siegfried if she returned, an ambiguous expression which might mean anything from loss of status to death by blood-feud. But she has allowed herself to be persuaded by her relations, and when Siegmund begs her not to leave her son an orphan she at first over-looks this in her answer. Only when her refusal to go back with them is plain does she commend her 'dear little son' to the care of the Netherlandish warriors when they should arrive back home. Characteristically, this is the last we hear of the matter. If pressed, the poet would have admitted that it was very damaging to Kriemhild, for he hints as much through Siegmund's amazement. But, as so often, his rule is 'least said, soonest mended'. We note Kriemhild's failure as a mother and feel that after this she may perhaps be capable of anything.

It has been argued that in causing Kriemhild to remain at Worms, the poet made it possible to show her in the utter desola-tion of her widowhood, humiliated without an effective friend by Hagen's distrainment of her treasure, and despairing of revenge and then only recalled to action by Etzel's suit through Rüdiger. The poet does achieve all this: but it would be wrong to regard it otherwise than as a virtue born of necessity. In staying behind in Worms, Kriemhild sacrificed her child and Siegfried's, and pros-pects of immediate revenge by forces perhaps as strong and brave as Etzel's and infinitely more willing to fight for her.

When the plot demands it, the leading characters follow old ways. Otherwise they follow the new. In historical terms this means that, in our poem, acts rooted in the Heroic Age alternate with others more typical of the poet's own chivalric period. This does not necessarily imply a contrast, since the latter grew out of the former and the knight inherited some of the qualities of the Germanic warrior, and similarly with their women. Thus natural links between the two outlooks exist and it is not to be thought that because *we* must not build bridges there are gaping rifts within the characters. In raising the question of Kriemhild's motherhood I have already drawn attention to the most challeng-ing problem.

Our Hohenstauffen poet was understanding to an astonishing

1. Even at this late date one's kinsmen were one's family, one's allies, club-mates, and mutual benefit and insurance society: but Kriemhild's kinsmen had utterly betrayed her.

degree of the archaic mentality of his main characters, but there are times when he gives up, as for example with Siegfried and Brunhild, who become figures of fun when showing their strength (pp. 65, 128). Another aspect of his attitude towards character is seen in his treatment of Hagen. Although Hagen shows himself indifferent to the Church and Christian morality, his solicitude for his comrades is such that he urges them to be confessed before battle. Why? The scholar who claimed that Hagen had matured to a state of sublime selflessness showed himself not unmarked by the time and place in which he lived. A less bewildered and more consciously cynical interpretation would be that Hagen as an experienced commander knew that men fight better confessed than unconfessed. But the answer that begs fewest questions is 'good commanders do just this on such occasions'. Following the plot on the one hand and avoiding indefensible inconsistencies on the other, the characterization of Hagen is, as another has said, strictly *ad hoc*. This leaves us an area in which to look for development within the characters, with the warning that such development is not the supreme law of their being.

THE CHARACTERS

It has been truly said that the conception of Kriemhild holding the two halves of the epic together for the first time would not have been possible before courtly authors like Thomas of Britain (p. 312n. 2) and Chrétien de Troyes[1] had achieved the form of the biographical romance. But although Kriemhild – a mere woman – is the first character to be named, and only weeping and then silence follow her death, it would be wrong to read the *Nibelungenlied* as her biography. If the wealth of deeds, to which she contributes so mightily, is held together by her personality they are not capable of being absorbed by it. The fine moments of Siegfried's death-scene are swiftly engulfed in her agony and mourning. But in the second half there grows inexorably something that defies treatment only in relation to her, something that defeats her in the moment of her triumph: the clear-sighted and fatalistic heroism of Hagen, heroism as darkly splendid as Siegfried's was bright, and achieved at far greater cost.

Kriemhild begins as a charming young princess and ends as a

1. The author of *Erec* and *Yvain* and other epoch-making romances (fl. 1160 – *c*. 1185).

vâlandinne[1] or 'she-devil', a woman who has sacrificed her nature to revenge, the business of men. I will follow this clue through the maze of the action.

In the opening scene, in which her mother reads her dream of a falcon, Kriemhild divines what a tragic love could do to her, and she resolves to avoid the joy of love forever and so avoid its pain. When her falcon comes, however, she accepts him gladly, and when on the second night of her wedding he returns from a strange absence, unlike the fretful Brunhild she allows him to silence the question on her lips. We are never told whether she knows the truth about his taming of Brunhild; but it is with pride, not jealousy, that she allows the court to think that he enjoyed King Gunther's Queen. She is very much in love with her young husband. When he and she make their preparations to leave Worms a delicate symmetrical arrangement in the fourth lines of the first two strophes of Chapter Eleven informs us that Siegfried will be master; for when she hears that he is soon to take her home, *she* is *glad* to learn it, but when he hears that she first intends to secure her share of the Burgundian patrimony, *he* is *loath* to learn it – and nothing comes of her intention. But then she shows much spirit and some lack of tact in asking Hagen, of all men, to follow her north as her liegeman. Nothing comes of this, either, for as Hagen angrily explains, the place of those of Troneck had always been at the court of Burgundy. And so they depart. The next significant moment comes ten years later when the pair have returned to Worms. Although Brunhild has planned the confrontation, it is Kriemhild who tactlessly provokes the quarrel by praising Siegfried in superlative terms, reviving imperial claims which he has long since abandoned on being tamed by her love. Although she withdraws so far as to offer Brunhild parity in husbands, the damage has been done. Brunhild means to establish her own precedence and this brings out the worst in Kriemhild. Nothing less than the manifest utter defeat of Brunhild will content her now. Some of Kriemhild's concern for her status may have been inspired by pride in her husband, but it is shot through with self-love. In the scene in which Hagen tricks her into divulging the whereabouts of Siegfried's vulnerable spot she relates without resentment how her husband had beaten her for her loose talk.

1. The neutral Dietrich first uses this term, rather too early for full effect. Hagen uses it at the end when he lies (or stands) bound at her mercy, and one might think him biased. Her death at the hands of Hildebrand seems to imply the poet's own verdict.

'How perfectly matched this couple must have been!' we are bound to exclaim, 'if this imperious woman could so sweetly accept a thrashing from her husband.'[1] It is on her love for Siegfried that Hagen plays, and we may well think it excessive, because blind, since in the very words with which she owns her fault towards Brunhild she begs Hagen not to let Siegfried pay for it. Her unconscious fears at what she has done express themselves in warning dreams. And when her chamberlain announces a corpse on the threshold she knows everything in one revealing flash. She resolutely insists on the public proof of Hagen's guilt by the ordeal beside the bier. For those with eyes to see (and only Hagen appears to have them) the future can be read at the graveside. Until now we have suspected that Kriemhild was inordinately attached to her spouse. When, weeping tears of blood, she has his magnificent coffin raised for a last look at his face, we know it. Her love was Siegfried's and her own undoing, and it will prove the undoing of them all. Now comes the most tenuous part of the clue, Kriemhild's resignation from motherhood, with which I have dealt above (pp. 314f.). After residing at Worms for some time she goes through a reconciliation with Gunther, but not with Hagen, whereupon her brothers betray her anew over Siegfried's treasure, with Hagen as the driving force; for Hagen clearly sees that she is winning allies with her bounty. When Etzel sends to woo her she is persuaded to surrender her person to him and to overcome her scruples against re-marriage and a pagan husband, only when Rüdiger, by his oath of alliance, has placed the instruments of vengeance in her hands. Her invitation to her brothers seems inspired by both revenge and homesickness. In the series of confrontations with Hagen in Hungary, of which she gets the worst only because she is a woman, her passion for revenge is goaded to frenzy. She was certainly careless about her son Ortlieb, but since the poet behaves so irresponsibly here, it is futile to discuss her reactions (pp. 302f.). Now comes a whole list of warriors, from both sides, whom she sacrifices to her revenge: Bloedelin, Iring, Rüdiger (why does she weep when Rüdiger at last resolves to fight? The poet leaves us with yet another enigma, which has not failed to draw the unwary), then Gernot and Giselher, who refuse to buy their lives with Hagen's, and finally, in cold blood, Gunther. Strangely enough, it is overlooked by the com-

1. If such chastisement was customary, this will have softened the blows; but one wonders whether a queen might be thrashed, even by a king.

mentators (it may take a compatriot of Mrs Pankhurst's to see it)
that these sacrifices are due equally to Hagen. After all, he did
murder Siegfried and he now glories in it; and the only thing that
is needed to avoid the destruction of the house whose faithful
guardian he claims to be is for him to walk out of the hall and die
fighting. But Hagen does not see this. He drags them all down with
him, and such is the poet's sympathy that Hagen wins most of the
kudos. This is not without its bearing on our assessment of Kriem-
hild's situation. The poet's gift of glory to Hagen, though Hagen
only partly deserves it (it is all at Kriemhild's expense), is inspired
by male prejudice. Our poet's pride of sex makes him as mean
towards Kriemhild here as Homer's pride of race made him
momentarily ungenerous towards Hector, when he would not
suffer Hector to slay Patroclus until first Apollo had shattered
him and then a nobody, Euphorbus, had struck him between the
shoulders, thus cheating the Trojan leader of his glory. For just as
Brunhild as a woman was expected to behave with docility on the
nuptial couch, however much she may have been deceived (p. 92*n*.),
so Kriemhild, whatever her wrongs, as a woman was forbidden to
pursue revenge to the destruction of good warriors. Discussing the
scene in which Isolde stands sword in hand over Tristan, her
uncle's slayer,[1] I drew a comparison with Kriemhild, and if the
comparison was apt it will work the other way round. Women must
not take up the sword to slay. Their womanhood should prevent
them. Isolde's feelings acknowledge, Kriemhild's violate this rule.
The events of the last chapter confirm this. Dietrich, the one figure
who rises above the conflict, sets aside his own good grounds for
vengeance and delivers Gunther and Hagen to Kriemhild, bound,
with a recommendation to mercy, thus contradicting his premature
verdict that she was a she-devil.[2] She is given her chance to find
her woman's nature; but this she cannot achieve. The grim years of
widowhood and exile have robbed her of the power to do so.
Though outwardly she may have warmed to Rüdiger's daughter
(p. 169) and proved a worthy successor to Queen Helche (p. 176),
her heart is frozen over. Yet, as we have seen (p. 307), the hot
fount of her revenge was her love for her young husband, thwarted
and turned to hatred for his slayer, a love that we may well call
vast when we measure it by its obverse. Impelled by this fury that
possesses her, she now kills Hagen, the finest warrior of them all.

1. *Tristan*, Introduction, p. 28.
2. See p. 217. The ineptitude cannot be explained away.

and, masculine pride thus having been outraged,[1] she at once pays the price for so far overstepping her bounds. A woman whose will was as strong as a man's risked being branded as a monster. Such women were far less rare in the heroic Age of Migrations, when warriors had need of them. But men of the high Middle Ages thought them either comic or objectionable. Indeed, it has been well said that Kriemhild could never have been invented in our poet's generation. The marvel is that he could re-create her.

Kriemhild's antagonist Hagen[2] is not easy to assess because the very events that elicit his good qualities spring from his darker nature. This blend of the heroic and the sinister has appealed mightily to German writers in the past. One critic saw in Hagen's bearing the self-assertion of the ethical personality against odds, overlooking (or brushing aside) the fact that Hagen was a murderer. Another, as we saw, viewed him in a Christian or near-Christian light as a man who had attained to selfless care for his dear ones. It would of course be unprofitable to try to measure so magnificent a figure with a conventional moral tape. But we shall get nowhere with this enigmatic personage until the nature of his guilt has been established.

Hagen was not present at the quarrel of the queens, no doubt in order that the impact of Brunhild's grief upon him might be the greater.[3] Shortly afterwards, he came and found Brunhild in tears. He asked her what was the matter and she 'told' him, and he then swore that Siegfried should pay for it. Although he had time and opportunity to amplify and if necessary correct Brunhild's account, which (whatever its content) must have been one-sided, he never wavered in his intention to kill Siegfried. What counted more with him than the truth was the fact that the language of the ring and girdle had appeared to be confirmed by the tears of his queen, witnessed by all. He therefore went to work on Kriemhild craftily, though Kriemhild was the sister of his lord and also his own kinswoman. Other motives than revenge for tarnished honour lurk below the surface. We gain some insight into Hagen's self-

1. Old Hildebrand's voice rises to a shrill falsetto as he raises his sword to make an end of her.

2. During the growth of the Nibelung story in medieval Germany, Hagen gained in stature at the expense of both Gunther and Brunhild (see pp. 391f.).

3. But also, surely, because in his presence the transactions between the two queens and their husbands must have taken another course.

control and political acumen during the first clash with Siegfried
when, in his youthful arrogance, Siegfried challenged Gunther to
fight for their two kingdoms: for on this occasion Hagen permitted
himself no more than the reproach: 'He ought to have refrained.
My lords would never have wronged him so . . .' (p. 30), leaving
threats and bluster to his nephew Ortwin. Kriemhild's invitation
to Hagen to follow her to the Netherlands as her (and therefore
Siegfried's) vassal must have galled him, and his angry refusal is no
doubt aimed against her husband as much as against herself
(p. 96). Siegfried's pre-eminence irked Hagen. He could not suffer
his king to be outshone. Failing to persuade Gunther on the point
of his marital honour, he suggests to him that if Siegfried were
dead, Gunther would be lord of many lands, and this Hagen may
well have believed, since, as Siegfried lies dying, Hagen exults at
having ended his dominion, and he asserts that there will now be
few to oppose the Burgundians (pp. 117, 132). To this must be
added Hagen's first expression of a wish that Siegfried's treasure
should come to Burgundy, long before the queens have quarrelled,
when Siegfried and Kriemhild's visit was being mooted. Here the
poet is said to have 'sown the seed' of Hagen's intention to acquire
the hoard. (Chapter 12, p. 105.)

The trait which explains most of Hagen's deeds is his political
clearsightedness followed by ruthless action. It has been well said
of him that he 'represents the type of responsible statesman who
has to do what he sees is necessary, even against public opinion and
against a weak sovereign'. The quarrel of the queens convinced him
that the time had come for Siegfried to go, leaving him to choose
but the means. Hagen foresees so clearly that his house must
perish if his lords go to Hungary that he scarcely needs con-
firmation either from the fairies' prophecy or from his experiment
with the Chaplain – so that the incidents in which they occur are
to be interpreted as a demonstration in epic terms of his superior
insight. The dullest member of the audience now knows that
Hagen knows. All that can follow for Hagen is resignation, which
in so active a man means dedication. It is this same clearsighted-
ness which explains his brutal slaughter of the innocent Ortlieb.
The appearance of Dancwart at the door tells him that the moment
for the inevitable battle has come, and so he summons fate punc-
tually himself. His words and deeds are governed by supreme
economy. Only once does he reverse a decision, when his foolish
lord makes the invitation to Hungary an issue not of policy but
of courage. Stung by Giselher's taunt, Hagen accepts the challenge,

with the outcome he so clearly surveys, and withdraws his opposition (p. 191). In this scene Hagen had reminded Gunther of their fell deed. Accused by the blood at Siegfried's bier (p. 137), he had been too proud to deny his guilt. And later, face to face with Kriemhild, he had again owned it (p. 222). And when at last she had him at her mercy, he truthfully observed that things had turned out just as he thought they would.

Hagen's motive for murdering Siegfried was therefore political rather than personal in a petty sense. So long as Siegfried could be used to further the Burgundian interest, as in the war against the Saxons or the wooing of Brunhild, Hagen used him without prejudice. But when he sensed a threat in Siegfried, he made away with him, and his action was as impersonal as it was efficient.

With the one exception of the fateful visit to Hungary, it is always Hagen who forces the pace when important decisions have to be made. He is the power behind the throne. Thus the degree of Hagen's guilt is great, and when he is about to incur it, the poet admits it and even tends to harp on it (pp. 123f.). Nevertheless, in the second half of the poem, increasingly, when the plot requires grim resistance from Hagen the poet seems to overlook Hagen's guilt and gains sympathy for him in his reversal of fortune as for one betrayed.

Hagen, we are told, was a tall man of impressive appearance and gait, with eyes that struck terror in the beholder.[1] For all his splendid presence, his was no face that a girl would wish to kiss (p. 207). He was nevertheless capable of kindness, as well as of stern loyalty towards kinsmen whom he cannot always have esteemed. He approves of the proposed marriage between Giselher and Rüdiger's daughter with benignity as well as policy. Towards Eckewart, and even more towards Rüdiger, he shows perfect chivalry and tact: for in returning Eckewart's sword on the frontier he restores his honour,[2] and in asking for Rüdiger's shield in battle he makes it possible for him to rise above his tragic dilemma and give proof of his affection for the Burgundians and also to reassert himself as the Bestower of Gifts (p. 271). To do this,

1. p. 216. The one-eyed Hagen comes from the epic of Walther of Aquitaine, cf. p. 381.

2. p. 204. 'Honour' is the esteem in which society holds a man, as so often in the plays of Shakespeare, cf. *Richard II*, I, 1: 'The purest treasure mortal times afford ...'

it has been argued, Hagen asserts the claims of friendship against those of his fealty to Gunther, for to accept Rüdiger's gift is to bind himself to Rüdiger, thus bringing about his neutrality. Such warm regard for the reputations of others as Hagen shows, and such readiness to redress them, if tarnished, are rare qualities, and this may help to explain why Hagen felt bound to restore Brunhild's esteem at any cost, after Kriemhild had shattered it. Honour was what he understood best. Hagen's high moral qualities in the second half are underlined by the poet's presentation of Volker and Dancwart as his physical superiors, and his greater depth also appears at once if we compare him with another vassal-in-chief, Hildebrand, who fails to deal with young hotheads, or with the amiable young berserk Wolfhart, who dies happy to have been slain by a King (p. 283). And again, Hagen's great stature is seen when we confront him with the shifty kings of Burgundy. For, having judged a situation and taken action, Hagen abides by the deed, he is not assailed by vain regrets. Hagen remains unbroken to the end, active, and yet resigned to the fate which (unlike Siegfried) he has long foreseen.

True to his style, the poet offers no direct hint whether Hagen in any way purges his guilt. Kriemhild indeed subjects him and his companions to a purgatory of steel and fire from which they emerge with enhanced loyalty towards each other. But Hagen's brutal killing of Ortlieb is an unpromising entry into any purgatory, and the notion had better be dismissed. Our poet fell short of Homer morally as well as artistically: he failed to relate Hagen in his greatness to Hagen at his depths. We understand and accept Hagen with gratitude as an ancient heroic figure in a medieval setting. But we feel no need to glorify either him or his 'Nibelung spirit', as they have been glorified anachronistically in these days of industrial civilization. Marvel at Hagen we surely must. But with their perverse 'will to death', Hagen and his friends are best viewed from a distance.

Kriemhild and Hagen are evenly matched in their grim magnificence, and the poet pits them against each other with great skill. The ruined love of a passionate woman and the 'honour' of a masterful man are terrible forces to be reckoned with. The poet makes it wholly credible that they should hold each other in check for so long.

The three Burgundian kings form the centre of a highly dangerous court. Although nothing of importance can be undertaken without Gunther's at least tacit consent, whether it be a murder or a grand theft of treasure, his younger brothers Gernot and Giselher are always free to speak their minds. Gernot's role is that of a middle term between his elder and younger brother: sometimes he is Cox to Gunther, at other times he is Box to Giselher. Giselher's part is that of 'junior lead'. The hypocrisy and treachery of all three towards their sister are differentiated broadly in descending degrees. Yet a word of caution is necessary here. It may well be that the poet would not have approved of this additive approach to his characters, and that when he makes them protest their honesty and innocence he means both them and us to believe it – for the moment.

Gunther is a king in name but in little else. In the last scenes, in which all show themselves as doughty fighting men, he, too, hardens into a hero and so may be thought to atone somewhat for his past. He is also a very courteous man – so courteous and smooth that it is difficult to catch his drift. Before the poem begins he has already learnt to rely on Hagen. Confronted with the imponderable threat of young Siegfried, and with Ortwin calling for swords, he is sorry that Hagen stays silent so long (p. 30), and it is significant that when Hagen does speak up he is 'Hagen the strong'. On such strong men can weak kings lean. But Gunther had to be weak in the first half of the poem because the plot required it. Only a weak man would have left the winning and taming of his wife to another. Gunther, however, is not only weak but also vain and deceitful. He finds it possible to aspire to the love of a woman beyond his own power to woo, and as her publicly acknowledged conqueror to make her his wife. But his reward for aspiring so far above himself is farcical humiliation. When Siegfried, at his own suggestion, so far demeans himself as to hold Gunther's stirrup as his 'vassal' while Brunhild and her ladies look on, Gunther feels exalted (p. 60). On their return from Iceland, Siegfried had to remind Gunther that Kriemhild's hand was to be his reward. But perhaps this may be excused, on the grounds that no man should seem in a hurry to give away his sister. Gunther's yellow streak is skilfully hinted at as early as the fourth chapter. An attack by Liudegast and Liudeger has been announced, and Siegfried sees Gunther anxious and silent. Frankly asked by Siegfried why he has so much changed from his former happy ways, Gunther replies with an unwarrantable insinuation:

I cannot tell everyone about the vexation I have to bear, locked away in my heart ... One should complain of one's wrongs to proven friends.

An Introduction to a Second Reading

It is an answer that would pain the heart of any honest man. No wonder Siegfried changes colour violently (p. 34). When counter-measures are agreed on, Siegfried goodnaturedly asks Gunther to stay at home with the ladies – and Gunther does so, although Siegfried himself is a king, and there is a king in the field against them.

In the last analysis Gunther's weakness can be made to bear the whole responsibility for the tragedy. Faced on the nuptial couch with the choice between the physical enjoyment of Brunhild and the truth, he might have chosen the latter: but in fact he chose the former.

Although Gunther denies it later (p. 146), he connived at Siegfried's murder. He at first resisted Hagen's suggestion. Then the argument that, were Siegfried dead, Gunther would rule many kingdoms made him 'sad'. And when Hagen proposed a secret murder, Gunther showed alert interest in the means, and, satisfied on this score, he did not withhold his consent (p. 118). On this we have the poet's observation:

The king followed his vassal Hagen's advice to evil effect, and those rare knights began to set afoot the great betrayal.

When the deed is done, however, Gunther breaks out into laments, only to be checked by murderer and victim alike, in words that leave us in doubt which of the two despised him the more (p. 131). In view of his share in the murder of Kriemhild's husband, Gunther's facile protest 'after all, she is my sister', twice uttered, sickens us: when Hagen suggests taking her Nibelung treasure (for which Gunther then fabricates an alibi) (p. 148), and when Hagen advises against her marriage with Etzel (p. 156). A strange thing, plausibly grounded in the character of a weak and perfidious man, is that when the Burgundians set out for Hungary, Gunther places his reliance in the dubious reconciliation between Kriemhild and himself, which he has in any case already dishonoured (p. 148). On the way there, Gunther even fails to stand up for his own Chaplain when Hagen throws him into the Danube (p. 197). And in Etzel's hall he trusts to his glibness to justify Hagen's slaughter of Ortlieb to the outraged father. It is long after the fighting has begun, when he refuses to buy his life at the expense of Hagen's, that he moves into a more favourable light, which holds him till the end. It is widely thought that the two heroic lays from which the *Nibelungenlied* descended were of Burgundo-Frankish origin, and it must be admitted that in Gunther's character there is enshrined a blend of perfidy, cowardice, cunning, finesse, and physical courage that strikes one as peculiarly Merovingian.

Apart from the doubling role already referred to, Gernot is almost without function in the poem. Yet several times he steps forward from the background to test the situation before it is safe for Gunther to commit himself, or to supplement an official act of Gunther's. It is Gernot who bids Siegfried welcome when he is still thirsting for a fight – whereupon they pour out Gunther's wine, which, once drunk, will be binding on all (p. 31). Gernot acquits himself well at the Saxon wars, but he is of course overshadowed by Siegfried. It is Gernot who produces the compromise which results in the sinking of Kriemhild's treasure. Like his elder and his younger brother, he is very courteous. After Gunther, for reasons that escape us, has overlooked the death of Helche when welcoming Rüdiger, Gernot offers their condolences (p. 155). And when Volker, publicly and apparently without prior discussion, has brought the question of a royal marriage with Rüdiger's daughter to the highest pitch of embarrassment, Gernot eases the situation with a gallant and tactful statement, only to have Hagen intervene and make a match not with him as the bridegroom but the other 'young king', Giselher (pp. 208f.). Gernot receives some prominence in the battle in Etzel's hall, from having inherited Giselher's traditional role as the recipient of a sword from Rüdiger, a gift with which he will slay the donor (p. 274). His high-sounding exchange with Rüdiger merges into another between Giselher and Rüdiger by means of the ambiguous line: 'Then said the son of fair Uote of Burgundy'. The context shows that Giselher is meant (p. 270).

The role of Giselher as a youth of tender years persists throughout the poem, as we have seen. And we have also seen how the poet sends Giselher into action with reckless disregard for his 'character' when gentle speech is needed. For he scarcely intended us to think of Giselher as a nauseating old hypocrite, which is what Giselher amounts to if we simply add him up. Giselher is clearly intended to present a foil of youth, innocence, and loyal affection to the dark figures of Gunther and Hagen. But, as the poet unfolds his story, all three attributes are dissipated. Giselher's youth vanishes in a whirl of years, his innocence and loyalty (at least towards his sister) in the storm of events. The word '*triuwe*' – 'loyal affection' – is always on his lips, yet he never once takes effective action against treachery. It was in his knowledge and power to have warned Kriemhild and Siegfried (p. 117). After a protest which proves as ineffectual as Gunther's, no sooner is he back with his brothers from the planned alibi which enables Hagen to sink the treasure, than we are told: 'Giselher especially would have liked to give proof of his affection'. But this does not prevent him from acting his part in the feigned dismissal of Hagen from royal favour (pp. 148, 149*n*.). This conceded, the counterclaim that Giselher is unmatched in the poem for the certainty and clarity of his feeling for what is true, just, and noble may, for what it is worth, also be conceded. It is only Giselher's will and ability to practise what he preaches that are in question. His latent worth comes out in battle. When Dietrich tells the Burgundian leaders in confidence how matters stand with Kriemhild and they see how things must end, Giselher is notably absent (p. 215). Only gradually does it dawn on the 'young' man that they are doomed. But as their fate becomes clearer and clearer to him, he matures visibly, so that he can at last look death steadily in the face. When he advises that the corpses be thrown from the hall he gains the commendation of no less a man than Hagen (p. 249). Next, his childish faith in his sister's mercy breaks down (p. 260). On Rüdiger's arrival on the scene of battle, his hope flares up again, only to be damped once more when this bond, also breaks (pp. 268f.). He now finally accepts his fate and grows to royal and heroic stature, fully deserving the tribute in death of his gallant victor and victim, Wolfhart (p. 283). Giselher seems to have retained his sister's affection through all the crooked course of their lives, for, homesick in Hungary, she dreams that she is kissing him (p. 177). Nor does Giselher show bad conscience towards her. It is quite conceivable that life at a medieval court as in other places where politics are paramount, bred up schizophrenic attitudes. Only when one's own position was secure could one give way to natural affection. Such may have been the very air that our poet breathed.[1] Nevertheless, it is when trying to assess Giselher, of all the characters in this poem, that we sense the risks we take in dealing with the figures of medieval epic in terms of modern characterization. In the background there is always the knowledge that the truly 'young' Giselher of an earlier epic on the destruction of the Burgundians, in which his

1. It would be no more surprising in this poet than in Gottfried if he had discharged diplomatic or political duties in life, apart from writing.

role is readily understood, has been stretched back over the years into the very different separate plot that ended in the death of Siegfried.[1]

All the foregoing characters lived together serenely in high estate at Worms, so we are told in the first chapter, and long might they have continued to do so but for their becoming involved with two people of very different calibre.

Siegfried and Brunhild go together. Each has a quasi-mythical aura. Each is of a different order from that of normal men and women, both in their superhuman strength and in the nature of its limitations. Their excess of strength breeds fear and respect for each. Yet at times it also invests each with an air of burlesque. Each is broken and done with before the first part of the poem is over, and from the same fundamental cause: entanglement in ordinary human affairs through love. There is a hint of prior acquaintance between Siegfried and Brunhild, and there is an indefinable suggestion that something has gone wrong between them. For the conditions set for Brunhild's wooers are such as to exclude all but Siegfried, and it is in fact Siegfried who fulfils them, though on behalf of another man and to win another woman. Nevertheless, beyond the lurking suspicion that Siegfried in some way meant much to Brunhild, all remains wrapped in mystery, and must forever remain so.

When we first meet Siegfried, he has still to emerge from a wildness which we divine from his dragon-slaying past in Hagen's description (p. 28) but which surprises us in a prince of the Netherlands so tenderly nurtured as he is said to be (p. 20). The violence and impetuosity with which he challenges Gunther to fight for their two kingdoms come as a great shock to the urbane court of Burgundy. It is only by a desperate exercise of tact that the cooler heads at Worms manage to avoid a battle with the stranger and stave off a nameless threat to their society. Despite young Siegfried's courtly trappings, the scene partakes of the timeless confrontation of civilized men with barbarians. Siegfried's love for Kriemhild, however, soon tames him and even induces him to demean himself as Gunther's 'vassal' after they have met, an act which at the same time automatically excludes him as a possible suitor for Queen Brunhild (p. 63). When Kriemhild and Siegfried are married this slight imbalance is redressed. The second part of the poem may show Kriemhild as a woman with all the makings of a virago, but the first makes it clear that Siegfried's mastery

1. See Appendix 4, p. 395.

was never in doubt and that his tenderness and superabundant virility made him a perfect match for his spirited young wife. Having crowned his high endeavours in war, adventure, and love, Siegfried matures rapidly into a charming man with an open nature, who is ever ready to help a friend. Also, in appropriate contexts, he can still give expression to his huge vitality through roughest horseplay, as when he captures a bear and looses it among his companions. At such times he is of course a figure of fun. But Siegfried is not one of those boring heroes who suffer from too much bone in the head, as might be inferred from this incident with the bear. He owes his treasure to knowing how to play *tertius gaudens*, no easy gambit. Whatever we think of its ethics, his handling of Gunther's wooing expedition is masterly. After his frank and friendly nature and his courtesy have exposed him to his murderer, and the poet has bedded him so fittingly upon the flowers, his dying words reveal a character as sensitive and intelligent as it is loving and considerate for the wife and child he will be leaving. This is no ox that falls beneath the axe but a human being possessed of all the qualities that make a man truly noble.

How far can such a character be responsible for his own tragic end, conceding that Siegfried has been elevated appreciably by the last poet in the interests of the new fashions of chivalry and love-service, and in order to make his murder more detestable? It has been said that Siegfried died because he talked. This is true so far as he need not have divulged the whereabouts of his vulnerable spot to his wife any more than Samson with Delilah. But if we were to think that he had told Kriemhild in words of his taming of Brunhild, there is no evidence to support it – the poet has seen to that (p. 312). Rather is it to be thought that in handing over Brunhild's ring and girdle to Kriemhild he said nothing. For had he said anything he would have told the truth, and Kriemhild would then have had to lie to call Brunhild his paramour. Siegfried's fault will have been his surrender to his wife of the tokens of Brunhild's virginity, leaving their silent accusation uncorrected. Whether he had already incurred guilt through planning and carrying out the deception of Brunhild in Iceland is another question. As in ancient Greece, Germanic and then medieval German heroes were permitted to be resourceful on occasion if abnormal circumstances seemed to call for it. Nevertheless, despite this caveat, it is undeniable that Siegfried twice violated the will of a woman whose only fault (if fault it be) was to have taken extreme precautions to find a suitable mate, and this, he must have known, was dangerous, if not immoral. Siegfried took this risk upon himself in pursuit of his own love, and he paid for it with his life.

Both Siegfried and Achilles were mighty heroes with a vulnerable spot, and therefore both died young, though Siegfried (as our poet tells the tale) enjoyed ten or eleven years of married life. The great difference between them is that Achilles consciously chose fame and early death with all the insight and apartness which this knowledge brought him, whereas Siegfried lived without care and had to learn the bitter lesson in the last few moments that remained to him after he had been treacherously struck down.

The figure of Brunhild has suffered a great decline in the *Nibelungenlied*, compared with what it must have been in the original lay, in which, so it seems, she was a woman whose sense of outraged honour at having been wooed by one warrior for another made her press ruthlessly for the elimination of her 'first man',[1] so that it has been claimed in respect of our Brunhild that the poet failed in his task. For this decline, two interconnected reasons are urged. First, that as feelings grew to be more refined, the starkness of the old plot was toned down, as when Siegfried was no longer permitted to deflower Brunhild. Second, that a 'heroic' woman of ancient Germanic stamp, to whom honour was all, could not maintain her place in the poetry of the chivalric age, which was dominated by the great lady of the court. Brunhild's display of physical strength both in the arena and on her nuptial couch furnished opportunities for burlesque of which a minstrel poet might safely avail himself – and tragedy and burlesque do not accord well within one character.

Just as in Worms Siegfried admits to knowledge of Brunhild's ways (p. 53) and of the ocean paths to her distant court (p. 58), and on his arrival there recognizes her land (p. 59) and her person (p. 60), so he in turn is recognized by one of her attendants (p. 62). And Brunhild herself knows of 'mighty Siegfried' (p. 62), assumes that he has come to woo her (p. 62), does not fear him so far as to accept him, unless he defeat her in her contests (p. 62), and when the visitors present themselves, addresses Siegfried by name before Gunther, although it is clear from protocol that Siegfried must be Gunther's 'vassal' (p. 63). Corrected by Siegfried on this score, Brunhild then addresses herself to Gunther

1 See Appendix 4 below.

without any show of emotion. When Siegfried returns from his expedition to Nibelungland, Brunhild offers him a greeting that marks him out from his followers (pp. 73, 73n.). Until Brunhild takes her seat at the wedding feast, there has been no sign of distressed feelings. Custom would have sanctioned consummatino of her marriage in Iceland, with her kinsmen and warriors within call (p. 75), and had she harboured suspicions then, this would have been the best place in which to clear them up. But it is only when she sees Kriemhild sitting at Siegfried's side that her feelings get the better of her and she bursts into tears (p. 86). According to the text (and what else have we to go by?) Brunhild's reason for weeping is that it troubles her to see her sister-in-law sitting as bride to a vassal, and she threatens not to consummate the marriage unless she learns why this is so (p. 88).[1] Gunther's reply adds nothing to the eloquent fact that Kriemhild and Siegfried are sitting opposite, in the seat of honour: he says that Siegfried is a king as mighty as himself and thus a fitting mate for his sister. Gunther's evasiveness, surely is an insult to a young bride with whom he is due to spend the remainder of his life. His answer ought to have provoked her to ask why Siegfried acted in Iceland as though he were Gunther's vassal. But no such question is asked. It takes the knotty form, reiterated at the bed-side, that Brunhild demands to know why Kriemhild has been married to Siegfried. Outwardly at least, for the next ten years Brunhild will cling to the idea that Siegfried was Gunther's vassal, until her quarrel with Kriemhild brings matters to a head, though now she will refuse Gunther her favours unless he answers her question. Gunther of course cannot do so and he resorts to force, with lamentable results. Outward forms of etiquette and protocol in the Middle Ages could have left no queen in doubt as to the sovereign status of a king in Siegfried's position: yet for ten years Brunhild is at grips with the problem how Kriemhild can hold her head so high despite Siegfried's imagined servile status.[2] Finally, when her insistence provokes Kriemhild to call her a paramour, her thought is that if Siegfried has boasted of enjoying her he must die (p. 114). She is not mollified by Gunther's superficial solution of the crisis, whereby Siegfried clears himself by his readiness to swear an oath, nor does she, on the other hand, explicitly demand Siegfried's death. Her tears and her account of what happened during the quarrel are enough to

1. Kriemhild's tears when Rüdiger at last resolves to fight are even less explained.
2. Such expressions as *eigenman* are used, implying 'unfree' status.

seal Siegfried's fate. Hagen takes over (p. 116),[1] and Brunhild all but disappears from the story. At the end of the first part of the poem, after the murder of Siegfried, Brunhild sits indifferent in her pride while Kriemhild weeps.[2] Later, she is shown to be inaccessible to Etzel's envoys (p. 187). And during the last night that she will ever spend with Gunther, as 'the Queen', unnamed, she pleasures him as a dutiful wife (p. 191).

The poet gives us very little guidance during all these events. After her tears at the banquet, and just before the two queens are escorted to their nuptials, the poet assures us that 'As yet there was no enmity between them' (p. 87). And when, after ten years, Siegfried and Kriemhild revisit Worms, and Siegfried sits as before in the seat of honour (p. 108), Brunhild's feelings are said, in an ironical double-entendre, to be 'still friendly enough towards him to let him be (live)' (p. 109n.). It is surely better to take the poet at his word here, rather than impute, without evidence, feelings of sexual jealousy to Brunhild. The poet's hints also have the function of pointing forward to the time when Brunhild will quarrel with Kriemhild and then wish to have Siegfried killed.

I have several times drawn attention to the dangers of 'explaining' the characters beyond what the poem gives us, and the danger is nowhere greater than in elaborating on Brunhild's silences. It is not permissible to resort to Northern versions of the story in order to show that Brunhild loved Siegfried, nor can we prove that such versions of the story were known to Austro-Bavarian audiences for them to fill in the background themselves. We must abide by the version before us. Here the salient fact seems to me to be Brunhild's fixed idea that Siegfried was Gunther's liegeman, to which she adheres tenaciously despite all too tangible evidence to the contrary. Surely this is either her last legal hold on a situation that is growing beyond her, or, if she really believes it, a vital illusion? For if she accepts it as true that mighty Siegfried is a sovereign king, she must admit that she has been most shamefully deceived, and cheated of the one eligible mate in the story. The decisive moments of her life were those in which Siegfried and Gunther came to Iceland and she was wooed and won, and it is to this time of decision that she reverts when she insists that Sieg-

1. In terms of the growth of the story Hagen is ousting Brunhild from her role of inciter to the murder.

2. In an early form of the lay, perhaps in the original lay itself, she had answered Kriemhild's shriek on finding her husband dead with a laugh as loud and shrill.

fried is a vassal, because then she witnessed all the outward signs of it. By implication she reverts to that time also during her wedding night when she demands to know the truth, else Gunther shall not lie with her. For Brunhild must divine that only the man who vanquished her at the game of war can vanquish her at the game of love. Although a second deception settles this issue superficially, doubt still lurks in her mind. She had taken it for granted that, if any, Siegfried was to be her mate, so that now when she has been won by another, she is forced to believe (or at least to act as though she believes) Siegfried to be Gunther's vassal. Her tragedy is that pride and suspicion force her in the end to destroy her own defences and learn with certainty of her deception.

Great has been Brunhild's fall since the proud days in Iceland. Whereas she had once commanded and if need be fought to express her will, in the new state to which her womanhood has reduced her (p. 93) she has to live by her wits like any other lady in medieval society. When she sets to work to persuade Gunther to invite Siegfried and Kriemhild, she speaks 'subtly' (p. 100).[1]

'Whatever heights of power a royal vassal might have reached [she says], he should not fail to do his sovereign's bidding.' Gunther smiled at her words, since whenever he saw Siegfried, he did not reckon it as homage.

The man who had no right to possess Brunhild, smiles in a superior way at the perplexity his deceit has occasioned. But what was Brunhild thinking? *Did* she intuitively feel cheated of her rightful mate? A situation of this sort offers a poet of the Heroic and Modern Ages great opportunities, and they were and have been taken.[2] But, for the reasons given, the odds were against it in Austria at the beginning of the thirteenth century, and all that we are offered are tears, riddles, and silence.

Of the remaining figures, that of Rüdiger is by far the most interesting. In his association with the Burgundians he probably does not go back beyond the immediate, epic, source of the second half of our poem (p. 392). He is thus not deeply involved in primary events, and this makes it possible for him to be shown as possessing more recent 'medieval' as well as 'heroic' qualities.

1. '*in einen listigen siten*'.
2. See the résumé of the Old Icelandic *Atlakviða* on p. 373. Brunhild was a character as if predestined for Friedrich Hebbel, and he uses his opportunity to the full in his *Die Nibelungen*.

As ambassador and suitor by proxy for Kriemhild's hand he shows some skill, only failing, in his honest enthusiasm for his mission, to divine Kriemhild's ulterior motives for consenting, so that he binds himself to her personally for the future beyond his oath of allegiance to his queen (p. 161). In this, however, his hand was forced: Rüdiger had to succeed on his lord's behalf, and such were Kriemhild's terms. As host at Pöchlarn, his warmth and generosity are above praise (Chapter 27). His testing time comes when the fighting has begun in Hungary and his sovereigns demand that he fight for them. It is torment for Rüdiger to have to make up his mind. On the one hand he is bound by his feudal oath to Etzel and his personal oath to Kriemhild (pp. 266f., 161): on the other, he feels in honour bound to the Burgundians, and very strongly bound indeed, both because he had been their host and escort (p. 267) and because of the marriage tie between his daughter and Giselher (which, however, remained unconsummated). The terrible dilemma in Rüdiger's heart is that he is gripped by conflicting obligations, on the one hand of law and ethics, on the other of custom and sentiment, obligations the common meeting-ground of which was 'honour' or reputation in the eyes of the world, the best part of a medieval warrior, so that whatever choice Rüdiger makes, whether to fight on the one side or on the other, or to abstain, he is disgraced. This anguish causes him to speak of his 'soul'.

> There is no denying it, noble lady, [he says to Kriemhild] that I swore to risk my life and position for you: but that I would lose my soul I never swore. Remember, it was I who brought those highborn kings to the festival here. (p. 266)

Fine as the words sound, Rüdiger is overstating his case. No man can lose his soul for an offence against custom, rather than against Christian teaching. Socially and humanly lamentable though it was to have to fight men with whom he had such close ties of friendship, no confessor would have detected sin in it. Rather would he have found sin in a breach of the sacred oaths that bound a liegeman to his lord, or in the scanting of a private oath, such as that of Rüdiger to Kriemhild. Rüdiger knows this in his heart, and it is a magnificent tribute to friendship within the harsh code of feudal society that he does not consent to do the one possible thing until Etzel and Kriemhild have demeaned themselves by kneeling to him (reversing the normal roles of lords and vassals) and until he himself has offered to return his fief, preferring poverty and exile; after which his king and queen have no recourse but to beg him to have pity on them! (Here is a feast of high sentiment, and there is more to come.) Thus shamed into accepting an obligation from which he has technically freed himself – the feudal oath of the period in any case had a clause exempting the vassal from the duty to fight to his own dishonour – Rüdiger prepares to enter the fray, now a loyal vassal who sacrifices everything to his lord, but also a broken-hearted man. To him in this state Hagen's request for his shield (p. 271) comes as a marvellous deliverance. It at once conveys that Hagen fully understands Rüdiger's position as a vassal and it gives Rüdiger a chance to show himself for the last time as the generous man that he is and so grow again to full stature. Rüdiger is now fit to die. He need fear no longer for his 'soul', by which we understand his 'worldly honour'. Posthumously, too, his honour is redeemed, for although he sought death as the solution of his dilemma, he slew his slayer, and slaying him, slew a king.

The scene that ends in Rüdiger's death has been rightly recognized as one of the great beauties of the poem. Momentarily, a bridge of magnanimous understanding is flung across the chasm of hostility. The earlier poet planned it that Rüdiger and his son-in-law Giselher should slay each other, with Giselher using Rüdiger's gift-sword (pp. 380, 383); but our poet judged this no longer tolerable, and transferred Giselher's role to Gernot (p. 274). He wrested the last bit of high-flown sentiment out of a situation in which a beloved host stands committed to fight his guests, friends, and relations, and one notes that there is rather too much talking, with some smack of heroics, as in the exchange between Rüdiger and Volker (p. 272) or when Gernot tells Rüdiger that he will try to deserve his gift sword dearly – if need be by killing the donor (p. 273). The question of Rüdiger's 'soul' is not logically pursued, for when he decides to fight we are told he will hazard both body and soul (p. 268). But perhaps this is bitter irony. Hearing Giselher place the bonds of the kindred above those of marriage, Rüdiger begs God to have mercy on them (p. 271). And when at last he fights he enters the fray in a berserk fury and dies without a further thought of his salvation. To assert, as has been claimed, that Rüdiger suffers a Germanic fate with a Christian character, is to deny to pagans the sentiment of friendship. But it must be admitted that the exploitation in poetry of a conflict between duty and friendship was not possible much before this time, when the ferment of Christian civilization was loosening the tongues of poets.

The remaining characters call for little discussion, since they are for the most part types.

The Austro-Bavarians inherited a favourable image of Attila ultimately from his allies, the Ostrogoths, so that the Etzel of the *Nibelungenlied* is far from being a Scourge of God. Rather does he remind us of other great kings of medieval literature, of King Arthur and Charlemagne, in his role of an amiable *roi fainéant*. For example, when in his courage he is about to enter the fray in person he is pulled back with decisive result by his shield-strap! (p. 250). But for his blissful unawareness of what was brewing under his very nose there would have been no catastrophe (p. 393). The arrogance of others is blamed, however, for his having been kept in the dark (pp. 231f.). We see him smiling benignly on one and all until Hagen makes his brutal remark on Ortlieb's ill-fated look, and even then Etzel shows gentlemanly restraint (p. 237). It is hard not to visualize him anachronistically as blinking good-humouredly over his spectacles. Nevertheless, where he perceives action to be necessary his response is swift and decisive. When Volker, his guest, is in danger of being killed by the indignant Huns whom Volker has so wantonly bereaved, King Etzel races out on to the scene from a window at breakneck speed, despite his years, and quells the disturbance (pp. 234f.).

Dietrich, a king in exile, alone succeeds in preserving his neutrality nearly to the end. Although much beholden to Etzel, he is evidently not so closely bound to him as Margrave Rüdiger, nor has he sworn an oath to Kriemhild. As a comrade-in-arms of Hagen's from the days when Hagen was hostage to Etzel, he warns the Burgundians on their arrival and takes the field against the two survivors only when he learns the terrible news from Hilde-brand that his hot-headed war-band, all that remains to him in the world, has been drawn into battle against orders and slain to a man, bar Hildebrand. The stunning impact of this news all but unmans him, yet he recovers himself and goes to Gunther and Hagen. His reproaches to them, and the self-conquest which his generous terms imply (p. 287), reveal lofty greatness of soul. With Dietrich there is least risk in speaking of a Christian character.

Dietrich's Master-at-Arms, old Hildebrand, shows a great descent from the magnificent figure of the ancient Lay of Hildebrand.[1] In our poem he is an old campaigner with a somewhat professional air, despite his noble birth. His failure to restrain his nephew Wolfhart even with a high tackle suggests a devoted sergeant-major attempting to deal with a rash young officer, and it is amusing and revealing that when Wolfhart breaks loose Hildebrand races him to be first in the battle. On his return as sole survivor, part-architect of his lord's ruin, he adopts a hangdog air. His tendency to bandy insults with his betters, perhaps inherited from misunderstood memories of his tragic altercation with the son he had to slay, is sharply curbed by Dietrich. His running away from Hagen is a slur on the name of Hildebrand, and we do not mind that Dietrich's former role of executing Kriemhild has fallen to him.

Volker the 'Fiddler' or 'Minstrel' is a typical figure of heroic epic in whom accretion through successive stages of growth is evident. Although important minstrels might belong to a lord's household and even own a fief, their status was normally plebeian.[2] Nevertheless, we are expressly told that Volker was a noble lord with many good warriors of Burgundy as his vassals, but that he was called 'Minstrel' because of his skill with the fiddle.[3] In our poem he is, then, a gentleman amateur. His public tribute to Gotelind in Pöchlarn of a song to his own accompaniment, for which she rewards him richly with bracelets, does not quite tally with what we know of the cult of Minnesang (p. 212n.). We do not know the words of Volker's song. But we do know that no plebeian at this time would have been permitted to address a lady directly on the subject of love, a fact which accords with Volker's noble status. During a pause in the carnage in Etzel's hall, Gunther turns to Hagen to comment on Volker's prowess in 'fiddling' on Hunnish helmets,[4] and Hagen voices his regret that he sat higher in the hall than Volker, whom he had chosen as his comrade-in-arms. Here we have a reference to Volker's humbler status, and we can safely assume that this German Taillefer had been a minstrel of plebeian status in the epic source of our poem and a favourite figure with

1. For a modern rendering of this lay see *The Penguin Book of German Verse*, introduced and edited by Leonard Forster, Penguin Poets, D 36 (1957), pp. 3ff. Although the poem is incomplete in the manuscript we know that Hildebrand had to slay his son in battle.

2. See Appendix 1, p. 354.

3. In reality, the viol.

4. A metaphor inherited from the epic of *c.* 1160: see the summary of the *Thiðrekssaga*, p. 383.

its poet, who was himself a minstrel, and that the 'last' poet (that is, our poet) went the whole way in ennobling in rank a figure who was already felt by admiring audiences to be noble at heart. Volker's fortunes were assured, once he had been picked as Hagen's battle-companion, yet in our poem he still bears the traces of a self-made man. In the opening chapter, he is introduced as a man of flawless courage, and when he is presented to Rüdiger's daughter in recognition of his great courage he is honoured by a kiss normally reserved for social equals (p. 207). It was said above that Volker's superior physical prowess serves to underline Hagen's greater depth of character, and it is also true that Volker's light-hearted, musical temperament provides a foil to the grim and sceptical side of Hagen. Although Volker is at one with Hagen in his foreknowledge of the doom that awaits them, he does not let it weigh on him at Pöchlarn, where, in his vivacious manner, he is the life and soul of the party and even paves the way to a marriage.

It was no doubt owing to the ambiguity of this 'noble fiddler' that the last poet and his continuators between them introduced Volker thrice (pp. 18, 186, 198). And it is a strange coincidence, if coincidence it be, that documentary evidence is to hand, from Flanders in the earlier part of the twelfth century, of an enfeoffed minstrel of the same name, *Folkirus joculator*.

AFFINITIES WITH DRAMA

Two ideas have been confirmed as true by this review of the leading figures. First, characters tend to lose their consistency if one goes beyond an episode or related group of episodes, and consistency may be jeopardized if one leaps from one half of the poem to the other. And second, even in vital passages, the poet often prefers to let actions speak for themselves. This latter feature, which is perhaps favoured by the compact shape of the strophe (pp. 348ff.), is suggestive of drama, and we may well inquire whether other features of the poet's art point in this direction.

The ancient Germanic heroic lay was a short epic-dramatic poem in which tense dialogue furnished the crises, and it is undeniable that over the centuries our poem has inherited much of the spirit of the lay, despite the different aims of epic. The various clashes between Kriemhild and Hagen, and the exchanges between Rüdiger, Wolfhart, Hildebrand, and Dietrich on the one side and the Burgundian heroes on the other, speak for themselves.

Beyond this, two contrasting 'dramatic' styles have been discerned, one the general style of our poet's predecessors, the other his own contemporary style of presentation. The former culminates in powerful symbolic gestures: Kriemhild flaunting Brunhild's ring in triumph (to which our poet has added her girdle) (pp. 114, 115); the flinging of Siegfried's corpse on to Kriemhild's bed (which our poet has toned down to depositing it on her threshold) (pp. 133, 378); Kriemhild's reading of Siegfried's unscarred shield to the effect that he has been murdered (p. 134); Hagen's killing of the ferryman on the way to Hungary; his breaking the oar and smashing the ferry (p. 198); and his lacing on of his helmet more tightly on arriving at Etzel's court (p. 216). The second style has aptly been called 'scenic'. The last poet can 'produce' a whole episode within the bounds of a single scene like a true dramatic artist, as in Chapter 29 when he makes Hagen and Volker leave Gunther standing in Etzel's forecourt, walk over the broad space, seat themselves against the palace wall on a bench, and sustain the curiosity of the Huns who stare at them as though they were strange beasts – whereupon Kriemhild espies them through a window, prostrates herself before her warriors in order to move them to avenge her, descends the Stair – the scene of so many fights and flytings to come – and draws close to the two heroes, who grimly keep their seats while Hagen displays Siegfried's sword Balmung on his knees ... (pp. 219ff.). Or there is the dramatic appearance of Dancwart at the top of that same Stair, viewed from within the hall, with drawn sword, and all bespattered with gore (p. 242). Or to revert to an outstanding example from the first part, the quarrel of the queens in Chapter 14 in three stages: at the tournament, and then, with the prima donnas magnificently gowned and with supporting ladies on either side, at the cathedral door on the steps, before and after mass.

The last poet tried to retain all the pictorial gestures of his sources, although (as we have seen with the ring and girdle) he was not above tampering with them if need be. But he also signally added to them in the scene in which Hagen requests and receives the shield of Rüdiger (p. 271). As to the poet's own scenic effects, he tended to reserve them for the high points of his narrative. In one instance in which he stints us of all indication of time and place, his very bareness contributes to the close atmosphere of the

1. Those who like everything to be profound may equate the Ferryman with Charon and the Danube with the Styx, as they may regard the Palace Stair as a Bridge to the Underworld.

transaction, namely where courtiers plot the death of Siegfried (pp. 116f.).

The total visual effect of the *Nibelungenlied*, however, is gaunt and dim compared with that of the *Iliad*, which even distinguishes an upper and lower air and glories in the accurate evocation of movement. With regard to this latter quality, of all those writing in Germany at the beginning of the thirteenth century, Wolfram von Eschenbach alone could challenge Homer.

Considerations of dramatic effect often swamp those of epic in our poem. Since the days of the heroic lay there had been the well-used stylistic device, also known to our poets, of indirect speech changing to direct without transition. The splendid set speeches in which Homer abounds have no parallel in the *Nibelungenlied*. Instead we find naturalistic dialogue, dramatically presented, which Homer on the other hand avoids. Similarly also, the stately repetitions of set utterances in Homer (halving a beginner's work with his lexicon) have no counterpart in the German poem.

The dramatic features of the *Nibelungenlied* are innate. Whereas there was no secular drama in German at this time there was of course the liturgical drama of the Church as well as agrarian ritual in the village, both of which may have contributed towards forming the 'symbolic' style of our poet's sources. On the other hand, there was as yet little book reading in private among the laity.[1] Instead, however, poems like *Parzival* and *Willehalm* (to name works that were eminently suited to such treatment) were publicly recited, and one does not need to be endowed with much feeling to know that they must have been recited with every resource of voice and gesture, though documentary evidence is lacking. Certain genres of contemporary love-song (like that of the *Tagelied* or *alba*) were also surely performed with mime, and, no doubt, so were those racy ditties that dealt with peasant frolics. The setting in which we imagine the *Nibelungenlied* to have been performed – we do not know whether it was sung, chanted, or intoned – may thus have been not too remote from that of cabaret, though naturally on a far more serious plane. Yet all evidence is lacking, so that it is not possible to contradict those who argue that the poem was chanted in a liturgical style with a 'deadpan' demeanour.

1. One work that must have been read privately as well as recited publicly was the *Tristan* of Gottfried von Strassburg.

An Introduction to a Second Reading

THE ETHOS OF THE POEM

Has the *Nibelungenlied* a 'meaning'? That is, can its action, together with the poet's *obiter dicta* and hints between the lines, be shown to serve a dominant group of ideas and sentiments, whether they amount to 'a message', a 'philosophy', or a more or less consistent attitude towards life? In the case of the *Aeneid* or *Paradise Lost* one would think that this question could be answered in the affirmative, for all their rich diversity. But from what has already been said about the *Nibelungenlied* it will come as no surprise that, in its case, the question is not easy to answer.

In his penultimate strophe the last poet offers the comment that Etzel's high festivity has ended in sorrow, for joy must always turn to sorrow in the end. In the first strophe (whose internal rhymes declare it to be the work of a later hand),[1] by pairing fame and toil, joy and lamentation, with the negative element always in the second place, a redactor suggests from the outset that joy will turn to sorrow. Thus the poem is set in the framework of a simple yet effective pessimism. Throughout the poem we are told sententiously of the dire consequences of this or that deed, and, as the story unfolds, we must admit that joy does give way to sorrow in the end, since almost every festivity in the *Nibelungenlied* is clouded by untoward events. The victory-feast at which Siegfried meets Kriemhild for the first time is gay enough (but we know that Siegfried is being pulled irrevocably from his orbit by the power of love). The wedding-feast at Worms is marred by Brunhild's tears and all the dark things they stand for. Siegfried and Kriemhild's visit to Worms ends in the murder of the former. Etzel's festivity, the one that gave rise to the poet's final comment on the nature of joy and sorrow, ends in carnage and destruction. No resolution of the conflict of joy and sorrow is offered. Sorrow is left to reign supreme.

When we consider that the *Nibelungenlied* was recited to Christian courts of the high Middle Ages, we are rather taken aback. Christians, believing the Crucifixion to have been not a tragedy but a triumph, are nothing if not optimists, and their optimism duly left its marks on the tragic themes inherited from the heathen past by medieval men in Germany. In thirteenth-century poetry, fathers no longer kill their sons at the dictates of

1. See Appendix 2, p. 358.

honour,[1] sons-in-law no longer kill the fathers who pursue eloping daughters.[2] The Arthurian romances – the narrative literature par excellence of the courts – are singularly lacking in stark themes of any kind and always end on a note of harmony restored, and thus of hope. If anything very drastic happens in a tale of this period, as when Helmbrecht the farmer's son turns robber and is first mutilated by the sheriff and then lynched by the outraged villagers, it is sure to be a cautionary tale. There was great hope that by noting young Helmbrecht's terrible end one would be able to muster sufficient self-control to escape his fate. Was the *Nibelungenlied*, which had the only plot whose ancient, tragic outlook defied all essential change through the centuries, perhaps a cautionary tale or a great penitentiary sermon in verse on pride, with the Pride and Fall of the Burgundians as example?

There is something to be said for this idea as long as it is duly subordinated to the other, dominant qualities of the epic. It would be an exaggeration to claim that hundreds of years of Christian teaching had eradicated the sentiments of the blood-feud among the German nobility of the period, yet these nobles knew where they stood before the Church in matters of revenge. Thus any great story of revenge which, like the *Nibelungenlied*, dwelt sententiously though not pontifically on the inevitable consequences of high-handed deeds, could not fail to impress the listeners in a moral and cathartic sense. The fall of the Burgundians must have amounted to more in their eyes than an admirable feat of vengeance by Kriemhild or an abominable misfortune to the Burgundians, according to which side they took, if they paid attention to how the story is told. Like most heroic poets, our poet leaves the moral to his listeners. But he furnishes us with a hint or two in his use of words meaning 'pride', 'haughtiness', 'arrogance', or 'high spirits' at significant points.[3] Such hints, hedged about with his usual taciturnities as they are, sometimes

1. In the Younger Lay of Hildebrand, father and son go home in friendliest fashion to the housewife. Contrast the older lay, referred to above, p. 337*n*. 1

2. In the epic of *Kudrun*, as against the old *Lay of Hild*.

3. The motive of 'pride' is brought in, for example, at the following points. Kriemhild is proud and unapproachable as a maiden; hearing of her beauty, young Siegfried resolves to win her against the advice of his father and mother, whom he should have honoured, and despite their warning concerning Hagen's proud temper; when Siegfried arrives at

raise more problems than they solve (p. 296), yet never do they take on a priestly or theological tone. Just as not one of the heroes, not even Rüdiger, gives a thought to his heavenly salvation as he dies, so not one of these references to 'pride' is linked with anything but death and destruction, and not always explicitly with them. So far as the good of his characters' souls is concerned, our poet offers no comment. Thus, although we must assume that the *Nibelungenlied* was written by a Christian poet for Christian audiences, and that he leaves loose ends for thoughtful Christians to take up if they so please, the mood which the theme induced was not a Christian mood, and the result is not a Christian poem.

From a loftier ethical point of view, the *Nibelungenlied* is a poem of dire retribution for proud and arrogant deeds, with physical courage and group loyalty offering some purgation. The tragic events of which it tells are a web woven to a greater or lesser degree, in their blind arrogance, by all its leading characters. But whereas Homer lets it be known that the forces which punish *hybris* are divine, it is quite astonishing that our poet, writing in a priest-ridden age, offers not a word of guidance whether the sanction behind his retribution be impersonal Fate or the Providence of the Holy Trinity. We may well suspect the latter, for what else are we to think? But it is significant for the whole art of this singular and reticent person that he never once implies it.

Worms he challenges Gunther with the most thick-skinned arrogance; before the wooing of Brunhild, Siegfried warns the others (who later fully agree) of Brunhild's haughty ways, and when she has been vanquished he exults over her fall; when Siegfried takes Brunhild's ring and girdle, the poet himself tells us that the deed was perhaps inspired by high-spirited pride; when the two queens quarrel they of course accuse each other of overweening pride; and when Hagen has Siegfried's corpse set down on Kriemhild's threshold, the poet again intervenes to accuse Hagen of arrogance; Brunhild then sits exulting in her pride; in Hungary Kriemhild knows she can count on Hagen's pride not to deny the murder, and indeed he has given repeated evidence of this side of his nature during his dealings with the Bavarians; before the fighting breaks out we are told that it could all have been halted by Etzel but for the arrogance of those concerned; and during the battle 'proud' or 'arrogant' becomes a standing epithet to Hagen's name. As was said during discussion of Siegfried's purloining of the ring and girdle, the motive of 'pride' can be used as a blanket for motives which the poet either can or will not give in detail. It is enough for him that the deed has dire effects: such effects must have been occasioned by pride.

343

An Introduction to a Second Reading

The poet yielded his imagination to his un-Christian subject-matter to an extent that baffles us in a Christian of the high Middle Ages. Was his heart breaking with all the wicked ruin of his story? If it was, he kept his feelings to himself. He did not attempt to put them into words.

THE TWO-FOLD TEXTURE OF THE POEM

Those who come to the *Nibelungenlied* from other traditions of heroic poetry are struck and even troubled by its contrasting textures.[1] Some passages, like the exchanges between Siegfried and Kriemhild, they find unbelievably gentle or 'soft'; others almost incredibly savage. These contrasts, they say, go far beyond modulations from the major to the minor key, from warlike to peaceful pursuits, such as may be considered normal in heroic epics. And these critics note quite rightly that the double texture of the *Nibelungenlied* must be due to the poet's endeavour to accommodate his grim heritage to the new Romance fashions. For the chivalric ideal and the cult of courtly song were penetrating the sterner and more conservative south-eastern marches of the Empire from the West during the very generation in which our poet was at work, and in attempting to bridge the two divergent cultures he was accepting his greatest compromise, a compromise which, like the others, was forced upon him from without. It would not have been possible for the poet, had he so wished, to resist such modern influences at this time at any leading court of Austria. We may, despite obvious influences from courtly narrative, disregard the assertion that the *Nibelungenlied* was intended as a Kriemhild biography roughly to be classed with *Iwein* and the like (p. 316); while, on the other hand, to claim that the stylized

1. Whereas the Germanic element in the theme of the *Nibelungenlied* remains surprisingly strong, very little indeed survives stylistically. The old alliterative measure gave way everywhere to rhyme during the ninth century, and so the ancient epic formulae, in which much might have been conserved, were disrupted, offering a marked contrast with the fossil formulae embedded in the continuing hexameters of the *Iliad*. As echoes of the ancient epic manner we may note: the tendency of narrative to shift at crises into dramatic dialogue; a predilection for understatement; the laconism; and a few circumlocutions of kenning type, like '*trost der Nibelunge*' ('Refuge' = 'king', then 'leader of the Nibelungs', applied not only to Gunther but in a modified form also to Hagen) (pp. 192*n*. 3., 215*n*. 2.), and *fürsten wine* ('beloved', 'friend of a king' = 'queen'.).

love scenes, ceremonies, tournaments, and displays of finery are the price which the poet paid for having a *Nibelungenlied* at all, might be to underrate his creative interest in what is of lesser interest to us. To acquire the full sense of how this poet stood at the hinge of old and new, we need only compare the *Song of Roland*.[1] Writing about A.D. 1100, the last poet of the *Roland* needs to make few concessions to the arts of peace. As to the love of woman, there is very little of it – notoriously little in the eyes of our love-sick age, whose ideas on the subject go back in unbroken succession to the twelfth century but no farther. Chiding Roland for his rashness in failing to summon the Emperor betimes with his horn, Oliver tells him that he will never lie in the arms of Oliver's sister Aude. And when Charles returns without Roland, Aude dutifully dies of grief. This is all. When young warriors of archaic stamp love each other as Roland and Oliver do, their sisters may be thrown in to seal the bond. So it was with Siegfried and Gunther, and so it remained, until new and imperious conceptions of love forced their way into Austria.

Great epics are said to arise from an awareness on the part of a new and more literate age that an old order is passing away even in memory. If this is so, the *Nibelungenlied* came at the latest possible moment, at a time when modern notions threatened altogether to engulf the ancient subject-matter. That they did not do so entirely – and this may be accounted a marvel – can be set down to two factors. First, an earlier epic on the Fall of the Nibelungs (see p. 391), dated '*c*. 1160', came at the *right* time, before Romance fashions were making themselves felt. There is some danger of inviting ridicule by indulging in laments for lost poems whose beauties can only be surmised, but of this we may be sure: *Diu Nôt* was a very powerful, concentrated epic of unified texture, to which the poet of the *Nibelungenlied* owed an incalculable debt. The second factor that contributed to the rise of a great heroic epic as late as *c*. 1200 was the unique imagination of the last poet, who, building on *Diu Nôt*, found it possible to recapture and elaborate richly upon the temper of a past age, and at the same time work creatively in terms of the new, giving each of two fundamentally opposed generations what it wanted, though at an unavoidable cost in consistency.

But our poet, in the main, does not confront new and old haphazardly. He subdues the ancient spirit to contemporary

1. A New Translation by Dorothy L. Sayers, Penguin Classics, L 75 (1957).

notions of form. The putting of old wine into new skins, too, has its dangers, but the poet manages it without much damage to the vintage and even laces his beverage on occasion. As his story unfolds, its tone grows ever sterner. The modern and courtly veneer is progressively stripped off to reveal harsh political realities. A state of affairs that can be recognized as an ideal present begins to recede into the past, at first gently, then more swiftly till it reaches breakneck speed, yet not before the graces of contemporary society have been dwelt on lovingly for the last time at Pöchlarn. Already at the beginning there is a sharp reminder of the conflict between seemly order and uncurbed violence when Siegfried challenges Gunther at Worms, but with the roles reversed. For it is Siegfried (who will be so reliable when Kriemhild's love has tamed him) that offers a threat to society, while the Burgundians, as yet unmasked, appear as its upholders. And at the end, the noble figure of Dietrich survives, after Rüdiger has gone down, to give us hope for the modern generation.

THE POET'S ACHIEVEMENT

After this lengthy discussion it is time baldly to set forth the positive achievement of the last poet.

Taking two sources for the first half of his poem, and the older epic *Diu Nôt* for the second, and placing in Hagen's mouth only what his audience needed to know from various lays on Siegfried's youth, the last poet fashioned a great epic of revenge with two crises (see p. 7). He succeeded largely in harmonizing two plots with conflicting elements, and he braced them together not only by the motive of revenge, which had long exerted an influence on them, but also through the unity of some of the characters and even through their mutual relations, above all in the case of Kriemhild and Hagen. He created new episodes (Chapter 8, p. 296, Chapter 15, p. 304, Chapter 29), one of them of outstanding quality, 'How Kriemhild upbraided Hagen and he did not rise to greet her' (Chapter 29). He created new characters, preeminent among them Dancwart and Wolfhart. He sometimes showed considerable independence in his treatment of existing characters. For instance, he reshaped Siegfried in the role of a charming and well-bred prince, retaining some of his rougher characteristics for comic and dramatic effect. He also enriched the characters of Rüdiger and Hagen above all in their exchanges over

Rüdiger's shield. In fusing the Kriemhild of the first and second parts, he revealed to us the soul of a woman frustrated in love (p. 319), and altogether he gave Kriemhild a new prominence. He added much social and psychological refinement to what he found in his sources. Thanks to the patient work of scholars, who have never ceased to feel the challenge of this epic, it is now possible to make these statements on the work of the last poet with some assurance. There is much that we should still like to know. But we know that we could only know this if we had the poet's lost sources before us, those sources which the very success of his great epic was soon to condemn to oblivion.

CONCLUSION

The *Nibelungenlied* is inferior to the *Iliad*, which far surpasses it in the beauty of its structure, the maturity of its ethos, the magnificence of its language, its astonishing power of conjuring up line, mass, colour, and movement, and indeed in most other respects. Our poem is bare of the grand and weighty diction that we find in *Beowulf*,[1] nor has it any natural setting so charged with 'atmosphere', elegiac or otherwise, as the scene at Grendelsmere. The only notice taken of the beauties of nature is when Siegfried falls to die upon the flowers, a masterly touch, though nature here serves as a backcloth.[2] Our poem knows no supreme moment of the heroic imagination, like that of the *Roland* when the hero at last blows his horn, and blows so loud that his temples burst while Charles catches its echoes in far-off France. The zest, colour, and robust good sense of the *Cid* are absent from the tense and ruthless *Nibelungenlied*, whose moments of high chivalry are a little overdone. It lacks the naïve charm of the *Cattle Raid of Cooley*, that prose epic with a perfect plot, in which the bulls of Ulster and Connaught settle what heroes have left unsettled. Yet, when all these loose comparisons have been made, such are the strength, vitality, and tension of the *Nibelungenlied* that it could be claimed with great force, as I myself would claim, that it is the world's best heroic epic bar one.

1. Mr David Wright regrets the loss of this diction in translation, and gives convincing reasons for not attempting to reproduce it, in his *Beowulf*, Penguin Classics, L 70, 1957, pp. 22 ff.
2. The moon peeping from the clouds and lighting up bloodstained armour, and the rays of the sun at dawn after the night-action, are briefly but beautifully described (pp. 202–3).

A NOTE ON THE TRANSLATION

*

My thoughts on translating from medieval German are recorded at the end of the Introduction to my rendering of Gottfried's *Tristan* (pp. 31ff.). There is no need to repeat them here. But the problems that face a translator of the *Nibelungenlied* in particular require comment, and this, in the nature of things, cannot fail to throw light on formal aspects of the poem.

In some ways the present task was lighter, in other ways heavier than with *Tristan*. Gottfried was a man of letters as well as a poet, and in his more sententious passages his syntax, aptly tailored to his thought, could be elaborate, whereas the poet of the *Nibelungenlied* is mostly simple and direct, as befits his more dramatic art. Gottfried may obscure his meaning by the very elegance of a highly articulated paragraph, best mastered on the written page, whereas our poet may do so through his reliance on the spoken word. He sometimes interrupts his constructions in a way that can only be called chuckle-headed. In all but his plainest narrative Gottfried uses a wealth of rhetorical devices to colour his poem, whereas our poet keeps to the tradition which he inherited, using an impersonal style whose few surviving tropes in the ancient heroic manner are concerned mostly with understatement.

The dominant fact with which an English translator of the *Nibelungenlied* has to reckon is its strophic nature. The reasons why I rejected the possibility of a verse rendering of *Tristan* apply here with redoubled force. True, the lines of the Nibelung-strophe are twice as long as those of the couplets in which the *Tristran* is written, halving the compulsion of rhyme. But the Nibelung-strophe is reared on a balance between quantity and stress that cannot be imitated in modern English.[1] We do not know whether the poem was sung, chanted, or recited, though the last is by far the least likely, so that the balance between quantity and stress was, or approached to, that of song. To offer a cheap imitation of this effect in terms of English prosody with its different treatment of cadences would be a wicked waste of effort. Nor have we any

1. The same is true of modern German. Some German dialects, however, like the archaic Swiss German of Berne, could carry it admirably.

proven stanza in English that could do the work of the Nibelung-strophe.

Even for a gifted poet there would scarcely be any choice but prose. Yet to accept prose, as I have done, is not to escape the dominion of the Nibelung-strophe. Not only is it built in terms of 'sprung measure', not only are its cadences different from those of elevated English poetic usage,[1] but its last half-line also has a highly characteristic lilt. Through all its variations, the strophe therefore has a very definite shape which exerts a more marked influence on the presentation of the content than is ordinarily the case. In order that the reader may judge of this shape, I give the rhythmic patterns of three strophes, the first with monosyllabic masculine cadences in its first couplet, the second with disyllabic masculine and the third with (heavy) feminine cadences in the same position (see p. 350).

True to archaic usage,[2] this strophe tended to be constructed paratactically rather than hypotactically, as can be seen from the above examples, and this went naturally together with end-stopped lines. But when the strophe was used at book length, enjambement within the strophe and then even from one strophe to the next occurred (the latter, however, only rarely), marking a victory of the eye over the ear. Despite such tendencies, the strophe of the *Nibelungenlied* is normally a balanced and self-contained unit with a marked *rallentando* in the last half-line owing to its extra filled bar, which invites reflection, and sometimes dark and gnomic utterance, before the measure renews its forces at the beginning of the next strophe. The prose-translator is thus faced with a permanent and twofold problem: (i) how to take his already swifter narrative past the pause; and (ii) nevertheless how to absorb the reflective elements, which, when they are of a cryptic nature, sometimes require a major effort of interpretation. This problem could not always be solved, and I am only too well aware of the fact. In cases where the original proved more stubborn than I am, those who are familiar with its style and diction could easily detect the boundaries between the strophes in my English, and then proceed to reconstruct the poet's text. Conscious of this as I was, I might easily have eluded the tyranny of the strophe and covered my tracks by abandoning what the poet had said. But if

1. The cadences are nearer to those of English sung and danced nursery or folk rhymes, from the common Germanic inheritance.

2. Its parent 'Kürenberg-strophe' was undoubtedly a lyrical-epical form.

one is prepared to go this far, where does it end? I refused to take this course. I have naturally allowed myself some freedom in expanding and also in varying my expression of the poet's thought, when dealing with cryptic and at the same time stereotyped lines, especially when, as so often, they point to future woes. But in

---

(1) Ez wúohs in Búr- gòn- dèn   ein vil é-del má-ge- dìn,

dáz in ál-len lán- dèn   niht schǿ-ners móh-te sín,

Kríem- hìlt ge- héi- zèn: si wárt ein scǿ-ne wíp,

dar úm-be múo-sen dé-ge- nè   víl ver- líe- sèn den líp.

(ii) Óuch er-kén-neich Há-ge-nèn   von sí-nen jún-gen tá-gen; 1

des mác man vón dem réc- kèn   líh-te mír ge- sá-gen.

in zwéin und zwéin-zec stúr-mèn   hán ich ín ge- sé-hen,

dá vil má-ni-ger vróu-wèn   ist hér-ze- lèi- dè ge- sché-hen.

(iii) Den tróum sî dô ge- sá-ge- tè   ir múo-ter Úo- tèn, 2

si-ne kún-des níht be- scéi- dèn   báz der gúo- tèn:

'der vál-ke dén du zíu- hèst,   daz íst ein é-del mán.

in wél-le gót be-hüe-tèn,   du múost in scíere vlóren hán.'

---

1. This disyllabic cadence is presumably 'feminine' to English ears: but in medieval German it is 'masculine', a merely disyllabic equivalent of the monosyllabic *-dîn* in (i). Cf. the 'feminine' cadence *Úotèn*, where *Úo* – fills a whole bar, in (iii). All lines but the fourth end in a full bar's rest.

2. There is a trisyllabic sub-variety of this disyllabic cadence taking the same musico-metrical time: e.g. Hágenè | ♪♪ | ♪♩ | .

availing myself of this freedom I was aware of the need to avoid licence. Licence is for poets, not translators.

I also found the various overlapping synonyms for 'knight', 'warrior', 'hero', 'fighting-man', and for '(fair) women', 'ladies', 'maidens', together with their regular epithets, rather trying. With regard to epithets, as a counsel of perfection I had to test whether they were used freshly and aptly to suit the individual occasion. I found that they were sometimes apt (whether by direct statement or less often by irony) but more frequently that they were 'automatic'. In this respect, then, the *Nibelungenlied*, goes with the other heroic epics composed in a traditional style. It would be foolish to expect of our poem the standards of a Virgil or a Milton in the use of the epithet.

Another source of difficulty was the poet's naïve traditional style, abounding in clichés and superlatives: *vil* ('much', 'many') and *manec* ('many') were often a torment. I might have to find three or four words evoking the idea of 'many' within one strophe. I have wriggled there. It was part of the price I had to pay for attempting the perilous leap from traditional performed strophic narrative to modern prose, which most of us soak up through the eyes without jerk of tongue or twitch of lips.

A confession which requires a paragraph to itself is that on perhaps as many as three occasions I have mentally transposed a line or half-line from one strophe to another before translating it. Had I not done so, the reader would have been offended by the poet's indifference to logic.

The *Nibelungenlied* was 'translated' into modern German several times during the course of the nineteenth century in imitation Nibelung-strophes. The intention (as the associated illustrations confirm) was the frankly Romantic one of wafting the reader back to the Middle Ages on clouds of ancient-sounding words. Since such efforts leave a considerable portion of the original untranslated, they do not deserve the name of translation. They in fact mirror the poem with a permanent factor of distortion. I have not consulted such renderings, nor even more recent renderings, since their authors were not known to me as scholars. But in our own time Professor Helmut de Boor, the editor of the text on which I based my translation,[1] has offered a rendering in a quasi-Nibelung strophe. This I have often consulted, and with profit, for a translation by one who has edited the text and furnished it with an

1. *Das Nibelungenlied*. Nach der Ausgabe von Karl Bartsch (Deutsche Klassiker des Mittelalters), Wiesbaden, 1956, following branch *B.

excellent commentary must command respect. But although Professor de Boor's rendering often helps one to his reading, where his commentary is discreetly silent, it is evident that here, too, the tyranny of rhyme and metre has forced him away from the poet's sense more often than he could have wished. Professor de Boor's is a pleasing, at times racy, at times archaizing rendering, skilfully rhymed. Having done his duty by the text as a scholar, Professor de Boor was free to give the poem to a wider public in this form, and with all the better conscience for printing the medieval text on the opposite page.[1]

The *Nibelungenlied* has been done into English verse and prose several times in the past. In 1848 J. Birch published a verse translation, and he was followed in 1850 by W. N. Lettsom. In 1877 A. Forestier entered the field with 'Echoes from Mistland, or the Nibelungen Lay revealed to lovers of romance and chivalry', a prose translation published in Chicago. In 1887 A. G. Foster-Barham presented a prose translation, and ten years later Margery Armour presented another, which, because it was later incorporated in the Everyman's Library and also because of its own merits, became the best known since Edwardian times, though it was in fact not the last to be made. I did not have the heart to consult the nineteenth-century renderings because they were based on obsolete editions of the original or their titles proclaimed the follies which must inevitably be found within, or there were errors of German in their very titles (if correctly reported). The rendering of Margery Armour[2] is in the prose that was considered appropriate in her own generation. I have expressed my views elsewhere on the hybrid English that was favoured in those less hard-bitten days[3] and will say no more now, except that, fearing to be influenced by my predecessors, who were writing while Nibelung scholarship had not yet come of age, I decided not to consult their versions.

In French there is a prose rendering by Professors Maurice Colleville and Ernest Tonnelat,[4] the latter of whom also translated *Parzival*. I respect their work, and I have consulted it frequently and with profit. It was an eloquent lesson in English history, as I compared renderings, to see how English and German sometimes went together in idiom against French, and then English and

1. *Das Nibelungenlied:* In Urtext und Übersetzung (Bremen, 1959).
2. *The Fall of the Nibelungs* (Everyman's Library, No. 312).
3. *Tristan,* p. 34.
4. *La Chanson des Nibelungen* (Paris, 1945).

A Note on the Translation

French against German. In their translation, Messieurs Colleville and Tonnelat number the strophes, and they print them as typographical units. It was not their aim to make the narrative flow according to modern French requirements. With the interest of students, above all, in mind, they clearly decided not to throw themselves bodily into the story. Their rendering, then, remains cool, literal, analytic, minutely aware of the poet's meaning, and (to a very considerable extent) accurate.[1]

The Nibelunglied: Translated with an Introduction and Notes by D. G. Mowatt. Everyman, Library No. 312 (1962) appeared after my own work was finished. It replaces Margery Armour's rendering in the series and retains its number.

1. There are many instances in which Professor de Boor's version disagrees with Professors Colleville's and Tonnelat's, and no few in which mine disagrees with both.

APPENDIX I

The Status of the Poet

*

NOTHING is known about the poet[1] beyond what we learn from his work. It was evidently a convention that the authors of heroic poems, which were written in a more traditional and popular style than the fashionable romances of the knights, should remain anonymous. No author of a heroic poem names himself during the earlier history of medieval German poetry. On the evidence of the *Nibelungenlied* alone we can only guess at the poet's status, and there is no agreed guess.

Some think that the poet may have been a ministerialis, or 'unfree' knight bound to the service of a lord, that is a man of the same status as his great contemporaries Hartmann von Aue and Wolfram von Eschenbach. Others think of him as a menial cleric with a turn for poetry in his mother tongue. Yet others take him to be a superior sort of 'minstrel', a type of poet that whether in fact or theory, belonged to the nondescript class of wayfarers or strolling entertainers, somewhat suspect, because rootless, plebeians. Yet there are well-authenticated instances of 'minstrels' who were not only members of the households of lords lay or spiritual, but also sometimes settled owners of fiefs, well-to-do, valued men capable of discharging a variety of useful offices for their masters. These guesses virtually exhaust the possibilities, for it is unthinkable that the *Nibelungenlied* was the work of a secular lord, an ecclesiastic, a monk, a merchant, or a peasant.

Despite forthright and even ill-tempered assertions that our poet must have been a knight, the evidence for this claim is weak. Interest in courtly customs, ceremonies, and dress is of course not decisive, since courtly patrons at this time will have expected it.[2] Our poet's sensitive outlook may have matured below the salt. A man of humbler origins than a ministerialis could have had

1. Despite the manifold additions and revisions which the poem underwent as shown by the MS tradition, it cannot be doubted that there was a gifted poet whose version put all others out of the running. See Appendix 2, pp. 358ff.

2. See the section on 'The Two-fold Texture of the Poem', p. 344.

ample opportunity of conversing with his betters as Haydn and others would in a later age, had he been as gifted. But if, against probability, he was indeed a ministerialis, we may be thankful that he kept any enthusiasm he had for the new French fashions of chivalry within such reasonable bounds, since he might easily have ruined his theme. There is, however, a powerful argument, hitherto overlooked, why the poet is unlikely to have been a knight of any sort. It applies to his idea of a hunt. No nobleman who wished to be accepted as such by his fellows would have concocted so absurd a sequence of events as those narrated in Chapter 16, for no student of the hunt can take them seriously. It is quite the flimsiest affair of the chase among all the more respectable narratives of the German Middle Ages. This is at one with the remarkable fact that in an epic in which there is so much fighting there is not a single military technicality such as one finds in other heroic epics like the *Iliad* and the *Song of Roland*, or even in contemporary Arthurian narratives like *Parzival*.

Perhaps the best reason for thinking of the poet as a cleric is that he could cope with over two thousand quatrains on parchment. Yet there are grounds for believing that non-clerical poets could do the same – competition was growing keen in the field of literary entertainment. This would justify us in thinking of the poet as 'semi-clerical', if we like, that is as having enjoyed some schooling. Another reason for thinking him a cleric might be his assumed connexion with the Bishop's City of Passau. Yet the very bishop in whom many would see his chief patron, Wolfger, later Patriarch of Aquilea, generously supported lay poets, the most famous of whom was Walther von der Vogelweide. But if the poet was in fact a cleric, which of course does not necessarily mean a priest, he had a remarkable capacity for thrusting ecclesiastical considerations aside and abandoning himself to the ethos of his subject-matter, which, as we have seen, is far from Christian. We have reviewed the argument that the *Nibelungenlied* may be a sermon on the Fall of Pride, and found that if it is, it is a very unclerical sermon.[1] The most clerical touches in the whole epic, perhaps, are two instances in which the poet praises natural at the expense of counterfeit complexions (pp. 83, 206), and a passage in which he dwells, with much tolerant humour and even complacency, on the long-drawn-out greetings of the ladies (p. 83). This is all, and it amounts to very little. On the other

---

1. See pp. 341f., where the ethos of the poem is discussed at length.

hand, God, the Devil, Church, and the mass are mere narrative conveniences to this poet, or they are part of the normal social background. The warning in Chapter 31 should be heeded, for surely we know where we stand when a man of Hagen's stamp, having dragged a chaplain from the sacred utensils of his mobile altar and thrown him into the Danube without provocation, reminds the Burgundians to confess their sins. Nor is there a note of zeal or disapproval when he tells of Christian living cheek by jowl with pagan at Etzel's Court (p. 170). If the poet was indeed a cleric he doffed his cassock and folded it neatly away before taking up his quill. He would have been the most facile cleric in medieval German literature, had he in fact been a priest. Much has been said above on his astonishing lack of candour in attributing motives for the deeds he narrates.

We are left with the least hazardous surmise, that the author of the *Nibelungenlied* was a lay poet of plebeian status who had acquired the art of letters at a school and then considerable personal culture in the household of a lord. Are there any positive arguments in favour of this conception?

There is the general argument that heroic poetry in German during this period was purveyed by the miscellaneous and not easily definable 'minstrel' class, and we shall see that what can be reconstructed of our poet's main sources was strongly marked by the 'minstrel' style, which he adopts and refines. There is in the narrative of our poem some very special pleading on behalf of superior minstrels, in part inherited and retained from a minstrel predecessor, in part our poet's contribution. King Etzel sends a leading vassal, the Margrave Rüdiger, to Burgundy to sue for the hand of Kriemhild, yet to invite her royal brothers to Hungary he dispatches the minstrels Werbel and Swemmel, highly favoured men within their own class, but very small fry beside Rüdiger. One might be tempted to explain this away by arguing that minstrels were the accepted go-betweens, secret agents, and tools for dirty work of their day, and that this pair were appropriately chosen to lure the Burgundians to their doom (for which, incidentally, one of them paid with his hand) (p. 243). But however this may have been in the poet's source,[1] as he tells the story they were chosen for their mission not by Kriemhild but by Etzel, and

1. The issue is obscured in the *Thiðrekssaga*, the one parallel source which could help us, because the Eddic motif of Etzel's lust for Burgundian gold is introduced here. Yet it seems that in the common source Kriemhild chose a pair of minstrels as being most apt to her purpose.

in good faith. Another explanation offered is that the Burgundians might have harboured less suspicion towards an invitation conveyed by men of so peaceful a profession. In real life they are unthinkable as royal ambassadors for such an occasion, and it is best to ascribe them to the wistful and perhaps ironic imaginings of a poet on the fringe of high society. And here, no doubt, is the point: what gifts were lavished on Werbel and Swemmel, going and coming on their embassy! (pp. 181, 188). It is both amusing and touching to see in what princely fashion these minstrels – already worth a thousand marks each from the takings at Kriemhild's wedding – live for the brief space of their royal mission. The same theme of largesse is touched on with a rather personal show of impersonality when Kriemhild rewards the messenger for his news of the Saxon war: 'Such gifts encourage one to tell such news to great ladies (p. 43).' And then there is the enigmatic figure of Volker, Hagen's comrade-in-arms. We know for sure (p. 379) that the poet inherited Volker from his source for the second part of his poem, and there are some grounds for believing that Volker may have been of minstrel status in it.[1] Our poet, however, presents Volker as a nobleman who brings thirty of his own vassals to the wars, and he gives him prominence in battle. Volker nevertheless retains his viol and his title of 'Fiddler' and 'Minstrel' as a sobriquet, and he plays the army to sleep. He is further distinguished by being made to sing to Lady Gotelind to his own accompaniment, earning the favour of a rich reward. Thus the poet by implication thrice advances the claims to honour of 'minstrels': in diplomacy, at court before the ladies, and on the field of battle. It is hard to imagine either a poor knight or a menial cleric doing this for his professional rivals.

The safest guess is, then, that the strange genius who wrote the *Nibelungenlied* was a semi-clerical poet by profession, technically of the order of *vagi* or wayfarers, though probably sedentary for much of his life.[2]

---

1. The significant metaphor of his 'fiddling' on the helmets of his enemies is known from the *Thiðrekssaga*; see p. 383n. 1.

2. Such minstrels or *ioculatores* are known from the documents, for example, for the King of Germany (*Rupertus ioculator Regis,* i.e. of Emperor Henry VI); for Duke Leopold VI (VII) of Austria (the minstrel's name was Eberhard and he made a gift of red cloth to a monastery); and for a later Bishop of Passau (the minstrel was Wolfker, and he gave a German book to the monastery, *c.* 1221).

APPENDIX 2

The Manuscript Tradition, Bishop Wolfger of Passau, and the Homeland of the Last Poet

*

THERE is a strongly held view that the poet's patron was Bishop Wolfger of Passau. The evidence adduced in favour of this view is that Wolfger's remote predecessor in Passau, Bishop Pilgrim (971–91), whose bones had been raised as recently as 1181, occurs several times favourably in the poem. But before this can be discussed, something must be said about the MS tradition.

Until recently it was held that the extant MSS could be arranged in two groups, *B and *C. *C was to be regarded as a later recension, and *B as an earlier recension beyond which it was impossible to ascend in pursuit of the text of the 'last poet'. Some even went so far as to say that the reconstructed prototype *B could be virtually equated with that text. Conflations between these groups were set at a minimum, although it was admitted that some strophes from *C had been adopted by all MSS of group *B, especially in the first chapter of the poem. Recent work, however, challenges this position. It shows that authentic Nibelung legend could enter the poem at any stage of the MS tradition, that the dividing lines between the groups are more blurred than had been hitherto supposed, and that in any case the value of MSS A[1] and C for reconstructing the poet's text had been underestimated. Nevertheless, this new view does not dispense with the assumption that there was a vulgata or that there was a Passau recension of the text, as indeed it could not deny the existence of a common text and a Passau version, since all complete surviving MSS of the poem are followed by the elegiac *Klage*, the obvious intention of which is to set the seal of the city of Passau on the *Nibelungenlied* in order to enhance its Bishop's prestige. On the other hand, the new view claims that it is not technically possible

1. An early MS of considerable importance, once even thought to constitute a class of its own, so that an edition of the *Nibelungenlied* was based on it.

to assert or deny that the Passau version was identical either with the vulgata or with the text of the last poet.

Bishop Pilgrim of Passau occurs both in the *Klage* and in the *Nibelungenlied*, and it would be of cardinal importance if it could be proved either that he was taken into the *Klage* from our poem, or vice versa. If the *Klage* had the priority, then the passages featuring Pilgrim and Passau in the *Nibelungenlied* as we have it would be interpolations, and the text into which they had been inserted could have arisen elsewhere than in Passau. But if our *Nibelungenlied* had the priority, then either as the work of the 'last poet' or as a recension thereof, it very probably arose in Passau. In the event of the poet's version having been made in Passau, his patron would not be far to seek, since from 1191 to 1204, the worldly Wolfger von Erla in Lower Austria,[1] a great patron of vernacular poets, was Bishop of Passau.

Unfortunately the required proof of priority between the epic and the *Klage* in respect of the allusions to Passau cannot be furnished. Nevertheless there are very strong reasons for believing that the *Klage* was the donor and the epic the recipient in this one respect, and I shall proceed to give these reasons, whilst repeating that the argument cannot be strictly proved in terms of textual criticism.

First, a word must be said on the nature and purpose of the *Klage*.

The *Klage* is a garrulous elegiac poem in court couplets, deriving its interest and subject-matter from the *Nibelungenlied*, which, as stated above, it always follows in the manuscripts, whatever their alleged grouping. This concoction serves to remind us what little understanding of the last poet's achievement the average listener then had, for it picks up the pieces after the catastrophe in more than one sense, replacing severed heads on their bodies and regaling the audience with an 'inside story' gleaned from the survivors with all the zeal of modern newspaper reportage. Even those who, like the Bavarian lord Else, fell foul of the Nibelungs on their way to Hungary, are interviewed, and none gives the answer 'no comment'. In order that we may believe this shallow fabrication we are assured that after diligently searching for eye-witnesses, Kriemhild's uncle, Bishop Pilgrim of Passau, commanded the history to be written in Latin from beginning to end! But Pilgrim flourished in the days of the Hungarian, not of the

1. That Wolfger was 'von Ellenbrechtskirchen' in Bavaria has long been disproved.

Hunnish incursions.[1] By A.D. 1200, however, secular literature in Germany was throwing off its ecclesiastical shackles, and the citation of spurious sources in order to launch a new story was coming into fashion. Grub Street was just round the corner, and it was very smart of a precursor to take up the theme of the Nibelungs so soon after our poet had laid it down and to capture the attention of his public by raising the curtain over the scene on which the poet, in the austerity of his art, had thought fit to drop it. Yet this was a blessing in disguise. Just because from early days the *Klage* followed the *Nibelungenlied* in the manuscripts and scavenged the leavings, it helped to preserve the marvellously curt and powerful ending of the epic. 'I cannot tell you what happened after this,' says our poet in muted tones, when the swish of Hildebrand's sword and Kriemhild's shriek have died away and general lamentation has broken out – but the hack who wrote the *Klage* could, and so the temptation to meddle with the end was unwittingly frustrated.

The *Klage*, then, is an example of literary opportunism, the intended beneficiary of which is the city of Passau, and more particularly its Bishop, presumably Wolfger, who had been to Palestine in 1197 and so gained the title of 'Pilgrim', the proper name of the bishop in the story; and credit was claimed for the older Pilgrim's having ordered the Nibelung story to be recorded in Latin, without which (it is implied) there would be no *Nibelungenlied*. Surely it is far more probable that a garrulous poem, which is essentially a fabrication designed to associate the Nibelungen with Passau, should make one of its bishops their uncle, than that an austere poet should do violence to his style in order to do so? In its allusions to Passau and its Bishop, the *Klage* presents an organic whole, whereas the allusions to Passau and its Bishop in the *Nibelungenlied* are sketchy and fitful. They could be accounted for entirely in terms of what is said on the subject by the *Klage*, and in one case, if the passage is removed as an interpolation, some important narrative illogicalities are removed with it. After their engagement with the Bavarians, Dancwart urges his men to press on through the night, although they are beginning to complain of weariness. '... we cannot rest before dawn. Then, as soon as we find an opportunity, let us lie down in the grass,' he says. 'We cannot tell you where they camped,' the poem continues. News of their approach reaches Passau. Soon they are

1. Attila the Hun is a character in the *Nibelungenlied*, in which he appears under the High German form of 'Etzel'.

received, and they spend a day and a night there, resting. How strange, then, that they should be travel-weary again and have another rest on approaching Rüdiger's domain, and that the cadences of the strophe which tells us this are of archaic type. If we omit the Passau strophes, however, it becomes clear that the men are travel-weary because of the long, forced night-march which makes them so disgruntled, and that the line 'We cannot tell you where they camped' is a clever piece of patchwork to cover up the interpolation.[1]

In the other major allusion to Passau there is some evidence in favour of its being an interpolation (however skilfully contrived) which has never been discussed. After Kriemhild leaves Passau on her way to Hungary, she arrives in due course at Eferding, some fifty-two kilometres farther down the Danube valley, though not directly by the river. On this, the poet's comment is highly significant: 'Had certain lords of Bavaria (whom I could name) succeeded in robbing them on the roads in their usual style they might possibly have harmed the visitors, but the noble Margrave prevented it' (p. 362). Thus on arriving at Eferding, Kriemhild, thanks to Rüdiger, has escaped what would otherwise have been inevitable molestation by 'certain lords of Bavaria'. The man who wrote this, and he was presumably the 'last poet', was thus himself no Bavarian, and the hostility which he evinces was neighbourly detestation such as we find on all borders under feudal conditions, and later. Eferding at this time was a market town belonging to Passau, but, in our context, of far greater importance than its connexion with the bishopric is the fact that it was safely beyond the jurisdiction of Bavarian lords. This picture is confirmed by another passage (p. 181) in which it is said that Werbel and Swemmel, coming from Hungary, had not passed *right through* Bavaria before they found Bishop Pilgrim. The normal place in which to imagine him is in Passau, in which case Etzel's envoys will have traversed *part* of Bavaria before reaching that city.

Round about A.D. 1200, the frontier between Bavaria and Austria did not follow the Inn into Passau as it does today. On the Austrian Margraviate's becoming a Duchy in 1156, the frontier began to move west of the Enns. The addition of the Duchy of Styria in 1192 consolidated this tendency. In A.D. 1200 the frontier

1. It is not possible to say what the suggested interpolation replaced. There may well have been a neutral mention of Passau, since in the absence of a bridge at Schärding *c.* 1200, the bridge at Passau (since *c.* 1143) was the obvious way over the Inn.

(which of course must not be conceived in too linear a sense) ran north-west along the Hausruck and the Grosse Mühl, leaving Eferding to the east and surrounded by the possessions of the 'reichsfrei' lords of Schaunberg whose lands were included in 'Austria'. Farther to the west of Eferding there was the lord of Viechtenstein (on the Danube below Passau), a member of the Bavarian family von Wasserburg higher up the Inn. The whole eastern bank of the Inn from Schärding to Passau belonged to the County of Neuburg, whose Count between 1188 and 1204 was the Bávarian Count Berthold III of Andechs, also Margrave of Istria and Duke of Meran and Dalmatia. The County of Neuburg remained in this family till 1209, when it probably fell to the Duke of Bavaria. The County of Schärding also belonged to the Counts of Andechs, who, like the lords of Schaunberg, were 'reichsfrei'. In 1192 those of Andechs had been in feud with the Duke of Austria, and Passau had been damaged during the hostilities. Farther west still, to the south-west of Passau, in Bavaria, there were the lords of Ortenburg, who were at war with Passau in 1199. Thus west of Passau and also east of it approaching Eferding there was a region dominated by Bavarian lords of independent outlook.

If the last poet of the *Nibelungenlied* had been in the service of the Bishop of Passau it is less likely that he would have alluded to the surrounding Bavarian nobility in the terms cited above, even though Bishop Wolfger was of an Austrian and not a Bavarian noble family; for Passau was pre-eminently a Bavarian bishopric despite its deep reach into Austria. It makes far better sense if a poet in the service of an Austrian lord, above all within the old, traditional frontier of the Enns, says: 'Had certain lords of Bavaria[1] succeeded in robbing them on the roads *in their usual style...*' than if a poet of Passau were to say so.

If this argument has any weight, based as it is on contemporary conditions in a small area, then (i) the contention that the passages alluding to Bishop Pilgrim and Passau are interpolated, receives independent support; (ii) the claim that the last poet served a lord in the Austrian Duchy is strengthened; and (iii) the success of the clergy of Passau in appropriating the decisive version of the epic to themselves by means of a new recension and the addition of the *Klage*, is underlined. This latter feat would have some smack of literary forgery, but there were no laws of copyright

1. *genuoge* (polemical indefinite) *ûz* ('of', 'from', titular, implying feudal allods) *Peyer lande*, NL 1302, 2.

then. At this time far more serious forgeries, both sacred and profane, abounded in furtherance of political ends. Scholars have wondered how Passau could leave its stamp upon the whole surviving MS tradition of the *Nibelungenlied*. The answer, surely, is that it used the weapon in which it excelled, its chancellery and scriptoria, whose influence is strong even in the Austrian ducal chancellery, despite the trade war that embroiled the two powers and despite Austria's long struggle to free herself from Passau and have a bishopric of her own – nothing of which, incidentally, makes it impossible for a Babenberger Duke to die in the arms of a bishop of Passau, as, in 1198, Frederick I died in Wolfger's.

Scrutiny of the considerable number of divergent strophes furnished by the redactor of group *C (and it seems that we may still speak of such a redactor) reveals his temperament and his aim. He was no poet but a rationalist, who, like many a person in the audience, required an explicit statement of motives and general clarity, whatever the cost. He also wished to raise Kriemhild morally at the expense of Hagen and Gunther. Examples of his innovations speak for themselves. As a dutiful widow, Kriemhild not only makes gifts to the Abbey of Lorsch for the good of Siegfried's soul, but (at the suggestion of her mother, who founded the abbey)[1] she also has his body exhumed and taken there for reburial – Siegfried's body, for one last look at which (according to *our* poet) Kriemhild had had his coffin raised and broken open, as she wept tears of blood on his fair face ! In an attempt to whitewash Kriemhild, the redactor causes her twice to say that her men are to harm only Hagen, and he tells us on his own behalf that she had not foreseen such carnage, having planned only Hagen's downfall, but the Devil saw to it that all had to suffer Hagen's fate. Another opinion which the redactor offers is that had there been no Christians in the field against the Nibelungs the latter would have survived against all odds.[2] But at another point, after Kriemhild has expressed concern about marrying the heathen Etzel, Rüdiger (himself a Christian) is made to say that Etzel was not altogether a heathen but merely a renegade – the matter could be arranged. (Our poet was far more discreet (p. 162).) When Gunther's chaplain reaches the shore after Hagen's attempt to drown him (p. 198), the redactor adds an exchange of curses which Gunther ends with a promise of compensation for the ducking – and best wishes to the Queen in Burgundy ! Lastly, shocked by the tradi-

1. *C here elaborates a hint in the *Klage*.
2. This is taken from the *Klage*.

tional passage, retained by our poet, in which Hagen transports what has grown to be a whole army across the Danube in a one-man ferry (p. 197), the redactor adds a strophe to explain that it was a very big boat capable of shipping eighty men at a time, and that many had to pull at the oars.

To sum up a rather complex situation. As with the *Iliad*, though not always for the same reasons, scholars have been struck both by the cumulative nature of the *Nibelungenlied* and by the work of creative organization undertaken by a single poet whose version silenced his competitors. It is not possible to arrive at the text of such a poet through the manuscripts now available. A vulgate text and a Passau recension are discernible, but it is not possible to say whether they are one and the same. It is probable that Passau laid its hand on the tradition, as a compliment to Wolfger von Erla, and so heavily that its version left its mark on all others. It is also probable that the last poet (or failing him, a predecessor of the redactor of Passau) was of the Duchy of Austria, east of the Enns, and of neither Bavaria nor Passau. Branching off from a version earlier than *B, there was a more modern, rationalistic version *C with additional pro-Kriemhild strophes.

APPENDIX 3

The Date of the Poem

*

As with all of the better known heroic epics, it is difficult to date the *Nibelungenlied* with accuracy. The question is only meaningful if we ask when that version was composed which put all other versions out of the running and which is said to have been written by 'the last poet'? This version cannot be recovered by the process of critical editing, so that any passages in the poem which can be dated will require a separate proof that they were part of the last poet's version: but in the nature of the case such proof cannot be strictly given. Apart from the criterion that strophes with caesura rhyme are later than the 'last poet', it must be left to an aesthetic judgement to decide whether a given passage belongs to that poet's text or not, with all the risk that this entails.

The last poet's version, in my view, will have antedated the Passau recension, and if the latter was made in the interests of Bishop Wolfger, the most likely candidate, this gives us the broad period of 1191–1204. If the Passau recension was completed before 1204, the version of the last poet will have been completed some time before that. This agrees broadly with four other independent indications of date, none of which, individually, can be regarded as unimpugnable. Taken together, however, these four indications suggest that the Passau recension can scarcely have been completed by May 1204, when Wolfger ceased to be Bishop.

The first concerns the passage in Chapter 17, in which Kriemhild causes Hagen to stand beside Siegfried's bier, whereupon the wounds bleed anew and accuse him as the murderer (p. 137). Although the poet says that the like often happens today, he does not take it for granted, but explains the whole happening. This ordeal is not known from legal records in Germany until the fourteenth century. Thus we are to some extent justified in looking for a literary source. In Hartmann von Aue's *Iwein*, the same motif occurs. Iwein, who slew Laudine's husband with a blow of which the author disapproved, watches the funeral procession from nearby, in his state of invisibility, whereat the wounds bleed afresh. Like the Nibelungen poet, Hartmann, too, makes a fuss on introducing this ordeal: 'Now we have often been told for a truth that if one man has slain another . . .' The formulation here is more guarded. Hartmann does not *know* of its having happened 'often', only that he and his listeners had 'often' been *told* it. Hartmann may be speaking the truth: yet his immediate source is the original of his adaptation, the *Yvain* of Chrétien de Troyes, which introduces the motif without fuss. The corpse was carried past Yvain, the wounds bled anew, and this was proof positive . . . Now Hartman's *Iwein* was almost certainly begun a year or two before A.D. 1200, and the ordeal scene occurs early in the second thousand lines, so that if *Iwein* was published episodically, Chapter 17 of the *Nibelungenlied*¹ was written not earlier than 1199; whereas if *Iwein* was published entire, the date becomes 'not before 1203–4'. These dates depend on the assumption that the passage in the *Nibelungenlied* was in fact prompted by that in *Iwein*. Here it must be noted that Kriemhild employs the idea of an ordeal beside the bier deliberately and judicially, whereas in *Yvain* and *Iwein* the presence of an invisible manslayer is inferred postfactually and incidentally. Historians of German law assume that since this ordeal is found in the documents in the fourteenth century it will have existed in practice before, and in fact they quote our passage from the *Nibelungenlied* as the earliest evidence of the ordeal as such.

The second indication of date has been found in quasi-Saracenic names of precious fabrics. When Kriemhild and her maidens prepare the magnificent clothes which Gunther and his companions intend to wear in Iceland, in Chapter 6, they take Arabian silk as white as snow and good silk from Zazamanc as green as clover (p. 56). The people of distant Iceland, however, are as well provided with Oriental luxuries as are those of Burgundy, for in the next chapter Brunhild takes the field in a tabard of silk from Azagouc (p. 65); and in Chapter 14, the orphrey which Kriemhild flaunts as Brunhild's maiden girdle is said to be from 'Ninnive' (p. 115). Such exotic fabrics and names are out of keeping with the general style of the *Nibelungenlied*, and are to be taken as extreme examples of its newly acquired taste for courtly pomp and ceremony. If Zazamanc, Azagouc, and Ninnive could be given contemporary reality, that is, if they were actual cities renowned for their fabrics, there would be no problem: but they are not. All attempts to identify Zazamanc and Azagouc as place-names, let alone as manufacturing towns, have failed. Ninnive, of course, is known from the Bible. Thus we are at the familiar level of fantastic

1. Always assuming that the ordeal was an integral part of it.

intelligence of the East, whose mystery grows with fantasy. Those who recognized these names as of literary origin in such a context did not have far to seek: all three occur in the *Parzival* of Wolfram von Eschenbach, whose bizarre and exuberant imagination could coin or new-mint exotic names by the bushel. The whole of the first book of *Parzival* is situated in Morocco and gravitates between Zazamanc and Azagouc, whose most extraordinary products, there, are gigantic jewels. But in Wolfram's fifth book, in which he forages for things of splendour with which to adorn the scene before the Holy Graal, and in the sixth, in which he introduces Oriental characters, we find two of the above three place-names associated with precious stuffs. Eight ladies who serve the Graal wear mantles of brocade[1] of Azagouc, greener than grass. Other ladies wore brocade from Ninnive. Zazamanc and Azagouc are not known from sources earlier than *Parzival* and the *Nibelungenlied*. Ninnive is named in a version of the Alexander legend of *c.* 1190, that is precisely in a story which tended to jumble up the Orient of the past with that of the present. Wolfram names Ninnive and Babylon together in *Parzival*, Book I, confusing the ancient city with medieval Babylon (Old Cairo) in Egypt. Stylistically there can be little doubt who coined the names Zazamanc and Azagouc. The *Nibelungenlied* names many places that existed, but the only other fabulous names that it has are Isenstein and Nibelungland, which are in an entirely different vein. Wolfram, on the other hand, has exotic names galore, even when allowance is made for the many fantastically corrupted versions of real place-names which he cites.

If it be granted, then, that by Chapter 14 the Nibelung poet had borrowed three fabulous names from *Parzival*, what follows for chronology? The books of *Parzival* were written in the order III to VI-I-II-VII to XVI, and even then subjected to revision. Pseudo-oriental interest becomes perceptible in the sequence V–VI–I. Book VII was written at the earliest after the summer of 1203, and a pause is assumed between it and Books I–VI, so that if the exotic names of Books V–VI–I are not the result of revision, Chapters 6 to 14 of the *Nibelungenlied* were composed about 1203 or later – unless the exotic names here, too, were introduced by a redactor, say by the redactor of the Passau version.

The third indication of date is bound up with the amusing figure of Rumold, Lord of the Royal Kitchen. Rumold is introduced to the listener as a stranger on two different occasions. First, in what German critics call 'the play-bill' in Chapter 1, in which

1. Actually *samit*, from *hexamitos*, a Byzantine product.

he is said to be lord of the Kitchen and a rare warrior (p. 18), and, second, in Chapter 25, where a brave and loyal vassal of the Burgundian kings steps forward on the eve of their departure for Hungary. 'His name was Rumold, and he was a doughty warrior', the poet continues. Rumold wishes to know who is to be regent during their absence, and he voices his regret that none can turn his lords from their purpose. Gunther then puts him in charge of his land and of his son. Some have thought this must be a different Rumold from the famous Rumold in Chapter 24, since in the scene in which he is made regent his courage is emphasized, he is not given the title 'Lord of the Kitchen', and he is introduced as if unknown: whereas in Chapter 24 he tries to dissuade the Burgundians from going to Hungary by promising to make them luscious dishes and by telling them to live on their great wealth and make love to pretty women (p. 185), constituting the famous 'Advice of Rumold' (*Rumoldes rât*), over which Wolfram will laugh in his *Parzival*. At the end of Chapter 12, we see Rumold busying himself with his 'subjects', the spacious cauldrons, as though he were a head cook (p. 105). The best explanation of all these anomalies is one that has recently been put forward; that in the epic source of the second half of the poem a cook offered his Sancho-like advice to the departing warriors, but the scene was transferred to the point where the Burgundians deliberated whether to accept Etzel's invitation, thus leaving a vestigial scene at the eve of departure, and that, at the same time as he transferred the episode, the last poet raised Rumold from head cook to Lord of the Kitchen to give him standing at the council, where his gross materialism serves to offset Hagen's proud fortitude. Then, since a lord must have courage, however much of a figure of fun he might be (like all cooks in medieval literature), the virtue of courage is added to Rumold. The harmonized item in Chapter 1 comes last, presumably from recension *C.

The significance of this for the dating of our poem is that in his more elevated role Rumold holds an office which first appears under Henry VI in Italy in 1194. The family of von Rothenburg (ob der Tauber) held the imperial office of Lord High Steward until c.1200. But Heinrich von Rothenburg, belonging to another branch of the family, held the title of 'Lord of the Kitchen' in Germany from 1201 till 1217 and beyond. Walther von der Vogelweide has a poem of *c.* 1203 in which he makes devastating play with the notion of bureaucratic cooks carving up the imperial joint: 'Let them advise the cooks ...'. And this conjunction of 'advice' and 'cooks' may well allude to 'Rumold's Advice', in passing. Thus if the audience of our poet was meant to think of the new office of 'Lord of the Kitchen' in Chapters 24 and 25, the passages concerned will have been written *c.* 1201–2, though possibly earlier.

A fourth indication of date, perhaps a rather slender one, has been found in Etzel's wedding with Kriemhild in Vienna. There was a wedding of unusual magnificence in Vienna in 1203, between Duke Leopold VI of Austria and Theodora Comnena, granddaughter of the Emperor Isaac of Byzantium.

Taking the above four indications of date at their face value and reserving the objections that could be laid against them singly, and also assuming that the *Nibelungenlied* was published entire, the following table is obtained:

Chapter 6 and 7	*c.* 1203
Chapter 17	1203–4
Chapter 22	1203 and later
Chapter 24 and 25	1201–2, plus or minus

There is a remarkable unanimity in these four indications of date, and if any reliance can be placed on them they suggest that our poem was published entire, not by episodes. If the passages concerned were the work of the 'last poet', this really leaves no time for a completed Passau version before Wolfger ceased to be Bishop in May 1204, yet it does not exclude the possibility that such a version had been commissioned by or for Wolfger while he was still bishop there. His elevation to the Patriarchate of Aquilea followed the sudden death of its Patriarch.

This may not be regarded as an entirely satisfactory result. But in my view the solution of the problem is not to be found in the conclusion that the text of the last poet and that of the Passau version must be one and the same thing. However convenient chronologically, such a conclusion would raise other and more intractable problems, as I have tried to show in Appendix 2.

APPENDIX 4

The Genesis of the Poem

*

MORE is known about the evolution of the *Nibelungenlied*[1] than about that of any other great heroic epic, so that in this respect the study of our poem is exemplary. If classical scholars knew as much about the prior stages of the *Iliad* as is known about those of the *Nibelungenlied*, the question who or what was 'Homer' would be largely settled, and the Higher Critic could lie down with the Unitarian. The reason why the *Nibelungenlied* enjoys this favoured position is, of course, that anterior sources of a historical or near-historical nature exist, and also parallel versions and allusions of archaic stamp.

These sources fall into the following classes: (*a*) Latin laws and chronicles from the sixth century onwards; (*b*) a tenth-century or perhaps ninth-century Latin epic on Walter of Aquitaine; (*c*) lays on the Death of Sigurð (= Siegfried) and the Fall of the Niflungs (= Nibelungs) recorded in the thirteenth-century *Edda* but composed some hundreds of years earlier, together with cyclically associated Eddic lays, and, for supplementation, the thirteenth-century prose *Volsungasaga*, which is largely based on epic poetry but also presupposes the *Thiðrekssaga*; (*d*) the thirteenth-century prose *Thiðrekssaga*, a conflated compilation of the legendary life and deeds of Thiðrek (= Theoderic, Dietrich), made in Bergen in Norway from narratives furnished by North German merchants, above all from Soest in Westphalia; (*e*) an invaluable passing reference to an oral version of the Nibelung story in a 'historical' author writing in Latin; (*f*) some passing references to characters or background in Old English heroic poetry; (*g*) later medieval German, Danish, and Faroese poems, songs, or ballads, on some part of the general subject-matter, from the thirteenth century until recent times.

My aim in this Appendix must be to give in English, from these varied sources, only the essential information from which the growth of the *Nibelungenlied* has been inferred in outline.

1. In the footnotes to this section 'Nibelungenlied' is abbreviated as 'NL'.

(*a*) The *Lex Burgundionum*, composed before A.D. 516, mentions among the predecessors of the reigning King Gundobad (*c.* 480–516), four kings: Gibica, Gundomaris, Gislaharius, and Gundaharius. Of these, only Gundaharius is known to the Latin chronicles. He is said to have gained territory for his Burgundians on the left (Gallic) bank of the Rhine between the years 406 and 413. In 435–6 he was defeated by the Roman Aetius, and in 437 overwhelmed in battle by a Hunnish army, possibly in alliance with Aetius. Gundaharius and his whole kindred are said to have been slain. The Huns in this battle were not led by Attila, who was elsewhere.[1] The chronicles record that Attila died of a haemorrhage during his nuptials with a presumably Germanic wife Ildico in 453. Seventy years later, Marcellinus Comes reports that Ildico had murdered Attila.[2] This all applies to the subject-matter of the second half of the *Nibelungenlied*. As to that of the first half, we are not so favourably placed. The names Siegfried and Brunhild are known from Merovingian sources, but apart from the general background of treachery and murder no convincing parallels can be adduced. The atmosphere that surrounds Siegfried and Brunhild is in any case semi-mythical or redolent of folktale.

(*b*) Characters known from the *Nibelungenlied* occur in *Waltharius* (tenth or even ninth century). Gibicho, King not of Burgundy but of Franconia in this source,[3] sends Hagano to Attila as a hostage. But on the death of Gibicho, the latter's son Guntharius abrogates the treaty, and Hagano escapes to his lord. When a second hostage, Waltharius, escapes from Attila with his destined bride Hiltgund, a third hostage, he passes through Frankish territory and is attacked in the Vosges by Guntharius and his vassals. Hagano holds back from fighting with his old comrade-in-arms until Waltharius slays a beloved kinsman of Hagano. Guntharius and his men are recognized by Waltharius as *nebulones Franci*,

1. See, however, p. 389*n.* 1.

2. Towards the end of the ninth century, Poeta Saxo gives as the motive her desire to avenge her father. This had no echo in any version that we know. It is quoted here merely in order to show how easily a bare account in a chronicle may become colourful and circumstantial, like heroic legend in general.

3. Hildigund, Waltharius's destined bride, is the daughter of a king of Burgundy: thus Franconia cannot be assumed to have included Burgundy here.

which, although derisive ('Frankish rascals' or 'windbags'), surely alludes to the dynastic name of Nibelung (pp. 301f.).

(*c*) (i) (I omit all mention here of the Eddic lays of Young Sigurð and also of the later songs in the German and Scandinavian languages on the same topic, which would have gone to make a sub-section (*g*) below, because there is so little agreement among scholars about them, and because the *Nibelungenlied*, in any case, has so little to say on Young Siegfried (p. 27).

(ii) Eddic lays on the Death of Sigurð. Of these there are two. The older and more important, *Brot* is (as the title conveys) a fragment giving the second half only of a lay composed *c*. 1100. The more recent *Sigurðarkviða en skamma* is an eclectic poem which borrows from the source of *Brot* and from various other lays and sentimentalizes the suicide of Brynhild as due to love for Sigurð, adding little touches of pagan lore as she prepares her funeral pyre. The various lays of Guðrun (= Kriemhild) also allude elegiacally to the theme. A cautious reconstruction of the content of the missing part of *Brot* followed by a paraphrase of its content must suffice here.

The young dragon-slayer Sigurð becomes the sworn brother of Gunnar and Hogni, Gjuki's sons, and marries Guðrun, their sister. Gunnar wishes to woo Brynhild, who will only marry the man who can satisfy her test of his manhood (i.e. pass through her wall of flame?). Sigurð promises to help. Gunnar fails to pass the test, and so Sigurð changes shapes with him. Naming himself 'Gunnar' he passes a chaste night or nights with Brynhild, with his sword Gram between them. He gives Brynhild's ring (which Brynhild will have bestowed on him in the normal course of events) to Guðrun. Bathing in the river, the two women dispute which of their husbands takes precedence. It is possible that Brynhild taunted Guðrun with Sigurð's apparently ignoble descent,[1] only to be overwhelmed by Guðrun's flaunting of her ring. (This humiliation must be assumed to have been a public one.) Brynhild has been mortally insulted. Pale with anger, she goes to Gunnar and lies to him: Sigurð had anticipated Gunnar's rights, she implies, and she will not suffer two husbands in one hall. Gunnar decides that Sigurð must die. (Here conjecture ends, and the text of *Brot* begins.)

Hogni questions this, but Gunnar urges Sigurð's broken oaths. Hogni ascribes Brynhild's accusation to her jealousy of Guðrun's

1. Cf. NL, p. 112, and *Thiðrekssaga*, p. 377.

happy condition. Guthorm,[1] a younger brother, who is not bound to Sigurð by oaths, is primed with magic to do the deed. He kills Sigurð south of the Rhine,[2] while a raven foretells destruction by Atli.[3] Only Hogni answers, in balladic terms: 'We slew him – his stallion bows its head over his master's body.' Claiming that Sigurð would have ruled them all, had he lived, Brynhild laughs with triumph so that the whole palace rings. Guðrun's answer is to curse Gunnar and threaten revenge.[3] Gunnar broods sleeplessly on the raven's words, and Brynhild, Buðli's daughter,[4] wakes at early dawn. She will either tell or withhold what is on her mind, as she pleases. They all keep silent, since few know a woman's ways, and how, weeping, she may tell of deeds to which, laughing, she egged men on. She narrates her dream of Gunnar riding to his foes in fetters and of the annihilation of the whole mighty race of Niflungs. The oaths of blood brotherhood which Gunnar swore to Sigurð, she says, were perjured, and Gunnar gave him a poor reward for always placing Gunnar first! It was evident when he came to woo her (Brynhild continues) how well Sigurð kept his oaths to Gunnar: for he laid his gold-bedizened sword between them, whose edges, outside, were tempered in fire, but, inside, bated with venom . . . [5]

(iii) Eddic lays on the Fall of the Niflungs. There are two, of which the more important is the *Atlakviða*, attributed to the ninth century.

Atli sends a messenger over the pathless Myrkvið[6] to invite Gunnar to visit him, promising rich gifts and territory. Proud in his knowledge of his own great wealth, Gunnar asks his younger brother Hogni for his opinion. – Why did their young sister send a ring twined round with wolf's hair? Surely to warn them that, if

1. Possibly a Nordic transformation of the ancient Godomar.

2. This mention of the Rhine is less likely to be a memory from Merovingian times than an echo of recent Low German versions.

3. The mention of Atli and Guðrun's threat of vengeance show an early tendency to relate the 'Death of Sigurð' and the 'The Fall of the Niflungs' more closely to each other (see pp. 388ff.).

4. This makes her Atli's sister. Cf. NL Etzel as Botelung's son, p. 168*n.*

5. The presumption is that Brynhild will take her own life, a theme of which much is made in the later *Sigurðarkviða en skamma*.

6. 'Gloomy forest'. Possibly a memory of the great forest known as the *Hercynia silva* or Firgund, north of the Roman road from the Rhineland to the Danube.

they came, their path would lead them to wolves? Gunnar's kinsmen refrain from advising him, for it is Gunnar's to command them, and it is of his own great spirit that Gunnar exclaims: 'May wolves rule over the heritage of the Niflungs, if Gunnar stays away!'

They set out amid the tears of their people, cross through the pathless Myrkviŏ, and as they approach the land of the Huns its marches quake beneath the hooves of their steeds.

Atli sits in his hall drinking wine, while his watchmen stand guard. Their sister was the first to see them enter. 'You are betrayed, Gunnar!' she cries. 'Go quickly – what chance have you against the cunning of the Huns? Better would it have been had you worn your chain-mail!' 'Too late now, sister, to assemble the Niflungs . . . from the red rock of the Rhine,'[1] replies Gunnar, who is taken and bound at once. Hogni, however, cuts down seven men and thrusts an eighth into the fire before he is over-powered.

The Huns ask Gunnar whether he will buy his life with his treasure? 'The heart of Hogni must lie in my hand,' he answers. They cut out the heart of Hjalli, the Cook, which Gunnar derides as it lies quivering on the plate. But Hogni laughs when they cut out his heart from the living flesh. 'Here I have the heart of Hogni the warrior – little does it quiver where it lies on the plate. Not so much did it quiver when it lay in his breast!' Now Gunnar can defy Atli. 'I was always in doubt while the two of us lived; but now I have none, when I alone am alive! The Rhine shall rule over the ore for which princes battle . . . over the god-given heritage of the Niflungs. In the swirling waters Gaulish rings will gleam, rather than the gold shine in Hunnish hands!' Gunnar is taken on a waggon at Atli's command and cast into the snake-pit, while Gudrun[2] curses her oath-breaking husband in his hall. Alone in his pit, Gunnar plays his harp till he dies. Thus should a brave ring-lavisher[3] deny men his gold!

Guŏrun welcomes the returning Atli with a golden goblet. Plying him and his warriors of the drooping moustaches with

1. The rock in the whole region of Worms is red, and this phrase might be a genuine survival, in keeping with the poetic tradition, not fully supported by history, that Worms was the chief city of the Burgundians. See p. 389*n*. 1.

2. This is the first time that the 'Kriemhild'-figure is named (see p. 385).

3. Literally, 'ring-hailer', that is, 'prince'.

drink and dainties till they are helpless, she then taunts Atli with having eaten his own sons.[1] There is a clamour along the benches, wild and tuneful lament and cries of woe below the rich tapestries – the Huns are weeping, all except Guðrun, who weeps not at all ... The goose-white woman opens the treasure house and gladdens the house-carls with gifts of gold. She then gluts the sword with the blood of Atli as he lies on his bed, unable to defend himself, unleashes the hounds and sets fire to the hall, in whose flames she perishes with all her victims.

No young woman in chain-mail has acted thus since then to exact vengeance for her brothers.

The twelfth-century Eddic *Atlamál* covers roughly the same ground, but at greater length and in a less heroic and more homely, sentimental manner. Its main source is held to be the *Atlakviða*, of which it makes surprisingly little use. Its women's dreams of warning and the rowing of the warriors till the planks and rowlocks break, are best regarded as late borrowings via the Danish from a Low German source similar to that of the *Thiðreks-saga* (p. 380). Despite its polar bear,[2] the description 'The Greenlandish', which it shares with the *Atlakviða*, is difficult to uphold.

(d) The gist of the story unfolded in the thirteenth-century *Thiðrekssaga* is as follows:

Sigurð, son of Sigmund, King of Tarlungland, is born, in the forest, of Sisibe, daughter of the King of Spain. She places him in a pot of glass, and he is accidentally sent floating downstream into the sea. When he reaches the coast he is suckled by a doe. He grows very fast. A smith Mimi finds him in the forest, names him Sigurð,[3] and rears him. Sigurð grows so strong that Mimi asks his brother Regin, a dragon, to kill him. Sigurð is sent to burn charcoal, the dragon appears, and Sigurð beats him to death. He cooks pieces of the dragon to still his hunger, and, scalding his finger in the broth, licks it and at once understands the conversation of two birds who are saying that he ought to kill the plotter Mimi. He smears his body with dragon's blood, except where he cannot reach between the shoulders, and his skin becomes horny. Return-

1. This is not the only classical motif that is found in Germanic heroic poetry.

2. White bears occur in Scandinavian literature that has nothing to do with the Icelandic colony in Greenland.

3. As this is narrated, it is pure chance that the *Sig* element of Sigmund's lineage is preserved.

ing home he receives from Mimi splendid armour and a sword 'Gram', with which he kills his foster-father.

Sigurð comes to Brynild's castle, and there he starts a fight by breaking down the gate. Hearing the tumult, Brynild remarks that this must be Sigurð, son of Sigmund (p. 62). She welcomes him, names his parents, and asks his errand. He answers that he has come for the steed Grane. Only Sigurð succeeds in taming it. This done, he mounts and rides away.

The scene changes to Niflungland. In the absence of its king Aldrian,[1] an incubus embraces his queen in her sleep. Later, this fairy tells her that their son will be a hero. When he is born, he is named Hogni. He grows to be tall and ill-favoured. His legitimate brothers are Gunnar, Gernoz, and Gislher,[2] who, however, was a child (p. 326). Their sister was Grimhild. Gunnar succeeded Aldrian on his death.[3]

Sigurð, who has become Thiðrek's vassal, goes with him to Niflungland and is there married to Grimhild with half of Gunnar's kingdom for dowry. He proposes that Gunnar should marry Brynild and he offers his aid, for he knows all the ways (pp. 53, 58) that lead there. Thiðrek, Gunnar, Hogni, Sigurð and their companions go to Segarð, where Brynild receives Gunnar well, but Sigurð ill, knowing that he has broken his promise, made when they last met, to marry no other but her.[4] Sigurð begins to negotiate on Gunnar's behalf, excusing himself on the grounds that Grimhild was a better match for himself because she had a brother. With Thiðrek's assistance a marriage is arranged between Gunnar and Brynild. The house is cleared for the nuptials, but Brynild will not suffer Gunnar's embraces and hangs him on the wall by their girdles, releasing him only at dawn. After the third such night, Gunnar remembers that Sigurð and he are sworn brothers, and he requests Sigurð's aid. Sigurð explains that Brynild's nature is such that scarcely any man could measure his strength with hers so long as she remained a virgin, whereupon Gunnar empowers him to take Brynild's maidenhead, on condi-

1. Cf. NL, p. 194. There is a confusion here: Aldrian was really the name of the fairy, not of the King.

2. In the MSS also Gisler, and Gilser.

3. Now follows a review of many heroes, among them Gunnar, Hogni, and Sigurð; then there are campaigns and battles in which Sigurð, too, is involved, but they are of no concern to the *Nibelungenlied*.

4. This was not related at the appropriate point.

tion that he keeps the secret. That night, Sigurð goes to the couch, and Gunnar leaves in Sigurð's clothes, so that all think he is Sigurð. Sigurð swiftly deflowers Brynild and, when morning comes, draws a ring from her finger, substituting another. Gunnar and Sigurð exchange clothes, and no one is the wiser. After the festivity Gunnar appoints a regent and returns with his bride to Niflungland, where he rules in peace with Sigurð, and with his brothers Hogni and Gernoz.[1]

Niflungland flourishes as never before owing to the harmony in which Gunnar and Sigurð rule in Werniza.[2] One day Queen Brynild enters her hall in which Grimhild is already seated. 'Why do you not rise before your Queen?' asks Brynild. 'Because you sit in my mother's high seat, in which I am no less entitled to sit,' retorts Grimhild. 'I own this city and land now,' Brynild answers, 'so run into the woods and seek the paths of the doe, behind your husband Sigurð!' 'Who took your maidenhead and who was your first man?' asks Grimhild. Brynild offers the reply which she believes to be true, but Grimhild gives her the lie and displays Brynild's ring as proof that Sigurð was her first man, and now Brynild regrets that so many have overheard their quarrel and she blushes as though blood were flowing from a wound. In silence she leaves the city and soon meets Gunnar, Hogni, and Gernoz, who are returning from the hunt. She tells them that Sigurð has broken his oath and told Grimhild everything and that Grimhild has publicly exposed her, and she demands that her own shame be avenged. Hogni asks her to behave as though nothing has happened and Gunnar promises vengeance. They ride in; but Sigurð is still away at the hunt. When he returns some days later he is welcomed as usual. Hogni and Gunnar proclaim a new hunt, and Hogni goes to the cook and orders breakfast to be strongly salted, and then to the butler, telling him to be slow to pour out drink. At breakfast they are met by Sigurð, who wishes to join the hunt. Thereupon all set out except Hogni. Hogni goes secretly to Brynild,

1. There now follow adventures of other warriors, including the escape of Waltharius with Hildegund (see p. 371) and Thiðrek's flight from Ermanrik and refuge with Roðingeir and Attila, and subsequent adventures. Events narrated in this group of adventures include the death of Nauðung and of Attila's sons whilst in Thiðrek's care, both touched on in the *Nibelungenlied* (see pp. 211, 277n).

2. Worms, Lat. *Borbetomagus*, Medieval Latin *Wormatia*, Middle High German *Wormez*.

and she begs him to kill Sigurð that day, promising him precious gifts as a reward. The hunters hunt till they bring down a great boar, which Hogni kills with his spear. Weary and thirsty, first Gunnar and Hogni and then Sigurð lie down to drink from a brook. Hogni then rises, seizes a spear, and plunges it between Sigurð's shoulder-blades. Wounded as he is, Sigurð says he could not have expected it of his brother-in-law and that his shield would have been shattered, his helmet smashed and his sword notched (p. 339), before this would have happened, and that it would have cost them all their lives. As Sigurð dies, Hogni observes that they had hunted a boar all the morning and scarcely managed to kill him together, but that now he alone has brought down a bear or bison. They carry the corpse home and are espied from the tower by Brynild, who descends in order to congratulate them. She tells them to take Sigurð to Grimhild, who is asleep in her bed. 'Let her now embrace the dead man!' They break open her door and throw the corpse into her arms. She awakes and sees him dead. She finds his shield and helmet unscarred. 'You must have been murdered!' she cries.[1] Hogni denies it: 'It was a wild boar that gave him his death-wound.' 'You and no other were that boar, Hogni,' she replies. They leave her to her tears. She and her vassals bury Sigurð.[2]

Learning of Sigurð's death, King Attila of Susat (Soest) sends his nephew, Duke Osid, to woo Grimhild for him. In Niflungland Osid makes his proposal to Gunnar, Hogni, and Gernoz. Gunnar is willing, if his brothers are too, and Hogni thinks it a great honour and a possible source of further aggrandisement. Approached by Gunnar and Osid, Grimhild replies that she would not dare to refuse so mighty a king as Attila. The marriage is arranged, and Attila and Thiðrek are fetched and escorted into Werniza, with a great show of affection between Thiðrek and Hogni. At the leave-taking after the wedding celebrations, Gunnar gives Grani to Thiðrek, and Gram to Margrave Roðingeir.[3] In Attila's country Grimhild weeps daily for Young Sigurð.

One night, after seven years, Grimhild asks Attila to invite her brothers, who have kept back Sigurð's treasure from her. If he will help her to regain it, she will share it with him. Attila lusts after

1. Cf. the similar words NL p. 391n.1; *du lîst ermorderôt*, an archaic form of the verb and surely an ancient half-line.
2. The adventures of other heroes intervene.
3. Known to the reader of the *Thiðrekssaga* from other adventures unconnected with the Nibelungs.

gold more than any other man.[1] He knows of Sigurð's great wealth, gained from the dragon, the wars, and also inherited from Sigmund. 'We are denied it all,' he answers. 'Yet Gunnar is our dear friend.' He gives Grimhild permission to invite her brothers, and shortly afterwards she sends two minstrels to Niflungland, luxuriously equipped and clothed, with a letter bearing Attila's and her seals. The message which they deliver in Werniza is that Attila has grown too old to rule and that he therefore invites Gunnar and his brothers to rule in his stead until his baby son Aldrian shall come of age. In conclave, Hogni advises against acceptance, urging that this is a trap laid by the perfidious Grimhild. Gunnar rejects his advice, affirming that it is as bad as the advice which Hogni's father gave his mother,[2] and that if he is afraid he need not come. Hogni prophesies total destruction if they go to the land of the Huns, and then, stung by the taunt about his mother, goes to his sworn friend, Folkher, and commands his men to prepare themselves. Queen Oda[3] tells of having dreamt that there were so many dead birds in the Hunnish land that none was left alive in Niflungland, presaging disaster if they make the journey. Hogni derides her dream. She wishes Gislher at least to remain; but he insists on going. Gunnar assembles his men and they depart.

They march to where Rhine and Danube flow together, but find no ferry. Hogni holds the night-watch down-stream, and seeks a ferry. In the bright moonlight he comes upon a lake called Moere,[4] in which two mermaids from the Rhine are bathing. Hogni hides their clothes and refuses to return them unless they tell him whether he and his companions will cross the river, and if they do, whether they will ever come back. The mermaids answer that he and his companions will cross but not return, and Hogni hews them in half for their pains. Farther down, Hogni espies a man in a ship and hails him, saying that he is to fetch a man of Elsung's. The ferryman will not work for nothing, and remembering that he is newly married and how much he loves his beautiful wife, he accepts Hogni's proferred ring of

1. This is the Nordic view of Attila, see (c) ii above. It is intrusive in this account based on a Low and then ultimately Upper German source. Cf. the mild and generous figure of the *Nibelungenlied*.

2. A malicious reference to Hogni's conception, p. 376.

3. The Low German form of 'Uote'.

4. A reminiscence of the Danubian crossing at Mehring (NL Mœriogen, see Appendix 5, p. 398).

gold.[1] Meanwhile, Gunnar and his men have found a tiny boat and they get wet in it when it capsizes. They now go aboard Hogni's ship, and he rows so hard that he rows the oars and rowlocks to pieces.[2] Rising to his feet with a curse on the shipwright, he cuts off the ferryman's head. Asked why he has done so, Hogni tells Gunnar that it is to prevent news of their approach reaching Hunland. Reproached by Gunnar, Hogni answers: 'Why should I refrain from doing wrong? I know that not one of us will return.' Now Gunnar steers, and the rudder breaks in his hands. Hogni repairs it, and they have almost reached land when the ship capsizes. They struggle ashore, repair the ship, and ferry the rest of the army across. Then they march till evening, when Hogni keeps watch. Out reconnoitring, he finds an armed man sleeping. He throws the man's sword to a distance and wakes him with his foot. Missing his sword, the man laments that his lord will find his kingdom ill guarded, and that Roðingeir will find his lands invaded. Hogni approvingly returns his sword and gives him a ring of gold. The man names himself as Ekkivarð, and on learning who Hogni is, warns him to be on his guard in Hunland. He points the way to Roðingeir of Bakalar,[3] with whom they can stay the night. Forewarned by Ekkivarð, Roðingeir makes his castle festive, while Hogni fetches his companions.

In Bakalar the guests dry themselves at two fires. Gudelinda, sister of Duke Nauðung, who was slain at Gronsport (cf. NL, p. 211), remarks on their bright armour and relates how piteously Grimhild weeps daily for Sigurð. In conversation with his wife that night, Roðingeir plans to offer their daughter to Gislher in marriage. The next day the guests are entertained, and then Roðingeir makes them gifts: a helmet for Gunnar, a shield for Gernoz, his daughter and Gram for Gislher, who gratefully accepts both. Asked what he would like, Hogni requests a shield that hangs on the wall, and Roðingeir gives it him, telling him that it was Duke Nauðung's, whom Viðga slew with the sword Miming,[4] memories that make Gudelinda weep. Gunnar and his men leave that same day.

After some days' ride, the Niflungs arrive in Soest drenched

1. In the corresponding scene in NL, p. 195, the ferryman's rank has been raised, but, quite typically, he still accepts largess.
2. Cf. the parallel in the *Atlamál*, p. 375.
3. Middle High German *Bechelâren*, Modern German *Pöchlarn*.
4. The incident is overlooked in the medieval German minor epic, *Die Rabenschlacht*.

with rain.[1] They are met before the gate by Thiðrek. As they ride in, Grimhild sees them in their shining armour from a tower. 'How fair this green summer season is!' she says. 'My brothers march in with many a new shield and many a gleaming mail-shirt and I am now thinking how Sigurð's great wounds harass me!'[2] Then, weeping bitterly, she goes out to meet them.

Attila has fires lit for them and they dry themselves without removing their armour, but, beneath their mantles, Grimhild can see their mail-shirts. Observing his sister, Hogni puts on his helmet and laces it tightly. 'Have you brought me the Niflung treasure?' she asks. 'I have brought you the Devil, and my shield, helmet, and sword ...' (cf. NL, p. 217) he answers. She goes and kisses Gislher, who asks why she is weeping. When she tells him that it is because of Sigurð's wounds, Hogni retorts that they should leave Sigurð in peace – Attila ought to be as dear to her now as Sigurð was. Done is done. Grimhild leaves, Thiðrek summons the Niflungs to table, and he and Hogni go out arm-in-arm, to where Attila gives a splendid feast.

The next day Thiðrek comes and warns Hogni of Grimhild's weeping, and the Niflungs go through the town for recreation. Attila watches them from above, with Blodelin at his side, and he is reminded of when he and Queen Erka[3] knighted Hogni. As they pass through the town, Hogni and Folkher doff their helmets to observe the ladies, and it can be seen that Hogni is slender-waisted but broad-shouldered, with a long sallow face and but one glaring eye (p. 322n.1), a fine figure of a man. Attila orders a feast in an orchard. Meanwhile Grimhild incites Thiðrek to avenge her, promising to help him to avenge himself on Ermanrik and Sifka in return,[4] but in vain. She now turns to Duke Blodelin, who declines, fearing Attila's wrath. Attila is equally unresponsive to her prayers. Out in the orchard she commands the Niflungs to give up their armour, but Hogni replies that his father had never taught

1. There is clearly some doubling of the motif of drenched clothing here, the function of which was to provide a glimpse of the Niflungs' armour.

2. Cf. NL, p. 213, and also *Atlakviða*, p. 374, where Guðrun is the first to see her brothers, and for good reason.

3. The Queen Helche of the *Nibelungenlied*.

4. According to the later medieval German poems of the Dietrich cycle (offshoots of which are of course incorporated in the *Thiðrekssaga*) Ermanerich ousted Dietrich from his kingdom at the prompting of Sibech.

him to give up his weapons to a woman, and then laces his helmet more tightly. They sit down to feast, the Niflungs in their armour, though their shields and spears are lodged away. Hogni, however, has taken the precaution of posting squires as sentinels. Grimhild now wins over Irung by promising to fill his shield with gold and to be his friend. Grimhild returns to her seat in the orchard and is joined by Aldrian, her son by Attila. She dares him to buffet Hogni on the cheek, which he does, whereupon he is dispatched by Hogni, who throws his severed head at Grimhild's breast. 'We shall have to pay dearly for the good wine that we have drunk here, and I shall settle the first debt with sister Grimhild' (cf. NL, p. 243). He then beheads Aldrian's tutor 'as he deserves' (cf. NL, pp. 243, 302f.) Attila rises and orders the destruction of the Niflungs. As they rush from the orchard the Niflungs slip up on fresh ox-hides that Grimhild has had stretched before the gate. Seeing their escape barred, they turn and slaughter all within. But Thiðrek goes home with his vassals, while Grimhild arms and incites men all day. That garden in Soest is still called 'Homgarden'. Seeing that they are increasingly outnumbered, Hogni breaches the wall and the Niflungs pass through, but are stopped in the street by Blodelin and overwhelmed. Yet Hogni leaps up the stairs to a hall[1] and with his back to it, defends himself against all comers. He is then joined by Gernoz, Gislher, and Folkher. They call to Thiðrek in his battlement, but he asserts that he must stay neutral. Gunnar, fighting alone till dusk, is taken prisoner by Osid, who takes him to Attila, and Attila at Grimhild's prompting casts him into a snake-pit, where he dies. The tower is still at the centre of Soest. The news of Gunnar's capture makes the Niflungs run berserk, and they slay in the streets till nightfall. During the night Huns keep streaming in . . . Hogni marshals the Niflungs and in order to obtain light to fight by before they are again outnumbered, he sets fire to the buildings around. The Niflungs go in to the attack.

By daybreak, however, the Huns are reinforced, and large-scale fighting breaks out anew. Gernoz slays Blodelin, rousing Roðingeir to battle. Bathed in blood up to his shoulders, Hogni has forged far ahead. He breaks into a hall to rest himself,[1] while Roðingeir attacks the Niflungs, and then, entering the hall, faces Hogni. Espying her chance, Grimhild has the hall set on fire and eggs on Irung, who hacks off a lump of flesh from Hogni's thigh.

1. The original setting reasserts itself, against that of localization in Soest.

Grimhild now adorns Irung's helmet with gold and sets him on again, but this time he is killed. (There is still an 'Irung's Way' in Soest.) Shortly afterwards, Gislher slays Roðingeir with his gift-sword, Gram (see p. 335). Folkher cuts his way through to Hogni, who thanks him for making his sword sing so on Hunnish helmets.[1] Seeing his friend Roðingeir dead, Thiðrek orders his men to arm, and soon his sword Ekkisax is singing on Niflung helmets, so that Hogni is forced back towards Gernoz and Gislher. Thiðrek beheads Folkher, and Master Hildebrand fells Gernoz with Lagulf. Meanwhile Hogni and Thiðrek are locked in battle, and then Gislher and Hildebrand. As Attila descends from his towers, Hogni begs for peace for the boy Gislher, since he was innocent of Sigurð's death – 'It was I that struck his death-wound!' 'I do not say it because I doubt my power to defend myself,' adds Gislher, 'but my sister can testify that I was only five years old and was lying abed with my mother when Sigurð was killed.[2] But I have no desire to outlive my brothers.' And he runs at Hildebrand and to his death. Observing that their friendship looks like breaking, Hogni challenges Thiðrek to fight it out alone, and this they do. Thiðrek grows angry to be resisted so long by a fairy's son, and Hogni flings back the taunt of 'devil' at Thiðrek,[3] who now grows so angry that he breathes flames at Hogni which force him to surrender. Meanwhile, Grimhild has fetched a brand, and she thrusts it into Gernoz's mouth to see whether he still lives, and this kills him. But Thiðrek observes it, and reminding Attila of all the carnage Grimhild has caused, receives his permission to kill her, devil that she is. Thiðrek takes Hogni to his quarters, where, after his wounds are bound, he begets a son who is to be named Aldrian and to whom he bequeaths the keys of Sigurð's Niflung treasure. The land of the Huns is empty of famous men, fulfilling Queen Erka's prophecy of what would happen if Attila wed a Niflung.

1. The 'singing' of the sword on helmets is an ancient trope in Germanic heroic poetry, of which the 'fiddling' of Volker in the *Nibelungenlied* is a colourful sophistication. It is possible that this reference to Folkher's singing sword implies a reference to his having been a minstrel in the common source; see pp. 337f.

2. Cf. NL, p. 238, where the saying has been transferred to Dancwart, and p. 259.

3. The popular motif of a fire-breathing warrior attached itself to Dietrich early and so made it possible for disapproving churchmen to refer to his 'diabolical' nature.

(e) In Book XIII, vi, 7 of his *Gesta Danorum*, Saxo Grammaticus narrates how in A.D. 1131 Canute Lavard, Duke of Slesvig, for whom an ambush had been laid, was warned by a bard who sang a 'most beautiful song' on the famous betrayal of her brothers by Grimilda.

(f) (i) In *Beowulf* (eighth century) [Siegfried's father] Siegmund (in the form Sigemund, the Wælsing, cf. Norse 'Volsung'), is named as having slain a dragon and gained his treasure, a regular achievement in terms of ancient lore, whereas his son Siegfried in the *Nibelungenlied* achieves these feats separately.

(ii) *Widsið*, which contains an accumulation of ancient information ascending in part even to the time before the Anglo-Saxon Conquest, knows Gifica as ruler of the Burgundians, and it also knows Guðhere (Gunther) as a generous patron of 'heroic' poets.

(iii) Like the Old High German *Hilderbandslied* (ninth-century MS, composed c. 650), *Deor's Lament* (early eighth century) knows of Ðēodric's (Dietrich's) exile lasting thirty years.

(iv) The two fragments of the epic *Waldere* (Walter of Aquitaine, MS c. A.D. 1000, composition c. 750) know Gūðhere as ruler of the Burgundians, and also Hagena.

(g) For example: (i) The crude and confused late medieval German *Lied vom Hürnen Seyfrit*; (ii) The Danish ballads *Sivard Snarensvend*, *Sivard og Bryhild*, and *Grimhilds Hævn* (with parallels from other Scandinavian countries and islands), some of which descend from the common source of the second half of the *Nibelungenlied* and the corresponding chapters of the *Thiðrekssaga*.

The questions how the foregoing sources are interrelated, and how the Nibelung story grew and ramified, naturally determine each other. But they are vexed by the absence of important stages of growth, both in the set form of poems, whether oral or written, and also, it must be conceded, in the looser form of legend. Nevertheless, certain leading facts emerge, and it is to these that I shall address myself, ignoring temptations to refine, of which there are endless legitimate instances. Furthermore, of the two possible ways of furnishing the key to this material – the ascent to the lost original sources through analysis, or descent from them to the surviving texts – the latter is obviously to be preferred here, since it allows of a minimum of argument. The reader has the main facts before him in sections (*a*) to (*g*) above, and can form his own opinion of the acceptability of the bald assertions which follow.

As has been inferred for the *Iliad* and as is certain for the *Song of Roland*, the prime source of the Nibelung legend was a historical event (see (*a*) above). At some time during the fifth or sixth centuries, using historical memories already enshrined in heroic lays, a poet composed a lay on the destruction of the royal house of Burgundy and the death of Attila in revenge.

Attila, wedded to a Burgundian princess, lusts for her brothers' treasure, succeeds in luring them to Hunland[1] *despite the warnings which she sends them and other warnings given in 'Burgundy', fails to extort an answer from them as to where they have hidden their hoard, has them killed, and, together with his sons by this wife, is in turn killed by her and burned in his own hall.*[2]

Who were the leading characters of this lay? What were their names? And where was the lay composed? Attila, Gundahari, and a sister of Gundahari belonged to it with certainty. That Gundahari was designated 'son of Gibeca' is also certain.[3] The 'Ildico' of the chronicles may have been assimilated to the Burgundian dynasty, whose names alliterate on 'G', by addition of the element 'Grim–' '(fierce'), although there are phonological difficulties on the way from 'Grimhild' to 'Kriemhild'. Or the Norse 'Guðrun' (from 'Gunþrun'), which accords so well with 'Gunþahari', is the original Burgundian name of the sister. It is probable that Gislahari was featured as a very young brother in order to emphasize the total extirpation of the royal family, as stated in the chronicles. Whether Gundomaris/Godomar first appeared in this lay or in the one in which Siegfried is slain is uncertain. He occurs as 'Guthorm'

1. Once a Burgundian princess, be she named (?Grim)hild or Gunþrun, is made into Attila's wife, an *invitation* to her brothers (instead of the historic attack by a detachment of Huns) becomes possible and even likely.

2. The elements of this construct, if it has any validity, are thus remarkably well preserved in the Eddic *Atlakviða*; see (*c*) iii, above.

3. The *Nibelungenlied* behaves very oddly and against all known tradition both in Germany and in Scandinavia, in making the non-alliterative Dancrat father of the Burgundian kings and in bestowing the name of 'Gibech' on a vassal king of Attila. (King Gibicho, the King of the Franks in *Waltharius*, was also a tributary of Attila's: but there he was rightly father to Guntharius.) See pp. 17, 117. 'Gjuki' is the regular Norse equivalent of 'Gibeca'.

in *Brot*, and he may have been succeeded by 'Gernot' in the German tradition.[1] One is tempted to exclude Hagano from this lay; but if he was not an original character in it, he must have been introduced into the tradition relatively early[2], and where from, unless from the lay of Siegfried's death? Hagano is not known to history. His name does not alliterate with the names of the Burgundian kings. Thus he could not be their full brother. And so perhaps the door was left open for the incubus.[3] Whether the dynastic name of 'Nibelung' occurred in this lay, whether it was already associated with the Burgundian treasure or imported only later from Siegfried's treasure, is not amenable to proof, but this last is far less likely. The presentation of Attila in a negative light rules out the possibility that this lay was composed among the Huns' Germanic allies, say the Goths, or among those who (for one reason or another) shared the Gothic attitude towards Attila, like the Langobards. The conjecture has therefore been hazarded that the lay on the Fall of the Burgundians outlined above was composed among the Burgundians or Franks in Northern Burgundy of the Merovingian period, where Burgundians and Franks lived close together.

At another time, presumably later in the sixth century and again in Northern Burgundy, a poet made a lay on the wooing of Brunhild and the death of 'Sigifrid'. Whether or not the family into which 'Sigifrid' had married was originally the royal Burgundian family is not susceptible of proof, yet the identification must soon have been made. In other words, this second lay was originally or subsequently associated with the first lay in a 'cyclic' sense, as often happens during the growth of oral literature. This cyclic association, however, generated a tension between the two lays which, as we have seen above (pp. 301ff.), was not fully composed even by the deliberate attempt of our Austrian poet to harmonize the two plots. *Why should 'Grimhild' try to save brothers who had murdered her dear husband?* Blood-ties were all important in that age: but was it not asking a great deal that a widow should side with such brothers? As we shall see, there was a sequel to this conflict.

Once the Burgundians had been introduced into this second lay,

1. Guthorm, not bound by oaths, murders Sigurð in *Brot*, having perhaps ousted Hogni in that role; see (*c*) ii above.
2. He is firmly entrenched as 'Hogni' in the *Atlakviða* (ninth century).
3. Called 'Aldrian' in extant sources; see NL, p. 194, and (*d*), p. 376.

whether from the beginning or subsequently, the plot may already have run thus:

'*Sigifrid*' *who* (as associated lays narrated in detail) *comes unknown from abroad and who, thanks to his great strength, has slain a dragon and won treasure and a horny skin with but one vulnerable spot, now marries* '*Grimhild*' *and thus becomes the brother-in-law of Gunþahari. He helps Gunþahari to win Brunhild, who is so very hard to woo that only* '*Sigifrid*' *can surmount the obstacles, which he does in Gunþahari's shape. Whether he deflowers Brunhild or not,*[1] *as her accepted lover he receives a ring from her, and this he gives to* '*Grimhild*'. '*Grimhild*' *and Brunhild later quarrel in public over the standing of their men.*[2] *Brunhild twits* '*Grimhild*' *with* '*Sigifrid's*' *obscure origin, and* '*Grimhild*' *retorts by displaying Brunhild's maiden ring – Brunhild has been this man's bedfellow! Brunhild then either lies to Gunþahari or tells him what she believes to be the truth about her wedding night, and she demands vengeance. In order to restore her honour,* '*Sigifrid*' *is treacherously killed through his vulnerable spot:* by whom, cannot be shown; as to *where*, it suits the law of the talion that it should be *in bed* (as one Norse tradition relates[3]) rather than *out hunting in the forest* (as German tradition has it).[4] If the former was the original motif, we might add '*Grimhild's*' *piercing shriek of grief, as she wakes with* '*Sigifrid's*' *body in her arms,*[5] *answered by Brunhild's resounding laugh of triumph.*[6]

'Sigifrid' appears above in inverted commas because it cannot be proved that the hero's name was in fact Sigifrid, though it must have contained the element *Sigi–* ('victory'). He and Brunhild are,

1. The Norse tradition tells of chaste nights, with Sigurð's sword between the pair; German tradition of the mid twelfth century certainly had defloration (see pp. 298f, 376). It is not at all necessary to the plot that 'Sigifrid' should deflower Brunhild. It is more probable that Brunhild's hardness to win was exaggerated into an Amazonian virginity which demanded superlative athletic feats from her suitors, but the taking of which robbed her of her excessive strength, as stated explicitly in the *Thiðrekssaga*; see p. 376.

2. The setting is uncertain. 'Bathing in the river', as in *Brot*, is certainly an archaic motif. 'Before the high seat in the hall' cannot be excluded, cf. *Thiðrekssaga* (see p. 377). 'At the cathedral door', as in the *Nibelungenlied*, is, no doubt, later.

3. *Sigurðarkviða en skamma*.

4. *Nibelungenlied*, *Thiðrekssaga*, and presumably a southern borrowing in *Brot*: 'Sigurð died South of the Rhine'.

5. *Sigurðarkviða en skamma*.

6. *Brot*. The women's cries might be reversed, according to whether Brunhild's triumph or Grimhild's grief was uppermost in the poet's mind.

or have been fused with, characters from a sphere other than that of Germanic princes. There is an aura of fairytale magic about them. Yet such imaginative motifs are not essentially foreign to Germanic heroic poetry. There is the Daedalus-like figure of Wayland the Smith, who makes himself wings to fly, or (if this comes too near to purely technological prowess) there are Ermanrik's stallions, who cannot endure the beautiful eyes of Swanhild and only succeed in trampling her when her eyes are covered. One strongly suspects that Hagen had the role of murdering Siegfried in this lay, without being able to prove it, for Norse tradition does not know him as Sigurð's murderer. Was Hagen perhaps the original slayer of the husband of another Hild, his sister, with whose name his name would alliterate? Did such a Hagen, with an elf for father, originate in this more fabulous of the two lays? We can never know the answer to these questions. The only part which Hagen plays with any consistency in the southern and northern branches of the legend is that of the realist who warns his king. As such he might have inherited second-sight from an elvish father. But all this is too tenuous to build on.[1] All that we can be sure of is that without a definite role Hagen could never have survived as a character, and that as the slayer of mighty 'Sigifrid' he *would have been* assured of survival.

The reader will have long since noticed a marked discrepancy between the German tradition of the *Nibelungenlied* on the one hand, and the Norse tradition on the other, concerning the motive for inviting the Burgundians to Hunland. The latter tradition makes the invitation come from Atli, and Atli's motive is lust for the Niflung treasure, while the role of Guðrun is to try to warn her brothers, and, having failed in her purpose, to wreak vengeance for them on her husband. According to the German tradition, however, it is Kriemhild who inspires the invitation through an indulgent Etzel, and her motive is revenge on her brothers for the murder of her husband. In other words, (i) in the Norse versions, the solidarity of the kindred, that is of blood-relations, takes precedence of marriage-ties, whereas in the German versions the reverse is true; (ii) the early Norse versions of the Fall of the Niflungs ignore, or all but ignore, the existence

1. The *Atlakviða*, for example, does not present Hogni in this role. Gunnar asks Hogni's advice on receiving Atli's invitation: but the lay then says emphatically: 'His kinsmen did not prompt him, nor did any other relation ... Gunnar commanded there, as a king should ...' Whether this emphasis implies a revision in Gunnar's favour of Hogni's role as adviser is unknowable.

of the lays which sang the death of Sigurð, whereas the German versions presuppose his death in corresponding lays.

Since the whole legend of the Nibelungs grew from the historically attested destruction of the Burgundian kingdom on the Rhine by a Hunnish army, later identified in legend with the army of Attila,[1] there can be no question but that the Norse version is the more and the German version the less archaic. There must have been a stage in the evolution of the legend in Germany, at which a poet or narrator substituted the later motive for the earlier, with all that this entailed, and in so convincing a manner that his version won the day. When and how did this come to pass?

Judging by the account of Saxo Grammaticus (see (*e*) above), this change must have been made by A.D. 1131, since he refers under that date to a lay in which 'Grimhild' betrays her brothers. But, it has been argued, we can go farther back in time than this. The figure of Attila in the *Nibelungenlied* and in the *Thiðrekssaga*[2] is presented in a favourable light, as in the entire heroic tradition of Austro-Bavaria: therefore the time when Attila's lust for gold gave way to Kriemhild's thirst for vengeance on her brothers must have been when the original Burgundo-Frankish lay on the fall of the Burgundians was assimilated to the Austro-Bavarian cycle. The question when this assimilation took place, however, cannot be answered precisely. Gunther and Hagen are already associated cyclically with Attila in the ninth or tenth century Latin *Waltharius* (see (*b*) above): but this poem does not permit us to speculate how Gunther and Hagen (who appear not as Burgundians but as Franks) would have stood to Attila at their downfall, nor does it so much as mention Grimhild. The great Swiss scholar Andreas Heusler[3] favoured an eighth-century date for this assimilation

1. It seems that Attila moved up the road from Passau to Worms before burning Metz on Easter Day 451, after which one no longer hears of Burgundians on the Rhine. This might well have merged in memory with the total defeat of the Burgundian dynasty in 437 at the hands of other Huns (see (*a*) above).

2. Despite the occasional intrusion of Norse traits due to conflation with Norse poems known in Bergen.

3. Who so generously acknowledged his debt to the Scottish scholar W. P. Ker for his insight into heroic poetry. Heusler's work is in process of modification by a younger generation in the direction of a greater complexity, but on the whole with very little effect on fundamentals. Heusler knew that his reconstruction offered only the barest outline of how the legend grew.

to the Austro-Bavarian cycle; but although this is not improbable, it cannot be proved. The substitution of the one motive for the other is in any case a complex matter: (i) it implies a neutral or benevolent Attila; (ii) it implies knowledge of the death of Siegfried as narrated in an independent lay; (iii) it implies an understanding of the claims of marital interest against those of the kindred. As to (i), this in fact accords with the Austro-Bavarian image of Attila, attested since the eighth century; as to (ii), it is in any case plausibly assumed, though not strictly proved, that a lay on Siegfried's death had existed since the sixth or seventh century; as to (iii), it has been argued, paradoxically though not convincingly, that it would only have been after a period of Christian influence that a much-wronged widow in a poem could be allowed to take vengeance on her brothers.

Whenever this great change took place in Germany, it is best interpreted as a brilliant feat of opportunism on the part of a discerning poet faced with the task of assimilating the lay to a tradition in which Attila was admired, and moreover a tradition in which cyclic tendencies were strong, so that glaring discrepancies like that of a woman siding with brothers who had wronged her, had, if possible, to be composed.

A further consequence of this change in motive is that Kriemhild's revenge on Etzel had to be jettisoned. But the poet who transformed the plot used what fragments of the old ending he could. He still caused Kriemhild to sacrifice a son, by provoking a Burgundian warrior;[1] and she still set fire to Etzel's hall, only not to burn him but her brothers.[2]

No such fundamental break in development can be discerned in the case of the succession of lost German lays that dealt with 'the death of Siegfried' or (if Brunhild was their dominant figure) with 'the humiliation and revenge of Brunhild'.

Although the emergence of a Kriemhild who avenges a murdered husband on her brothers can be taken as some evidence of the mutual attraction of the two plots, there is as yet no sign that these plots were ever treated together in one and the same poem. Rather is there evidence that the lay of Siegfried and Brunhild was variously expanded into longer lays that must have fallen short of epics, while the ruin of the Burgundians was worked up into a great epic poem known to scholars as '*Diu (ältere)*

1. Cf. the buffeting of Hogni; see (*d*) above, p. 382.
2. See (*d*) above, p. 382, and NL, p. 261.

Nôt'.[1] The evidence is indirect in both cases, since it is based upon inference: for not a line of these poems survives unless it is embedded more or less unrecognizably in the text of the extant *Nibelungenlied*.[2] Yet the inferences in question are sound.

The reader cannot have failed to notice quite detailed correspondences between the *Nibelungenlied* and the *Thiðrekssaga*. The two narratives are in the main very closely related to one another, and comparison reveals their common sources. The second part of the *Nibelungenlied*, and the parallel passages of the *Thiðrekssaga* derive from the lost epic, *Diu Nôt*, except that the *Thiðrekssaga* has suffered a major disturbance in this portion through its reliance on a version which localized the last stand of the Nibelungs in a 'Hunnish' Soest. With regard to the first half of the *Nibelungenlied*, comparison with the *Thiðrekssaga* shows that the former conflated two divergent lays dealing with Siegfried and Brunhild, a conflation which led to some typical inconsistencies of narrative.

The lost *Nôt* is dated 'about A.D. 1160', partly because of the archaic language and versification which peep through the text of the second half of the *Nibelungenlied*, partly because the Nibelung strophe, a highly stylized quatrain of lyrical provenance, is thought to have been in existence by this time: for '*c.* 1160' is the date ascribed to the Austro-Bavarian Minnesinger von Kürenberg, who |may well have invented it for his love-songs. *Diu Nôt* must have been a powerful poem, fierce, ruthless, and instinct with a gaunt beauty, such as one finds again in the old Romanesque churches of Germany. There can be no doubt but that *Diu Nôt* was an Austrian poem, and that even if it was preceded and followed by cumulative accretions, it was given shape by a great poet.

The two lays of Siegfried and Brunhild are even less tangible as works of the poetic art.

By 1160, in all three sources (*Diu Nôt* and the two lays of Siegfried and Brunhild), the figure of Hagen had long achieved a commanding stature. However it may have been in the original lays, by this time Hagen has long established himself in Germany as the slayer of Siegfried on the one hand, and consequently as the

1. 'Last Stand', a title taken from the last word of the extant poem, which ends: *daz ist der Nibelunge nôt.*

2. For example, some such phrase as *du lîst ermorderôt* must have stood in a lay of Siegfried and Brunhild at the point where Kriemhild first sees her husband's corpse. Cf. p. 378*n*.1.

presiding spirit of the Burgundian defiance on the other. The figure of Gunther in the Fall was bound to suffer from ever closer assimilation to the figure of the King who failed first to win his queen and then to kill her traducer's husband, as in the lays of Siegfried and Brunhild. He was bound to suffer to the extent that another, more kingly person should embody the Nibelung spirit. With a benevolent Attila it was possible at any time for Attila's most admired guest and warrior, Dietrich, to enter the story, and Dietrich will scarcely have had to wait for the poet of *Diu Nôt*. It is with reasonable confidence that we ascribe to this poet the introduction of great-hearted Rüdiger, another of Etzel's vassals, though as yet free of his terrible clash of loyalties; for in the *Thiðrekssaga* Roðingeir attacks at once on hearing of the death of Blodelin (p. 382). Volker, too, may well have entered at this stage of epic expansion in *Diu Nôt*.

The desire of the poet of the *Nibelungenlied* for fashionable refinement in behaviour, clothes, and ceremonies is so obvious that scholars have rightly taken it as a general rule that where the *Thiðrekssaga* offers a cruder version of an incident, this must have been adopted from the common source, whereas the *Nibelungenlied* has sublimated it. Another rule of more general application is that where the logical sequence is clear in the *Thiðrekssaga*, but obscure or 'blinded' in the *Nibelungenlied*, it must be the former which preserves the common source.[1] Both rules are exemplified, as we saw, in the case of Siegfried's wanton purloining of Brunhild's ring (and girdle) (pp. 93, 377). One or other or both rules will also apply in respect of the following incidents: (i) (In the lay or lays of Siegfried and Brunhild): the dead Siegfried was thrown into Kriemhild's bed (see (*d*) above, p. 378), not laid upon her threshold (NL, p. 133). (ii) (In *Diu Nôt*): Hagen will have killed the mermaids (see (*d*) above, p. 379), not bowed his thanks (NL, p. 195); Giselher will have killed his father-in-law Rüdiger with the latter's gift-sword (see (*d*) above, p. 383), Gernot will not have done so (NL, p. 274).

1. There is of course less opportunity for applying such rules to the *Iliad*, since there are fewer truly parallel sources. One parallel that has attracted much attention of late is the weighing of the fates of Achilles and Memnon by Hermes in the reconstructed cyclic epic, the 'Memnonis', and of the fates of Achilles and Hektor by Zeus in the *Iliad*. Prima facie, the former is the more archaic, since the scales and the role are more appropriate to the Guide of Souls, Hermes: yet this interpretation does not command universal assent among Homeric scholars.

As to the conflations between the two lays of Siegfried and Brunhild that have been detected in the *Nibelungenlied*, not all the motifs of the second can be reconstructed. Motifs in the *Nibelungenlied* which came from the second source were: Siegfried's reluctance to help Gunther win Brunhild except in return for Kriemhild (NL, p. 54); the need for Brunhild to be won by contest (p. 53), bringing with it the need for the cloak of invisibility (p. 54), a 'daylight' motif which nevertheless recurs in the darkness of the bedroom scene unnecessarily, apart from the strength it confers (p. 90). The test of the lover in the first source was the defloration of Brunhild. Thus, in the conflated account of the *Nibelungenlied*, Brunhild is won twice over, though the motif of defloration is blinded, and possibly, in agreement therewith, Siegfried's chaste dealings with Brunhild are adopted from the second source.

Some scholars consider that the epical *Nôt* of *c.* 1160 will not have plunged into the story of the Fall of the Nibelungs without an introduction which briefly narrated Siegfried's murder and the main events that led up to it. If this was so, it is possible that the account of these happenings in the *Thiðrekssaga* was based on such an introduction, and that the poet of the *Nibelungenlied* conflated it with his second source for Siegfried and Brunhild.

At the conclusion of these remarks it must be stressed once again that the foregoing offers but the barest outline of the growth of the Nibelung story so far as the *Nibelungenlied* is concerned. In actuality the descent of the legend was very much more complex. Some of this complexity can be filled in. There are many minor motifs, like that of Kriemhild's watch for her brothers from the tower (NL, p. 213, and (*d*) above, p. 381)[1], or that of the land-guard Eckewart, who is found sleeping by Hagen (NL, p. 203, and (*d*) above, p. 380), about which a good deal could be said. But I have had to pass it over. The matter would fill a book.[2] Nevertheless, the reader will have seen that despite our comparative wealth of knowledge, some leading elements, like the role of Hagena in the original lays, cannot be safely defined, which gives some measure of our ignorance, too.

The growth of the *Nibelungenlied* in barest outline, then, can be suggested in the diagram on page 394, which gives no idea of the various cross influences that we know to have occurred.

1. Cf. Guðrun's welcome in the *Atlakviða*, see (*c*) iii.
2. It has filled Andreas Heusler's masterpiece *Nibelungensage und Nibelungenlied* (1920 etc.), which the interested reader is recommended to consult.

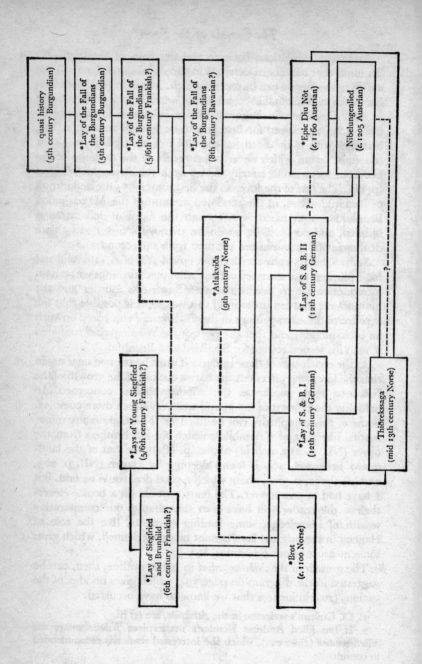

quasi history
(5th century Burgundian)

*Lay of the Fall of
the Burgundians
(5th century Burgundian)

*Lay of the Fall of
the Burgundians
(5/6th century Frankish?)

*Lay of the Fall of
the Burgundians
(8th century Bavarian?)

*Epic Diu Nôt
(c. 1160 Austrian)

Nibelungenlied
(c. 1205 Austrian)

*Atlakviða
(9th century Norse)

*Lay of S. & B. II
(12th century German)

*Lays of Young Siegfried
(5/6th century Frankish?)

*Lay of S. & B. I
(12th century German)

Thiðrekssaga
(mid 13th century Norse)

*Lay of Siegfried
and Brunhild
(6th century Frankish?)

*Brot
(c. 1100 Norse)

The Genesis of the Poem

To conclude, 'The last poet' took one or more shadowy lays of Young Siegfried, took two parallel lays of Siegfried and Brunhild and the weightier epic poem *Diu Nôt,* and out of them fashioned the *Nibelungenlied.* Of the Young Siegfried lay or lays he retained only what was needed to account for subsequent events, and he placed this with great skill in Hagen's mouth as a brief report. The two lays of Siegfried he fused together, though not with complete success, and he expanded and even padded out their matter to make the first half of his epic. To make its second half, he expanded the epical *Nôt,* though to a lesser degree, and he reworked it and refined it. In doing all this, and whilst introducing new beauties of his own, even of episodic length, he was inhibited, by his conservative attitude towards his audience and towards his art, from harmonizing his sources as discreetly as he might otherwise have done. But this poet's great achievement and his petty failings, so hard for us moderns to reconcile, have been treated above in my 'Introduction to a Second Reading': yet a better guide to what the poet built, when all the talking is done, will be found in the translation which precedes it.

APPENDIX 5

The Geography of the Poem

*

THE geographical indications of the *Nibelungenlied* range from the precise and local to the vague and semi-mythical. The local indications, as one would expect, concern places in Danubian Austria and its western and eastern approaches. Then there are two regions of broader focus: the one centred on the Burgundian capital of Worms[1] in the west, the other centred on Etzel's city of Gran[2] (Esztergom) in the east.[3] The northern lands ruled by Siegfried, the Netherlands, Norway, and 'Nibelungland', are merged mythically, with Siegfried's capital, Xanten on the Rhine, in the foreground. Far away over the sea there is a mythic Iceland, with 'Isenstein' for capital.

It is probable that each stage of growth of the legend left its deposit of geographical names in our poem, but their stratification cannot be disentangled. Nevertheless, the western frontier of the old Austrian Margraviate on the River Enns of before 1156 can be distinguished when the Margravine Gotelind rides there to welcome Kriemhild. The various comings and goings between

1. The Roman fortress Borbetomagus. Destroyed A.D. 407, when Alemanni, Vandals, and Alans crossed the Rhine, then presumably fell to the incoming Burgundians when they established themselves on the left bank of the Rhine with Roman permission in 413. Historical proof is lacking that Borbetomagus/Wormatia was the capital of the Burgundians. The ninth or tenth century *Waltharius* makes Wormatia the capital of Guntharius (but since at that time it was in 'Franconia', Guntharius and his men appear as Franks).

2. 'Gran' is named only once as Etzel's town (*stat*). Otherwise the reference is to 'Etzel's walled town' (*Etzeln burc*). There can be no doubt that the two are identical. Gran/Esztergom was the capital of King Bela III of Hungary (1173–96) as of the whole Arpad Dynasty, and it may well be that this wealthy king, whose relations with Austria were so good, was in the mind of our poet when writing of Etzel.

3. '*Ungerlant*', '*Ungern*' (Hungary) and '*daz hiunische lant*', '*zen Hiunen*' ('Hunland') etc. are identical in the eyes of the poet, since it does not occur to him to distinguish between ancient Huns and his own contemporaries in that region.

Worms and Gran, along what was a vital part of the ancient route between France and Constantinople, will have been typical rather than precise at earlier stages of the Fall of the Burgundians, like the journey to Atli's land in the *Atlakviða* (p. 373). But in our epic, as these journeys approach the Duchy of Austria, they come to be more realistic, though as will be seen below, full realism is not attempted.

In the following itineraries the places at which it is certain that a night was spent are given in italics.

No stages are given for Rüdiger's journey to Worms other than the very general indications Hungary, Vienna, Pöchlarn, Bavaria, and then twelve days (from the Danube?) to the Rhine.

On the return journey with Kriemhild no stages are given before Pföring on the Danube. The normal route of an earlier period will have taken her across the Danube here: but at the time of our poem the best crossing was at Regensburg. The party then rode down through Bavaria to *Passau*, a distance of 125 km. (pp. 166f.).[1] No stages are given for this long stretch, so that it would not matter much if Passau had not been named, although the theory that the Passau sections are interpolations does not of itself exclude the possibility that Passau was named here without Bishop Pilgrim.[2] (After the Burgundians leave Pöchlarn for Etzelnburc on a later journey, no mention is made of Vienna, though we must imagine them to have passed through it: so why need Passau have been mentioned in an earlier account of Kriemhild's journey?) The mention of Passau in our text is highly circumstantial. Allusion is made to it by means of a rather gnomic circumlocution: 'a monastery still stands there today, where the Inn flows into the Danube'. Only then is Passau named. The reference, remarkably enough, is not to the Cathedral, so that one could be forgiven for thinking that the author of this formulation was personally connected with the monastery; but whether with St Nikola or Kloster Niedernburg remains open.[3] Kriemhild's party now go to

1. The distances given in this Appendix are as the crow flies, but I do not let my crow cross the Danube. All places named after Pföring are of course south of the Danube.

2. *c.* 1200 there was probably only a ferry at Schärding, but there was a bridge over the Inn at Passau (since *c.* 1143). Thus Kriemhild is more easily imagined as crossing the Inn at Passau.

3. If the scenic aspect of the monastery was uppermost in the writer's mind, Niedernburg (situated at the tip of the eastern promontory of Passau where Inn, Danube, and Ilz flow together) will have been meant.

Eferding (52 km.) (p. 167), cross the Traun, are met at the town of *Enns* (37 km.), continue to Pöchlarn (57 km.), Melk (where they pause only to drink wine on the road, 9 km.), Mautern (26 km.), *Traismauer*[1] on the River Traisen (14 km.), *Tulln* (22 km.), *Vienna* (18 km.), *Hainburg* (47 km.), Wieselburg/Moson (if correct for 'Mîsenburc', 21 km.), *Gran*/Esztergom (upwards of 80 km. by water). Kriemhild, according to the poet's conception, leaves Austrian soil some time after setting out from Vienna, and Hainburg is in Hungary. Kriemhild's journey to Hunland was of more recent date in the growth of the epic than the journey of the men of Burgundy. It cannot even be proved that her journey was given in detail in *Diu Nôt*: much of it might therefore be the work of the last poet. Not being bound by tradition here, as he was with the journey of the Burgundians, he could afford to be more circumstantial on this occasion.

Werbel's and Swemmel's route is: Hungary–Pöchlarn–Passau(?) (p. 181), and then, by ways which the poet cannot name, in twelve days' time to Worms (cf. Rüdiger's journey to Worms, above.) Returning, they ride through Swabia, Passau (?) (Pilgrim receives their news), Pöchlarn, Gran (explicitly).

The journey of the Burgundians ran: Worms, towards the River Main, up through East Franconia towards 'Swanevelt', formerly 'Swalefeld', and so, on the twelfth morning, to the Danube somewhere near Mehring (cf. Rüdiger's and the minstrels' journey in the opposite direction). This very odd route has been explained as due to a conflation of an older and a more up-to-date route. After the building of the bridge at Regensburg (1146), the route from Northern Franconia ran: Worms–Miltenberg–Würzburg–Nuremberg–Regensburg–Passau. When the Burgundians go through the old Swabian Gau of Swalefeld (on the River Swalb, an eastern tributary of the Wörnitz) towards Mehring, they are abandoning the newer route for the older. Now the mention of Mœre in the *Thiðrekssaga* (see (*d*) above, p. 379) shows that the place at which the Burgundians crossed the Danube in *Diu Nôt* was at Mehring (*Mœringen* in the *Nibelungenlied*). Thus when our poet changed from new to old in mid-route, tradition once again was too strong for him. Had he preferred to be up to date and let his Burgundians cross over the new bridge at Regensburg, it would have cost him most of Chapter 25 and all of Chapter 26! But, characteristically,

1. MSS ABHJdg have 'Zeiselmauer' in obvious error, but group *C has correctly, 'Traisenmauer'. 'Zeiselmauer' is not on the River Traisen, but on the Danube between Tulln and Vienna.

he gave the moderns in his audience what he could, namely the *beginning* of the modern journey – and then, having no choice, reverted to tradition for the rest. The Burgundians, then, cross the Danube at Mehring, some kilometres upstream from Pföring, where Kriemhild had crossed. Like her, they ride through Bavaria, and our text has them come to *Passau*; but this passage obviously interrupts the logical flow of the narrative (pp. 360f.). The *Not* had the Burgundians ride on wearily till they found Eckewart sleeping on Etzel's frontier (pp. 202f., 380). But whether the last poet or a revisor of Passau introduced Passau at this point can never be known for certain, though (as I have tried to show) the latter alternative is far more likely. The next stage from Passau is Pöchlarn (146 km.), which implies a journey as little realistic as from Mehring to Passau (*c.* 130 km.).[1] From here they ride down the Danube through Austria (with no mention of Vienna) to 'Hungary'. Now that the Burgundians are approaching their fate, not even the circumlocution 'Etzel's Town' or 'Etzel's Fortress' is used, let alone the specific 'Gran'. The Nibelungs, who had passed through country that was intimately known to the poet and his patrons, draw away into a distant past to meet their legendary fate, in a place grown shadowy and remote. In the imagination of this poet, time and space conspire to impart an atmosphere of myth to the 'Last Stand of the Nibelungs'.

1. Geographical notions tended to be jumbled by two contradictory factors, owing to the stratification of periods in the *Nibelungenlied*. On the one hand, the Hungarian frontier is in a contemporary position near Hainburg: on the other Etzel celebrates his wedding in Vienna, and his vassal Rüdiger, the Margrave, appears to be Margrave of Austria with his western frontier on the Enns. Thus strangely are past and present blended.

APPENDIX 6

A Glossary of the Characters' Names

*

THE forms used in the text of the translation are in some cases Middle High German, in others Modern German, according to how I judged they would sound in English or how well known they already were to the English reader. That the same Middle High German sound should appear in some names as -t but in others as -d is indefensible philologically; but in offering this lame apology to scholars, I must admit how much I have enjoyed the luxury of doing as I please on this privileged occasion.

The normal Middle High German form of 'Siegfried' is 'Sîvrit'; that of 'Brunhild' is 'Prünhilt'; that of 'Rüdiger' is 'Rüedegêr', with -üe- pronounced as a diphthong; -e at the end of a name is pronounced as a weak vowel, as for example in Helchè.

To assist those who read Appendix 4, the Norse forms of the characters' names are given below in round brackets when parallels occur. Names of those who play no part in the poem are given an asterisk.

ALBERICH: A dwarf; Lord Treasurer to the Nibelung dynasty and then to Siegfried, who took the treasure and wrested the cloak of invisibility from Alberich.

*ALDRIAN: father of Hagen and Dancwart. (The name has been shifted in the *Thiðrekssaga*, from the fairy incubus, father of Hogni, to Gunnar's father. See p. 376.)

AMELUNG: dynastic name of Dietrich's family, applied collectively to his vassals.

ASTOLT: a lord of Melk/Mölk.

BALMUNG: Siegfried's sword; stolen from him by Hagen, who is slain with it by Kriemhild. Listed here because in heroic poetry swords are persons.

BLOEDELIN (Blodelin): brother of Etzel; slain by Dancwart.

*BOTELUNG (Budli): father of Etzel.

BRUNHILD (Brynhild, Brunild): Queen of Iceland; married to Gunther. See pp. 331f.

*DANCRAT: father of Gunther, husband of Uote. (Unaccountably displaces Gibech, q.v., in this role. See p. 171.)

DANCWART: younger brother of Hagen; vassal of the Burgundian kings, more particularly of Giselher, see Chapter 8; slain by Helpfrich.

DIETRICH (Thiðrek): Theoderic the Great, the favourite hero of upper Germany. Lord of the Amelungs; lives in exile at Etzel's court; engaged to Herrat.

ECKEWART (Ekkivarð): Burgundian Margrave; accompanies Kriemhild to the Netherlands and then to Hungary; found sleeping on Rüdiger's frontier by Hagen. Considered by some to have been conflated from two different characters of the same name.

ELSE (Elsung): Lord of the Marches on the southern, Bavarian bank of the Danube; brother of Gelpfrat.

ETZEL (Atli, Attila): Attila, king of the Huns; son of Botelung; husband of Helche, then of Kriemhild.

GELPFRAT: Bavarian Margrave; brother of Else.

GERBART: a vassal of Dietrich.

GERE: Margrave, and kinsman of the Burgundian kings.

GERNOT (Gernoz): the second eldest co-king of Burgundy; slain by Rüdiger, whom he slays. See p. 326.

GIBECH: a tributary king under Etzel. (Otherwise in heroic tradition, both in Germany and in Scandinavia, father of Gunther. Norse Gjuki. Replaced by Dancrat in our poem. See p. 385.)

GISELHER (Gislher, Gilser): the youngest of the three co-kings of Burgundy. Legally married to Rüdiger's unnamed daughter, but owing to his failure to return from Hungary neither consummates the marriage nor 'takes her home'; 'Young'. See pp. 326ff., 301.

GOTELIND (Gudelinda): wife of Rüdiger.

GUNTHER (1) (Gunnar): son of Dancrat and Uote; senior king of Burgundy; brother of Gernot, Giselher and Kriemhild; marries Brunhild; connives at the murder of Siegfried; beheaded in bonds by order of Kriemhild. See pp. 324ff.

GUNTHER (2): son of Siegfried and Kriemhild.

HADEBURG: a Danubian water-sprite; prophesies to Hagen.

HAGEN (Hogni) eldest son of Aldrian; brother of Dancwart; kinsman and vassal of the Burgundian kings; lord of Troneck; former hostage at Etzel's court; murders Siegfried; slain in bonds by Kriemhild. See pp. 320ff.

HAWART: Danish prince living in exile at Etzel's court; overlord of Iring; slain by Hagen.

*HELCHE (Erka): Etzel's first queen; maternal aunt of Herrat.

HELMNOT: a vassal of Dietrich.

HELPFRICH: a vassal of Dietrich; slays Dancwart.

HERRAT (Herraŏ): daughter of Nantwin; maternal niece of Helche; betrothed to Dietrich.

HILDEBRAND (Hildibrand): Dietrich's tutor and Master-at-Arms; maternal uncle of Wolfhart; 'executes' Kriemhild. See pp. 336f.

*HILDEGUND: the beloved of Walter of Spain, q.v.

HORNBOGE: a vassal of Etzel.

HUNOLD: Lord Chamberlain of Burgundy.

IRING: vassal of Hawart; slain by Hagen.

IRNFRIED: Landgrave of Thuringia; lives in exile with Etzel; slain by Volker.

KRIEMHILD (Guŏrun in ancient Norse tradition, but Grimhild in the *Thiŏrekssaga*): daughter of Dancrat and Uote; sister to Gunther, Gernot, and Giselher; wife of Siegfried and then of Etzel; mother of Gunther by Siegfried and of Ortlieb by Etzel; slays Hagen with her own hands; slain by Hildebrand. See pp. 316ff.

LIUDEGAST: King of Denmark; brother of Liudeger; makes war on Burgundy and is captured by Siegfried.

LIUDEGER: King of Saxony; brother of Liudegast; captured with his brother.

*NANTWIN: father of Herrat.

*NIBELUNG (1): lord of Nibelungland; father of Kings Schilbung and Nibelung, to whom he bequeathed his treasure.

NIBELUNG (2): a king of Nibelungland; son of the foregoing, brother of Schilbung; slain by Siegfried over the treasure.

NIBELUNGS (Niflungs): in the first part of the poem, the dynasty of Nibelung (1) and their followers; in the second part, an alternative name for the Burgundians.

*NUODUNG (Nauŏung): kinsman of Gotelind; slain by Witege in another epic; Hagen is given his shield; his bride is promised to Bloedelin by Kriemhild as a lure to battle.

ORTLIEB: son of Etzel and Kriemhild; about six years of age when slain by Hagen. (Named 'Aldrian' in the *Thiŏrekssaga*.)

ORTWIN: Lord High Steward of Burgundy and lord of Metz; maternal nephew of Hagen.

PILGRIM: Bishop of Passau; brother of Uote, and so maternal uncle of Kriemhild and the Burgundian kings.

RAMUNG: Duke of Wallachia and vassal of Etzel.

RITSCHART: a vassal of Dietrich.

RÜDIGER (Roðingeir): Margrave, and lord of Pöchlarn; vassal of Etzel; husband of Gotelind; becomes the father-in-law of Giselher; slain by Gernot as he slays him. See pp. 333ff.

RUMOLD: Lord of the Kitchen in Burgundy; appointed regent when his lords leave for Hungary. See pp. 367f.

SCHILBUNG: a king of Nibelungland; son of Nibelung (1); brother of Nibelung (2); slain by Siegfried over the Nibelung treasure.

SCHRUTAN: a vassal of Etzel.

SIEGFRIED(1) (Sigurð): son of Siegmund and Sieglind; lord of the Netherlands, Norway, and Nibelungland; marries Kriemhild; murdered by Hagen; avenged by Kriemhild. See pp. 328f.

SIEGFRIED(2): son of Gunther and Brunhild.

SIEGLIND(1): queen of Siegmund, and mother of Siegfried. (Sisibe in the *Thiðrekssaga*.)

SIEGLIND(2): a Danubian water-sprite questioned by Hagen.

SIEGMUND (Sigmund): King of the Netherlands; husband of Sieglind; father of Siegfried.

SINDOLD: Cup-bearer of Burgundy.

SWEMMEL: minstrel to Etzel; with Werbel, envoy to Worms.

UOTE (Oda): dowager queen of Burgundy; widow of Dancrat; mother of Gunther, Gernot, Giselher, and Kriemhild; sister of Bishop Pilgrim of Passau.

VOLKER (Folkher): lord of Alzei and vassal of the Burgundian kings; gentleman-musician with the sobriquets of 'The Fiddler' and 'The Minstrel'; Hagen's chosen comrade in arms; slain by Hildebrand.

*WALTER 'of Spain': hero of the epics *Waltharius*, *Waldere*; former hostage of Etzel, from whom he escaped with his beloved Hildigund; waylaid in the Vosges by Gunther and his vassals, with Hagen refusing to fight him, as an old comrade in arms, until forced by circumstances to do so. See pp. 218, 288.

WERBEL: minstrel to Etzel; with Swemmel, envoy to Worms.

WASKE: Iring's sword.

WICHART: a vassal of Dietrich.

*WITEGE (Viðga): a famous hero of the Dietrich Cycle; the slayer of Nuodung.

WOLFHART: maternal nephew of Hildebrand; vassal of Dietrich; slain by Giselher slaying him.

WOLFBRAND: a vassal of Dietrich.

WOLFWIN: a vassal of Dietrich.

FOR THE BEST IN PAPERBACKS, LOOK FOR THE 🐧

Aeschylus	The Oresteian Trilogy (Agamemnon/The Choephori/The Eumenides)
	Prometheus Bound/The Suppliants/Seven Against Thebes/The Persians
Aesop	Fables
Ammianus Marcellinus	The Later Roman Empire (AD 354–378)
Apollonius of Rhodes	The Voyage of Argo
Apuleius	The Golden Ass
Aristophanes	The Knights/Peace/The Birds/The Assembly Women/Wealth
	Lysistrata/The Acharnians/The Clouds
	The Wasps/The Poet and the Women/The Frogs
Aristotle	The Athenian Constitution
	Ethics
	The Politics
	De Anima
Arrian	The Campaigns of Alexander
Saint Augustine	City of God
	Confessions
Boethius	The Consolation of Philosophy
Caesar	The Civil War
	The Conquest of Gaul
Catullus	Poems
Cicero	The Murder Trials
	The Nature of the Gods
	On the Good Life
	Selected Letters
	Selected Political Speeches
	Selected Works
Euripides	Alcestis/Iphigenia in Tauris/Hippolytus
	The Bacchae/Ion/The Women of Troy/Helen
	Medea/Hecabe/Electra/Heracles
	Orestes/The Children of Heracles/ Andromache/The Suppliant Women/ The Phoenician Women/Iphigenia in Aulis

Hesiod/Theognis	**Theogony and Works and Days/Elegies**
Hippocrates	**Hippocratic Writings**
Homer	**The Iliad**
	The Odyssey
Horace	**Complete Odes and Epodes**
Horace/Persius	**Satires and Epistles**
Juvenal	**Sixteen Satires**
Livy	**The Early History of Rome**
	Rome and Italy
	Rome and the Mediterranean
	The War with Hannibal
Lucretius	**On the Nature of the Universe**
Marcus Aurelius	**Meditations**
Martial	**Epigrams**
Ovid	**The Erotic Poems**
	Heroides
	The Metamorphoses
Pausanias	**Guide to Greece** (in two volumes)
Petronius/Seneca	**The Satyricon/The Apocolocyntosis**
Pindar	**The Odes**
Plato	**Early Socratic Dialogues**
	Gorgias
	The Last Days of Socrates (Euthyphro/ The Apology/Crito/Phaedo)
	The Laws
	Phaedrus and Letters VII and VIII
	Philebus
	Protagoras and Meno
	The Republic
	The Symposium
	Theaetetus
	Timaeus and Critias

Plautus	**The Pot of Gold/The Prisoners/ The Brothers Menaechmus/ The Swaggering Soldier/Pseudolus**
	The Rope/Amphitryo/The Ghost/ A Three-Dollar Day
Pliny	**The Letters of the Younger Pliny**
Plutarch	**The Age of Alexander** (Nine Greek Lives)
	The Fall of the Roman Republic (Six Lives)
	The Makers of Rome (Nine Lives)
	The Rise and Fall of Athens (Nine Greek Lives)
	Plutarch on Sparta
Polybius	**The Rise of the Roman Empire**
Procopius	**The Secret History**
Propertius	**The Poems**
Quintus Curtius Rufus	**The History of Alexander**
Sallust	**The Jugurthine War** and **The Conspiracy of Cataline**
Seneca	**Four Tragedies** and **Octavia**
	Letters from a Stoic
Sophocles	**Electra/Women of Trachis/Philoctetes/Ajax**
	The Theban Plays (King Oedipus/Oedipus at Colonus/Antigone)
Suetonius	**The Twelve Caesars**
Tacitus	**The Agricola** and **The Germania**
	The Annals of Imperial Rome
	The Histories
Terence	**The Comedies** (The Girl from Andros/The Self-Tormentor/The Eunuch/Phormio/The Mother-in-Law/The Brothers)
Thucydides	**The History of the Peloponnesian War**
Virgil	**The Aeneid**
	The Eclogues
	The Georgics
Xenophon	**Conversations of Socrates**
	A History of My Times
	The Persian Expedition

FOR THE BEST IN PAPERBACKS, LOOK FOR THE 🐧

PENGUIN CLASSICS

FOR THE BEST IN PAPERBACKS, LOOK FOR THE 🐧

PENGUIN CLASSICS

William Hazlitt	**Selected Writings**
Thomas Hobbes	**Leviathan**
Samuel Johnson/ James Boswell	**A Journey to the Western Islands of Scotland** and **The Journal of a Tour to the Hebrides**
Charles Lamb	**Selected Prose**
Samuel Richardson	**Clarissa**
	Pamela
Richard Brinsley Sheridan	**The School for Scandal and Other Plays**
Christopher Smart	**Selected Poems**
Adam Smith	**The Wealth of Nations**
Tobias Smollett	**The Expedition of Humphry Clinker**
	The Life and Adventures of Sir Launcelot Greaves
Laurence Sterne	**The Life and Opinions of Tristram Shandy, Gentleman**
	A Sentimental Journey Through France and Italy
Jonathan Swift	**Gulliver's Travels**
Sir John Vanbrugh	**Four Comedies**

FOR THE BEST IN PAPERBACKS, LOOK FOR THE 🐧

PENGUIN CLASSICS

FOR THE BEST IN PAPERBACKS, LOOK FOR THE 🐧

PENGUIN CLASSICS

FOR THE BEST IN PAPERBACKS, LOOK FOR THE 🐧

PENGUIN CLASSICS

Jacob Burckhardt	**The Civilization of the Renaissance in Italy**
Carl von Clausewitz	**On War**
Friedrich Engels	**The Origins of the Family, Private Property and the State**
Wolfram von Eschenbach	**Parzival**
	Willehalm
Goethe	**Elective Affinities**
	Faust Parts One and Two (in 2 volumes)
	Italian Journey
	The Sorrows of Young Werther
Jacob and Wilhelm Grimm	**Selected Tales**
E. T. A. Hoffmann	**Tales of Hoffmann**
Henrik Ibsen	**The Doll's House/The League of Youth/The Lady from the Sea**
	Ghosts/A Public Enemy/When We Dead Wake
	Hedda Gabler/The Pillars of the Community/The Wild Duck
	The Master Builder/Rosmersholm/Little Eyolf/ John Gabriel Borkman
	Peer Gynt
Søren Kierkegaard	**Fear and Trembling**
	The Sickness Unto Death
Georg Christoph Lichtenberg	**Aphorisms**
Friedrich Nietzsche	**Beyond Good and Evil**
	Ecce Homo
	A Nietzsche Reader
	Thus Spoke Zarathustra
	Twilight of the Idols and **The Anti-Christ**
Friedrich Schiller	**The Robbers** and **Wallenstein**
Arthur Schopenhauer	**Essays and Aphorisms**
Gottfried von Strassburg	**Tristan**
August Strindberg	**The Father/Miss Julie/Easter**

FOR THE BEST IN PAPERBACKS, LOOK FOR THE 🐧

PENGUIN CLASSICS

ANTHOLOGIES AND ANONYMOUS WORKS

The Age of Bede
Alfred the Great
Beowulf
A Celtic Miscellany
The Cloud of Unknowing and Other Works
The Death of King Arthur
The Earliest English Poems
Early Irish Myths and Sagas
Egil's Saga
The Letters of Abelard and Heloise
Medieval English Verse
Njal's Saga
Seven Viking Romances
Sir Gawain and the Green Knight
The Song of Roland